The Age of Cultural Revolutions

James Gillray, *The Fashionable Mama, —or—The Convenience of Modern Dress* (1796). A commentary on the then-current preoccupation with maternal breast-feeding [note the picture on the wall], this image suggests that the emphasis affected even the design of the fashionable lady's evening dress. By permission of the British Library.

The Age of
Cultural Revolutions

Britain and France, 1750–1820

EDITED BY

Colin Jones and Dror Wahrman

UNIVERSITY OF CALIFORNIA PRESS

Berkeley   Los Angeles   London

"Misogyny and Femininism: The Case of Mary Wollstonecraft" originally
appeared in *Constellations: An International Journal of Critical and Democratic
Theory*, vol. 6, no. 4 (December 1999): 499–512.

University of California Press
Berkeley and Los Angeles, California

University of California Press, Ltd.
London, England

Library of Congress Cataloging-in-Publication Data

The age of cultural revolutions : Britain and France, 1750–1820 / edited by
Colin Jones and Dror Wahrman.
    p.   cm.
    Chiefly, selected papers of a conference entitled "Dissolving boundaries;
historical writing towards the third millenium" held 1997 at the University
of Warwick.
    Includes bibliographical references and index.
    ISBN 0–520–22966–5 (cloth : alk. paper)—ISBN 0–520–22967–3 (pbk. :
alk. paper)
    1. Revolutions—Europe—History—18th century—Congresses. 2. Great
Britain—History—1760–1789—Congresses. 3. Great Britain—History—
1789–1820—Congresses. 4. Great Britain—Economic conditions—18th
century—Congresses. 5. France—Politics and government—1789–1815—
Congresses. 6. France—History—1789–1815—Congresses. 7. Political
culture—France—History—18th century—Congresses. 8. Political
culture—Great Britain—History—18th century—Congresses. I. Jones,
Colin, 1947– II. Wahrman, Dror.
    D295.A44 2002
    940—dc21   2001003114

Manufactured in the United States of America
10 09 08 07 06 05 04 03 02
10 9 8 7 6 5 4 3 2 1

The paper used in this publication is both acid-free and totally chlorine-free (TCF). It meets
the minimum requirements of ANSI/NISO Z39.48–1992 (R 1997) (*Permanence of Paper*). ♾

To the memory of Lawrence Stone

CONTENTS

ACKNOWLEDGMENTS

The idea for this volume arose out of a conference organized by Colin Jones and Dror Wahrman at the University of Warwick in 1997, entitled "Dissolving Boundaries: Historical Writing towards the Third Millennium." Of the authors in the volume, James Chandler, Carla Hesse, Thomas Laqueur, Michael McKeon, Sarah Maza, Gareth Stedman Jones, Carolyn Steedman, and Barbara Taylor gave papers at that conference. We also wish to thank other speakers and commentators on that occasion—David Bell, Maxine Berg, John Brewer, Marilyn Butler, Erica Carter, Stuart Clark, Thomas Crow, Robert Darnton, Geoff Eley, Anne Janowitz, Ludmilla Jordanova, Marcia Pointon, Rebecca Spang, and Peter Wagner—for their contributions to the thinking behind this volume. We also acknowledge with thanks the British Academy and the University of Warwick for financial assistance in running the conference. The late Lawrence Stone, despite failing health, agreed to give the concluding remarks for the conference, in what was one of his last public performances of this kind; we dedicate this volume to his memory.

CONTRIBUTORS

David A. Bell is Professor of History at Johns Hopkins University. He is the author of *Lawyers and Citizens: The Making of a Political Elite in Old Regime France* (1994), which won the Pinkney Prize of the Society for French Historical Studies, and *The National and the Sacred: The Origins of Nationalism in Eighteenth-Century France* (2001). He is currently working on a project entitled "Napoleon and the Cult of War."

James Chandler is George M. Pullman Professor in the Department of English and a member of the Committee on the History of Culture at the University of Chicago. He is author, most recently, of *England in 1819: The Politics of Literary Culture and the Case of Romantic Historicism* (1998) and coeditor of *Questions of Evidence: Proof, Practice, and Persuasion across the Disciplines* (1994). He is currently at work on the *New Cambridge History of English Romantic Literature,* as well as on a book about the sentimental in theater, print, and cinema.

Paul Friedland is Assistant Professor of History at Bowdoin College. He is the author of *Political Actors: Representative Bodies and Theatricality in the Age of the French Revolution* (forthcoming) and is currently working on a study of executioners and the logic of executions in old regime France.

Carla Hesse is Professor of European History at the University of California, Berkeley, and the cochair of the editorial board of *Representations,* an interdisciplinary journal in the humanities and interpretive social sciences. She has published extensively on the literary culture of the French Revolution and is the author of *Publishing and Cultural Politics in Revolutionary Paris* (1991) and *The Other Enlightenment: French Women and the Problem of Modernity* (2001).

Colin Jones is Professor of History at Warwick University. His books include *The Charitable Imperative* (1989), *Reassessing Foucault* (coedited with Roy Porter, 1991), and *The Medical World of Early Modern France* (with Laurence Brockliss, 1997). He is currently completing a history of eighteenth-century France for *The New Penguin History of Modern France*. His next research project is on the cultural history of the mouth and smiles.

Gareth Stedman Jones is Professor of History of Political Thought at King's College, Cambridge. His publications include *Outcast London: A Study in the Relationship between Classes in Victorian Society* (1971) and *Languages of Class: Studies in English Working Class History, 1832–1982* (1983).

Thomas W. Laqueur is Professor of History at the University of California, Berkeley. He is the author most recently of *Making Sex: Body and Gender from the Greeks to Freud* (1990) and is completing a book about death and modernity.

Michael McKeon is Professor of English Literature at Rutgers University. He is the author of *Politics and Poetry in Restoration England* (1975) and *The Origins of the English Novel* (1987) and the editor of *Theory of the Novel* (2000). His essay in this volume is the subject of his current book project.

Sarah Maza is Professor of History and Jane Long Professor of Arts and Sciences at Northwestern University. Her work focuses on the cultural history of eighteenth- and nineteenth-century France, with an emphasis on the study of the social imaginary. Her most recent book is *Private Lives and Public Affairs: The Causes Célèbres of Prerevolutionary France* (1993). She is currently completing a book-length essay on the construction of the "bourgeoisie" in French politics and culture between 1750 and 1850.

Carolyn Steedman is Professor of History at Warwick University. Her books include *The Tidy House* (1982), *Landscape for a Good Woman* (1986), *Childhood, Culture, and Class in Britain: Margaret MacMillan* (1990), *Past Tenses* (1992), and *Strange Dislocations: Childhood and the Idea of Human Interiority, 1780–1980* (1995).

Barbara Taylor teaches history at the University of East London and is director of the international research project "Feminism and Enlightenment, 1650–1850: A Comparative History." She is the author of *Eve and the New Jerusalem: Socialism and Feminism in the 19th Century* (1983) and other articles on the history of early feminism. Her new book, *Mary Wollstonecraft and the Feminist Imagination*, will be published in 2002.

Dror Wahrman is Associate Professor of Cultural History at Indiana University and the associate editor of the *American Historical Review*. He is the author of *Imagining the Middle Class: The Political Representation of Class in*

Britain, c. 1780–1840 (1995) and several publications on the history of Palestine and early photography in the Middle East. He is completing a book on the eighteenth-century origins of modern understandings of identity, tentatively entitled *The Making of the Modern Self*.

Kathleen Wilson is Associate Professor of History at the State University of New York, Stony Brook. Her book *The Sense of the People: Politics, Culture, and Imperialism in England, 1715–1785* (1995) won prizes from the Royal Historical Society and the North American Council on British Studies. Her forthcoming book, *The Island Race: Englishness, Empire, and Gender in the Eighteenth Century*, addresses questions of identity and modernity within the oceanic intercultures produced by British imperialism. Her current project is entitled "Theater, Culture, and Modernity in the English Provinces, 1720–1820."

Introduction

An Age of Cultural Revolutions?

Colin Jones and Dror Wahrman

I

In *The Age of Revolution,* the first volume of his masterly four-volume oeuvre on the history of the modern world, the British Marxist historian Eric Hobsbawm sought the origins of this modern world in what he dubbed the "dual revolution": a transformation incarnated in the French Revolution of 1789 and "the contemporaneous (British) Industrial Revolution." If, Hobsbawm argued, the focus of his work was on these two countries to the omission of many other aspects of the history of the wider world, that was "because in this period the world—or at least a large part of it—was transformed from a European, or rather Franco-British base."[1]

Although Hobsbawm's vision, with its clear Marxian echoes, was not new, the striking "dual revolution" formulation crystallized and endorsed a particular view of the experiences of the French and British nations in the late eighteenth and early nineteenth centuries and of their significance, a view found in many other contemporary works. The following year, for example, saw the publication of the colossally influential *Making of the English Working Class,* by fellow Marxist E. P. Thompson, which reenacted a similar vision, with the French Revolution and the English Industrial Revolution as major (if nondeterminist) actors on its historical mise-en-scène. The dual revolutions model is thus a convenient heuristic starting point from which to assess some of the changes that have occurred in this historical field over the last four decades.

1. E. J. Hobsbawm, *The Age of Revolution, 1789–1848* (New York and London, 1962); see the introduction, p. xv.

The basic assumptions of the dual revolutions scheme can be summarized as follows. First, it presupposed that the divergent experiences of the two countries deserved in each case the epithet *revolution,* designating radical discontinuity and disjuncture.[2] Second, it iterated a kind of division of revolutionary labor between the two countries. On the one hand, the social and economic dislocations associated with rapid industrialization from circa 1750 unbound the English Prometheus, making the country the world's "first industrial nation" (to evoke the titles of two other influential texts of the 1960s).[3] On the other hand, France's destiny was more significantly marked by the transformative modernization of the country's political institutions, which became the (rocky) cradle of human rights, representative government, and popular sovereignty. Third, implicit in such a view of the contrasting histories of England and France during this period was the wider assumption that, taken together, these two cases were in some key senses exemplary and paradigmatic: that together they provided the matrix from which modernity sprang and which, when propelled outward, continued to transform the world to the present day. Fourth, the kind of explanatory framework employed by Hobsbawm privileged social class: as he explained, "the great revolution of 1789–1848 was the triumph not of 'industry,' as such, but of *capitalist* industry; not of liberty and equality in general, but of *middle class* or *'bourgeois' liberal* society."[4]

Over the last generation, much of the historical writing in this field involved either direct attacks on or more subtle subversions of most of the methodological and conceptual foundations on which the dual revolutions vision had been constructed. On the one hand, scholars have proven eager to break their revisionist lances on the historical meta-narrative it offered— that of "revolutionary" socioeconomic change in England and sociopolitical change in France. At the same time, many of its methodological assumptions—not least the validity of the very search for a meta-narrative—likewise came under increasing fire. On the other hand, despite the multi-pronged and thorough undermining of the arch of dual revolution, this period (the late eighteenth and early nineteenth centuries) and this site (the societies of Britain and France) continue to attract scholars who share the gut feeling, which struck Hobsbawm, Thompson, and others, that here

2. It is hardly a coincidence that the decisive shift in the meaning of the term *revolution* itself, from its earlier connotation of the return of former forms of existence to its modern understanding of radical rupture, dates to this same period; cf. M. Ozouf, "Revolution," in F. Furet and M. Ozouf, eds., *The Critical Dictionary of the French Revolution* (Cambridge, Mass., 1989).

3. D. Landes, *The Unbound Prometheus: Technological Change and Industrial Development in Western Europe from 1750 to the Present* (London, 1969); P. Mathias, *The First Industrial Nation: An Economic History of Britain, 1700–1914* (London, 1969).

4. Hobsbawm, *The Age of Revolution,* p. 17.

were to be found keys crucial to understanding the formation and the character of the modern world.

It is the purpose of the present volume to revisit this pivotal historical site, bringing together scholars involved in the recent rethinking of the transformations during this period in the Franco-British context. Together, the following essays allow readers a firsthand insight into the ongoing process by which our understanding of the nature and salience of this particular period is being reshaped and reformulated.

In this introduction, we seek to contextualize these contributions within key trends in the study of this period. We shall begin by highlighting recent developments that have come together from different quarters to undermine the dual revolution template. We shall demonstrate how, even though the contrast between England and France has not borne up particularly well, the sense that these years witnessed key revolutionary developments has shown surprising durability. However, we suggest—and our contributors shall make clear—that these revolutionary developments can perhaps be thought of most fruitfully less as primarily social, economic, or political transformations than as cultural ones.

II

Let us begin with a reminder of the multiple cracks that have been detected in the dual revolutions narrative, first with regard to its substantive contents. On the English side, as has often been pointed out, the notion of an abrupt socioeconomic "revolution" that radically transformed the economy and the social structure—a vision associated especially with W. W. Rostow's famous "take-off" model—has been in decline since the late 1970s. Instead, current interpretations of eighteenth-century English economic growth stress its protracted, gradual, and—importantly—uneven nature. While some sectors, or some regions, did experience remarkable growth rates toward the end of the century, others had experienced change much earlier, while others still had not witnessed any radical change deep into the nineteenth century. Moreover, the transformation of English (and in some cases British) social structure was also found to have been in fact a remarkably long-term process, with "middle" or "bourgeois" social groups increasingly visible from much earlier in the eighteenth century: England did not have to wait for an industrial revolution to develop what E. P. Thompson referred to as an agrarian bourgeoisie, or Paul Langford as a bourgeois aristocracy, or indeed even for what one recent writer has described as eighteenth-century "middle-class culture."[5] So much, then, for the vision of the

5. The literature on these issues is much too vast to list here. On economic growth, key contributions include N. F. R. Crafts, *British Economic Growth during the Industrial Revolution*

late eighteenth and early nineteenth centuries as a distinctive period of economic and social revolution in England, abruptly ushering in modern industrial society and bourgeois hegemony.

If the economic historians of England replaced revolution with uneven gradualism, those of France brought their own socioeconomic stories to a virtual standstill. From the Braudelian emphasis of the *Annales* school on the importance of the *longue durée,* through Emmanuel Le Roy Ladurie's *histoire immobile* stretching from the late Middle Ages to the mid-eighteenth century, to Pierre Goubert's synchronic picture of the Ancien Régime between the sixteenth century and about 1750, the long-term, slowly evolving picture was pretty much the same. These and similar works were often laconic on the developments of the late eighteenth century, thus leaving room, at least implicitly, for the possibility of change *after* their chosen time frame. And yet, while the *Annaliste* accounts perhaps fudged the question of more radical change after the mid-eighteenth century, the very nature of their narratives was resolutely gradualist and thus inhibited a "revolutionary" view.[6] French society and economy were therefore left waiting patiently at the station for the railroad that, only from late in the nineteenth century, would—Eugen Weber dixit (more or less)—transport them into the modern age.[7]

This gradualist, even glacial picture of the Ancien Régime economy had, of course, immediate consequences for the other pillar of the dual revolutions scheme, that predicated on the radical sociopolitical effects of the

(Oxford, 1985); R. Samuel, "The Workshop of the World," *History Workshop Journal* 3 (1977): 6–72; and (trying to reverse the trend, but with a hundred-year framework in mind) M. Berg and P. Hudson, "Rehabilitating the Industrial Revolution," *Economic History Review* 45 (1992): 24–50. On bourgeois elements in eighteenth-century social structure, see E. P. Thompson's essays republished in his book *Customs in Common* (London, 1991); P. Langford, *Public Life and the Propertied Englishman 1689–1798* (Oxford, 1991); J. Smail, *The Origins of Middle-Class Culture* (Ithaca, N.Y., 1994); and M. Hunt, *The Middling Sort: Commerce, Gender, and the Family in England 1680–1780* (Berkeley, 1996). The consequences of these revisionist accounts are discussed in D. Wahrman, *Imagining the Middle Class: The Political Representation of Class in Britain, c. 1780–1840* (Cambridge, 1995), pp. 1–6 (and see there for further references).

6. Fernand Braudel, whose influence on French post–World War II historiography cannot be overestimated, famously steered clear of the vagaries of "event-history" and political controversy. Significantly, when toward the end of his life he did attempt a history of France as a whole (*The Identity of France,* London, 1988 [French edition, 1986]), it was largely in terms of the importance of determinations that preceded 1789 (and often the early modern period to boot), and that made the study of recent history into one of long-existent marks and traces. For E. Le Roy Ladurie's emphasis on *l'histoire immobile,* see his article with this title in *Annales E. S. C.* 29 (1974)—reprinted as "History that Stands Still" in id., *The Mind and Method of the Historian* (London, 1981). Cf. Pierre Goubert, *L'Ancien Régime,* 2 vols., Paris, 1969 and 1973 (the first volume translated as *The Ancien Régime* [London, 1973]).

7. E. Weber, *Peasants into Frenchmen: The Modernization of Rural France, 1870–1914* (Stanford, 1976).

French Revolution. For if the French Revolution was supposed to bring to power a suddenly empowered bourgeoisie, where was this bourgeoisie supposed to have sprung from, and where could it be seen? Already in the mid-1950s, Alfred Cobban, the spiritual progenitor of a whole generation of revisionist historians of the French Revolution, had questioned whether this was a "bourgeois revolution" at all. Not only was the eighteenth-century economy increasingly seen as too backward to produce a conquering bourgeois class; prosopographical analyses revealed the revolutionaries themselves to have been an uncapitalist (and therefore, arguably, unbourgeois) crew—disgruntled state-office holders, vindictive Grub Street journalists and hack writers, starving peasants, lawyers on the make, and the like. Pre-revolutionary France had produced not a class-conscious bourgeoisie but an interclass elite of landowners—the "*notables*"—who were (a nice gradualist touch) both the main influences on and the principal beneficiaries of the revolutionary process. And while the counterpoint has been made that a more expansive definition of *bourgeois,* to encompass not only industrial capitalists (à la Cobban) but also middling groups increasingly plugged into expanding markets, might bring a revolutionary bourgeoisie back into the frame, this commercial-society-centered perspective could in itself be contained within the gradualist mode.[8] Likewise, the work of François Furet, attacking the "Jacobino-Marxist catechism" in French Revolutionary historiography, sought to replace Marxism with a Tocquevillian perspective that turned the revolutionaries into unwitting abettors of long-term changes in political and administrative developments.[9] Then again, the belated but influential heyday of Jürgen Habermas's *Strukturwandel der Öffentlichkeit* (published in 1962, but having a wide impact only from the late 1980s) reinforced the same effect: his emphasis on the structural aspects of the "bourgeois public sphere" allowed historians to reinstate the importance of bourgeois social characteristics without attributing the Revolution to a revolutionary bourgeoisie, thus maintaining a slowly evolving, gradualist perspective.[10]

Overall, then, each revisionist rewriting of eighteenth-century history on either side of the Channel was undermining one side of the "dual revolution" and in the process pulling the rug from under one narrative of the revolutionary rise of the bourgeoisie—be its engine an economic or a political

8. This is the argument developed in C. Jones, "Bourgeois Revolution Revivified: 1789 and Social Change," in C. Lucas, ed., *Rewriting the French Revolution* (Oxford, 1991).

9. F. Furet, *Penser la révolution française* (Paris, 1978); translated as *Interpreting the French Revolution* (Cambridge, 1981).

10. J. Habermas, *The Structural Transformation of the Public Sphere: An Inquiry into a Category of Bourgeois Society,* trans. T. Burger (Cambridge, Mass., 1989 [originally 1962]). For one influential reading of Ancien Régime France through a Habermasian lens, see R. Chartier, *The Cultural Origins of the French Revolution* (Durham, N.C., 1991).

one. Together, moreover, they also placed in doubt the contrastive juxtaposition of France and England. Thus, the interclass, unified, enduring French elite of the *notables* seemed now little different from E. P. Thompson's unified and enduring "agrarian bourgeoisie" in England; Jonathan Clark's explicit agenda was to point out how little did England's "Ancien Régime" differ from its continental counterpart; and John Brewer's exposure of the eighteenth-century British state as more active and effective than its seeming invisibility had led us to believe likewise reintegrated it into the paradigms of continental history, undermining its supposed exceptionalism.[11] Among economic historians, François Crouzet was one who realized the consequences of the gradualist revisionism of English industrialization for the supposed contrast that had underpinned the dual revolution account, pointing out that in fact the French economy had performed well in the eighteenth century, even outperforming the British in many sectors.[12] Once again, the consensually reiterated black-and-white contrast between the two countries appeared rather shaky.

The clear-cut juxtaposition of England and France as supposedly opposite models became fuzzier still as a result of changes in the geographical perspective of history writing at the same time: on the one hand the trend toward regionalized studies, on the other the shift to globalized perspectives. Regionalization has been particularly strong in France, where the classics of post–World War II historiography have been regional studies intent on uncovering local differences, locating internal cultural frontiers, and dissolving national certitudes—indeed, with such success that Paris, for centuries the prism through which historians tended to view French history, has become, in relative terms, a historiographical also-ran.[13] England has also seen its share of regional emphases, especially by the economic historians who replaced sweeping accounts of the Industrial Revolution with an insistence on the regional, uneven aspects of industrialization; at the same time, the status of "England" itself was shaken, as historians began looking at it within the broader context of "the four nations" in the British Isles. Overall, therefore, national comparisons began losing their edge, since it was no longer clear what was the unified, salient entity to be compared. At the other end of the spectrum, the relative globalization of historians' perspectives in the 1980s and 1990s could only have the effect of highlighting the extent to

11. J. C. D. Clark, *English Society 1688–1832* (Cambridge, 1985); J. Brewer, *The Sinews of Power: War, Money and the English State, 1688–1783* (New York, 1989).

12. F. Crouzet's series of articles and book chapters are conveniently collected, and added to, in his *De la supériorité de l'Angleterre sur la France: L'économique et l'imaginaire (XVIIe–XXe siècle)* (Paris, 1985). See also P. O'Brien and C. Keyder, *Economic Growth in Britain and France 1780–1914: Two Paths to the Twentieth Century* (London, 1978).

13. A useful synthesis of the achievement of this mass of doctoral studies is F. Braudel and E. Labrousse, eds., *Histoire économique et sociale de la France*, vol. 2, *1660–1789* (Paris, 1970).

which Britain and France, competing as they were on the world stage for commercial and political dominance, subjected much of the rest of the world to similar pressures. To a sugar-producing Caribbean slave out in the "periphery" (to adopt the language of world-systems analyst Immanuel Wallerstein)—whether in English Jamaica or in French Saint-Domingue—the "core" states, England and France, must have looked pretty much alike.[14] Once again, the presumed opposites found themselves on the same side of the pertinent divide.

III

The cumulative outcome of so much historical writing from a wide range of angles has been to muddy almost out of all recognition the once neat contrast between the politically precocious France and the economically pioneering England. The dual revolutions framework appeared by now a "colossal wreck" whose elements lie, as in the "Ozymandias" of Percy Bysshe Shelley, as testimony to bygone power, like "two vast and trunkless legs of stone" in the revisionist wilderness where "the lone and level sands stretch far away."

At the same time, while empirical research has been eroding the bases of the dual revolutions model from one flank, new theoretical and methodological developments have been gnawing at them from another, shifting the grounds in terms of foci of investigation, structures of argument, criteria of relevance, and prioritization of historical causation. History's own "revolution" of the last generation, that which is often put together under the rubric of "cultural history," has of course permeated its fields of inquiry far and wide.[15] But it is curious, as we shall see, how many of those historiographical breakthroughs in fact did have the second half of the eighteenth century in mind.

This was hardly true, however, of the earlier signs of the cultural turn, which were neatly attuned to those gradualist forces undermining the vision of the dual revolution. Crucial here was the inspiration that the early "new cultural history" took from anthropology, especially cultural anthropology (in the Geertzian mold). Anthropology did not provide the best tools for analyzing historical transformations, and when change was addressed, it was most often of the glacial kind, fitting resolutely within the slow-changing,

---

14. I. Wallerstein, *The Modern World System*, vol. 2, *Mercantilism and the Consolidation of the European World Economy, 1600–1750* (New York, 1980). Even within Europe, moreover, comparative historians have tended to open up a differential gap more between an Anglo-Franco-Dutch northwestern region and an eastern and/or southern geographical expanse marked by large landowners, state centralization, and a weak mercantile sector.

15. A useful introduction remains L. Hunt, "Introduction: History, Culture, and Text," in L. Hunt, ed., *The New Cultural History* (Berkeley, 1989), pp. 1–22.

gradualist mode. Small wonder, then, that the preferred terrain of this type of history writing in the 1970s and early 1980s—the work of Natalie Zemon Davis, Keith Thomas, or Carlo Ginzburg, for example—was the late medieval and early modern period, that long stretch of Le Roy Ladurie's *histoire immobile,* stopping short of the more unruly shifts of the late eighteenth and nineteenth centuries. In France, this preference was reflected in the *Annaliste* interest in *mentalités*—the mental equipment supposedly antecedent to the formulation of ideas that Braudel characteristically depicted not as forces of change but rather as "long-term prisons" *(prisons de longue durée).*[16] Similar was the effect of the long-delayed discovery of the work of the German sociologist Norbert Elias on the "civilizing process," which likewise provided an account of gradual, centuries-long cultural change that freely drew on early-twentieth-century ethnography.[17]

In the 1980s and 1990s, however, new perspectives came to the fore that focused attention once again on radical change. Drawing their inspiration more from literary criticism and cultural studies than from anthropology, these investigations were often (though not always) by self-description "postmodern," a posture that forced their practitioners to engage with the nature and origins of the modern. What these new perspectives had in common was the insistence on the historically specific, constructed, contingent, and politically freighted makeup of seemingly natural, inevitable, and given social "realities" or "experiences," be they notions of difference between people, relationships predicated upon such notions, group identities together with the allegiances that they entail, or individual identities predicated on a belief in a unified, centered subject. We can single out three different (if at times overlapping) developments that pointed in this direction with particular force: feminist criticism, linguistic studies of class and politics (at times referred to as "the linguistic turn"), and the scholarship inspired by the writings of the French philosopher Michel Foucault. These culturalist emphases continued to undermine the contrast between France and England, a contrast that had been predicated on economic or political perspectives. But at the same time, by drawing attention once again to key shifts in the late eighteenth and early nineteenth centuries as the supposed cradles of modernity, they have provided a different dimension for what could perhaps be better called "an age of cultural revolutions."

Feminist historiography, even before it embraced the linguistic turn, had already done a good deal to resuscitate the dual revolutions paradigm for this period. This body of scholarship suggested that the essence of bour-

16. F. Braudel, *Écrits sur l'histoire* (Paris, 1969), p. 51.
17. N. Elias, *The Civilizing Process,* vol. 1, *The History of Manners,* and vol. 2, *Power and Civility* (New York, 1978 [originally 1939]).

geois society, as it came into being in the nineteenth century, was situated in its gender relations, in particular the sharply delineated separation of the public and the private, the confinement of women to the domestic sphere, and the explicit masculinization of the political one. The origins of this configuration were sought, rather predictably, in the French Revolution on one side of the Channel, and in the late-eighteenth-century birth of a new class society on the other. For France, a host of writers—affirming the predictions of political theorist Carole Pateman—made the case for the French Revolution as a decisive shift in the position of women. In the influential words of Joan Landes, "the exclusion of women from the bourgeois public was not incidental but central to its incarnation," a constitutive component of republican revolutionary ideology.[18] Some authors (including Sarah Maza and Dena Goodman) have sought to push back the origins of this demarcation into the late Enlightenment, yet without giving up the notion of a radical break.[19]

In England, Catherine Hall and Leonore Davidoff rewrote the history of the emergence of modern class society in the period 1780–1850. Their 1987 account centered around the middle class—newly formed within a changing economic order—but located its key manifestation in the new gendered reconfiguration of public and private, effected through the intertwined grip of domestic ideology and Evangelical religion. This view has since been complemented by Anna Clark's analysis of the emergence of modern gender relations in the making of the English working class—linking, as Thompson had done, industrial with consequent political developments in her account of the crucial developments of the same half century.[20] Together, these studies reestablished the narrative of rupture in the late-eighteenth-century emergence of bourgeois society—characterized as it now came to be by its "modern" gender configurations—through a primarily political path in France or a primarily socioeconomic one in England. Needless to say, they were also immediately countered by skeptical revisionists who pointed out the long-term continuities of women's experi-

18. J. Landes, *Women and the Public Sphere in the Age of the French Revolution* (Ithaca, N.Y., 1988), p. 7. J. Scott, "'A Woman Who Has Only Paradoxes to Offer': Olympe de Gouges Claims Rights for Women," in S. E. Melzer and L. W. Rabine, eds., *Rebel Daughters: Women and the French Revolution* (Oxford, 1992), pp. 102–20, and see the other contributions to this collection. See also C. Pateman, *The Sexual Contract* (Stanford, 1988).

19. D. Goodman, *The Republic of Letters: A Cultural History of the French Enlightenment* (Ithaca, N.Y., 1994). S. Maza, "Women, the Bourgeoisie, and the Public Sphere," *French Historical Studies* 17 (1992): 935–50.

20. L. Davidoff and C. Hall, *Family Fortunes: Men and Women of the English Middle Class, 1780–1850* (London, 1987). A. Clark, *The Struggle for the Breeches: Gender and the Making of the British Working Class* (Berkeley, 1995).

ences that belied, once again, the emphasis on the late-eighteenth-century discontinuities of social experience.[21]

At the same time, however, a second wave of feminist historiography— taking its cue from a large body of theoretical writings, such as those of Denise Riley and Judith Butler—was shifting its focus from women's experiences to the constructions of gender as a mode of differentiation. This was a fundamental step in the evolving perspective of the new cultural history— that is, the shift of focus from supposedly "objective," anterior social reality, and the impersonally observable aspects of the social process, to their representations, to the historically specific constructions of the meanings attributed to such realities. This perspective also received reinforcement from discussions of racial and ethnic difference, especially in the emerging field of postcolonial studies—a field that has hitherto been less apparent in this than in later periods (at least among historians, as opposed to literary critics). For the history of gender, nobody has been more influential in advocating this move than Joan Scott. Scott insisted on a linguistic understanding of the operations of gender, stressing that there was "a connection between the study of 'language' and the study of gender, when both are carefully defined." This perspective then led her to a wider rejection of "experience" as a category of analysis that presupposes the system of signification that we would like to examine critically, shifting the analytical probe once more to the workings and internal dynamics of language.[22] And again, once the conceptual and representational histories of sex, gender, heterosexuality, and homosexuality began to be written, the period under discussion here appeared at least for some scholars to be a crucial one for the setting in motion of those modern understandings that the feminist critique was now at such pains to destabilize. Thus, Thomas Laqueur influentially posited the late eighteenth century as the juncture when premodern western European understandings of sex—understandings that had been around since the Greeks—underwent a decisive shift into modernity, while Wahrman has proposed that this period witnessed a radical break in the crystallization of modern understandings of gender.[23]

21. For the English case, see A. Vickery, "Golden Age to Separate Spheres? A Review of the Categories and Chronology of English Women's History," *Historical Journal* 36 (1993): 383– 414. The long-term perspective is also central to A. Fletcher, *Gender, Sex, and Subordination in England 1500–1800* (New Haven, 1995).

22. J. W. Scott, *Gender and the Politics of History* (New York, 1988), p. 55. Id., "Experience," in J. Butler and J. Scott, eds., *Feminists Theorize the Political* (New York, 1992), pp. 22–40. D. Riley, *"Am I That Name?" Feminism and the Category of "Women" in History* (Minneapolis, 1988). J. Butler, *Gender Trouble: Feminism and the Subversion of Identity* (New York, 1990).

23. T. Laqueur, *Making Sex: Body and Gender from the Greeks to Freud* (Cambridge, Mass., 1990); id., "Orgasm, Generation, and the Politics of Reproductive Biology," in C. Gallagher and T. Laqueur, eds., *The Making of the Modern Body* (Berkeley, 1987), pp. 1–41. See also

Meanwhile, revisionist historians of class and politics in France and Britain have likewise found themselves moving into the realms of language and representations. Perhaps inevitably, the development of what came to be called "the linguistic turn" in the historiographies of both countries, from the mid-1980s onward, again followed the double helix of the dual revolutions paradigm. In the French case, language provided a rich new key to the revisionist (or was it by now "postrevisionist"?) interpretation of the French Revolution. Lynn Hunt and Keith Baker, following a path originally blazed by François Furet, highlighted the role of democratic ideology and language in providing the script for the revolutionary assemblies after 1789—a script that was unworkable: once the revolutionaries had adopted a Rousseauist version of the general will into their constitutional arrangements and political aspirations, the Terror of 1793–94 became implicit, even inevitable. So, Simon Schama, putting the icing on the revisionist cake, could contend that 1794 would in essence be 1789—only "with a higher body count." Hunt in particular highlighted both the enabling and the limiting aspects of French revolutionary language, seeking to show (as she put it elsewhere) "the ways in which linguistic practice, rather than simply reflecting social reality, could actively be an instrument of (or constitute) power." Indeed, the very conspicuous seam between the two parts of Hunt's influential 1984 book *Politics, Culture, and Class in the French Revolution*—one of social analysis, the other linguistic—was in itself an unmistakable (if unwitting) testimony to the interpretive shift that she has been so important in pushing forth.[24]

For England, the breakthrough was signaled by the work of Gareth Stedman Jones (paralleled, independently, by William Sewell in France), especially the pathbreaking essay "Rethinking Chartism" of 1983, subsequently taken up by Patrick Joyce and Dror Wahrman. Pointing to the continuity of working-class political language in the first half of the nineteenth century with that of the eighteenth, Stedman Jones put in question the

L. Jordanova, *Sexual Visions: Images of Gender in Science and Medicine between the Eighteenth and Twentieth Centuries* (Madison, Wis., 1989); L. Schiebinger, *The Mind Has No Sex? Women in the Origins of Modern Science* (Cambridge, Mass., 1989), esp. chap. 7; id., *Nature's Body: Gender in the Making of Modern Science* (Boston, 1993); and D. Wahrman, "*Percy*'s Prologue: From Gender Play to Gender Panic in Eighteenth-Century England," *Past and Present* 159 (May 1998): 113–60.

24. Furet, *Interpreting the French Revolution*. L. Hunt, *Politics, Culture, and Class in the French Revolution* (Berkeley, 1984). See also K. Baker, *Inventing the French Revolution* (Cambridge, 1990), and S. Schama, *Citizens: A Chronicle of the French Revolution* (New York, 1989). A peculiarity of French historiography that increased the receptiveness to these language-based departures, one may add, was the Francocentric subdiscipline of the history of the book, which placed texts at the center of investigation as key cultural artifacts; it is hardly a coincidence that so many key figures in the textually sensitive cultural history of the late 1980s and the 1990s (such as Robert Darnton, Roger Chartier, Natalie Davis, and Carla Hesse) were also inhabitants of these intellectual quarters.

Thompsonian social-historical account of the turn-of-the-century making of the English working class. In its place he insisted on the primacy and constitutive importance of political language as endowing political behavior with meaning. Closely prefiguring Scott's feminist critique of "experience," Stedman Jones wrote that "we cannot therefore decode political language to reach a primal and material expression of interest since it is the discursive structure of political language which conceived and defined interest in the first place," a point that sounded the trumpet for the conceptual assault on "class" (especially by Joyce). Wahrman's reworking of the origins of class society in the late eighteenth and early nineteenth centuries similarly employed a framework that gave precedence to language and representations—with their own contingent dynamics—over the supposedly inexorable pressures of anterior social processes, in explaining the emergence of a newly resonant map of social categories centered around the image of the rising middle class.[25]

The third strand we chose to single out within the development of cultural history, the pervasive—if sometimes nebulous—influence of French philosopher Michel Foucault, of course underlies much of the work we have already discussed. We say "nebulous" because Foucault's intellectual thumbprints are evident not only among committed Foucauldian scholars, but much more broadly in the sensibilities of many historians who do not venture at great lengths into the thickets of postmodern theory. Most of the moves associated with the cultural-historical perspective have been prefigured in some form by Foucault (however incompletely, or imprecisely, as has often been pointed out): the shift from "social reality" to representations and discourse; the emphasis on the deceptive, freighted, historically specific nature of our assumptions about supposedly stable concepts, be they our organizing concepts of thinking about history, or the historical subjects themselves; the consequent insistence on taking no presupposition as a given; and the rejection of a notion of undivided, unconflicted subjects

---

25. G. Stedman Jones, *Languages of Class: Studies in English Working Class History 1832–1982* (Cambridge, 1983), p. 22; note the virtually identical suggestion in Baker, *Inventing the French Revolution*, p. 6. See also P. Joyce, *Visions of the People: Industrial England and the Question of Class, 1848–1914* (Cambridge, 1991); D. Wahrman, *Imagining the Middle Class: The Political Representation of Class in Britain, c. 1780–1840* (Cambridge, 1995); and W. H. Sewell, *Work and Revolution in France: The Language of Labor from the Old Regime to 1848* (Cambridge, 1980). If the history of the book was a "local" forte that helped such analyses of France, then the so-called Cambridge school of the history of political thought can be seen as the English equivalent: inspired by Quentin Skinner and J. G. A. Pocock, these scholars took apart key texts in their subdiscipline to reveal a palimpsest of different and not necessarily compatible political languages that underlay them, thus belying their view as coherent unities. Again, it is hardly a coincidence that Stedman Jones (like Keith Baker) had been well versed in the Cambridge insights into political language, which he then brought to bear on his revisionist account of the emergence of modern industrial class society.

with clear purpose and agency.[26] It may be noted in this context that the influence of Foucault (whose *Folie et déraison: Histoire de la folie à l'âge classique* dated back to 1961), precociously detectable in literary theory and cultural studies, took some time to make its way into the historical academy: the trickle turned into a flood only when it fused with the mutually reinforcing new cultural turn of the 1980s and 1990s.

Most important for our purposes here, the particular periodization highlighted in this volume is also Foucauldian. Apart from a return toward the end of his life to classical antiquity, the crucial historical shift on which Foucault focused his efforts remained that from the late eighteenth to the early nineteenth centuries, with the emergence of the modern always in mind. This was true of the more historically inclined of his works, such as *Birth of the Clinic,* which traced the genealogy of the "Paris School" of the 1790s and thereby the emergence of modern scientific medicine; *Madness and Civilization,* which explored the emergence of the lunatic asylum, particularly in France and England, in the same decade; and *Discipline and Punish,* which offered a profound rumination on the emergence of a more disciplinarian society. It was also true of his more philosophical studies—*The Order of Things* and *The Archaeology of Knowledge*—which highlighted this period as marking a fundamental shift in the western episteme.

So Foucault and his followers—like the feminist historians and the linguistic "turners"—have for the most part retained a heavier investment in notions of radical rupture and discontinuity than much of the social, economic, and political revisionism that was the backdrop to their writing. And again, it is worthy to note how many of those who privilege discontinuity over continuity in the making of the modern persist in latching onto the late eighteenth and early nineteenth centuries as the significant moment of rupture. It is as though the revolutionary arch over this period is being reerected, even while its content is changing before our eyes. For, as we have suggested, the new "revolutionaries," in contradistinction to the social gradualists, have been cultural revolutionaries.

IV

The cultural turn has if anything only widened the range of analytical approaches in play. Some historians are keen on going down the postmodern path (or rather down *a* postmodern path of their preference) as far as it will go. Others are intent on providing syntheses, feeling that the bathwater may well still contain a baby or two. Still other historians have recently

26. Among a vast literature by and on Foucault, see the cultural historical angles opened up in J. Goldstein, ed., *Foucault and the Writing of History* (Cambridge, Mass., 1994), and C. Jones and R. Porter, eds., *Reassessing Foucault: Power, Medicine, and the Body* (London, 1993).

been sounding the tocsin, suggesting that we have traveled too far along this path and should now pull away from the brink. In particular, one interesting countertrend can be described as an anticonstructionist backlash: wondering, as Barbara Taylor does in this volume, whether historians have overemphasized the cultural construction of subjectivity to the preclusion of deep, trans-historical mechanisms that are a precondition to becoming human at all. For Taylor (as for other historians recently—notably Lyndal Roper),[27] psychoanalysis is one obvious place to look for a way forward: her test case here is that of the purported misogyny of Mary Wollstonecraft, which Taylor proposes to explore within the context of Wollstonecraft's feminism through a recourse to the level of underlying unconscious fantasies—what she calls "the psychic history of feminism."

Methodology is most explicitly the concern of Gareth Stedman Jones's essay: he uses a recent analysis of current French historiography to probe the methodological and conceptual weaknesses of the *Annales* tradition, which in the recent past, as we have suggested, has been one of the most significant vessels of socioeconomic gradualism. He finds the spirit of renewal within the *Annales* camp inhibited by an alliance with the social sciences, restricting an engagement with language—and thus with key aspects of cultural-historical analysis.

Broadly speaking, most of the essays in this volume fall into one (or more) of the three strands we identified in the cultural-historical analysis of this period. Like Stedman Jones, Sarah Maza represents the class-oriented linguistic turn as she investigates language to determine the salience of class in the analysis of the French Revolution. Looking at discussions of the Third Estate and at the French National Guard in the early stages of the Revolution, she asks what is the significance of the fact that these two sites most likely to flag up a "revolutionary bourgeoisie" in fact reveal a language that eschews any terms that draw social ("class") distinctions between people.

Other contributions speak directly to the feminist critique of this period. Michael McKeon uses the literary history of the genre of domestic fiction to map changing notions of public and private—or "domesticity"—in England in relation to historical developments in wider realms, including the family and the state, political theory, and political economy. In the process McKeon posits a model of "cultural revolution," which strives to reconcile change with continuity, looking back as well as forward. Carla Hesse, for her part, encourages a radical revision of one of the pervasive tenets of the feminist historiography of this period in France: the notion that the revolutionary decade saw (after a brief window of opportunity) the progressive

27. L. Roper, *Oedipus and the Devil: Witchcraft, Sexuality, and Religion in Early Modern Europe* (London, 1994). Cf. W. M. Reddy, "Against Constructionism: The Historical Ethnography of Emotions," *Current Anthropology* 18, no. 3 (June 1997): 327–51.

confinement of women to the domestic, private realm. On the contrary, her authorship statistics suggest a greater, rather than lesser, visibility of women in the public world of print throughout the decade following the French Revolution. At the same time, however, she shows how the pressures of discourses intended to essentialize female nature and roles led to a gendering of representational strategies in print—involving, in particular, the insistence on the fictive and indeterminate nature of female identity—which has persisted well into the twentieth century.

Alongside these contributions to the critiques of class and gender, our volume includes two chapters that involve an exploration of race. As we have suggested, this question has so far made less of an impact on the historical study of this period; but the essays of David Bell and Kathleen Wilson demonstrate the potential in the period for analyses of this type. Bell uses one bloody incident in the Seven Years' War, together with the widespread propaganda it generated, to show the construction in France of what looks like an embryonic racism directed against perfidious and "barbarian" Albion. In this discourse, honed in the American periphery in the presence of colonists and "savages" but directed against France's closest neighbors, he identifies the seeds of more modern, racially based forms of nationalism. Similarly, Wilson is interested in how new ideas of difference—difference of race, ethnicity, and nationality—were linked to emergent modernity in Britain. Her essay explores the consequences of the "Second Age of Discovery"—of Captain Cook's encounters with the South Pacific—for the changing meanings of Englishness as they were elaborated in a variety of discourses: scientific, historical, and theatrical.

Paul Friedland's and Thomas Laqueur's chapters can be seen as examples of the more diffuse, Foucauldian investigations of the origins of modernity. Friedland identifies a key transformation en route to modernity in the understandings of representation itself. Looking in parallel at the realms of theater and politics in eighteenth-century France, he shows the shift in both realms from theories of re-presentation as concrete embodiment to notions of representation in their modern, metaphoric, abstract sense. This parallel development, he proposes, underlay the new notions of political representation enacted by the revolutionary assemblies, as well as the theatricalization of the political during the revolutionary period. Thomas Laqueur's chapter likewise suggests that this period, within western Europe as a whole, was pivotal, in this case in the construction of a new, more socially and spatially demarcated boundary between the living and the dead. In a defining moment of modernity, graveyards and cemeteries were moved from the heart to the margins of community life, installing a new conception—for Laqueur, a new bourgeois conception—of life and death. If for Maza the notion of the bourgeoisie as political actor requires further investigation, Laqueur suggests that one way forward is to extend the field of signification to forms of collective behavior regarding—literally—matters of life and death.

Carolyn Steedman shares Laqueur's interest in the cultural origins of bourgeois identity, which she situates firmly in a specific social context— that of the relationship between master and servant, a relationship that involved virtually all of England's propertied classes, and perhaps as much as 40 percent of the population, in the role of servant at some point during their lives. This ubiquitous relationship, Steedman argues, involved the formation of a legal and social understanding of the personhood of the lower classes, a new articulation of the consciousness of social inequality, and a fundamental molding of bourgeois subjectivity. In a very different way, James Chandler also locates—within literary works and with a literary-critical eye—a new form of subjectivity during this period, based on a new "sentimental probability." By this term Chandler refers to new, "modern" codes of expectation and understandings of chance, design, and causality, a framework born of eighteenth-century commercial and literary conditions that represented, in his view, a crucial moral and epistemological paradigm shift.

Finally, Dror Wahrman's concluding essay tries to draw together some common threads emerging from these contributions, proposing one way of thinking about a perhaps revolutionary transformation during this period. Beginning with evidence for a cultural shift in possible—and impossible— imaginings of configurations of sex and gender in the late eighteenth century, he draws upon other essays in this volume to suggest a radical break in this period in the understandings of identity itself—be it class, race, or gender identity—or indeed in prior understandings of an underlying self. Wahrman's speculations focus on one feature of modernity that, he argues, underlies all these developments, namely, the move toward essentialization—a strong candidate for the title of "cultural revolution."

The Places of the Dead in Modernity

Thomas W. Laqueur

This essay is about the origin and meaning of the spaces where we put the dead, about the history of the cemetery: a "fascinating and complicated development that reveals a whole new side of contemporary sensibility"; the "identifying mark of a culture," as Philippe Aries put it.[1] But more specifically, I want to suggest that the secular, explicitly landscaped memorial park—that is, the cemetery, as opposed to the churchyard or other sacred or customary space—is so precisely the invention of a critical period in the history of our times (the late eighteenth and early nineteenth centuries) that thinking about its origins and meaning might allow us to understand what, if anything, is distinctively modern about death, and particularly about putting the dead to rest in modernity.

How much can be said about the subject is not clear. As William Empson puts it in his poem "Ignorance of Death,"

> I feel very blank upon this topic
> And think that though important, and proper for anyone to bring up,
> It is one that most people should be prepared to be blank upon.

But even if there is little to be said about death, what we do with the dead is less shrouded in silence. We know that unlike the poor, the dead are not always with us. In fact, beginning in 1804 they began to move decisively away from the living into cities of their own: out of churchyards and other religious spaces in which their bodies had been jumbled together in close proximity to each other and out of the day-to-day comings and goings of the living, into geographically distant—and, for the middle class, far more

---

1. Philippe Aries, *The Hour of Our Death* (New York: Alfred A. Knopf, 1981), 476; id., *Images of Man and Death*, trans. Janet Lloyd (Cambridge: Harvard University Press, 1985), 238.

private—representations of where they had once dwelled. They moved onto/into their freehold properties in the necropolis.

Père-Lachaise, in Paris, was not the first cemetery built by Europeans (in 1804); Park Street, in Calcutta, opened in 1767 and soon filled with tombs that look like they might have come from roads leading out of a Roman city but in fact were on the edge of Sir Elijah Impey's deer park.[2] Certainly other colonial cemeteries take precedence, as do of course the Islamic cemeteries, especially those of Constantinople, which Mary Wortley Montagu and William Wordsworth and Samuel Taylor Coleridge and a host of others so admired. But these antecedents should not detract us from the fact that Père-Lachaise was, and was understood at the time to be, a radical innovation in the spatial geography of the dead in relation to the living and of dead bodies in relation to each other. It very quickly became the symbol of—almost a name for—a kind of burial place that triumphed wherever the bourgeoisie triumphed or hoped to triumph.

Like the poor, however, the status of the dead as a community unto themselves or as part of the larger community is always fluid and was especially so in the decades around 1800. The Reformation in the Protestant world had severed their direct ties to the living, and even where purgatory persisted the souls who waited there received far less attention by the end of the eighteenth century than they had earlier. In the nineteenth century the world of the dead was once again displaced. The novel space of the cemetery allowed a certain class of the living to imagine a new world order of the dead: one in which lineage gave way to history and in which there were no "strangers"— as there were in the churchyard—because anyone with means and talent could gain entry on the same category as anyone else; one in which the historical specificity of a place and the autarky of the parish gave way to self-consciously planned landscapes—picturesque, natural, fanciful, or dull— that could be anywhere and mean anything and belong to anyone. The Emperor of Brazil wanted a Père-Lachaise near his capital, and the Merchant Adventurer's Company wanted one in Glasgow.[3] It would, on the other hand, have been nonsensical to speak of exporting Stoke Poges, the parish churchyard that Thomas Gray supposedly imagined as the site of his most famous elegy and the most reprinted poem of the late eighteenth century; similarly, the Cemetery of the Innocents in Paris had meaning only there. Their essence lay in being where they were, and had been, since far enough back to become a hallowed and meaningful part of a landscape. In the cemetery, customary rights to communal use of certain ground or to

2. *The South Park Street Cemetery, Calcutta* (Calcutta: Statesman Commercial Press, Calcutta, 1978; reprinted by British Association for Cemeteries in South Asia, 1986), 8.

3. George Blair, *Biographic and Descriptive Sketches of Glasgow Necropolis* (Glasgow: Maurice Ogle, 1858), vii.

areas of the church in which landed property held an easement gave way to freehold property that anyone could buy in scores of locations. It was a world in which commercially available art produced a bricolage that could signify as much or as little as its purchasers wanted—arranged like a museum in some order or no apparent one—unfettered by tradition or the restraints of a common history or culture. The monuments in a church succeeded one another as styles succeeded each other over centuries.

Briefly put, I want to suggest that the cemetery reveals—and is the result of—two distinct but intimately related features of imagining death and the community of the dead in modernity. The first has to do specifically with the dead body. Increasingly absorbed into the language of medicine, hygiene, and chemistry, metaphysically meaningless, it became unbearably repulsive in its purely and essentially material decay. William Hale, archdeacon of London in the 1840s and '50s, may well have been self-interested in his opposition to the cemetery but he was right when he said that the motives of its proponents had "their origin in a philosophical [and I might add visceral] distaste for the emblems and the reality of death."[4] And as the decaying dead body became an object of scientific attention it became also a source of acute anxiety and distaste, an anxiety that, I suggest, was displaced onto the monument and onto custom-built places of memory. Père-Lachaise, as the leading English designer of cemeteries put it, was "dedicated to the genius of memory," a place where, like the ancients, we moderns can contemplate death "never *polluted* with the idea of a charnel house . . . nor the revolting emblems of mortality."[5] Memory cleanses.

The second feature has to do with community. The bourgeoisie who were the self-conscious creators and the exclusive—or in any case exclusively visible—inhabitants of the cemetery imagined therein a new world; a new community of the dead, represented in the clean, sweet-smelling, wholly novel, real, and symbolic geography of the cemetery, gave a certain weight, solidity, and credence to a new community of the living.

In order to suggest how oddly modern the cemetery is, I begin with the present and work backward. Two instances: My colleague Amos Funkenstein, the distinguished Jewish historian, died recently. He was born in Israel, the

---

4. William Hale, *Intramural Burial in England Is Not Injurious to the Public Health; Its Abolition Is Injurious to Religion and Morals* (London: Rivingtons, 1855). Hale in fact was remarkably clear about the philosophical and political stakes in the shift from a metaphysical—he would say religious—to a materialist understanding of the body and its place in the civic order. Well over a century before Foucault he argued that the civil registration of births and deaths—biological events—as opposed to the ecclesiastical recording of rituals such as baptisms and burials was tantamount to giving the police (i.e., the state) license to enter the most intimate moments and spaces.

5. John Claudius Loudon, *An Encyclopedia of Gardening*, new ed., rev. (London: Longman, 1835), entry 1562 (emphasis added).

son of a German-born rabbi; he spoke perfect but accented English and spent what appeared to be an enormously rich intellectual life conversing with Aristotle, St. Thomas, and Immanuel Kant, among others, in their own languages and on more or less equal terms. At the time of his death he held appointments at Berkeley and Tel Aviv. He is buried in Sunrise Cemetery, across from Hilltop Mall on Interstate 80 heading east to Sacramento. I had been there before—that is, I had taken the right exit for the cemetery rather than the left exit to Macy's—on only one previous occasion: when I was a pall bearer for the father of one of my colleagues, a man whom I had met only a few times. He had come from the Bronx to Berkeley to be near his son and died soon after the migration west. My former colleague from Tel Aviv and the father of one of my current colleagues from New York rest in the Jewish section of a cemetery (Christians and others are just around the corner or over the rise) whose location not far from the Richmond refineries was determined by nothing more important than—or perhaps I should say by something as important as—the price of real estate.

A second instance of the strangeness of laying the dead to rest in our era might be the case of my parents. Their ashes are in a flower bed next to the summer cottage in Virginia that they built in 1955, five years after coming to America. In a sense this is not so odd; they loved the place and I return there every year and have a sense of their presence. But their being there is the result of a very modern history. My father might perhaps have ended up in the great Wiessensee Jewish Cemetery in Berlin, with its acres of magnificent classical mausoleums, arcades, and tombs modeled on that of some late Roman consul, or near his father in Hamburg, who is marked by a tombstone that similarly, if more modestly, reflects the commitment in death of the German Jewish community to imagining themselves as the Jewish section of a German "*burgertum.*" It did not work out that way. His mother's ashes are somewhere in West Virginia. My mother's father's ashes are somewhere near a camp in Poland, and her mother's body somewhere in Israel.

I am by no means the first to find odd this dispersal of the dead, here and there in unlikely places. A visitor to San Francisco in 1855, for example, described the cemetery that had been built on sixteen acres of what had three years earlier been the "sad and desolate" scrubland of Yerba Buena: people had started to build all sorts of monuments there so that now everything appeared, he said, in "the best Parisian style" in imitation of "the sepulchers of Père la Chaise." But even more to the point is the observation in this source that "the places of their births [he was speaking of the dead] were so diverse." "Now they sleep side by side. . . . American and European, Asiatic and African are now the same filthy substance." That social distinctions are erased among corpses is, of course, a very old trope. But the reference here was not to the leveling in death of those seemingly fixed, ancient hierarchies that ordered the world of the living, but to the distinctions that western bourgeois society had created to define itself in relation to the rest of the world. White pride in not having the blood of "yellow, red, and black races," the pride of the "man of progress" over the "slavish native of warm climates," were, in the cemetery, leveled. The world of commerce, empire, and slavery was manifest both in the fine Parisian styles and in contemplating the "filthy substance" that was barely hidden by chaste monuments. Whatever all this meant, it spoke of a sort of new democracy of the dead in a space far away from the living.[6]

The problem of filth and of smell lies at the core of what the modern cemetery represents. The language of "public health" is the language of that new, secular conception of the dead body that is so delicately effaced—*not* represented—in a Père-Lachaise or a Highgate (north London) or a Mt. Auburn (suburban Boston). But it would be to miss the critical cultural meaning of these new spaces if we were to tell the history of the cemetery as the relatively simple story of heroic, prescient doctors, Enlightenment philosophers, and bureaucrats who recognized the danger to the health of the living of the corrupting flesh in their midst and agitated successfully to have it cast out. I want to make a case against such a functionalist account in order to emphasize the culturally more intricate role that public health and a scientific materialist worldview played in creating new spaces for the dead. If dirt is "matter out of place," as Mary Douglas famously defined it, the question before us is why the dead body came to be understood as "out of place" where it had been put since at least the sixth century and why specifically the cemetery, of all possible solutions to the problem of disposing of corrupting human flesh, became the solution to making the dead clean again.[7] It is not writ in heaven that, as happened in London in 1852, the Commissioners of Sewers should have replaced the Church as the legally recognized administrators of the city's burials. In short, I propose to treat scientists in the Enlightenment tradition in the way anthropologists look at the clean and the not clean in other cultures.

The problem of an overpopulation of corpses that so exercised eighteenth- and nineteenth-century reformers was certainly not new; what was new was how they understood it. It would, in fact, be difficult to know what "crowding" meant in the old regime of burial, in which one place had served generations of the dead for centuries, if not millennia. The vestry of St. Botolph Bishopgate noted in 1621 that the churchyard was "buried so full," there was scarcely room for a child; ever lengthening burial registers apparently do not reflect the problem. The Cemetery of the Innocents

---

6. Helen Marcia Bruner, *California's Old Burial Grounds* (San Francisco: National Association of Colonial Dames, 1945); the quote from the 1855 source appears on p. 22.

7. Mary Douglas, *Purity and Danger: An Analysis of Concepts of Pollution and Taboo* (London: Routledge and Kegan Paul, 1966).

absorbed some 2 million Parisians in an area of 60 by 120 meters during the seven centuries before its closure in 1780; that is roughly three hundred bodies per square meter. Clearly the ground had been "full" by any modern standard well before reformers turned their attention to the problem. When George Fox, the founder of the Quakers, was buried in the Friends' plot of Bunhill Fields—not a parish churchyard, of course, but almost its equivalent for dissent—Robert Burrow remarked it was large but "quite full": eleven hundred bodies, dead from the plague or martyrdom in prison, were already there. Ten thousand more followed Fox over the course of the next century. The prosperous or socially ambitious middling sorts who from the seventeenth century on chose burial within the church itself scarcely enjoyed more space, privacy, or rest. Ground beneath the pavement filled up fast. When Samuel Pepys in 1664 sought interment in the middle aisle of St. Bride's for his brother, the sexton promised—after accepting a sixpence tip—that he would "Jostle them [the other bodies] but [would] make room for him." There were more than a hundred burials commemo-rated—many others would not have had memorials—in the floor of Bristol Cathedral's south quire aisle alone. With the exception of family vaults—almost all belonging the landed families—the ground under the pavement of the church building was no more the property of one generation of occu-pants than was the churchyard.[8]

The compacting, composting, jostling, and intermingling of corpses and coffins in various states of repair was a permanent condition, an inevitable consequence of two doctrines: the first that of "ubi decimus persolvebat vivus, sepeliatur mortuus" (literally the right to be buried where one had paid tithes, but generally the common-law right to be buried where one had lived), and the second, implied by the first, the doctrine that the ground of the churchyard was, as Lord Stowell put it in the celebrated eighteenth-century case of Gilbert v. Buzzard, "the common property of the living, and of generations yet unborn, and subject only to temporary appropriation." Thus no body could claim any space forever, and, Stowell continued, "the time must come when his [the corpse's] posthumous remains must mingle with and compose a part of the soil in which they were deposited."[9]

8. Vanessa Harding, " 'And One More May Be Laid There': The Location of Burials in Early Modern London," *London Journal* 14 (2): 10–11 (1989); William Beck, *The London Friends' meetings: Showing the rise of the Society of Friends in London, its progress, with accounts of various meet-ing-houses and burial-grounds, their history* (London: F. B. Kitto, 1869), 329–30; R. Latham and W. Matthews, *The Diary of Samuel Pepys*, vol. 5 (Berkeley and Los Angeles: University of California Press, 1971), 90 (the quote is from 18 March 1664); Rodwell Warwick, *The Archaeology of Religious Places* (Philadelphia: University of Pennsylvania Press, 1989), 157.

9. Gilbert *v.* Buzzard and Boyer, Consistory Court of London, Hilary term, 1820, reported in Joseph Phillimore, *Reports of Cases Argued and Determined in the Ecclesiastical Courts at Doctors Common* (London: Joseph Butterworth and Son, 1827), 3, 167, 335–43.

Eighteenth-century population growth and urbanization certainly put more pressure on the system, but crowding was in the nature of the thing. Archaeologists estimate that the average English churchyard, in use for a millennium or so, might contain the remains of some ten thousand bodies. This explains the usual elevation of the ground above the level of the church floor and the lumpiness that is so striking in eighteenth- and nineteenth-century representations. In fact, these bumps are the last unleveled addition. From very near the beginning, grave diggers intercut, hacked through, turned over, tossed out earlier tenants to make room for new ones and every hundred years or so apparently leveled the ground and started again. The lumps we can still see today escaped still another round of recycling when the bodies stopped coming, and now, survivors from another age, they sit atop a layered jumble—a stratigraphy of bones—that extends at least a couple of meters above the subsoil. Or more. St. Giles in London was rebuilt because "filth and various adventitious matter" had already by 1730 raised the churchyard eight feet above the building's floor, and John Evelyn when he visited Norwich in 1671 observed that churches "seemed to be built in pits" because the "congestion of bodies had so raised the ground around them."[10] (Readers of Goethe's *Elective Affinities* will remember that one of Charlotte's landscaping innovations in the churchyard was that graves were to be leveled, as they are in the modern cemetery, and the ground kept smooth for resowing—part 2, chapter 1.) Crowded burial grounds and their attendant odors thus were not a discovery of the Enlightenment.

The question is the one that Alain Corbin raised about smell: in this case, why did corruption become pollution, why did the "exhalations arising from the putrefaction of dead bodies"—their odor—come to be regarded as so particularly noisome? As Archdeacon Hale argued in 1854, his churchyard of St. Giles Cripplegate was essentially made of the compost of seven hundred years of burial and smelled, at the surface and in samples taken from six feet down, like compost, like ammonia. "The earth," he said, "had the qualities which are attendant upon every heap of the farmer's treasure upon every highly cultivated field." How can the physiologist say, as ammonia evaporates, "avoid this place because it is dangerous to health"?[11]

The key claim of the proponents of cemeteries was less that the crowding per se had become unbearable, although this did play a big part in English discussions of the late 1830s and '40s, but that the public health dangers of

10. P. A. Rahtz, "The Archaeology of the Churchyard," in *The Archaeological Study of Churches*, C. B. A. Research Reports no. 13, edited by P. V. Addyman and R. K. Morris (London: Council for British Archaeology, 1976). Warwick, *Archaeology of Religious Places*, 146–47. Richard Morris, *Churches in the Landscape* (London: J. M. Dent and Sons, 1989), 421.

11. Alain Corbin, *The Foul and the Fragrant: Odour and the French Social Imagination* (Cambridge: Harvard University Press, 1986); Hale, *Intramural Burial in England*.

rotting human flesh were too evident to be ignored. That miasma causes diseases was widely accepted; that decomposing, putrefying flesh gives off unmistakable odors is beyond dispute. Hence, the case was made, anything smelling so vile—what they took to be vile—simply had to be pathogenic. Decomposing flesh killed and thus needed to be removed in the interests of the living. This was not an altogether implausible argument. Miasmas have been thought to cause diseases at least since Hippocrates; one need only consider the correlation of fetid swamps and various malarial fevers. And interest in the dangers of effluvia from live diseased bodies was strong among eighteenth-century doctors. But the insistence—in a rhetoric full of excremental allusions and the goriest possible chemical and olfactory detail—that corpses are especially dangerous was more novel.

Putrefaction had once been understood differently. Some dead flesh had the odor of saintliness in contrast to the odor of ordinary bodies—corporeal corruption, with all its attendant unpleasantness, represented an earthly state to be followed by a sweeter life eternal with a new, incorruptible body; or it was endured simply as part of the smelly order of things. More than facts or purported new knowledge are needed to explain why the grotesque pleasure in decay that characterized, for example, the eschatological traditions about which Caroline Bynum has recently written, or memento mori painting, was abandoned for a new sensibility in which rotting flesh pointed not to the next life or to something transcendental but to a shortened life here on earth—to explain, in other words, why the corpse became secular.[12]

In fact, dead bodies do not cause disease and, more to the point, contemporaries knew it. On the eve of publication of his famous and inflammatory 1843 report on interment in towns and cities, Edwin Chadwick got a chilling letter, the sort one would not want to get just before going to press from an expert in one's field. It was a comment on a draft version from his colleague and Benthamite fellow traveler Southwood Smith, and it was not encouraging: "The foundation of the whole subject," Smith wrote, "is that animal matter in a state of decomposition is injurious to health. . . . Now it appears to me that the Evidence of that fundamental truth in your report is neither so strong, so succinct nor so varied as it might be." Basically, he said, the report was not what was necessary to produce a powerful impression on the public mind, and he recommended "*greatly* [the word is underlined in the letter] strengthening the evidence." There was little poor Chadwick could do at that point.[13]

But he might have known. When the reforming medical journal *The Lan-*

---

12. Caroline Walker Bynum, *The Resurrection of the Body in Western Christianity, 200–1336* (New York: Columbia University Press, 1995).

13. Chadwick Papers, University College, London, Box 46.

cet discussed the question in the 1840s, various correspondents pointed out that the evidence that was being adduced for the danger of bodies, even when supplemented by such massive compilations of horrors as Dr. George Walker's 258-page-long *Gatherings from Graveyards, Particularly London* (1839), did not make the case. One physician, for example, pointed out how many dissections they all had done without getting ill.[14] And it did not go unnoticed that the very same doctors and public health advocates who were so eager to move dead bodies out of churchyards had also been the great advocates of the Anatomy Acts, which made the unclaimed bodies of the poor available for sustained medical use. The epidemiology that purported to show the dangers of intramural interment was also weak, entirely anecdotal, and easily parried by equally ad hoc counterevidence.[15] As Matthieu Orfila, the distinguished professor of jurisprudential medicine at the Sorbonne, pointed out in 1800, the evidence that dead bodies were particularly dangerous was either apocryphal, exaggerated, or irrelevant: purported injuries were not due to "putrid exhalations." He reported that he and his assistants had done many exhumations and autopsies, taking no special precautions, and had not taken ill. (The pathologists I have consulted say the same thing.)[16]

And little wonder. Dead bodies are probably less dangerous than infected live ones. A more technical look at this question will make clear that the doctors and their allies who argued so passionately for removing the dead from the midst of the living were driven by something beyond the science available then. One of the most cited of all cases—in England, Italy, and the United States—right up through the 1840s was first reported in 1771 by a Montpellierian physician named Haguenot. He had had little success combating the universally accepted custom of burying the dead among the living in and around churches, he said, and so he wished to report the following observations in the hope of changing public opinion. Called to the Church of Notre Dame, he noted a putrid odor as he approached the crypt; it became more intense as the "cave" was opened. He put a burning taper into the depths and it was extinguished, "as if it were plunged in water." Dogs, cats, and birds that were lowered into the cave died, within two minutes for the most robust of the beasts—cats—and within seconds for the most delicate—birds. Bottles lowered into the cave collected a gas that still had its effect but not as strongly as it did in situ. He concluded that the

14. *The Lancet,* 1839–40, pp. 1, 411–13; 1840–41, pp. 1, 201–2.

15. For a lengthy compilation of anecdotal evidence of the safety of graveyards, see *"Health of Towns": An Examination of the Report and Evidence of the Select Committee of Mr. Mackinnon's Bill* (London: John Snow, 1843).

16. Matthieu Orfila and Octave Lesueur, *Traité des exhumations juridiques* (Paris: Bechet Jeune, 1831), 10.

"mephitis" in the "*cave commune*" was dangerous not only because the air had lost its elasticity or because of the lack of air, but peculiarly because of "the corrosive exhalations of cadavers."[17]

This last move is telling. Bernardino Ramazzini, pioneer of occupational health, was certainly no great friend of unpleasant smells: inhaling foul air, he said, "is to contaminate the animal spirits." And he was very much part of the eighteenth-century movement to claim such unpleasantness for doctors; nothing should be too filthy or horrible for the physician to inspect. But Ramazzini clearly saw the problem of workers in the *fosse commune* as having a lot in common with those of workers in other enclosed spaces. Slaves in antiquity, for example, who were consigned to work in caverns, mines, sewers, and burial pits; tanners; oil pressers; catgut-string makers; grave diggers; and midwives, who breathed in the effluvia of various uterine fluxes, were discussed in succession. The problem here is smell and enclosed spaces, not particularly the smell of decaying human flesh.[18]

In another context all of this was sorted out more clearly. James Curry, of Edinburgh, argued persuasively that there was indeed a common problem in mines, sewers, pump wells, the holds of ships, and burial vaults: the absence of freely circulating air. He pointed out that the fumes from charcoal burning, fermentation, and other chemical processes also produce something that makes air unhealthy: carbonic acid—formed when carbon dioxide is dissolved in water. Decaying bodies, in short, were not the problem, and others who wrote on the subject of death from bad air from a different perspective—rescuing the apparently dead from their stupors—had no particular interest in them.[19]

So why was the argument about public health so successful? In each national or even local case there was a particular history. Père-Lachaise was the culmination of a long Enlightenment battle against clerical control of the spaces of death, and the neoclassical or romantic aesthetics of the new cemetery were the result of considerable debate during various phases of the French Revolution. In England major cemeteries were in place well before the public health campaign began in the late 1830s, although the sweet memorial spaces of a Highgate or Kensal Green or a Glasgow Necropolis were a choice by the middle classes for private memory and against the community of the lumpy churchyard or the crowded public crypt. Portuguese liberals faced the most significant popular protests of the nineteenth century in their efforts to close churchyards and place dead bodies under

17. M. Haguenot, *Mélanges curieuses et intéressans de divers obiects relative à la physique, à la médecine, à l'histoire naturelle* (Paris: Chez Joseph Robert: 1771), 6 ff.

18. Bernardino Ramazzini, *Diseases of Workers*, translated from the Latin by Wilmer Cave Wright (1700; reprint, New York and London: Hafner, 1964), chapters 14 and 18.

19. James Curry, *Observations on Apparent Death*, 2nd ed. (London: E. Cox, 1815), 72–75, 179.

the authority of doctors: the Marie da Fonte uprising, named after the woman who was regarded its leader.[20]

But at a more abstract level I want to suggest that a new group of people managed to capture smell for its worldview. Vicq d'Azyr, one of the leading French proponents of cemeteries and a widely translated authority, gave it away: in the old, superstitious days, he said, we carried "our beliefs so far as to persuade ourselves that the emanations from the bodies of the saints were capable of warming the hearts of the faithful and encouraging in them impressions favorable to zeal and piety." It was against this "superstition" that the Enlightenment fought. And once triumphant, the relation of the living to the dead would change: now carefully hidden, the body would appear, he hoped, only in its representation, in new memorial practices linked specifically to the disappeared body. Vicq suggested epitaphs on cenotaphs, mausoleums, or tombs, either empty where the bodies used to be, if necessary, or far better, in new memorial parks.[21]

Public health thus did lie at the heart of the new regime of the hidden dead body, but indirectly. Aries is, I think, right, although in a different context, when he suggests that doctors in the late seventeenth and eighteenth centuries frightened themselves to death. And so was Archdeacon Hale when he conjoined "the modern Hygienist advocating the entire separation of the mansions of the dead from the houses of the living for the sake of public health," and the modern Epicurean who holds the same view because "nothing is so painful to him as the thought or sight of death." Stripped of "superstition," revealed in all, and only, its natural boldness, doctors and the enlightened public retreated in the case of death's now exclusively materialist realities. Death, in other words, lost its lineage—its metaphysical centrality; the discourse and agitation of public health was more of a symptom than a cause of the displacement of the dead into new spaces.

I have so far sketched in a cultural interpretation of one path—the public health route—to the cemetery and have only gestured toward the other trajectory: the active imagining by an ascendant class of a new community of the dead. Now to give some content to the latter idea and to the process whereby it happened. It is not quite right, as Gray said in his famous *Elegy Written in a Country Churchyard*, that "The rude forefathers of the hamlet sleep / Each in his narrow cell for ever laid." In fact, as I have suggested, bodies were jostled quite a bit, and few enjoyed a narrow cell to be occupied forever. But it is the case that Gray's *Elegy* spoke of an ideal—a "congrega-

20. J. De Pina-Cabral and Rui Feijo, "Conflicting Attitudes to Death in Modern Portugal: The Question of Cemeteries," *Journal of the Anthropological Society of Oxford* 14 (1): 17–43 (1983).

21. Vicq d'Azyr, *An Essay on the Danger of Interment in Cities* (New York: William Gratten Printer, 1824), 28 ff. This piece was originally a translation, with comments by Vicq, of an Italian work.

tion of the dead," as the clergyman James Hervey wrote—a historically rooted community of the dead belonging alike to a particular place. It was an ideal that held enormous appeal on the eve of its destruction.[22]

Some, of course, had never belonged to the community, the most prominent group being the Jews, but including also "strangers" to the parish— that is, those with no customary claim to being buried there (vagrants, prostitutes). But the systematic breakup of parochial burial came from elsewhere. It came from the Puritans in New England, who at first buried their dead outside nucleated villages in nondescript places as an aggressive rejection of Anglican custom. The halfway covenant brought the dead back to the center as a sort of ideal community in a world that was now more fragmented both religiously and economically. That is, a gemeinschaft of the dead substituted for a less than perfect gemeinschaft of the living. Baptists and Quakers continued to be buried at the periphery.[23]

Quakers in England established separate burial grounds beginning in the 1660s and new Baptist chapels in the late seventeenth and early eighteenth centuries tended to have theirs as well, despite the fact that the Dissenting Deputies spent a good deal of effort during the eighteenth century assuring them a place in the parish churchyard. There were also moments of overt aristocratic rejection of the old system, such as Lord Carlisle's mausoleum— the first in Europe since Roman antiquity—at Castle Howard. And then there was empire: the extraordinary seventeenth-century freestanding tombs of the great East India merchants of Surat, whose Latin inscriptions and European pseudoheraldry on essentially Saracenic buildings set amid tropical foliage produced the sort of weird bricolage effect that would so attract and repulse visitors to the nineteenth-century cemetery. Then in the 1760s there was Park Street in Calcutta, and then many more colonial burial grounds almost all in the grandest neoclassical style. In fact, the dead of empire with no particular parish attachments were among the earliest inhabitants of the new cemeteries. Major John William Pew of the Madras Army; Lady Bonham, wife of the commander in chief of Hong Kong; Major General Casement of the Bengal Army; and various East India merchants are all buried at Kensal Green, for example.[24] Clearly the old community of

22. James Hervey, *Meditations among the Tombs* (London, 1778). Hervey was rector at Collingtree and Weston Favell in Northamptonshire. Although his sensibility in this regard is close to Gray's he was also an early supporter of Methodism, which famously did not respect parish boundaries and undermined the legitimacy of the churchyard.

23. John L. Brooke, "'For Honour and Civil Worship to any Worthy Person': Burial, Baptism, and Community on the Massachusetts Near Frontier, 1730–1790," in *Material Life in America, 1600–1800*, ed. Robert Blair George (Boston: Northeastern University Press, 1988), 463–85.

24. *Pictorial Handbook of London* (London: 1859), 287.

the dead was breaking down, and the cemetery became a radically new sort of space in which it was possible to imagine a new one.

In the church and churchyard, "custom" dictated that bodies be buried with their heads to the west and feet to the east, more or less in alignment with the liturgically prescribed orientation of the church, which in turn had some long-standing relationship to its built environment. Churchyards around churches thus stood on the sites of holy wells, or the chapels of Saxon manors, or earlier burial mounds, or at medieval crossroads. That is, they were historically rooted and they were located in the midst of daily life. Cemeteries were situated where land was cheap, which meant at a distance from commerce and alternative, better-paying occupancy. They were nowhere in particular, and within them graves were aligned in no particular direction. Their placement was in conformity to the dictates of landscape architecture. The Merchant Adventurers, for example, had profited in various ways from the land that became the Glasgow Necropolis; some of it had been leased for farming, some used as a quarry, and then in 1828 it was decided that a cemetery would be just the thing: "it afforded a much wanted accommodation to the higher classes, and would at the same time convert an unproductive property into a general and lucrative source of profit."[25] A good real estate deal. Liverpool's first cemetery was also in a quarry, a big advantage since it allowed for tombs in the style of the patriarchs. (Highgate had to build this feature.) Woking was on a railway line; likewise Camberwell and Rockwood in Sydney.

The most remarkable change wrought in the cultural geography of burial was the new segregation of the dead. Cemeteries, more successfully than the home ever was for women, succeeded in being really a "separate sphere." Not for the dead the "tumult of a populous city. . . . [T]heir business with this world is ended. . . . The price of corn, the state of the money market, or the rising or falling of the funds are matters which ought to be discussed far away from those we followed."[26] Not in front of the servants. No one wonder that William Hazlitt understood the fear of death as being the fear of no longer mattering in the world of affairs and, projecting back, of never having mattered at all. "People walk along the streets the day of our deaths just as they did before, and the crowd is not diminished. While we were living, the world seemed in manner to exist only for us. . . . But our hearts cease to beat, and it goes on as usual, and thinks no more of us than it did in our lifetime."[27]

This is not the awesome death that so disturbed Dr. Johnson; it is death

25. John Strang, *Necropolis Glasguenis* (Glasgow, 1831), preface, 28–37.

26. Thomas Miller, *Picturesque Sketches of London, Past and Present* (London, 1852), 270.

27. William Hazlitt, "On the Fear of Death," in *Selected Essays of William Hazlitt*, ed. Geoffrey Keynes (London, 1930), 168.

as being forgotten. Memory is its antidote, and the cemetery made possible an undreamed of elaboration of personal commemoration and contemplation, which the densely populated churches and churchyards of the old order allowed only for a very small elite. I do not want to attribute this profound development in how we remember the dead to the lifting of material constraints alone. But the late-seventeenth-century architect and playwright Sir John Vanbrugh was right when he argued that the cemeteries he proposed to replace churchyards would permit "noble mausoleums erected over the dead," while those now in aisles and under pews in parish churches had at best "little tawny monuments of marble stuck against walls and pillars." Or, probably nothing at all.

Burial in the parish churchyard and church was explicitly for parishioners. Others could and did, for a higher fee, buy the privilege of burial there, and matters were never as tidy as principle might suggest. But there were no public burial places in the old regime—arguably Bunhill Fields, perhaps Westminster Abbey and St. Paul's, but the exception proves the rule. The nineteenth-century cemetery was in its essence public, and its glory was that anyone who could afford a place could be there: "Russ sleeping next to Spaniard, Protestant next to Catholic, the Jew next to the Turk," claimed the Glasgow Necropolis, echoing Père-Lachaise.[28] The first burial there—in sight of the cathedral—was in fact a Jew.

The poor, of course, had not been as prominently buried in the churchyard as were the powerful, and rights to especially prominent places belonged in various complicated ways to local landed classes. And, of course, as the middling sorts during the course of the seventeenth century started to bury their dead in the floors of the church, the poor were further isolated outdoors. But they had to be there for the churchyard to be what it was: the sensibility that so attracted readers of Gray's *Elegy* depended on it.

In cemeteries they were hidden and expendable were it not that they were needed only to make the enterprise pay. The dirty secret was that in fact the new cemeteries could survive economically only by egregious cheating on the one grave, one body program of the public health reformers. Whether in the *fosse commune* of the French cemetery or the British shaft graves that, with careful planning, could hold thirty or forty bodies, the poor subsidized the middle classes. Unlike the churchyard imagined by Gray, the nineteenth-century cemetery could be "read" by, and was readable for, them alone.

There is also a peculiar aesthetic incoherence to the cemetery, which

28. Indeed, everyone could be near some symbol or sign of their religion: the Catholic could be near a pot associated with the Virgin Mary; the Jew could "slumber in a cave, like that of Machpelah in the field of Ephron"; a Presbyterian could be near the column of John Knox. See Strang, *Necropolis*, 47.

produced unease in viewers as diverse as the radical liberal political econo-
mist Harriet Martineau and the High Church Tory A. W. Pugin. Martineau
found it strange that the Egyptian gate at Mt. Auburn cemetery, with its
winged globe and serpent, should have a quote from Ecclesiastes—"then
shall the dust return to earth"—since it belied both the Egyptian theme and
the idea of death as sleep in nature motif that dominated the cemetery. She
was equally puzzled why the Trier-born, Boston-buried phrenologist Johann
Spurzheim rested under a tomb that was the facsimile of Scipio's (that
would be Publius Cornelius Scipio Barbatus, consul 298). It is not easy, she
said, "to conceive how anything appropriate to Scipio would suit Spurzheim." The answer turns out to be purely circumstantial and shallow but
also wonderfully liberating. The marble arrived just when Spurzheim died,
and the committee appointed to honor him saved time by purchasing it.[29]

Pugin was angrier at the "grossest absurdities" perpetrated by new cemetery companies. He objected to the superabundance of inverted torches,
cinerary urns—but of course no ashes—and other pagan symbols. The
entrance gates to the new cemeteries were usually Egyptian—a kind of orientalist fantasy in Pugin's view—which associated (falsely) discoveries along
the Nile with the idea of the catacombs that the companies were offering for
sale. Each gate was topped by Grecian capitals along a frieze giving the
cemetery's name; Osiris bore a gas lamp, and various "hawk headed divini-
ties" looked on. Hieroglyphics on the cast-iron gate meant nothing; "they
would puzzle the most learned to decipher." And so would the aesthetics of
the cemetery more generally.[30]

Different styles of monuments—you could buy whatever style you
wanted—were scattered about. There was in principle no symbolic order,
nor historical order. But there was a space in which one could mourn and
remember in whatever fashion one could afford in the company of a veritable museum of styles and even bodies: Abelard and Héloïse were moved
to Père-Lachaise, as was Molière; John Knox stood guard over the Glasgow
Necropolis.

All of this suggests that I have gone a very long way around to rediscover
the bourgeoisie: all that is solid melts into air, old verities are torn asunder.
One does not need an anthropology or an archaeology or a cultural geography of death—as one might need in studying the ancient Greeks or
Egyptians—to understand the nature of a new civilization that became
ascendant in the nineteenth century. But what I have tried to suggest is that
there is something uneasy about the bourgeois way of putting the dead to

29. Harriet Martineau, *Retrospect of Western Travel*, vol. 3 (London, 1838), 272 ff.

30. A. Welby Pugin, *An Apology for the Revival of Christian Architecture in England* (London,
1843), p. 12 and pl. 5. Pugin was, at the time, professor of ecclesiastical antiquities at St.
Marie's College, Oscott.

rest: a strong reaction to the decay of death, which was displaced onto public health and chemistry and memory; a profound dispersal of the places of the dead. I could point to other features of the new regime—the hodge-podge of memorial styles, the fabulous elaboration of the cult of death at the same time that death was being represented as merely sleep.

It always takes a lot of cultural work to put the dead to rest, but this work took on peculiarly modern forms after the rejection of a widely accepted transcendental account of death itself. It seemed to Enlightenment figures and those who followed in their tradition that substituting History—progress, health, moral and material advance—for religion and superstition would make matters easier. It did not turn out that way.

Jumonville's Death

*War Propaganda and National Identity
in Eighteenth-Century France*

David A. Bell

In the early morning of May 28, 1754, in the woods of what is now south-western Pennsylvania, a killing took place. The victims, a thirty-six-year-old French-Canadian officer named Joseph Coulon de Jumonville and nine soldiers under his command, had pitched camp for the night, on the way from their base at Fort Duquesne (present-day Pittsburgh), to Britain's Fort Necessity, more than forty miles to the south. Although supposedly at peace, France and Britain were each building chains of forts to support their rival claims to the great stretches of land between the Appalachians and the Mississippi in the great game of military chess familiar from the novels of James Fenimore Cooper. Jumonville's mission was to instruct the British to withdraw, immediately, from what the French considered their territory. At Fort Necessity, however, Indian scouts had not only informed the inexperienced twenty-two-year-old British commander about Jumonville's approach, but persuaded him it was the prelude to a French attack (the Indian leader Tanaghrisson, known as the Half King, had his own grudge against the French). The commander therefore moved to intercept the French with a detachment of his own and crept up on their encampment at dawn. It is unclear exactly who opened fire, but after a few confused volleys, the French were quickly overcome. Jumonville, wounded but alive, died under the Indian leader's hatchet. The Indians took several French scalps, and the newly seasoned British officer wrote boastfully to his brother back home in Virginia: "I heard the bullets whistle, and believe me, there is something charming in the sound."

This incident has long been familiar to North American historians. It marked not only the opening skirmish in what would soon develop into the Seven Years' War, but also a key moment in the career of the cocky young British officer—a man by the name of George Washington. In fact, it nearly brought Washington's career to a premature end. Scarcely a month after Jumonville's death, a large French force, led, dramatically enough, by Jumonville's brother, captured Fort Necessity in a pitched battle with Washington's forces. They then compelled Washington to sign a confession that he had "assassinated" an ambassador traveling under a flag of truce. Only Washington's slippery insistence that he had not understood the French text he had signed allowed him to avoid a damaging scandal. His detractors and admirers have argued about the incident ever since.[1]

Yet Jumonville's death, for all its importance to the outbreak of hostilities and to Washington's career, also had a prominent place in a very different theater of operations. During the Seven Years' War, both the French and British made wide use of printed propaganda, and the French side used Jumonville's death as a leitmotif, a perfect illustration of the English enemy's treacherous conduct. Pamphlets, songs, journals, and supposedly impartial collections of documents stridently condemned the English and Washington (sometimes misidentified as "Wemcheston"), while enshrining the dead officer as a martyr of the *patrie*.[2] The incident even gave rise to a sixty-page-long epic poem, Antoine-Léonard Thomas's now-forgotten *Jumonville*, which a widely read Swiss book on "national pride" singled out as the nec plus ultra of French xenophobia.[3] So all in all, it is no surprise that as early as 1757, the influential Jesuit newspaper *Mémoires de Trévoux* could comment that "all the world has learned of the treatment meted out to the Sieur de Jumonville."[4] Indeed, the unfortunate officer, his undistinguished life now eclipsed by his sensational leaving of it, gained such a posthumous reputation that collec-

---

1. For the most recent, complete, and impartial accounts of the incident, see Francis Jennings, *Empire of Fortune: Crowns, Colonies, and Tribes in the Seven Years' War in America* (New York, 1988), 67–70, and Richard White, *The Middle Ground: Indians, Empires, and Republics in the Great Lakes Region, 1650–1815* (Cambridge, 1991), 240–41.

2. Among works that discussed Jumonville's death, see Antoine-Léonard Thomas, *Jumonville* (Paris, 1759); [Jacob-Nicolas Moreau], *Mémoire contenant le précis des faits avec leurs pièces justificatives* (Paris, 1756); idem, *L'observateur hollandois, ou deuxième lettre de M. Van *** à M. H*** de la Haye* (The Hague, 1755), esp. 20–35; idem, *L'observateur hollandois, troisième lettre* and *cinquième lettre* (The Hague, 1755); *Petit catechisme politique des Anglois, traduit de leur langue* (n.p., n.d. [1757]), 4; [Claude-Rigobert Lefebvre de Beauvray], *Adresse à la nation Angloise, poëme patriotique* (Amsterdam, 1757), 7; Audibert, "Poëme," in *Recueil général des pièces, chansons et fêtes données à l'occasion de la prise du Port-Mahon* ("France," 1757), 48; Denis-Ponce Ecouchard ("Lebrun"), *Ode nationale contre l'Angleterre* (Paris, 1758), 2–3; Séran de la Tour, *Parallèle de la conduite des carthaginois à l'égard des romains, dans la seconde guerre punique, avec la conduite de l'Angleterre, à l'égard de la France, dans la guerre déclarée par ces deux puissances, en 1756* (n.p., 1757), 185–91.

3. Thomas, *Jumonville*; Johann Georg Zimmermann, *Vom Nationalstolze* (Zurich, 1768), 177. Zimmermann's work was published in at least four editions and translated into both French and English.

4. *Mémoires de Trévoux* (also known as *Mémoires pour servir à l'histoire des sciences et des arts*), 1756, vol. 2, pp. 1756–57.

tive biographies of "great Frenchmen," published in profusion in the waning decades of the ancien régime, included him right alongside icons of French military glory such as Bayard and Du Guesclin.[5] Certain poems remained well known enough in 1792 for the military engineer Rouget de Lisle to crib from them in writing the *Marseillaise,* including his lines, "Aux armes, citoyens!" and "qu'un sang impur abreuve nos sillons."[6]

To twentieth-century eyes, this atrocity literature seems quite unremarkable—indeed, by our woefully jaded standards, rather tame—and so it has attracted little attention.[7] Yet in several ways, it represented a considerable novelty. For the first time in French history, it presented a war neither as a duel between royal houses nor as a clash of religions, but as a conflict of irreconcilable nations. This shift is usually associated with the French Revolution, but in fact it took place several decades earlier. Second, it pioneered the use of religious imagery and motifs for the mobilization of the (secular) nation, something that illuminates the links between the crusading religious movements of early modern Europe and modern nationalism. Finally, it foreshadowed the development of racially based nationalism. It has been argued that the eighteenth century saw the rise of new, "essentialist" ideas on the subject of human diversity in France—even the birth of "modern racism."[8] The scholars in question, however, have looked mostly at French interactions with non-Europeans. In this essay, I would like to suggest that the essentializing of ethnic and racial differences began at the center as much as it did at the (perceived) periphery as the French struggled to differentiate themselves from the people with whom they often felt the greatest affinity and similarity, yet who had also emerged as the greatest

5. See Claude de Sacy, *L'honneur François, ou Histoire des vertus et des exploits de notre nation, depuis l'Etablissement de la Monarchie jusqu'à nos jours,* vol. 11 (Paris, 1784), 284–86, and Louis-Pierre Manuel, *L'année françoise, ou Vies des Hommes qui ont honoré la France, ou par leurs talens, ou par leurs services, & sur-tout par leurs vertus,* vol. 3 (Paris, 1789), 12–15.

6. Denis-Ponce Ecouchard's ("Lebrun's") *Ode aux Français* (Angers, 1762) contains the line "Aux armes, citoyens!" (p. 1), and also the *Marseillaise*-like line "L'ENTENDEZ-vous gémir cette auguste Patrie?" (p. 1). Lefebvre de Beauvray's *Adresse* contains the line "Va, pour s'entredétruire, armer tes bataillons / Et de ton sang impur abreuver tes sillons" (11). See David A. Bell, "Aux origines de la 'Marseillaise': *L'Adresse à la nation angloise* de Claude-Rigobert Lefebvre de Beauvray," *Annales historiques de la Révolution française,* no. 299 (1995): 75–77. Lefebvre himself may well have borrowed from N. de Coulange, *Ode sur les anglois au sujet de la Guerre présente* (Paris, 1756), 7: "Puissiez-vous aborder sur leurs propres Rivages / Et de leur sang parjure arrosant les sillons . . ."

7. A recent, important exception is Edmond Dziembowski, *Un nouveau patriotisme français, 1750–1770: La France face à la puissance anglais à l'époque de la guerre de Sept Ans,* Studies on Voltaire and the Eighteenth Century, no. 365 (Oxford, 1998).

8. See, for instance, Pierre H. Boulle, "In Defense of Slavery: Eighteenth-Century Opposition to Abolition and the Origins of a Racist Ideology in France," in *History from Below: Studies in Popular Protest and Popular Ideology in Honour of George Rudé,* ed. Frederick Krantz

apparent threat to their own honor, prosperity, and understanding of the world: the English.

There were two great "xenophobic moments" in eighteenth-century French history: the Seven Years' War, which started (two years before any formal declaration of hostilities) with Jumonville's death, and the Revolutionary Wars, which started in 1792 and lasted into the nineteenth century. The second certainly dwarfed the first in intensity. In the period 1792–94, Jacobin clubs across France were spitting forth hatred of that "enemy of the human race," William Pitt, and Robespierre was declaring to the National Convention, "I hate the English people." Bertrand Barère not only called the English "a people foreign to humanity, [who] must disappear," but convinced the Convention to pass a (thankfully little-obeyed) motion instructing French commanders in the field to take no English prisoners alive.[9] Yet the two moments have striking similarities. In both cases, the cosmopolitanism so often associated with eighteenth-century French culture abruptly disappeared from books and periodicals, to be replaced by snarling hostility to France's enemies. In both cases, this change occurred thanks above all to the concerted efforts of the French government, which sought to mobilize resources and public opinion behind the war effort. And the revolutionary literature in fact followed models developed in the earlier period, sometimes quite literally, as in the case of the *Marseillaise*. It is impossible to say, given the available evidence, whether the Seven Years' War literature had anything like the popular resonance of its revolutionary counterpart, which helped shape a wave of patriotic mobilization unparalleled in European history.[10] But at the very least—as the revolutionary borrowings themselves demonstrate—this earlier body of work put certain powerful ideas and motifs into broad circulation.

(Montreal, 1985), 221–41; Laurent Versini, "Hommes des lumières et hommes de couleur," in *Métissages*, vol. 1, ed. Jean-Claude Carpanin Marimoutou and Jean-Michel Racault (Paris, 1992), 25–34; Béatrice Didier, "Le Métissage de l'*Encyclopédie* à la Révolution: De l'anthropologie à la politique," in ibid., 13–24; and Ivan Hannaford, *Race: The History of an Idea in the West* (Washington, D.C., 1996). Earlier literature on the same theme includes Michèle Duchet, *Anthropologie et histoire au siècle des lumières* (1973; reprint, Paris, 1995), and Richard H. Popkin, "The Philosophical Basis of Eighteenth-Century Racism," in *Studies in Eighteenth-Century Culture* 3 (1973): 245–62. See also Henry Vyverberg, *Human Nature, Cultural Diversity, and the French Enlightenment* (New York, 1989).

9. Robespierre in Alphonse Aulard, ed., *La société des Jacobins: Recueil de documents pour l'histoire du club des Jacobins de Paris*, vol. 5 (Paris, 1895), 634; Bertrand Barère, *Rapport sur les crimes de l'angleterre envers le Peuple français, et sur ses attentats contre la liberté des Nations* (Paris, 1794), 18. On the treatment of Pitt, and on the "take no prisoners" decree, see Norman Hampson, *The Perfidy of Albion: French Perceptions of England during the French Revolution* (Basingstoke, England, 1998), 103–19, 142–43; on the subject see also Sophie Wahnich, *L'impossible citoyen: L'étranger dans le discours de la Révolution française* (Paris, 1997).

10. Dziembowski summarizes what evidence there is in *Un nouveau patriotisme*, 106–110.

EUROPEAN BARBARIANS

In modern accounts, the Seven Years' War is considered important not only for the decisive realignment of European power that it brought about (especially the triumph of Britain and Prussia, and France and Austria's decline), but also because it was a new sort of war. It could almost be called the first "world war," for the combatants battled each other not only in Europe, but also in North America, Africa, India, and on every ocean. They also spent unprecedented sums in the process, and the war hastened the development of several Western European states into vast fiscal-military machines, capable of keeping hundreds of thousands of men in the field, and scores of ships of the line on the high seas.[11]

French war literature changed no less dramatically. To begin with, there is the sheer volume: at least eighty items per year appeared in France during the war, more than double what had been produced during the recent wars of the Spanish and Austrian Successions (the second of which ended just six years before Jumonville's death).[12] The *Journal encyclopédique* commented wryly that "the future will scarcely believe it, but the war between the English and the French has been as lively on paper, as on the high seas."[13] Not since the Wars of Religion had French printing presses churned out such quantities of xenophobic polemic. Tracking the material's distribution is difficult, but at least one item, the issue of Jacob-Nicolas Moreau's newspaper *L'Observateur hollandois* (The Dutch Observer) that recounted Jumonville's death, sold eight thousand copies, an impressive figure for the period. Issues of the same paper were pirated by Dutch, Italian, and German publishers and were translated into several languages.[14] The burgeoning European periodical press gave considerable attention to the works, as did the British themselves, who responded in kind.[15] As a result, not only

11. See John Brewer, *The Sinews of Power: War, Money, and the English State, 1688–1783* (New York, 1989), and James C. Riley, *The Seven Years' War and the Old Regime in France: The Economic and Financial Toll* (Princeton, 1986).

12. This assertion is based on my own survey of the number of publications in the holdings of the French Bibliothèque Nationale that qualify as wartime propaganda, including plays, poems, and pamphlets. On wartime propaganda in the War of the Spanish Succession, see Joseph Klaits, *Printed Propaganda under Louis XIV: Absolute Monarchy and Public Opinion* (Princeton, 1976). On the Seven Years' War, see Nicholas Rowe, "Romans and Carthaginians in the Eighteenth Century: Imperial Ideology and National Identity in Britain and France during the Seven Years' War" (Ph.D. dissertation, Boston College, 1997), and Charles Gevaert Salas, "Punic Wars in France and Britain" (Ph.D. dissertation, Claremont Graduate School, 1996).

13. *Journal encyclopédique, par une société de gens de lettres,* August 15, 1756: 78.

14. The figure comes from Jacob-Nicolas Moreau, *Mes souvenirs,* vol. 1, ed. Camille Hermelin (Paris, 1898), 59–63. The issue on Jumonville is dated 1755.

15. As an indication of the diffusion of the works, see the lengthy and favorable reviews of Moreau's *Mémoire* in *Mémoires de Trévoux,* 1756, vol. 2, pp. 1734–90, and of his *Observateur*

Jumonville's death, but also other major themes of French propaganda, such as the triumphant early seizure of Port Mahon in Minorca from the unfortunate Admiral Byng and the heroic death of the Chevalier d'Assas in the battle of Clostercamp, had wide diffusion.[16]

The material also represented a new departure in its violence. Although unimpressive by twentieth-century standards, this violence still reached a level not seen in French war literature since the sixteenth century—certainly not in the thin, almost decorous productions of the recent War of the Austrian Succession.[17] The propaganda portrayed the English as "vultures," a "perjurous race," driven by "blind wrath" and "undying hatred," people who had removed themselves from "that universal Republic, which embraces all nations in its heart."[18] It consistently compared them to the grasping, mercantile Carthaginians and suggested that England would soon, quite deservedly, share Carthage's hideous fate.[19] This tone characterized the literature from the very start, before France's terrible defeats and the desperation that accompanied them.

Simply taking note of the numbers and the violence, however, doesn't advance our understanding very far. The crucial questions are what form the material took, and what strategies the authors employed. It is important to note, first of all, that almost without exception, and in glaring contrast to English war propaganda, the French material did not attempt to stir up religious hatred. For reasons that will be explored later, the French resisted this particular temptation, even though visceral hatred of Protestants still permeated much of French society and some French Protestants may in fact have had illicit contacts with the English enemy.[20]

Hollandois, ou deuxième lettre in *Journal encyclopédique*, July 1, 1756: 12–22. The British replied to the second in the pamphlet *L'observateur observé* (n.p., [1756]), which the *Journal encyclopédique* mentioned as well (p. 12). Lengthy and favorable reviews of Thomas's *Jumonville* include *Mémoires de Trévoux*, 1759, vol. 2, pp. 1116–33, and *Journal encyclopédique* 4, pt. 3 (1759): 123–40.

16. See the *Recueil général des pièces* and Rowe, "Romans and Carthaginians," 10–63.

17. For instance, Voltaire's *Le Poeme sur la bataille de Fontenoy* (Amsterdam, 1748). The only text I have found of a violence remotely close to that of the Seven Years' War literature is Pezé d'Anglincourt's *Ode à la France* (Paris, 1744), which calls on Louis XV to "cut off the ferocious heads of a Cohort of Brigands," but then almost immediately checks itself: "What am I saying? Where is my mind wandering? LOUIS, magnanimous victor, don't grant this barbarous desire" (6–7).

18. [Lefebvre de Beauvray], *Adresse*, 9; Coulange, *Ode*, 3; *Considérations sur les différends des couronnes de la Grande-Bretagne et de France, touchant l'Acadie et autres parties de l'Amérique septentrionale* (Frankfurt, 1756), 23.

19. On this comparison, see above all Rowe, "Romans and Carthaginians," 64–97, and Salas, "Punic Wars," 287–314.

20. The exception is Audibert, "Poëme," 47. On British anti-Catholicism in the period, see Linda Colley, *Britons: Forging the Nation 1707–1837* (New Haven, 1992), 11–54. The fascinating evidence of a possible plot involving French Protestants has been unearthed by John D.

Rather than tar the English as "heretics," the propaganda instead tended to stigmatize them as lawbreaking "barbarians" and to compare them, insistently and unfavorably, to American Indians. Moreau first used the theme in his 1755 description of Jumonville's death, accusing the English of "infamies which have distinguished peoples whom Europeans consider Barbarians," and of "this wild license which previously distinguished the northern Barbarians."[21] He also linked English "barbarism" to the long history of English civil discord and the proven inability of the English to refrain even from killing one another.[22] Antoine-Léonard Thomas virtually structured his poem *Jumonville* around the theme. He began the poem with a pointed Virgilian epigraph—"What race of men is this? What fatherland is so barbarous as to allow this custom?"—and continued relentlessly thereafter.[23] The Englishman was a "new barbarian" (p. 23), who committed "a barbarian homicide" (p. 4), and showed "a barbarian joy" in it (p. 24). The English were also enemies of law and peace alike, even at home ("slaves under Cromwell, and tyrants of their kings," p. 26). Thomas also asserted no fewer than four times that the Indians themselves, for all their qualities of "ferocity," "cruelty," and "roughness" (p. 44), were shocked and angered by Jumonville's killing (pp. ix, 22, 30, 44). Immediately after the description of Jumonville's death itself, Thomas addressed himself directly to the Indians:

At least your crude and ferocious uprightness
Follows simple nature's first laws.
The Englishman, a new barbarian, has crossed the seas
To bring this crime to the heart of your wilderness [p. 22].

Thomas clearly meant to situate both the Indians and the English at a vast remove from European norms of politeness and morality, but he put the latter even farther away. The *Mémoires de Trévoux* grasped the point perfectly in its review of *Jumonville*: "These Englishmen on the Oyo [Ohio River] . . . were more barbarian than the Iroquois and the Hurons. They, at least, shuddered when they heard of the attack on Jumonville."[24]

Other chroniclers of Jumonville's death joined in as well. The poet Lebrun echoed Moreau's words in his indignation at the "barbaric" con-

---

Woodbridge in *Revolt in Prerevolutionary France: The Price de Conti's Conspiracy against Louis XV, 1755–1757* (Baltimore, 1995).

21. [Moreau], *L'observateur hollandois, ou deuxième lettre*, 37, and *cinquième lettre*, 4.

22. [Moreau], *deuxième lettre*, 39. On French perceptions of British "turbulence," see the interesting remarks of Keith Baker in *Inventing the French Revolution: Essays on French Political Culture in the Eighteenth Century* (Cambridge, 1990), 173–85.

23. Virgil, *Aeneid*, book 1, lines 539–40.

24. Thomas, *Jumonville; Mémoires de Trévoux*, 1759, vol. 2, p. 1118. The newspaper also noted, in the poem, "a striking contrast between the simplicity and uprightness of the Savage, and the perfidy of the English" (p. 1132).

queror who gave lessons in crime to Indians much less deserving of the epithet: "Greedy despoilers of Land and Seas, / He teaches infamies to the Huron he disdains, and calls barbarian."[25] A historically minded *abbé* named Séran de la Tour, expatiating at book length on the frequently made comparison between England and Carthage, devoted two pages to this particular instance of "English barbarism"—and three more to the Indians' horrified reaction.[26] These authors too stressed the "discord" that lay at the heart of the English soul.[27]

The incident in the Pennsylvania woods provided the ideal illustration of the theme, but its use permeated nearly all the polemical anti-English literature of the Seven Years' War (most of which did not deal with events in North America). Again and again, French publicists decried turbulent English "barbarians" and compared them unfavorably with non-European peoples. A poem on a wide range of English atrocities asked, for instance, "In the deep lairs of vast Lybia, did one ever see so much barbarism reign?"[28] Satirical verses carrying a mock seal of approval from Tunis's "Royal Academy of Barbary" put a particularly sharp speech in the mouth of Montcalm, the French general who would soon find defeat and death on the Plains of Abraham:

> . . . Friends, you were born French.
> Don't imitate the Barbarism and the tone of the English
> In this horrid depredation.
> Let the savage nation act
> . . . .
> An Iroquois has far more mercy in him
> Than these Milords who buy their titles.[29]

Most insistently, Robert-Martin Lesuire devoted an entire novel to the theme: his 1760 anti-English screed, *Les sauvages de l'Europe* (The Savages of Europe, which had sufficient success to merit—somewhat incredibly—an English translation, and also another edition twenty years later, during France and Britain's next war).[30] "The English lie at mid-point between men and beasts," says Lesuire's hero. "All the difference I can see between the English and the Savages of Africa, is that the latter spare the fair sex."[31]

25. Lebrun, *Ode nationale,* 3.

26. Séran de la Tour, *Parallèle,* 187–91, 250. The book attracted sufficient attention to warrant a nine-page review in the *Journal encyclopédique* 3, pt. 2 (1757): 81–89. On the work, and the Punic War comparison in general, see Rowe, "Romans and Carthaginians," and especially Salas, "Punic Wars."

27. For instance, [Lefebvre de Beauvray], *Adresse,* 12.

28. Audibert, "Poëme," 49.

29. *L'Albionide, ou l'Anglais démasqué: Poëme héroï-comique* (Aix, 1759), 80.

30. Robert-Martin Lesuire, *Les sauvages de l'Europe* (Berlin, 1760; reprint, Paris, 1780); translated as *The Savages of Europe* (London, 1764).

31. Lesuire, *Les sauvages,* 18–19.

One further point about the theme is worth making. Polemical writing of this sort hardly lent itself to lexical precision, but nonetheless, from the 1750s through the 1790s, the texts mostly respected the distinction recently emphasized by Montesquieu between *barbarians,* on the one hand, and *savages* on the other, putting the English into the first category (Lesuire was a rare exception).[32] The latter term, in keeping with its origins in *selvaggi,* or forest-dwellers, in the early modern period generally implied creatures without fixed abode, law, or polite customs, possibly even without language—but also without guile or hypocrisy. It most often connoted a greater closeness to nature and man's original state. The more pejorative *barbarian,* by contrast, tended to connote a degree of social corruption and willful rejection of polite behavior (particularly respect for the law), and was most often applied to non-European peoples possessed of a high degree of social organization (such as the inhabitants of the Barbary coast).[33] As a concise example of the difference, consider that eighteenth-century authors spoke of "noble savages" but never of "noble barbarians."[34]

Overall, this setting of the English in relation to non-Europeans served an obvious polemical purpose. Nor was it an entirely new theme for French publicists. During the Wars of Religion, when the Spanish had filled the role of national enemy, Huguenots and *politiques* occasionally denounced *them* as "barbarians" and gleefully copied into their broadsides Las Casas's accounts of Spanish New World atrocities.[35] Still, the renewed predilection for the theme in the 1750s, like the dimensions of the wartime literature itself, *was* novel, and deserves explanation.

MOBILIZING THE NATION

In providing such an explanation, the first questions to consider are: Who wrote this literature, and what readership did they hope to reach? Although

32. Montesquieu, *The Spirit of the Laws,* trans. and ed. Anne Cohler, Basia Miller, and Harold Stone (Cambridge, 1989), 290–91. Book 18. chapter 11 is entitled, "On Savage Peoples and Barbarian Peoples."

33. On this terminology, see Anthony Pagden, *The Fall of Natural Man: The American Indian and the Origins of Comparative Ethnology* (Cambridge, 1982), 15–26; idem, *Lords of All the World: Ideologies of Empire in Spain, Britain, and France, c. 1500–c. 1800* (New Haven, 1995); idem, "The 'Defence of Civilization' in Eighteenth-Century Social Theory," *History of the Human Sciences* 1 (1): 33–45 (1988); Olive Patricia Dickason, *The Myth of the Savage and the Beginnings of French Colonialism in the Americas* (Calgary, 1984), esp. 61–94; Duchet, *Anthropologie,* 217.

34. My thanks to Stéphane Pujol for this observation.

35. See notably the *politique* pamphlets *La fleur de lys, qui est un discours d'un François retenu dans Paris* (n.p., 1590) and *Exhortation d'aucuns Parisiens, n'agueres eslargis de la Bastille de Paris, au peuple François* (n.p., 1592).

many of the texts in question appeared anonymously, it is still possible to make one broad generalization: to a large extent, operations were directed from above, by the royal ministry. As the hostile satirist Mouffle d'Angerville later put it, "these writings [were] produced under the auspices of the Ministry, whose secret sponsorship remained hidden, [so that they] seemed nothing but the effusion of a patriotic heart."[36] The key figure was Jacob-Nicolas Moreau, who effectively served as the crown's chief publicist during the last forty years of the old regime. Moreau first made his mark in 1755 with a caustic pamphlet directed against France's recalcitrant *parlements*, and soon afterwards the ministry engaged his polemical talents against the English as well (and later against the *philosophes*). As he recounted in his memoirs, the foreign affairs department provided him with plentiful funds, the services of a translator and clerk, and confidential papers. Thus supplied, he wrote pamphlets and the lion's share of two newspapers: the highly successful *L'Observateur hollandois*, and, later in the war, *Le Moniteur françois* (The French Monitor). He also published in book form, in both English and French, papers seized from Washington at Fort Necessity.[37] Considerable textual evidence suggests that the other authors took their source material, and their themes, directly from Moreau's writings.[38] Antoine-Léonard Thomas and the prolifically anglophobic lawyer Lefebvre de Beauvray also had ministerial connections.[39] War poetry flooded the pages of official periodicals such as the *Mercure de France,* and it seems likely that many of the more than 150 separate poems, songs, and *fêtes* collected in one 1757 volume had

36. Barthélémy-François-Joseph Mouffle d'Angerville, *Vie privée de Louis XV, ou principaux événemens, particularités et anecdotes de son règne,* vol. 3 (London, 1785), 84–85, quoted in Dziembowski, *Un nouveau patriotisme,* 106–7.

37. On Moreau's activities, see Moreau, *Mes souvenirs,* vol. 1, 57–63, and Edmond Dziembowski, "Les débuts d'un publiciste au service de la monarchie: L'activité littéraire de Jacob-Nicolas Moreau pendant la guerre de sept ans," *Revue d'histoire diplomatique,* no. 4 (1995): 305–22; see also Dieter Gembicki, *Histoire et politique à la fin de l'ancien régime: Jacob-Nicolas Moreau (1717–1803)* (Geneva, 1976). The papers taken from Washington were published as [Moreau], *Mémoire,* and translated into English as *A Memorial, Containing a Summary View of Facts, with Their Authorities, in Answer to the Observations Sent by the English Ministry to the Courts of Europe* (Paris, 1757).

38. Séran de la Tour, *Parallèle,* p. x, says he based much of his account on Moreau's *Mémoire.* Thomas's narrative also follows it closely. Thomas's epigraph from the *Aeneid* was quoted in Moreau's *Observateur hollandois, ou cinquième lettre,* 32. Also compare Moreau's *Observateur hollandois, ou deuxième lettre,* 37, with Lebrun, *Ode nationale,* 3, and the *Observateur hollandois, ou cinquième lettre,* 42, with *Considérations sur les différends,* 23.

39. Thomas belonged to the clientele of foreign minister Choiseul. See Jean-Claude Bonnet, *Naissance du Panthéon: Essai sur le culte des grands hommes* (Paris, 1998), 68. On Lefebvre de Beauvray, see David A. Bell, *Lawyers and Citizens: The Making of a Political Elite in Old Regime France* (New York, 1994), 172, 184, 192.

official sponsorship.[40] During the course of the war, the foreign ministry directly sponsored several other books and periodicals.[41]

At least at the beginning, the ministry's intended audience was not so much French as international. When it hired Moreau in 1755, it did so first and foremost with the goal of keeping the Netherlands neutral in the looming Franco-British conflict, which is why the Parisian lawyer took on the unconvincing persona of a sturdy Dutch burgher ("Monsieur Van ***") in his *Observateur hollandois*. His publication of Washington's papers formed something of an unofficial codicil to France's formal declaration of war. Yet the newspaper was published in French (the ministry left it up to enterprising Dutch publishers to undertake a translation), and when Moreau boasted of the sensation it caused, he meant the sensation in France itself, not the Netherlands.[42] Reading the paper, it is hard to believe that Moreau did not also have a prospective French audience in mind. For instance, in the issue centered on Jumonville's death, he wrote of the French: "When will this aimiable and generous Nation learn to amuse its imagination with objects worthy of occupying its reason? When will the love of the *patrie* which lives in the heart of all Frenchmen convey its heat to those many minds who occupy themselves wholly with arid and frivolous questions?"[43] It was not the sort of passage to stir the blood of Dutch readers.

As the war proceeded and the early French victories turned to ashes, France faced the prospect of massive defeat, including the loss of most of its overseas empire. In response, the war literature made its principal purpose all the more clear: to mobilize French readers behind the crown's war effort. Moreau's less successful second newspaper, *Le Moniteur françois*, openly spoke to a domestic audience, and Moreau recounted in his memoirs that a later pamphlet he wrote comparing France and England had as its goal "to bring back the confidence that we needed more than ever, and to raise up our courage." Similarly, in a work entitled *Lettre sur la paix* (Letter on the Peace), "I exhorted the nation to recapture the customs, courage and virtues of its ancestors."[44]

In the shift from a propaganda effort aimed at least partly at an international audience to one designed to stimulate domestic "confidence" and

40. *Recueil général.* The volume included pieces by military officers and members of the King's bodyguard, as well as several odes by Voltaire and pieces previously published in periodicals. It also included several pieces in the Provençal language.

41. See Dziembowski, *Un nouveau patriotisme*, 60–71, 173–82.

42. See Moreau, *Mes souvenirs*, vol. 1, 57–63.

43. [Moreau], *L'observateur hollandois, ou deuxième lettre*, 6.

44. Moreau, *Mes souvenirs*, vol. 1, 129 (the publication of the first work was hastily scotched when negotiators reached agreement on peace terms); Jacob-Nicolas Moreau, *Lettre sur la paix, à M le Comte de ***** (Lyons, 1763).

"courage," the literature of the Seven Years' War in some respects followed a model first elaborated earlier in the century, during the War of the Spanish Succession. Then too, although on a noticeably smaller scale, the ministry underwrote pamphlets to persuade neutral foreign observers of the justice of the French cause, for example Jean de la Chapelle's vituperative *Lettres d'un suisse à un françois* (Letters of a Swiss to a Frenchman).[45] As that war turned more desperate for the French, the crown issued several public letters, supposedly written by the king himself, in which Louis stressed his love for his people and his desire to secure a lasting and honorable peace. These letters, especially one written to royal governors, were read out from church pulpits across the kingdom.[46] Moreau consulted de la Chapelle in writing his *Observateur hollandois,* and several publications of the period of the Seven Years' War recalled Louis's letter in making their exhortations to the French.[47]

Yet in fact, the difference between the two sets of war literature is enormous. The first presented the war as a war of kings, of royal houses. De la Chapelle consistently attacked the perfidies and infamies not of Austrians, but of the "House of Austria," and the "Emperor." While he used the word *barbarian,* he did so not to describe the Austrian or English people, but rather the "House of Austria's barbarous maxims."[48] When the ministry appealed to the French nation, it did so in the guise of the king speaking, and not even to the nation itself, but to noble governors *about* the King's "faithful subjects."[49] The literature of the Seven Years' War presented the conflict between France and Britain in quite a different manner, as a war of nations. The anti-*philosophe* Elie Fréron's newspaper expressed this difference quite clearly: "There are wars in which the nation only takes an interest because of its submission to the Prince; this war is of a different nature; it is the English nation which, by unanimous agreement, has attacked our nation to deprive us of something which belongs to each of us."[50] In this light, the publicists' emphasis on Jumonville's death takes on added significance. It was not an emissary of the House of Hanover who had cut Jumonville down in the Ohio Valley. Indeed, Britain's King George II barely figured in the war lit-

45. Jean de la Chapelle, *Lettres d'un suisse, qui demeure en France, à un François, qui s'est retiré en Suisse, touchant l'estat présent des affaires en Europe* (n.p., 1704). See also Klaits, *Printed Propaganda,* 113–70.

46. Klaits, *Printed Propaganda,* 212–16; *Lettre du Roy a Mr le Marquis d'Antin du 12 Juin 1709* (Paris, 1709). The letter was written by a royal minister. See also André Corvisier, *L'armée française de la fin du XVIIe siècle au ministère de Choiseul: Le soldat,* vol. 1 (Paris, 1964), 105.

47. Moreau, *Mes souvenirs,* vol. 2, 559; Charles-Pierre Colardeau, *Le patriotisme, poëme* (Paris, 1762), 3; *Le patriotisme, poëme qui a été présenté a l'académie françoise pour le prix de 1766 et dont on n'a fait aucune mention* (Paris, 1767), 7.

48. De la Chapelle, *Lettres d'un suisse,* "Quatrième lettre," 1st pagination, E4v.

49. *Lettre du Roy,* 3.

50. "Projet patriotique," in *Année littéraire,* vol. 6 (1756), 43–44.

erature at all. No, the villain was an "English barbarian," and more generally, all "English barbarians." The victim, meanwhile, was no illustrious noble or prince of the blood. He was, as Thomas wrote in *Jumonville*, "nothing but a simple French officer"—but for that very reason the prototype of his nation: "Of the virtuous Frenchman, such is the character."[51]

The difference between the two bodies of propaganda was due above all, I would suggest, to the great changes in French political culture that had occurred in the forty years between Louis XIV's death and 1755. As much recent historical work has demonstrated, these years had seen a vast expansion in the circulation of printed matter in France, and also a growing tendency on the part of many different political actors to carry on political debate in print, before what they referred to as "public opinion." The changes took place with particular intensity after 1748, when long-running conflicts between the French *parlements* and the crown developed into a full-fledged constitutional crisis, and the crown, advised by none other than Jacob-Nicolas Moreau, decided to enter openly into public argument with its critics.[52] Furthermore, in this crisis, the *parlements* justified their positions by claiming to speak for the "nation," while the crown asserted the inseparability of nation and king, and also strove to present its own position as the truly "patriotic" one.[53] Therefore, not only were the French growing increasingly accustomed to seeing themselves as a "nation" and "*patrie*"; France's ruling elites had become accustomed, in certain important respects, to treating them as one—as a collectivity possessed of its own internal unity, and possessing certain legitimate "rights." It is therefore natural that the ministry, in organized propaganda efforts led by the same Moreau, should seek not only to mobilize the "nation" (in fact, the small percentage of relatively well-off pamphlet readers), but to attempt, symbolically, to involve them *in* the war effort by presenting the war not as a war of royal houses, but as a war of nations, in which every citizen had a stake. At the same time, it seems clear that the ministry attempted to stifle expressions of Anglophilia (which had flourished in print without much constraint during the War of the Austrian Succession), and particularly on the part of the *philosophes*, whose "cosmopolitanism" now became a target of intense official criticism.[54]

51. Thomas, *Jumonville*, xvi, 18.

52. The most important works here are Baker, *Inventing the French Revolution*, and Roger Chartier, *The Cultural Origins of the French Revolution*, trans. Lydia Cochrane (Durham, N.C., 1991).

53. On this point, see my forthcoming book on the origins of French nationalism and Liah Greenfeld, *Nationalism: Five Roads to Modernity* (Cambridge, Mass., 1992), 89–188.

54. These were the years of Moreau's famous anti-*philosophe* satire *Nouveau mémoire pour servir à l'histoire des Cacouacs* (Amsterdam, 1757), of Charles Palissot's *Les philosophes* (Paris, 1760), and many other anti-*philosophe* works, not to mention a hardening of censorship of the *philosophes* themselves. On the connection with the war, see Dziembowski, *Un nouveau patriotisme*, 119–30.

NATIONAL IDENTITY AND EUROPEAN UNITY

If the war was a war of nations, then it was not only a war *of* all the French, but a war *against* all of the English. The publicists needed to demonize not simply an enemy king, or his advisors, but an entire enemy nation. This shift from earlier modes of propaganda raised some formidable problems, however, as illustrated particularly by Moreau's contortions on the issue. In October 1755, in the *Observateur hollandois,* he wrote unctuously that he "didn't want to accuse a Friendly Nation"—but he immediately proceeded to ask how one could possibly "separate from the rest of the nation an officer [Washington] whose crime . . . seems to have been the signal for hostilities of all sorts." And he added a few pages later: "Yes, Monsieur, whatever wish you may have to justify the English nation, the facts speak too loudly against it."[55] Yet, a month later, he retreated from this position, in a fascinating disquisition on the English national character. "I do not attribute to all the English the excesses to which the bulk of the Nation seems pushed today," he began.

> I do more. I distinguish two Nations, one of which is presently the small minority, the nation of the wise. . . . But there is in England another nation, if you can even give this name to that ill-considered multitude who let themselves be carried away by opinion and subjugated by hatred. A tumultuous assemblage of all sorts of different parties, they are not a Nation who consult, who reflect, who deliberate; they are a people who cry, who agitate, and who demand war.[56]

As in the case of Jumonville, other writers followed Moreau's example. The *Mémoires de Trévoux,* for instance, excoriated the "English common people [*petit peuple*]" for "a ferocity which no longer belongs to the mores [*moeurs*] of Europe."[57] Another semiofficial French publicist, the abbé Le Blanc, denounced "the imbecility of these [English] Fanatics, who take for the voice of the People, the cries of a mindless populace which they themselves have excited."[58]

There was an obvious reason why the publicists distinguished so carefully between the tiny minority of benign English and the crushing majority of

55. [Moreau], *L'observateur hollandois, ou troisième lettre,* 3, 4, 12.
56. [Moreau], *L'observateur hollandois, ou cinquième lettre,* 6–8.
57. *Mémoires de Trévoux,* 1756, vol. 2, p. 1750.
58. [Abbé Le Blanc], *Le patriote anglois, ou reflexions sur les Hostilités que la France reproche à l'Angleterre* (Geneva, 1756), ii. These passages, incidentally, illustrate the suppleness of the publicists' vocabulary—Moreau's distinction between "nation" and "people" was essentially the same as Le Blanc's between "people" and "populace." On the history of the word *peuple,* see Gérard Fritz, *L'idée de peuple en France du XVIIe au XIXe siècle* (Strasbourg, 1988); see also *Images du peuple au XVIIIe siècle* (Paris, 1973).

malignant ones. As they knew quite well, making collective accusations against the English nation might not have much credibility for the French reading public, because that public had, for more than twenty years, consumed a steady diet of Anglophilic literature, which taught that the proper attitude to be taken to the nation across the Channel was not hatred, but rather reverence. From Voltaire's paeans to England in the *Philosophical Letters*, to Montesquieu's exaltation of the English constitution, to the general adulation of Locke and Newton, the major *philosophes* did their part. But "Anglomania" raged in many other domains as well, notably fashion and sport, while the eighteenth-century adoption of words such as *le club* and *le jockey* marked the true birth of Franglais.[59] A sizable literature grew up in the eighteenth century solely to inoculate the French against the "disease" of Anglomania, and it still could not prevent Mlle. de l'Espinasse from notoriously remarking that "only Voltaire's glory consoles me for not having been born English."[60]

Although no other foreign nation elicited anything like the visceral emotional response from the French that England did, "Anglomania" itself fit within a broader eighteenth-century phenomenon: French readers' growing awareness of their identity as Europeans. The idea of Europe as a political unit had a long and august pedigree, and the shadow of European empire had not yet vanished from the continent, but in the eighteenth century, writers began to perceive what we would now call a close European cultural unity as well.[61] Voltaire, for instance, wrote in his preliminary discourse to *Le poëme sur la Bataille de Fontenoy* (Poem on the Battle of Fontenoy—a war poem, in fact, but from the relatively decorous War of the Austrian Succession): "The peoples of Europe have common principles of humanity which cannot be found in other parts of the world. . . . A Frenchman, an Englishman and a German who meet seem to have been born in the same town."[62] A 1760 review from the *Journal encyclopédique* also put the point in a global context: "There is a perceptible and striking difference between the inhabitants of

59. See, on this phenomenon, Josephine Grieder, *Anglomania in France, 1740–1789: Fact, Fiction, and Political Discourse* (Geneva, 1985), and Frances Acomb, *Anglophobia in France: An Essay in the History of Constitutionalism and Nationalism* (Durham, N.C., 1950). Both draw heavily on Georges Ascoli, *La Grande Bretagne devant l'opinion française au 18e siècle* (Paris, 1930).

60. Quoted in Greenfeld, *Nationalism,* 156. Among the more famous examples of anti-Anglomanical literature are Louis-Charles Fougeret de Montbron, *Préservatif contre l'anglomanie* ("Minorca," 1757).

61. Among the voluminous literature on the idea of Europe, see esp. René Pomeau, *L'Europe des lumières: Cosmopolitisme et unité européenne au dix-huitième siècle,* 2nd ed. (Paris, 1995); Jean-Baptiste Duroselle, *L'idée d'Europe dans l'histoire* (Paris, 1965), 103–33; Derek Heater, *The Idea of European Unity* (New York, 1992), 61–90; Denis de Rougemont, *The Idea of Europe,* trans. Norbert Guterman (New York, 1966), 51–175.

62. Voltaire, *Le poëme sur la bataille de Fontenoy* (Amsterdam, 1748), "Discours préliminaire," unpaginated.

Asia and those of Europe. . . . But it is much harder, and takes much more discernment, to grasp the slight differences that separate the inhabitants of Europe from one another."[63] Rousseau approached the topic more critically in his 1772 *Considerations on the Government of Poland:* "Today, whatever one may say, there are no longer any Frenchmen, Germans, Spaniards, or even Englishmen: . . . there are only Europeans. They all have the same tastes, the same passions, and the same customs, because none of them have acquired a national form through a particular education."[64]

Many different factors spurred this new awareness, including improved communications, the burgeoning periodical press, the enormous cultural influence of France itself, and the decline of international religious animosities. But Voltaire's discourse and the *Journal encyclopédique* review suggest that a particularly important factor was the vertiginous expansion of interest in and information about non-European cultures during the eighteenth century. Michèle Duchet has remarked that one need read no further than *Candide* and the *Spirit of the Laws* to see how large a place the non-European world occupied in the French Enlightenment's imagination— and Duchet herself, following on several earlier works, has in any case provided ample further evidence.[65] Travel writing, Jesuit *Relations*, newspapers, atlases, orientalist novels, and synthetic works of philosophy all made the French familiar with a much larger range of human diversity than ever before, and this material served to put Voltaire's "common principles of [European] humanity" in very high relief.[66]

In the context of this new perception of a European identity, the *Mémoires de Trévoux*'s comments that the English common people displayed a "ferocity which no longer belongs to the mores of Europe" takes on particular significance and suggests why the image of the "English barbarian" had such powerful resonance in French war literature. The casting of the Seven Years' War as a war of nations, rather than a war of royal houses, conflicted directly with the growing perceptions of a common European identity, and of a close connection between France and England. How could Moreau, Thomas, and the other publicists make national differences *within* Europe

63. *Journal encyclopédique*, 1760, vol. 8, pt. 2: 104. The anonymous writer also commented, unpleasantly, that "the Orientals themselves recognize the Europeans' mental superiority."
64. Jean-Jacques Rousseau, *Considérations sur le gouvernement de la Pologne et sur sa réforme projetée*, vol. 3 of *Oeuvres complètes* (Paris, 1964), 960.
65. Duchet, *Anthropologie*, 32 and, more generally, 25–136; Gilbert Chinard, *L'Amérique et le rêve exotique dans la littérature française au XVIIe et au XVIIIe siècles* (Paris, 1913); Geoffroy Atkinson, *Les relations de voyages du XVIIe siècle et l'évolution des idées: Contribution à l'étude de la formation de l'esprit du XVIIIe siècle* (Paris, 1927).
66. See Karen Ordahl Kupperman, *America in European Consciousness, 1493–1750* (Chapel Hill, N.C., 1995), 1–24.

appear unbridgeably vast, when so much of the printed matter consumed by their readership implied, to the contrary, that all Europeans were increasingly alike, and that France should follow examples set across the English Channel? The power of the image of the "English barbarian" lay precisely in the fact that it symbolically removed the English from Europe—to the shores of Tripoli, or even further, to an outer darkness beyond even the "savagery" of Africans and American Indians. It revealed that the English, or at least most of them, only *appeared* to be fellow Europeans, because they lacked the requisite qualities of politeness and respect for the law and stood at the opposite end of a linear scale of historical developments. In sum, if representations of "savage" Americans and Africans figured centrally in the invention of the idea of the "civilized" European, they also provided a radical standard of alien and primitive behavior (of "otherness") against which to measure other European peoples, and to find them wanting.

It was not only in the conduct of war that French writers of the mid-eighteenth century found the English lacking in proper European qualities. They also highlighted the peculiarly turbulent character of English politics, which showed through in everything from election riots to the execution of Charles I.[67] They deplored the supposed English tendency toward "melancholy," and their aversion to sociability.[68] They also, especially, berated the English for avoiding and restricting social interchange between the sexes— an activity widely seen as crucial to the perfection of "society" and "civilization" (itself a word born in this period).[69] A booklet published during France and England's next war not only lamented the fact that the English banished women from the table after dinner, but associated this behavior with Africans and "Orientals."[70] The authors of the Seven Years' War literature could have expected a familiarity with all these unfortunate English traits on the part of their readers. But the use of the label *barbarian* took the portrait to a new

67. See Baker, *Inventing the French Revolution*, 173–85.

68. For considerations of the English as "melancholic" loners, see for instance Charles Duclos, *Considérations sur les moeurs de ce siècle* (Amsterdam, 1751), 64; François-Ignace d'Espiard de la Borde, *L'esprit des nations*, vol. 1 (The Hague, 1752), 275; Louis-Charles Fougeret de Montbron, *Le cosmopolite, ou le citoyen du monde* (London, 1753), 42; Gazon-Dourxigné, *Essai historique et philosophique sur les principaux ridicules des differentes nations* (Amsterdam, 1766), 115–16.

69. See, for instance, d'Espiard de la Borde, *L'esprit des nations*, vol. 1, 134; Antoine de Rivarol, *L'universalité de la langue française* (1783; reprint, Paris, 1991), 23. On the position of women as barometer of a society's advancement, see Daniel Gordon, *Citizens without Sovereignty: Equality and Sociability in French Thought, 1670–1789* (Princeton, 1994), 150–60, and Dena Goodman, *The Republic of Letters: A Cultural History of the French Enlightenment* (Ithaca, N.Y., 1994), 90–135.

70. *Lettre d'un jeune homme à son ami, sur les Français et les Anglais, relativement à la frivolité repochée aux uns, et la philosophie attribuée aux autres* (Amsterdam, 1779), 18.

extreme: it suggested that the English, unlike more pliable American "savages," had actually *rejected* joining the company of advanced nations.

THE SCHOOL OF ARTS AND HUMANITY

If the image of the "English barbarian" functioned symbolically to "de-Europeanize" the English, it also helped to place France itself at the symbolic center of Europe. The national self-image it helped to construct had little in common with the one often proposed for England by English publicists in this period: the image of a new Israel of the elect—a chosen people fundamentally set apart from others.[71] The French image was rather that of a new Rome, the open and welcoming center of a universal civilization. And here too the French war literature fit in well with the evolution of French nationalism and patriotism over the course of the eighteenth century.

Although eighteenth-century French patriotic writing tended to insist on the compatibility of patriotism with a universal human community, this attitude did not imply any modesty about France's own place in the family of nations.[72] Throughout the early modern period, dating back at least to Jean Bodin's *Method for the Easy Comprehension of History*, French writers had generally sought to identify the highest stage of human development not merely with Europe, but with France itself. Often, they grounded their arguments in theories of climate and came to the conclusion that France's temperate weather and fertility not only made it welcoming soil for spiritual achievement, but also gave the naturally moderate French—nature's true cosmopolitans—the best qualities of *all* nations.[73] In the eighteenth century, the most subtle and sophisticated contributors to climate theory (particularly Montesquieu and Buffon) eschewed these chauvinistic claims, but many others rushed in where they feared to tread. Antoine de Rivarol, for instance, wrote in his prize-winning essay, *L'universalité de la langue française:* "Nature, in giving [the Frenchman] a gentle climate, could not make him rough: it has made him the man of all the nations."[74] The Burgundian cleric and magistrate François-Ignace d'Espiard de la Borde similarly argued, in *L'esprit des nations* (The Spirit of the Nations), that "France, among all the nations, can take pride in the fortunate Temperature of its Climate and Minds alike, which produces no bizarre effects, either in Nature or Morals."[75] French mores were perfectly compatible with those of all other nations, and so "France," d'Espiard concluded, "is the principal Pole of

71. See Colley, *Britons,* 11–54.

72. This is a point that I develop fully in my forthcoming book.

73. For a brief summary of these works, see Vyverberg, *Human Nature,* esp. pp. 66–71. The arguments about temperate climate go back to Aristotle.

74. Rivarol, *L'universalité de la langue française,* 25.

75. D'Espiard de la Borde, *L'esprit des nations,* vol. 2, 25.

Europe."[76] During the French Revolution the messianic radical Anacharsis Cloots asked: "Why, indeed, has nature placed Paris at an equal distance from the pole and the equator, but for it to be a cradle and the metropolis for the general confederation of mankind?"[77]

From these arguments, another point followed as well: the French had the duty to act not only as the world's seat of learning (in keeping with the venerable promise of a *translatio studii* from Athens to Rome to Paris), but also as the world's schoolmasters.[78] Fellow Europeans might recognize France's superiority and of their own free will copy its fashions and learn its language. Beyond Europe, however, fulfilling the Frenchman's destiny as "the man of all the nations" demanded an early version of what the nineteenth century would call the nation's "civilizing mission."[79] This mission was in fact a tenet of early modern French imperialist theory. The French authorities in Canada, for instance, declared early on that all "savages" who accepted Catholicism would "be considered and reputed native French," while Controller General Colbert even encouraged intermarriage between Indians and French, "in order that, in the course of time, having but one law and one master, they may likewise constitute one people and one race."[80] Similar ideas permeated French travel literature and the popular Jesuit *Relations*, which Jesuit *collèges* pressed on their students.[81]

Not surprisingly, the ideas also appeared in the polemical literature of the Seven Years' War—and most strongly in precisely those texts which most insistently deployed the image of the "English barbarian." Thomas's *Jumonville*, for instance, describes the American Indians in terms that Colbert himself would certainly have approved:

> The crude inhabitants of those distant shores,
> Shaped by our lessons, and instructed by our customs,

76. Ibid., vol. 1, 145; vol. 2, 126.

77. Cited in Hans Kohn, *Prelude to Nation States: The French and German Experience, 1789–1815* (New York, 1967), 15.

78. On French notions of the *translatio studii*, spiritual counterpart to the *translatio imperii*, see Colette Beaune, *The Birth of an Ideology: Myths and Symbols of Nation in Late-Medieval France*, trans. Susan Ross Huston, ed. Fredric L. Cheyette (Berkeley, 1991), 275–78.

79. The most recent study of the "civilizing mission," Alice Conklin's *A Mission to Civilize: The Republican Idea of Empire in French West Africa, 1895–1930* (Stanford, 1997), acknowledges its Enlightenment origins, without, however, discussing them in depth.

80. F. A. Isambert et al., *Recueil des anciennes lois françaises*, vol. 16 (Paris, 1833), 423. Colbert is quoted from James Axtell, *The Invasion Within: The Contest of Cultures in Colonial North America* (New York, 1981), 68. More generally, see Axtell, 43–127, and Cornelius J. Jaenen, "Characteristics of French-Amerindian Contact in New France," in *Essays on the History of North American Discovery and Exploration*, ed. Stanley H. Palmer and Dennis Reinharz (College Station, Texas, 1988), 79–101.

81. On the influence of the Jesuit *Relations* in particular, see Duchet, *Anthropologie*, 76.

Reform the harshness of their savage mores
In the school of Arts and humanity
. . . .
Their hearts, simple and naïve in their ferocity
Respect the wise authority of the Frenchman.[82]

In the poem, the death of Jumonville itself provides the Indians with a salutary lesson. Until they witnessed it, nothing could overcome their "inflexible roughness," and they remained deaf to pity, taking it for weakness. But on seeing Washington's crime, "For the first time they feel themselves weaken / And one sees tears flow from their eyes."[83] The novelist Lesuire, in Les sauvages de l'Europe, also cast the French as educators, but in this case the unsuccessful educators of the savage English. As he had one of his few sympathetic English characters remark in a crucial scene: "Our [French] neighbors could, more than any other People, soften our mores, and teach us the bonds of society, which makes life precious, by making it pleasant; but here we make it a duty to hate them. As long as we hate the French, we will be barbarians" (emphasis mine).[84]

I do not wish to imply that these representations of England, France, and the relation between them held unanimous sway, even during the war. The heavy legacy of Anglomania did not dissipate so easily. Besides, as already noted, it is impossible to say how widely the general population embraced a political line consciously generated by the royal ministry. The important point is rather that these representations permanently expanded the field of French political discussion, suggesting new and significant ways of seeing nations, foreign and French alike, that would continue to reappear in French political culture (particularly during the Revolution).

What was most new and significant about them, ultimately, was the idea of an essential, unalterable difference between two nations. In the eighteenth century, when it came to defining the differences between peoples, the most common criteria were climate, political system, and position on a linear scale of historical evolution (according to which the Indians, for instance, were roughly equivalent to the early Greeks).[85] For this reason, historians have generally opposed eighteenth-century notions of human difference to nineteenth-century racially based ones, since, according to the earlier criteria, a people's characteristics could change over time (as in Buffon's claim that Africans transplanted to Scandinavia would eventually become white).[86]

82. Thomas, Jumonville, 8.
83. Ibid., 44.
84. Lesuire, Les sauvages, 61–62.
85. See Pagden, The Fall of Natural Man. For a more specific treatment of ways of seeing human difference in eighteenth-century France, see Vyverberg, Human Nature.
86. J.-Y. Guiomar, L'idéologie nationale: Nation, représentation, propriété (Paris, 1974), 31. See

Certainly the polemical writers of the mid-eighteenth century did not fail to link English defaults to all these factors, particularly the turbulence of English politics and weather ("a perpetually bloody climate," as the playwright Buirette de Belloy concisely put it).[87] But the tactic of stigmatizing the English as "barbarians," although rooted in notions of historical evolution, established new criteria of difference. For the writers who deployed it, even "savage" Indians (whose own "rudeness" and "ferocity" had a climatic explanation) did not stand beyond the reach of the French civilizing mission. The English did, however, thanks to their own perverse refusal of French wisdom. Unlike the Indians, they would never evolve beyond a fundamentally primitive historical state. Lesuire, in *Les sauvages de l'Europe*, again expressed this idea quite strikingly. At the very beginning of his novel, one character observes—in keeping with climate-based theories of difference—that Europe has two true barbaric peoples, both in the north: the Lapps and the English. But then he adds a further difference: "The second are barbarians in their hearts."[88] Similarly, for Lefebvre de Beauvray, the "cruelty of the fierce African" was something the Englishman carried "in [his] breast."[89]

TOWARD THE REVOLUTIONARY WARS

It is true that when France and Britain signed the Peace of Paris in 1763, official attitudes toward the enemy across the Channel abruptly shifted. Martyrs like Jumonville were no longer in demand, and the specter of the English barbarian rapidly receded. Lefebvre de Beauvray, who only recently had been spitting forth his eternal hatred of the "perjurous race" of Englishmen, suddenly revealed himself a secret Anglomaniac, rhapsodizing about "The French and English, united by talents/Emulators of each other always, but too often enemies."[90] Even in two prominent postwar stage plays often cited by historians as prime examples of French Anglophobia, a far more nuanced portrait of "English barbarians" emerged. In Buirette de Belloy's hugely successful (and officially promoted) *The Siege of Calais*, England's Edward III threatens in true "barbarian" fashion to execute summarily several burghers of Calais who dare oppose him. At the end, however, tamed by the example of French virtue he sees before him, he changes his

---

also William B. Cohen, *The French Encounter with Africans: White Responses to Blacks, 1530–1880* (Bloomington, Ind., 1980), 80.

87. Pierre Buirette de Belloy, *Le siège de Calais* (1763; reprint, Paris, 1826), 28. See also, for example, Audibert, "Poëme," 47; Louis Basset de la Marelle, *La différence du patriotisme national chez les françois et chez les anglois* (Paris, 1766), 41, and [Lefebvre de Beauvray], *Adresse*, 9.

88. Lesuire, *Les sauvages*, 7.

89. [Lefebvre de Beauvray], *Adresse*, 8.

90. Claude-Rigobert Lefebvre de Beauvray, *Le monde pacifié, poëme* (Paris, 1763), 6.

mind, renounces his claims, and departs for home.[91] In Charles-Simon Favart's *The Englishman in Bordeaux* (commissioned by the crown to mark the peace), a French marquise takes it upon herself to civilize an English prisoner of war named Brumpton, a brusque and ill-mannered man with whom she has nonetheless fallen in love (significantly, the French woman is the agent of civilization). Of course, she succeeds, and in the final scene Brumpton tells her: "And when Peace mixes up your nation and mine, /All my prejudices are destroyed."[92] In short, both plays featured English barbarians who nonetheless proved susceptible, in the end, to the wisdom of French ways.

Nor did the specter of the English barbarian stage much of a return during the American War of Independence. Although again at war with England, the French also found themselves allied with erstwhile English colonists, commanded by the chief barbarian of 1754 (one French volunteer fighting with the Americans simply refused to believe that the imposing commanding general was the same man as Jumonville's murderer).[93] When Robert-Martin Lesuire published a revised version of *Les sauvages de l'Europe* in 1780, he toned down his portrait substantially and called England "a rival Nation, and one which we should esteem, because it can bear comparison with us from many points of view."[94] French propaganda in this war, including new work by Lefebvre de Beauvray, tended to criticize the English mostly for excessive pride, and for their desire to establish a universal empire of the seas.[95]

Yet in other ways the pattern set in the 1750s remained influential. For instance, during the American War of Independence the ministry continued to use the press as a means to mobilize domestic opinion behind the war effort. After a major naval defeat, Foreign Minister Vergennes developed what his biographer calls a "veritable press campaign," with the objective, as Vergennes himself put it, of "reestablishing and permanently fixing

91. On Buirette de Belloy's play and its reception, see most recently Anne Boës, *La Lanterne magique de l'histoire: Essai sur le théâtre historique en France de 1750 à 1789* (Oxford, 1982), 63–70, 100–103.

92. C.-S. Favart, *L'anglois à Bordeaux* (Paris, 1763). On the play, see Boës, *La Lanterne magique*, 66, 97–98.

93. See Gilbert Chinard, *George Washington as the French Knew Him* (Princeton, 1940), 29. Chinard notes that during the American War of Independence, the French seem largely not to have drawn the connection between the young and middle-age Washington. This was possibly as the result of the earlier confusion over Washington's name ("Washington/Wemcheston") and the failure of most French publicists—including Thomas—to use the name at all.

94. Quoted in Grieder, *Anglomania*, 108.

95. For a summary of this literature, see Acomb, *Anglophobia*, 69–88. Lefebvre's work, a partial rewriting of his earlier *Adresse*, was published as Claude-Rigobert Lefebvre de Beauvray, "Fragments d'un opuscule en vers, intitulé *Hommages ou souhaits patriotiques à la France, par un citoyen*," in *Journal encyclopédique*, 1779, vol. 5: 105–9.

opinion."[96] In the course of this campaign, the ministry published an open letter from Vergennes to the French, which described patriotism in frankly religious terms: "The Frenchman, proud of the name he glories in, sees the entire nation as his family, and sees his zealous sacrifices as a religious duty towards his brother. He sees the *patrie* as the object of his worship."[97] Once again the ministry popularized the deeds of ordinary French warriors.

The early years of the French Revolution likewise did little to revive the concept of wars of nations. These were the years of the Constituent Assembly's Declaration of Peace to the World and its frequent proclamations about the brotherhood of peoples.[98] Such gestures, themselves predicated on the concept of France as the pole of civilization and the world's schoolmaster, expressed the hope that in the brave new world of 1789, there were no more barbarians, that all peoples would embrace the new gospel emanating from Paris. In 1789–90 Baron Cloots was predicting that one day people would take stagecoaches from Paris to Peking as they did from Bordeaux to Strasbourg, while Bertrand Barère was asking complacently: "What people would not want to become French?"[99]

But in 1793–94, as the war against the allied powers grew fierce, the ruling Convention changed tack. It enacted a series of repressive measures against foreigners living in France (including a never-realized proposal for them to wear tricolor armbands at all times), and its leading members again began resorting to the notion that the English had willfully set themselves outside the universal (and France-centered) human community. Furthermore, the Jacobins most committed to radical theories of popular sovereignty now forthrightly insisted that an irreconcilable and permanent hatred separated the English from the French, even as their moderate opponents continued to distinguish between a supposedly virtuous English people and England's depraved and corrupted government.[100] Robespierre declared famously on January 30, 1794: "I hate the English, because the very word recalls to me the idea of an insolent people who dare to make war on a generous people who have recovered their liberty."[101] Saint-Just angrily insisted: "Make your children swear immortal hatred to this other Carthage," and petitions from provincial Jacobin clubs dutifully echoed the message, in one case vowing "eternal hatred to this race of cannibals."[102]

---

96. J.-F. Labourdette, *Vergennes: Ministre principal de Louis XVI* (Paris, 1990), 205.

97. Quoted in ibid., 207.

98. See Albert Mathiez, *La Révolution et les étrangers: Cosmopolitisme et défense nationale* (Paris, 1918), passim, and Wahnich, *L'impossible citoyen*, 163–85.

99. Quoted in Mathiez, *La Révolution et les étrangers*, 56, and Georges Fournier, "Images du Midi dans l'idéologie révolutionnaire," in *Amiras: Repères occitans*, nos. 15–16 (1987): 85.

100. On the shift, see Wahnich, *L'impossible citoyen*, 243–327.

101. Quoted in Mathiez, *La Révolution et les étrangers*, 177.

102. Wahnich, 301–25 (the quotation is on p. 305), 323.

Bertrand Barère hammered the point home most brutally, in his *Rapport sur les crimes de l'angleterre envers le Peuple français* (Report on England's Crimes against the French People): "National hatred must sound forth; for the purposes of commercial and political contacts, there must be an immense ocean between Dover and Calais; young republicans must suck in a hatred of the word Englishman along with their mothers' milk."[103] Clearly, these leaders believed that to mobilize the French effectively against the nation that seemed, superficially, most to resemble them—indeed, which French leaders in 1789–91 often hailed as a political model—the supposed resemblance had once again to be exposed as the vilest sort of deception.[104]

In the service of this cause, not only did the revolutionaries engage in massive propaganda campaigns against foreign enemies, which dwarfed anything seen previously; they also rediscovered, with a vengeance, the image of the "English barbarian" and the concept of a "war of nations." In fact, they literally rediscovered the war literature of the 1750s, as shown by the ease with which old poems were simply republished under new names, and the way Rouget de Lisle borrowed lines from the earlier literature for the *Marseillaise*.[105] Meanwhile, as Sophie Wahnich has demonstrated in her recent analysis of "the foreigner in the discourse of the French Revolution" (which unfortunately treats this discourse in isolation, both from the old regime and from nonparliamentary sources), the radical Jacobins took up the theme of the English barbarian with particular intensity.[106] Provincial Jacobin clubs and speakers in the Convention railed against "these barbarous islanders, banes of humanity, whom nature has already separated from humanity by the seas"; the "barbarous character and spirit of these inhabitants of an island fertile in infamies"; and "the most ferocious, the most barbarous nation, the most debased of them all."[107] Barère's *Report on*

103. Barère, *Rapport*, 13.

104. Sophie Wahnich suggests that the shift in French sentiments toward England derived above all from the Jacobins' belief that in England, unlike in the other enemy nations, the people were sovereign and thus responsible for their government's actions (see Wahnich, *L'impossible citoyen*, 281–327). While this belief certainly helped shape Revolutionary discourse on the subject, I would argue that Wahnich overestimates its importance. The polemicists of the Seven Years' War employed similar rhetoric against the British without ever invoking English national sovereignty. The willingness to make pejorative characterizations of the English as a people had far more to do with the proximity and perceived similarity between the two nations.

105. See Bell, "Aux origines de la 'Marseillaise.'" The collection *Poésies nationales de la Révolution française* (Paris, 1836), 292, indicates that Lebrun's poem *Ode aux Français* was republished during the Revolution.

106. See the material quoted extensively in Wahnich, 252–80, and 318–27. Wahnich's book, which draws heavily on the techniques of linguistic analysis devised by Jacques Guilhaumou, rarely strays beyond the legislative records of the revolutionary assemblies (the *Archives parlementaires*) for source material.

107. Quoted in Wahnich, *L'impossible citoyen*, 323, 326; Hampson, *Perfidy*, 150.

England's Crimes fairly bristled with the charges once leveled against Jumon-ville's killers: "Caesar, in landing on the island [Britain], found only a fierce tribe *[peuplade]*," he declared. "Their subsequent civilization, and their civil wars and maritime wars have all continued to bear the mark of this savage origin." He accused the English of "corrupting the humanity of the savages" in America, and added his truly bone-chilling lines: "They are a tribe for-eign to Europe, foreign to humanity. They must disappear."[108] The ultimate fate of a people who had refused the revealed truth of superior French wis-dom was the same as Carthage's: extermination.

FROM WARS OF RELIGION TO WARS OF NATIONS AND RACES

In the polemical literature of the Seven Years' War, as throughout eigh-teenth-century French patriotic writing, religion was both the great absence and the great hidden presence. As previously noted, the authors almost entirely eschewed denouncing the English as heretics. And when compared with the anti-Protestant literature of the late-sixteenth-century Wars of Religion, or even with Jean de la Chapelle's early-eighteenth-century *Lettres d'un suisse* (which saluted the Hapsburg candidate for the Spanish throne as "CHARLES III BY GRACE OF THE HERETICS CATHOLIC KING [i.e., *Rey Catolico*]"), the difference is stunning.[109] Their very predilection for the image of the "English barbarian," with "barbarian" understood as the oppo-site of a civilized person, underlined their acceptance of the idea that mem-bership in a properly constituted universal community did not depend on religion, but on customs (*moeurs*) and cultivation. Religion had become a private matter, an affair of the inner conscience. It should no longer struc-ture international animosities.

Yet at the same time, the war literature resembled earlier, religiously inspired war propaganda so strongly, that it is hard not to see deep connec-tions between the two. First, the most important French precedents for using print matter on a massive scale to mobilize a population for foreign warfare were religious: particularly the efforts of the *politique* party that sup-ported Henri of Navarre against Spain. Second, almost the only French precedents for the wholesale demonization of an enemy nation, at least since 1500, were religious as well. In the Wars of Religion, even pamphlets aimed at Spanish Catholics most often cast their accusations in religious terms. If Philip II and his subjects were "barbarians," as the *politiques* said, it was precisely because they were false Catholics: secret atheists, or even Jews or Muslims. "What!" exclaimed the *politique* Antoine Arnauld in his 1590 pamphlet *Copy of the Anti-Spaniard*. "Should these Marannos become our

108. Barère, *Rapport*, 11, 12, 18.
109. De la Chapelle, *Lettres d'un suisse*, "Vingtième lettre," 2nd pagination, S3r.

Kings and Princes! . . . Should France be added to the titles of this King of Majorca, this half-Moor, half-Jew, half-Saracen [*sic*]?"[110] The representation of the English as barbarian false Europeans seems to stand as a secular parallel to these earlier exercises in xenophobia.

In addition, the discussion of "barbarians" and "savages" in the eighteenth century itself strongly recalls earlier religious modes of characterizing human diversity. Those writers who described the American Indians as rude, unfinished people in need of civilizing closely echoed the Jesuit missionaries who had seen the same Indians as lost souls in need of instruction in the true faith. Anthony Pagden has noted that for centuries, *barbarian* and *pagan* were virtual synonyms, while Michèle Duchet, in her pioneering study of Enlightenment anthropology, has pointed out that the *philosophes* themselves recognized the connections between the religious and civilizing "missions." It is difficult, she adds, "to conceive of a purely secular model of colonization, not only because history offers no examples of one, but because the very image of savages susceptible to persuasion, relayed by centuries of missiology, is still indissolubly linked to an ideal of evangelization."[111] Meanwhile, the description of the English as "barbarians" who willfully refused the benefits of French civilization echoed earlier condemnations of those groups that had seen, but willfully rejected, the revealed truth of the Gospels: heretics, and especially Jews. Rather eerily, the nefarious qualities attributed to the English in the eighteenth century—overweening pride, irrational hatred of other peoples, a desire to dominate the world, and also an unreasonable love of money and trade (the last a favorite theme for orators in the Convention—Barère called the English "a mercantile horde"), recalled those qualities that French writers commonly attributed to the Jews.[112] The comparison may seem unlikely, but consider this passage written by Elie Fréron in 1756: "The intolerance of the Jews in religious matters made the entire universe indignant at them. The intolerance of the Tyrians and Carthaginians in commercial matters hastened their destruction. The English should fear the same fate, for all Europe reproaches them for the same principles, the same views and the same vices."[113]

110. [Antoine Arnauld], *Coppie de l'antiespagnol, faict à Paris* (Paris, 1590), 12. In general, see Myriam Yardeni, *La conscience nationale en France pendant les guerres de religion (1559–1598)* (Louvain, 1971), 270–77, and Mack P. Holt, "Burgundians into Frenchmen: Catholic Identity in Sixteenth-Century Burgundy," in *Changing Identities in Early Modern France*, ed. Michael Wolfe (Durham, N.C., 1997), 345–70.

111. Pagden, *Lords of All the World*, 24; Duchet, *Anthropologie*, 210–11.

112. See Arthur Hertzberg, *The French Enlightenment and the Jews* (New York, 1968), 248–313. See also, for instance, Voltaire's infamous description of the Jews in the *Essai sur les moeurs et l'esprit des nations, et sur les principaux faits de l'histoire, depuis Charlemagne jusqu'à Louis XIII*, vol. 5 (Paris, 1804), 82–83. Barère is quoted in Wahnich, *L'impossible citoyen*, 318.

113. Quoted in Dziembowski, *Un nouveau patriotisme*, 84.

Finally, there is Joseph Coulon de Jumonville himself: an undistinguished man, common, simple and plain, but courageous—the very embodiment of French virtue. Previous annals of French military glory held very few precedents for a democratic hero of this sort. Volumes devoted to "great" or "illustrious" Frenchmen before the 1750s drew their military figures almost entirely from the ranks of the high nobility and "grands capitaines" (the principal exception was more properly a religious figure: Joan of Arc). Only from the 1760s would volumes of this sort start to include common soldiers, including Jumonville himself.[114] However, in the thick ranks of Catholic martyrs and saints, men like him abounded. In this sense, Jumonville has a strong claim to being the first martyr of modern France (in Thomas's pathetic description of his martyrdom, even as "his eyes close to the light," his "soul" finds "delight" not in God, but in "the tender memory of France").[115] He is also a direct predecessor of the Christlike boy martyrs of the French Revolution.

In concluding this essay, I would like to speculate on the implications of this view of Franco-English difference, not only for French nationalism, but also for French understandings of human diversity in general, and for the origins of race-based nationalism. It is true that, even in the Revolution, polemicists rarely described the differences between the English and the French in biological terms. The word *race* did occasionally appear, as in the phrase *race of cannibals* or *perjurous race*. Its usage in these contexts seems to denote something more than the common eighteenth-century definition of race as "lineage."[116] But most often the fault attributed to the British was a moral one, a failing of the spirit. It did seem somehow to infect the English people as a whole, generation after generation, but it did not have its origin in any specific physical difference detectable by biological science.

Yet by making national difference into something as fierce and unforgiving as religious difference had been during the era of the Reformation, the wartime polemicists helped readers to think of human diversity in a way that went beyond the detached, clinical observations of most Enlightenment authors. They suggested that national groups, which is to say groups bound together by a common origin rather than by common faith, had characteristics that climate, forms of government, and historical evolution could not by themselves explain or alter. It has been suggested that a new, "modern" racism, predicated on the notion of essential, normative differences between black and white, took hold in France sometime in the middle of the eighteenth century, above all as a means to justify the continuing enslave-

114. See note 5.
115. Thomas, *Jumonville*, 22.
116. On the meanings of *race*, see Boulle, "In Defense of Slavery," 222.

ment of Africans.[117] As intellectual background for the shift, historians cite the weakening of Christian theology and its insistence on the common descent of the human race from Adam ("monogenesis"), and the increasing influence of the biological sciences with their penchant for classification and ranking. The argument may be convincing as far as peoples of color were concerned, but European racial science in the modern period has been concerned with proving essential racial differences not only between Europeans and non-Europeans, but also within the European family itself.[118] The intellectual framework for investigations into these narrower racial differences was largely the same, but here the "science" developed in the service not of slavery and imperialism, but of nationalism.

And it is precisely here that the language of "savages" and "barbarians" was so important. It was not a scientific language in the least. But it set forth a problem that biological science could later answer: the problem of difference. As Anthony Pagden has written, when modes of explanation of human difference shifted, in the early nineteenth century, from the sociological to the physiological, they did so in part because the sociological modes seemed incapable of revealing why some peoples failed to make historical progress.[119] This was precisely the problem highlighted by the specter of the English "barbarian"—despite, or perhaps because of, the usual association of England with progress. The same problem would be repeatedly highlighted by emerging nationalist movements over the next century, when stigmatizing their enemies—notably the Jews. The language of barbarism suggested that the English, despite their membership in the white race, and in a common European civilization, in fact were fundamentally alien, as alien as heretics had been to the mother church. And not only alien, but inferior, and deserving of hatred, subjugation, and even extermination. In all the voluminous writings of the French Revolutionary period, there is no clearer forerunner of modern expressions of racial hatred than Barère's report on English crimes: "National hatred must sound forth." Without such a preexisting sense of deep, profound difference between nations, could nineteenth-century race science have carried any sense of conviction? Would its creators have even pursued their research in the first place?

Yet before the middle of the eighteenth century, such a sense of difference was lacking, at least in France. It began to arise only in the period of the Seven Years' War, in response to anxieties about France's changing position in the world and the demands of a rapidly evolving public sphere, as supporters of the French crown sought to mobilize the nation as a whole

117. Ibid. and Popkin, "The Philosophical Basis of Eighteenth-Century Racism."
118. See, for example, Hannaford, *Race*, 235–76.
119. Pagden, "The 'Defence of Civilization,'" 40–44.

against an entire enemy nation—to turn a conflict of monarchies into a national crusade that involved every individual citizen. The image of English "barbarians," who were even more alien than the already-frightening American "savages," helped teach the French this sense of national difference. It did so, moreover, without challenging the universalism that remained so important a force in French culture, and that would express itself so powerfully both at the start of the Revolution and again under Napoleon. The English were different precisely because they rejected the universal human civilization that properly revolved around France, as symbolized most vividly by their murder of Jumonville. In slaying him, the French publicists were implying, the English had not only taken the life of an unarmed ambassador, but also killed their own membership in the human race.

Pacific Modernity

Theater, Englishness, and the Arts of Discovery, 1760–1800

Kathleen Wilson

Britannia: Mark, votive Islander, thy fate is mine
For mine, the Queen of Isles, the mistress of the Main! . . .
Still shall my sons, by Cook's example taught
Thy new found world protect and humanize.

JOHN O'KEEFFE, *Omai, or a Trip Around the World* (1785)

The philosophical traveller, sailing to the ends of the earth, is in fact travelling in time; he is exploring the past; every step he makes is the passage of an age. Those unknown islands that he reaches are for him the passage of human society.

J.-M. DEGERANDO, *The Observation of Savage Peoples* (1800)

Historicism contents itself with establishing a causal connection between various moments in history. But no fact that is a cause is for that very reason historical. It became historical posthumously, as it were, through events that may be separated from it by thousands of years. A historian who takes this as his point of departure stops telling the sequence of events like the beads of a rosary. Instead, he grasps the constellation which his own era has formed with a definite earlier one.

WALTER BENJAMIN, "THESES ON THE PHILOSOPHY OF HISTORY" (1940)

The debates over "modernity" that have reverberated in European cultural theory and history since World War II have not unduly troubled most historians of eighteenth-century Britain. Suspicious of any species of "Whig" (that is, linear) history and confident that Continental theorizing bears little relevance to their inquires, British historians have been content to fight less epochal battles over the appropriate characterization of their period. Hence, whether England was an "aristocratic" or "bourgeois" society, an "ancien regime" or "commercialized" polity, marked predominantly by paternalism and deference or restiveness and resistance are the issues that have traditionally occupied many historians' attention.[1] Although such

---

1. The "commercialization" thesis has been most enthusiastically documented by J. H. Plumb and his students; see Plumb, *The Commercialisation of Leisure in Eighteenth Century England* (Reading, Eng., 1973); Neil McKendrick, John Brewer, and J. H. Plumb, *The Birth of a Consumer*

dichotomous readings have often been geared more toward advancing academic careers than productive debate, the status of eighteenth-century England as a progenitor of modernity has only recently begun to be taken seriously within the disciplinary wooden walls of Hanoverian history.

Certainly there is cause for skepticism about the historical returns of investigations into the location and meanings of modernity, not least since the term is twisted and turned to serve a variety of scholarly constituencies. Among more positivistic social scientists and historians, for example, modernity has been conceived as the story of "modernization"—that is, of those objective, ineluctably unfolding processes that are believed to have generated the structures and texture of "modern" life: urbanization, industrialization, democratization, bureaucracy, scientism, and technology.[2] But other historians and cultural critics, less interested in structural determinacies than with the meanings, ambiguities, and significance of a period's configurations, have engaged more fruitfully with the notion of modernity as an unfolding set of relationships—cognitive, social, and intellectual as well as economic and technological—which, however valued or construed, are seen as producing the modern self and its expectations of perfection or

---

Society: The Commercialisation of Eighteenth Century England (London, 1982); John Brewer, Party Ideology and Popular Politics at the Accession of George III (Cambridge, 1976); Roy Porter, English Society in the Eighteenth Century (London, 1982). See also Paul Langford, A Polite and Commercial People: England, 1727–1783 (Oxford, 1989). Edward Thompson and his followers have countered with the more dyadic, neo-Marxist model of patrician hegemony and plebeian resistance: E. P. Thompson, "Eighteenth Century English Society: Class Struggle without Class?" Social History 3 (1978): 123–65, and Customs in Common: Studies in Traditional Popular Culture (New York, 1991); Douglas Hay et al., Albion's Fatal Tree: Crime and Society in Eighteenth Century England (New York, 1975). Thompson's hostility to "French" (i.e., non-Marxist) theory is on display in The Poverty of Theory and Other Essays (London, 1978).

    J. D. C. Clark has done most to advance the argument that England was an "ancien regime" marked by aristocratic dominance, paternalism, and deference (while also excoriating "Whig" history and imported theory alike): see Clark, English Society, 1688–1832 (Cambridge, 1985); Revolution and Rebellion: State and Society in England in the Seventeenth and Eighteenth Centuries (Cambridge, 1986). His view has been supported by Jeremy Black, The English Press in the Eighteenth Century (Philadelphia, 1987), and John Cannon, Aristocratic Century: The Peerage of Eighteenth-Century England (Cambridge, 1984).

    2. For example, W. W. Rostow, The Stages of Economic Growth (Cambridge, 1960); I. Wallerstein, The Modern World System (New York, 1974); Richard Brown, Modernization: The Transformation of American Life, 1600–1865 (New York, 1976); Paul Johnson, The Birth of the Modern World: 1815–30 (New York, 1991). Sociologists such as Emile Durkheim, in The Division of Labor in Society, 2nd ed., trans. George Simpson (New York, 1964), and Max Weber, in The Protestant Ethic and the Spirit of Capitalism, 2nd ed., trans. Talcott Parsons (London, 1976), who stressed the costs and ambiguities as well as the benefits of modernization, provide more interesting sociological ruminations on modernity. For the critique of "modernization theory," see Andrew Webster, Introduction to the Sociology of Development (London, 1984), and John Tomlinson, Cultural Imperialism: A Critical Introduction (Baltimore, 1991).

progress.[3] Some, influenced by the re-theorizing of modernity among the so-called post-modernists,[4] have located in the discursive and institutional matrices of power and resistance shaping late-eighteenth-century European societies the genealogies of their own age's discontents and transfigurations. Others have examined the relations of power at home and abroad that underwrote and sustained Europeans' perceptions of modernity, demonstrating how the nation-state and imperialism stimulated forms of identification, exclusion, and belonging that have refused to fade.[5] In general, the most interesting work has focused on modernity as a discursive and cultural construct rather than a set of stereotypic processes or "forces," and some of the most exciting has looked at ways in which emergent ideas about nationality, race, ethnicity, and difference became central to the broader social and political transformations of the mid-eighteenth to early nineteenth cen-

3. Jürgen Habermas, "Modernity: An Incomplete Project," in *Postmodern Culture*, ed. Hal Foster (London, 1983), 3–15, and *The Structural Transformation of the Public Sphere*, trans. Thomas Burber and Frederick Lawrence (Cambridge, Mass., 1989); Marshall Berman, *"All that Is Solid Melts into Air": The Experience of Modernity* (New York, 1982), and *The Politics of Authenticity: Radical Individualism and the Emergence of Modern Society* (London, 1971). Historians of France have been more favorably impressed by the potential of these readings of Enlightenment and modernity than have their English counterparts, and esp. by Habermas's notion of the eighteenth-century emergence of the "public sphere": see, e.g., Lynn Hunt, *Politics, Culture, and Class in the French Revolution* (Berkeley and Los Angeles, 1984); Lynn Hunt, ed., *The Invention of Pornography: Obscenity and the Origins of Modernity, 1500–1800* (New York, 1993); Tom Crow, *Painters and Public Life in Eighteenth Century Paris* (New Haven, 1985); Sarah Maza, *Private Lives and Public Affairs: The Causes Célèbres of Prerevolutionary France* (Berkeley and Los Angeles, 1993); Joan Landes, *Women and the Public Sphere in the Age of the French Revolution* (Ithaca, N.Y., 1988); Roger Chartier, *The Cultural Origins of the French Revolution* (New York, 1991); and Dena Goodman, *The Republic of Letters: A Cultural History of the French Enlightenment* (Ithaca, N.Y., 1994). Exceptions among historians writing on England include Geoff Eley, "Rethinking the Political: Social History and Political Culture in Eighteenth and Nineteenth Century Britain," *Archiv für Sozialgeschichte* 21 (1981): 427–56; Lawrence Klein, *Shaftesbury and the Culture of Politeness* (Cambridge, 1994); and John Brewer, *The Pleasures of the Imagination: English Culture in the Eighteenth Century* (London and New York, 1997). The classic pessimist reading of the modernity inaugurated by the Enlightenment is Theodore Adorno and Max Horkheimer, *Dialectic of Enlightenment* (London, 1979).

4. That is, a disparate group of critics whose perceived unity rests on their intellectual debts to various French poststructuralisms as well as their shared belief in the discontinuity of the late-twentieth-century present with the "modern" period that came before it. The work of Michel Foucault, particularly in *Discipline and Punish: The Birth of the Prison*, trans. Roger Sheridan (New York, 1971), and *The History of Sexuality*, trans. Robert Hurley (New York, 1978), is of particular importance here, as is that by Jacques Derrida in *Of Grammatology*, trans. Gayatri Chakravorty Spivak (Baltimore, 1976), and *Writing and Difference*, trans. Alan Bates (Chicago, 1987). See also Fredric Jameson, *The Political Unconscious: Narrative as a Socially Symbolic Act* (Ithaca, N.Y., 1981), and Umberto Eco, *Travels in Hyperreality*, trans. William Weaver (San Diego, 1986).

5. Such as C. L. R. James, *The Black Jacobins*, 2nd ed., rev. (New York, 1989); Eric Williams, *Capitalism and Slavery* (London, 1967); Henry Louis Gates, Jr., ed., *"Race," Writing and Difference*

turies. To take one example, Paul Gilroy's notion of the "Black Atlantic" has been rightly celebrated for offering a new perspective on Britishness, history, and modernity from the 1700s to the present, a perspective that emphasizes the hybridity and heterogeneity of Anglo-American cultural forms and experience and thus contests the more absolutist definitions of nations proffered by historians of nationalism. His emphases on the cultural *métissage*, political hybridity, and double subjectivities produced by slavery and colonialism have stimulated the investigation of a "counterculture of modernity" that challenged European order, exposed the limits to economic and intellectual "progress," and highlighted the fictive nature of homogeneous "national" cultures.[6]

Clearly, the analysis of modernity has borne rich conceptual fruit as well as some vacuities, and it is a rash historian who would dismiss all efforts to interrogate modernity as ahistorical, dangerous, or irrelevant. For modernity need not be seen as *one* particular moment whose "origins" and characteristics can be identified with certainty and mapped onto a specific temporality between the sixteenth and twentieth centuries. Rather, "modernity," the latest point on the continuum of historical change, should be understood as an emphatically historical condition that can only be recovered, in Walter Benjamin's resonant phrase, in "time filled by the presence of the now."[7] Modernity in this sense is not one moment or age, but a set of relations that are constantly being made and unmade, contested and reconfigured, that nonetheless produce among their contemporaneous witnesses the conviction of historical *difference*. Such a conceptualization opens up whole new grounds for theorizing and understanding our histories that do not deny the specificity of a period's configurations or reduce the eighteenth century to the status of the great primordial swamp of a more "modern" world. As an epistemological strategy, the historicization of differential modernities can also disrupt the comforting belief in the dissimilarity of past and present and subvert our sense of historical progress.[8]

This essay will propose that such a reading of modernity can greatly

(Chicago, 1985); Nicholas Thomas, *Colonialism's Culture* (Durham, N.C., 1994); Frederick Cooper and Ann Laura Stoler, *Tensions of Empire: Colonial Cultures in a Bourgeois World* (Berkeley, 1997); Paul Gilroy, *The Black Atlantic: Modernity and Double Consciousness* (Cambridge, Mass., 1993); Homi Bhabha, *The Location of Culture* (London, 1994); Nicholas Mirzoeff, *Silent Poetry: Deafness, Sign, and Visual Culture in Modern France, 1700–1920* (Princeton, 1995); and Kathleen Wilson, "Citizenship, Empire, and Modernity in the English Provinces, 1720–1800," *Eighteenth Century Studies* 29 (1995–96): 69–96, *The Sense of the People: Politics, Culture, and Imperialism in England 1715–1785* (Cambridge, 1995), and *The Island Race: Englishness, Empire, and Gender in the Eighteenth Century* (forthcoming).

6. Gilroy, *Black Atlantic.*

7. Walter Benjamin, *Illuminations,* ed. Hannah Arendt (New York, 1969), 263.

8. A point also made by Thomas in *Colonialism's Culture,* 21.

enrich our understanding of English culture in the last quarter of the eighteenth century. The discontinuous and plural nature of the eighteenth-century experience—marked as closely by slavery as liberty; by racial, class, and gender exclusions as universality; and by fractured and double identities as unitary ones—requires nothing less than a modification of the boundaries by which "modernity" and "postmodernity" are demarcated and understood. In the continual reinventions of "the nation"—always a constructed, mythic, and contested rather than stable or self-evident unit of meaning and coherence—and the ideological signification of its activities at home and abroad may be found a place where, in Gilroy's phrase, a modernity begins in the "constitutive relationships with outsiders that both found and temper a self-conscious sense of western civilization."[9] Here we will focus on the nature and meaning of Englishness and belonging produced through British exploration in the "Second Age of Discovery." We will examine a convergence of shifts in scientific classification, history writing, and theatrical practice that helped produce new kinds of subjects and objects of knowledge and upheld novel notions of space and time that made possible the naturalization of certain kinds of identities whose traces refuse to disappear. Doing so suggests how the Pacific, like the Atlantic, became commodified in an imperial circuitry of identity, alterity, and exchange, in which Pacific discovery and its representations became emblems of English superiority and modernity, while also providing unintentional commentary on the English dependence upon supposedly backward Pacific cultures and people.[10] The representation of colonial encounters in the South Seas deployed the latest in visual and historical technologies to verify equally English ethnicity and English excellence in the arts of discovery in ways that idealized past imperial experience and shaped expectations about the national destiny. Through the ironies of imperial mimicry, British cultural producers coopted a range of Pacific peoples, artifacts, and topographies in a theater of discovery that demonstrated how both the history and modernity of late-eighteenth-century England was consolidated and understood through the mirror of Pacific others.

A NEW KIND OF NATIONAL HERO

Central, of course, to English exploration and triumph in the Pacific was Captain James Cook, and he appropriately takes center stage in this rumination on late-eighteenth-century thinking about modernity and English-

9. Gilroy, *Black Atlantic*, 17.
10. A fuller discussion of these themes can be found in my chapters "The Island Race: Captain Cook and the Construction of English Ethnicity," and "Breasts, Sodomy, and the Lash: Masculinity and Its Others Aboard the Cook Voyages," both in *The Island Race*.

ness. For through the figure of Cook and the widely circulated stories of his and followers' voyages to the South Pacific islands, an important component of English ethnicity—that of England as a unique "island race"—was authorized and renewed as central to Britain's national identity and imperial mission. Literary critics have argued that the topos of the island in European imaginative literature enabled reflections on origins and dominion, "the site of that contemplation being the uninhabited territory upon which the conditions for return or genesis are made possible."[11] For the English, the topographical and figurative significance of insularity had long served to structure certain crucial beliefs about the "national character" and destiny (significantly, despite the fact that England itself, of course, was not an island).[12] But the "discoveries" in the Pacific also turned islands, literally and figuratively, into historical vehicles for the self-realization of humanity and the attainment of a particularly English genius and mission.

The voyages inaugurating what is Eurocentrically called the Second Age of Discovery—Bryon, Wallis, Carteret, and Cook to the Pacific, Cartwright to Labrador, Phipps and Pickergill to the Arctic—provided new information about the diversity of humankind and the extremes of degradation, savagery, or refinement in which it could live that renewed old questions about the relative positions of Europeans and their "others." At the same time, the literary and visual representations of these achievements commodified a rhetoric of discovery that combined features of travelogues and scientific (i.e., "objective," empirical) description. The resulting "scientific reportage," as it is called here, modeled its techniques of comparative social analysis on the systems of classification initiated in natural science, ranking human societies according to nature, history, culture, and "stage" of civilization. Integral to eighteenth-century European imperialism and its larger taxonomic projects of ethnology, natural history, and global knowledge, such scientific reportage also influenced the representation of colonial encounters in a range of forums, enabling the exotic, unknown, and "discovered" to be appropriated, domesticated, and rendered plausible.[13] The

11. Diana Loxley, *Problematic Shores: The Literature of Islands* (New York, 1990), 3; see also Michael Seidel, *Robinson Crusoe: Island Myths and the Novel* (Boston, 1987), and Orest Ranum, "Islands and the Self in a Ludovician Fete," in *Sun King*, ed. David Rubin (Washington, D.C., 1992), 17–34 (thanks to the author for the last reference).

12. I use the term *national character* here and elsewhere to refer to its eighteenth-century meaning, that is, the distinctive set of manners, customs, and morals shared by a people within a specific territory. It should not be taken as my endorsement of the ontology of "national character."

13. It thus differed from earlier travelers' and explorers' tales, which focused on the fantastic, the exotic, and the economic. See James Hevia, *Cherishing Men from Afar: Qing Guest Ritual and the Macartney Embassy* (Durham, N.C., 1995), 84–85; Thomas Richards, *The Imperial Archive* (London, 1993); Jonathan Lamb, introduction to "The South Pacific in the Eighteenth Century," special issue of *Eighteenth Century Life* 18 (November 1994): 5–6.

impact on articulations of English distinctiveness and identity are strikingly illuminated in the apotheosis of Captain Cook, and it is to the production of Cook as a national hero that we will first turn.

Coming as they did in the midst of a welter of imperial troubles that were forcing English observers to question the long-vaunted moral superiority of British imperialism over its European rivals, Cook's Pacific explorations were crucial to reconstituting the imperial project as an essentially philan-thropic, knowledge-producing enterprise, designed to benefit all of human-kind. Cook's three voyages (1768–71, 1772–75, 1776–80) generated an industry of highly ethnocentric commentary, praise, and critique that com-menced with publication of Hawkesworth's *Voyages* in 1773 and continues to the present day. With a distinguished sponsorship that included the Royal Society, George III, and the Admiralty, and boasting trained naturalists, astronomers, and artists as well as navigators on board, the voyages were cel-ebrated for marking new departures in scientific observation, discovery, and collection of data. Through the vast quantities of "firsthand" information thereby acquired on different peoples and customs, the voyages also sup-plied the materials for a new "science of Man." Cook himself was lionized by the English public in ways that few figures of the era could match, coming to symbolize and embody the combination of intrepidity and humanism that was quickly vaunted as a central feature of the national identity.

Cook's personal fame and nationalist significance swelled with each voy-age, overtaking the celebrity that initially attended the naturalists Joseph Banks and Daniel Solander of the *Endeavour* voyage and reaching a cre-scendo in the years after his death in 1779. His renown reverberated at many social and political levels, but in all he was heralded as a particularly *English* hero, who embodied and extended his country's genius for naviga-tion and discovery, aptitude for science, respect for merit, love of liberty, and paternalistic regard for humanity. A reviewer in the *Annual Register* for 1784–85, for example, captured the public mood in his hubristic summary of the national aggrandizement that had resulted from Cook's exploits. Thanks to Cook, he stated,

> there is nothing now unknown of this globe, which can intitle any one to the character of a discoverer. . . . [O]ur success in exploring unknown regions, give posterity a convincing proof that we have a more decided superiority over the other countries of Europe, than could be derived from the most extensive conquests, and will hold us forth to future ages as the most powerful people upon this globe.[14]

Cook himself was immortalized in biographies, plays, painting, and poetry. All served as fulsome encomiums to the low-born man who became

14. *Annual Register* 27 (1784–85): 149–50.

a great commander by virtue of his own talents, the supreme English explorer whose amazing forays into undiscovered countries spread friendship and arts among native peoples while furthering the national reputation and standing throughout the world. Cook's superior abilities, judgment, and discipline, as well as his humble origins as a Yorkshire husbandman's son, his autodidacticism (he taught himself mathematics and astronomy while master of a warship serving off the coast of America during the Seven Years' War), and his humility (he is endearingly disparaging of his literary skills in his account of the second voyage)[15] became inextricable parts of his heroic character, the Everyman whose hard work and merit, "great qualities and amiable virtues," paid off for himself, his family, and his country. Cook's humanity was also lauded from all quarters, particularly from among those who had been repelled by the crass commercialism and aggressive militarism of earlier maritime adventures. Fanny Burney called him "the most moderate, humane and gentle circumnavigator that ever went out upon discoveries," and this verdict was confirmed by Hannah More, Anna Seward, William Cowper, Dr. Johnson, and Mrs. Thrale, to name a few. Cook's reputed respect for the diversity and commonalty of humankind and his efforts to bring indigenous peoples "within the pale of the offices of humanity, and to relieve the wants of their imperfect state of society" while shedding "some rays of light . . . on their infant minds," made him the exemplar for abolitionists of what could be accomplished once the progress of all was privileged over the profits of a few.[16] Even his resistance to the sexual charms of Oceanic women—in marked contrast to most of the rest of his officers and crew—as well as his monogamous marriage and manly offspring, were celebrated for confirming his credentials as a man of sensibility and an upholder of nonaristocratic morality. After decades of war and the celebration of leaders whose fame rested on more militaristic and sanguinary acts performed in the service of their country, Cook represented not only an alternative masculinity, but also a new kind of national hero, one who demonstrated both English pluck and humanity, sense and sensi-

15. Though "employ'd as a discoverer," Cook explained, he was but "a plain man, zealously exerting himself in the service of his country," and therefore begs the reader to "excuse the inaccuracies of style." J. C. Beaglehole, ed., *Journals of Captain James Cook on His Voyages of Discovery. The Voyage of the Endeavour 1768–71* (Cambridge, 1955), 380; James Cook, *A Voyage to the South Pole & Round the World*, 2 vols. (London: 1777), xxxvi.

16. Fanny Burney, *Early Diary* (London, 1908), 267; Hannah More, *The Slave Trade* (London, 1784); *The Lady's Magazine* 4 (1773): 345–46; Anna Seward, *Elegy on the Death of Captain Cook* (London, 1780); William Cowper, *The Task* (London, 1785); T. M. Curley, *Samuel Johnson and the Age of Travel* (Athens, Ga., 1976), 66, 69. Cook quote from Andrew Kippis, *Narrative of the Life of Captain James Cook* (London, 1788), 371. Many of these encomiums compared Cook to the Spanish conquistadors rather than to earlier and less "ethical" English explorers and traders, in a strategy meant to erase Britain's less salubrious imperial record, which recent events had done much to drive home.

bility, to best advantage. He was the explorer's "man of feeling" who died on the altar of national service with more blood brothers than bloodshed to his credit.[17]

Certainly Cook had his critics. One of the most notable was the Reverend Gerald Fitzgerald, the Dublin professor whose poem, *The Injured Islanders,* betrayed a woeful familiarity with its tale of native desecration by avaricious English men. Missionaries would later take Cook to task for a number of wayward actions, not least allowing himself to be treated as a deity by incognizant savages. And Cook's quick temper and sudden flashes of violence were all too well known to his crew.[18] Nevertheless, the idealizations are important for what they reveal about Cook's instantly mythical stature as a figure capable of reconstituting British imperial authority and English superiority, through what was now seen as the humanitarian enterprise of empire building. These various strands in Cook's apotheosis are amply displayed in a theatrical extravaganza in his honor that is worthy of detailed attention. In the age of the "first empire," English theater did much to consolidate and popularize ideas about English distinctiveness, and to socialize audiences into the typologies of gender, class, and national difference. Lauded as a key element in the emergence of a polished and polite urban culture, the eighteenth-century stage represented and disseminated topical "knowledge" about the world as a central part of its respectability and "civilizing" function. Indeed, in its representations of conquest (sexual and territorial), desire, and otherness (both racial and gendered), Georgian theater supplemented the encyclopedic gaze of print culture in staking out the grounds of identification in the formation of alterity and sameness. It was thus crucial in socializing English people into *recognizing* difference, and especially the historicity and distinctiveness of the English compared to other nations in history.[19] Moreover, the stage played a crucial role in circulating the texts, bodies, ideas, and people meant to incarnate the best of an English, and secondarily a British, national identity, all the while demonstrating both the syncretism of that culture and the performative nature of those essentialized identities that theater was meant to express, invoke, and mobilize. The performances of difference on the Georgian stage thus constituted a repository of social knowledge that literally and figuratively

17. For a more recent endorsement of Cook's upright and strictly nonmiscegenational interactions with native women, see Marshall Sahlins, *Islands of History* (Chicago, 1985), chap. 1.

18. For Fitzgerald, see Bill Pearson, *Rifled Sanctuaries: Some Views of the Pacific Islands in Western Literature to 1900* (Auckland and Oxford, 1984); for the debate on Cook's violence, see Gananath Obeyeskere, *The Apotheosis of Captain Cook: European Myth Making in the Pacific* (Princeton, 1992), and Marshall Sahlins, *How 'Natives' Think, About Captain Cook, for Example* (Chicago, 1995).

19. This argument is taken from my book *The Colonial Stage: Theater, Culture, and Modernity in the English Provinces, 1720–1820* (in progress).

embodied the categories through which self and other could be understood, while also revealing, through the skill and artifice of the actors, their fictive nature—making "visible the play of difference and identity within the larger ensemble of [social] relations," as Joseph Roach has noted.[20]

The Cook play *Omai, or a Trip Around the World* amplified and reconfigured some of the visual and figurative tropes at work in other literature and drama of the day, enabling English audiences to come to terms with Cook's, and their own, histories and destinies in particular ways. A pantomime written by the Irish playwright John O'Keeffe and the English composer William Shields, and designed by the Alsatian artist and theater designer Phillipe Jacques de Loutherbourg, it was produced at Covent Garden in December 1785, one and a half years after the official accounts of Cook's final voyage had been released by the Admiralty.[21] That the canonization of Cook as the most English of heroes was left to the talents of an Irishman and Frenchman did not seem to trouble contemporaries. All were profoundly invested in the superiority of the English as the premier "mimic men" and in the English stage as the premier site for the enactment of superior national virtue and character: the place where, in and through the bodies of the actors, past met present and English mastery at becoming the other was made evident, if only for the duration of the show. Pantomime of the late eighteenth century revolved around the story of the frustrated romance of Harlequin and his lover Columbine and their ultimate triumph over their nemeses, Pantaloon and the Clown, but its rapidly changing scenes allowed for both topicality and spectacle. The spectacular, mythic, and topical blended in this case to provide, as one contemporary put it, "the stage edition of Captain Cook's voyage."[22]

20. Although we arrived at these conclusions independently, Joseph Roach's recent book supports many of the contentions about theater and performance presented here. See Roach, *Cities of the Dead: CircumAtlantic Performance* (New York, 1996); the quote is on p. 4.

21. The pantomime has been extensively studied. This account is indebted to, but differs significantly from, those by Rudiger Jöppien, "Phillipe Jacques de Loutherbourg's Pantomime *Omai, or a Trip Round the World* and the Artists of Captain Cook's Voyages," in his *Captain Cook and the South Seas* (London, 1979), 81–133; Bernard Smith, *European Vision and the South Pacific* (New Haven, 1985), 115–22; and Greg Dening, *Mr. Bligh's Bad Language: Passion, Power, and Theatre on the Bounty* (Cambridge, 1992), 270–76, 293–98. This account is based upon John O'Keeffe, *Harlequin Omai* (London, 1785); [William Shields], *A Short Account of the New Pantomime called OMAI, or a Trip Round the World* (London, 1785); Newberry Library, Microprint of O'Keeffe, Airs, etc. for *Harlequin Omai*, British Library, Add. MS 38622, Plays, Coker Collection, ff. 164–187v; and O'Keeffe, *Recollections of the Life of John O'Keeffe*, vol. 2 (London, 1826), 113–14.

22. For pantomime, see David Mayer III, *Harlequin in His Element: The English Pantomime 1806–36* (Cambridge, Mass., 1969), and Ralph Allen, "Topical Scenes from Pantomime," *Educational Theatre Journal* 17 (1965): 289–300. The quote is from the *Morning Chronicle*, 21 December 1785.

The title of the pantomime that was to honor Cook was equally significant. It was borrowed from the first Polynesian visitor to England, called by
the English Omai, who in 1774 had been brought by Captain Furneaux of
the *Adventure* (the consort vessel of the second voyage). Omai quickly
became the darling of London society for the two years of his stay. Although
a Raiatean commoner from the island of Huahine, Omai in England performed the role of noble savage for the patrician set, lauded for his "natural" grace, politeness, and manners, and was presented to the king and
painted in suitably neoclassical style by Reynolds.[23] He was ultimately sent
back to eastern Polynesia in the specific role of "ambassador" for England,
meant to persuade local peoples of the felicities of British civilization and of
British proprietary rights to their land. Yet Omai in fact was only the most
well known of the series of native informants whose aid, friendship, and
local knowledge allowed the voyagers not only to "discover" heretofore
unknown island societies, but also to survive. Others included the Tahitian
priest, advisor, and navigator Tupaia, who joined the *Endeavour* when the
ship left Tahiti in 1769 (and died in Batavia the next year); Hitihiti and his
servant Poetata, from Bora Bora, who accompanied the *Resolution* on its
Antarctic search for the southern continent and mediated the navigators'
dealings with Maoris and Easter Islanders; and the aristocratic "queen"
Purea, gracious friend of Wallis and Cook and the object of much scurrility
at the hands of English pundits for her supposed romantic relationship with
Joseph Banks.[24] Hitihiti, whose services materially aided the second voyage
at several crucial junctures, and Tupaia, who literally gave his life for the mission, do not figure in the play, but Omai and Purea do, in ways that
attempted to honor them for important roles in the "discovery" process.
Significantly, the stage production bore the same relation to Omai, Purea,
and Cook's "real" circumstances as its representation of Pacific-English
encounters did to the empirical politics of exploration, imbricating all present in an "unstable interplay of truth and illusion."[25]

Indeed, the pantomime had a whimsical and romantic plot, which
involved Omai, here made heir to the throne of Tahiti and his betrothed,
the beautiful Londina, daughter of Britannia, setting chase across the world
to escape the evil spells of his rival, who wants to prevent their union and
hence that of the two kingdoms. The lovers' flight provided the theme of
the show, bringing them from a Tahitian *morai* to Hyde Park, Plymouth, and

23. See Burney, *Early Diary*, vol. 1, 321–37, vol. 2, 130–33; George Colman, Jr., *Random Records*, vol. 2 (London, 1830), 152–96.
24. See K. R. Howe, *Where the Waves Fall: A New South Sea Islands History from the First Settlement to Colonial Rule* (Honolulu, 1984); Nicholas Thomas, *In Oceania* (Durham, N.C., 1997), 1–7.
25. Michael Taussig, *Shamanism, Colonialism, and the Wild Man* (Chicago, 1987), 121.

Margate before whisking them across all the islands and continents Cook had visited or discovered, including Kamchatka; the Ice Islands, or Antarctica; New Zealand; the Tongan, or Friendly, Islands; and the Sandwich Islands. In doing so the pantomime set new standards in scenery and costume for topographic and ethnographic accuracy. Indeed, Loutherbourg's sets were technologically breathtaking. Loutherbourg had made a reputation in the past decade for his naturalistic and spectacular stage designs, which used top-lights, silk screens, transparencies, and mechanical figures and ships to create the illusion that the stage had become the world, the "imagined place of action."[26] In 1781 he introduced to Londoners the *eidophusikon*, a miniature theater without actors, which presented performances described as "Imitations of Natural Phenomena, represented by Moving Pictures" that were made to represent "views" of landscapes and events from all over the globe, from London to Tangiers, Japan, and India, in an uncanny predecessor of the newsreel. As Loutherbourg explained the device:

> [B]y adding progressive motion to accurate resemblance, a series of incidents might be reproduced which should display in the most lively manner those captivating scenes which inexhaustible Nature presents to our view at different periods and in different parts of the globe.[27]

This expertise at representing "natural" phenomena and temporal movement proved to be the perfect strategy for this pantomime, where primitive South Sea islanders, English icons, and comedic characters confronted each other in a bemused apprehension of historical and cultural difference.

For in *Omai* Loutherbourg proved that the English arts of theatrical representation were equal to the arts of English discovery, merging the naturalistic and mimetic to produce an ethnographic spectacle within a magical setting that showed off English civility and technological superiority to best advantage. Loutherbourg had probably familiarized himself with the collections of South Seas artifacts collected by Banks, as well as those displayed at Sir Ashton Lever's private museum in Leicester House; he also paid close attention to the various drawings, sketches, and paintings by the voyages' artists, William Hodges and John Webber. Hence his sets for *Omai* brought to stage design the same arts of perspective, light, and motion that had helped make navigation such a spectacular science. In conjunction with the ethnographic accuracy of the costumes and weapons and the use of such sophisticated equipment as the flying balloon, the sets brought home the visuality of exploration to English audiences. Popular actors provided key

26. Rudiger Jöppien, *Phillipe Jacques de Loutherbourg* (London, 1978), 12.

27. Ibid., 6; *Public Advertiser,* 21 February 1781; Jöppien, "Loutherbourg's Pantomime *Omai,*" 111n. The "views" included *A View of London from Greenwich Park, The Port of Tangier, Rocky Shore on the Coast of Japan,* and *Shipwreck of the Haslewell East Indiaman.*

performances, such as the lovely young Miss Cranfield as Londina, stately Elizabeth Inchbald as Britannia, and the ethnic specialist Ralph Wewitzer as a native prophet who paid homage to Cook in extempore chatter that was supposed to be Tahitian and was "translated" in the program (a tactic that mimicked the widespread printed circulation of antipodean vocabularies in voyage accounts and commentaries). All increased the appeal of a show that sparkled with its jumble of exoticism, science, spectacle, and "fact." "What can be more delightful than an enchanting fascination that monopolizes the mind to the scene before the eye, and leads the imagination from country to country, from the frigid to the torrid zone, shewing as in a mirror, prospects of different climates, with all the productions of nature in the animal and vegetable worlds, and all the efforts of man to attain nourishment, convenience and luxury, by the world of arts," gushed the critic for the *Times.* The critic in *Rambler Magazine* put it more succinctly, calling the pantomime "a school for the history of Man."[28]

As an entertainment about encounters in the "contact zone" when English islanders confronted the otherness of Pacific islanders (in a genre appropriated from Italian commedia dell'arte and using British actors), the pantomime enabled what Walter Benjamin has called the "flash of recognition" between disjunctive historical subjects and periods that staked out the grounds of similarity in the construction of historical difference.[29] Capturing Pacific peoples in the ethnographic gaze characteristic of the period's nascent social science, the representation allowed "travel," geographic and temporal, by aid of the latest in visual sciences and technologies, while the Pacific islanders so arrayed provided examples to English audiences of their earlier selves, "mirrors" of a past once deemed lost, but now paraded before them in proof of present-day English ingenuity, civility, and cosmopolitanism. At the same time, through the dissemination of apparently neutral topical and "scientific" knowledge, the pantomime demonstrated the role of theater in formulating the notion of an (idealized) history "as it really was," which was also at the heart of burgeoning vogues in painting and fiction (realms where mimesis also transformed the "real" into the ideal, the higher form of knowledge).[30] The music, too, was praised for its realism, Shield's songs described as "beautifully wild" and "capturing the vernacular airs of Otaheite" by includ-

28. The *Times,* 22 December 1785; *Rambler Magazine* (January 1786): 53. For vocabularies, see, for example, Sydney Parkinson, *A Journal of Voyage to the South Seas In His Majesty's Ship the Endeavour* (London, 1784), and Johann Reinhold Forster, *Observations Made on a Voyage Round the World* (London, 1778).

29. Walter Benjamin, "Theses on the Philosophy of History," in *Illuminations;* for the "contact zone," see Mary Louis Pratt, *Imperial Eyes: Transculturation and Travel Writing* (London, 1992).

30. This idealized notion of history is also discussed by Dening, *Bligh's Bad Language,* 292, and Smith, *European Vision,* 117–18, 121.

ing Tahitian words and imitations of the sounds of conchs and exotic animals. The pantomime thus permitted "science . . . [to] approach barbarity," as the critic for the *London Chronicle* so evocatively remarked.[31]

Not coincidentally, these genres are brought together in the final scene of the pantomime, which takes place in Tahiti. Omai, successfully wed to Londina, is installed as king and a grand marriage procession of all the peoples of the Pacific Islands takes place—Tahitian dancing girls and (male) attendants; Maori warriors, with a Maori woman and child; chiefs and men of the Marquesas, Easter Island, Friendly Islands, and Sandwich Islands, the latter in feathered and plain helmets; Tannese, Tartars, Russians, Kamchatkars, Oonalashkans, and residents of both sexes from Nootka and Prince William Sound. The parade is wound up by British tars and an "English Captain," who presents Omai with a sword. Two features are remarkable here. First, the British actors cross-dressed as Pacific "natives" solicit through their costuming both identification and its refusal from the audience, the exotic or homely costumes of the women setting off the more graceful, demure, and civilized garb of Londina, and the feathers, furs, tattoos, beaded collars, and rudimentary weapons of the men distinguishing their degree of civility from the audience's own. The *Times,* for one, loved this choice: "We highly approve of the procession in the last scene, as it shews in a *regular* and *successive* view, the various people whom Captain Cook visited, whereby the mind of the spectator has an opportunity of comparing at one view, the different nations with each other."[32] Second, this scene of happy miscegenation, dignified by the princely status of Omai, engages in interesting ways with contemporary English anxieties over "real" interracial sexual union at home, in the colonies, and in the act of "discovery." It suspended, for example, the shame over the congress between (lower class) British tars and Tahitian women that had been a source of venereal contagion on the island, and morally elevated the amorous connections imagined by pundits to have existed between the historical Omai and concupiscent aristocratic English ladies. Omai and Londina's union also, perhaps unwittingly, conformed to colonial legal codes against miscegenation, many of which attempted to prohibit black-white sexual relations but permitted intermarriage between "Indians" and whites, since Polynesians were consistently referred to as "Indians" in all the voyage accounts and commentaries.[33] Above all, perhaps, the scene enacted that desire for the Other that

31. O'Keeffe, *Recollections,* 114; *London Chronicle,* 22 December 1785.

32. The *Times,* 22 December 1785.

33. As Bridgett Orr has argued for a different but related example, such representations inscribed an "amourous civility" that made miscegenation but an "inevitable condition of discovery." "Southern passion," in "The South Pacific in the Eighteenth Century," special issue of *Eighteenth Century Life* 18 (November 1994): 216.

was and would continue to be an endemic feature of Englishness, while also highlighting its ultimate goal of possession: Omai becomes, through marriage, British-identified, bound to the British way of life and to British superiority in arts and arms (a tactic that anticipated English missionaries' use of transcultural marriage as the ultimate reward for the conversion of formerly heathen charges). "Away my useless spells and magic charms," the enchantress Oberea (representing the historical Purea) coos after watching the sexual and material exchange under way; "A British sword is proof against the world in arms."

These implications are deepened by the entry of the real (nonmiscegenating) hero of the piece, for as soon as the marriage ceremony ends, the English captain begins to sing a grand lament for Captain Cook. A giant painting of the *Apotheosis of Captain Cook* (the first of what would be a long line of similarly titled paintings) simultaneously descends on the stage, portraying Cook, resting in clouds over the Hawaiian bay where he had been "sacrificed," being crowned by Britannia and Fame. As the last in the series of "original" island races, Cook represents their final and most advanced form. The tripartite structure of the painting attests to this progression: the space of exploration and discovery, where the exact representation of landscape and British ships evoke an objective mapping of the "discovered" and exotic terrain where Pacific Islanders lived; the intermediate space, separating the human and celestial; and the space of the divine, rococo in style, where Cook, in a pose clearly influenced by Benjamin West's *Death of Wolfe* (1773), is deified while looking nobly and sympathetically at the human scene below. The voices of all the various peoples proclaim:

> The hero of Macedon ran o'er the world,
> Yet nothing but death could he give
> 'Twas George's command and the sail was unfurl'd
> And Cook taught mankind how to live.
> He *came* and he *saw*, not to *conquer* but to save.
> The Caesar of Britain was he:
> Who scorn'd the conditions of making a slave
> While Britons themselves are so free.[34]

Reaching back to, and surpassing, both "ancient" and "primitive" time, Cook, Omai, and the Pacific islanders thus became figures in the panorama of English progress and achievement, lessons in the "school for the history of man," the "mirror" of past and present. It was, as the playwright himself noted, an immensely gratifying moment for English audiences, who thereby participated in the progress and ultimate canonization of English imperialism itself as the agent of Enlightened civilization. George III, slave trader

34. O'Keeffe, *Harlequin Omai*, act 4, chorus.

and soon-to-be staunch opponent of abolition, was nonetheless moved to tears by the pantomime at the performances he attended, and the finale became one of the most popular songs of the late 1780s and '90s, published in newspapers, demanded by audiences at theaters, concerts, and assemblies, and sung at tavern societies. As J. Boaden, Kemble's biographer, recalled in 1825, "The success of this elegant entertainment seems to have stampt a character upon the theatre itself, which has since constantly adhered to it."[35]

The significance of *Omai* should be seen in several contexts. Certainly the dramatic presentation of contemporary English heroics in exotic or foreign settings was not new. The *Death of General Wolfe,* first staged in provincial theaters in 1763 (and perhaps influencing West's famous painting) remained a favorite afterpiece into the early 1800s and contained a similarly idealized historical tableau that aimed at exalting another exemplar of the glorious national character. An episode of less socially elevated but nationalistically useful heroism was represented to Birmingham audiences in the midst of the American war by Richard Brinsley Sheridan's interlude *The Storming of Fort Omoa,* taken from the pantomime of *Harlequin Fortunatus,* which featured (thanks again to Loutherbourg) the astonishing spectacle of a brave British tar scaling the wall of the fort while he furnished an unarmed Spaniard with a cutlass, conquered him, and then spared his life.[36] But Loutherbourg both before and after 1785 had transformed scene design, setting new standards of authenticity and "exactness" in stage representation, which quickly came to serve as a testimony to British national and imperial expertise. Spectacles set in India, for example, such as *The Choice of Harlequin, or the Indian Chief* (1782) and *Ramah Droog* (1798), boasted scenery based on the drawings of Indian architecture and topography by Tilly Kettle and Thomas Daniell, respectively, artists renowned for their "first-hand knowledge" of the subcontinent. "Exactness" also became crucial to future efforts to turn current affairs and fantasies into heroic history: *The Pirates* (1790) claimed to be an "exact representation" of the *Bounty* mutiny: the capture, rescue, and arrival at the Cape of Good Hope of Captain Bligh (played by none other than Ralph Wewitzer), and the celebratory dances of the "Hottentots" at his departure made up some of its central scenes. *The Death of Captain Cook,* a French ballet that in 1789 began a three-year tour of England and Ireland, also used gorgeous, naturalistic scenery to heighten the romantic plot about love and betrayal among Hawaiian islanders, ren-

35. O'Keeffe, *Recollections,* vol. 2, 114; J. Boaden, *Memoirs of the Life of John Philip Kemble,* vol. 1 (London, 1825), 311–12. *Omai* was staged fifty times in the 1785–86 season, and eight times in each of the two following ones (1786–87, 1787–88).

36. *The Death of General Wolfe at the Siege of Quebec,* Manchester Central Library, Playbills, Marsden St. Theater, 17 August 1763; *Aris's Birmingham Gazette,* 30 August 1780.

dering Cook's death all the more tragic and heroic.[37] Hence, *Omai*, with its blend of fantasy and ethnography, science and spectacle, crystallized the innovations in representation by which theater was able to transform historical idealizations into historical "realities" that helped structure and confirm English beliefs about their own distinctiveness and destiny.

Second, the pantomime exhibited a broader shift in contemporary understanding of historical time and primitivism, which moved away from cyclical, classically based models toward linear, locally inflected ones, thanks in large part to the proliferation of information about indigenous cultures. In this latter mode, the notion of the ancients as the moderns (or vice versa) gave way to a conception of the primitives as the ancients—that is, to a progressive notion of historical time that ranked societies according to their "stage" and accomplishments rather than supposed classical origins. The tension between the English mimesis of primitiveness and English men's actual displays of "primitive" behavior in the South Seas (through violence, murder, rapaciousness, and so on) was, of course, not addressed. Instead, *Omai* gave English audiences the simultaneous pleasure of reimagining themselves as historically alter—as a primitive island race—and confirming their "real" status as modern, advanced, civilized, tolerant, progressive: the superior Island Race.

THE PROGRESS OF NATIONS

To see how and why this was so, we must turn to some of the uses made of Cook's voyages in scientific literature. Cook's discoveries in the South Pacific initially fostered within Britain a craze for descriptions of the customs and manners of South Sea islanders, feeding the appetite for the exotic, eroticizing the primitive, and bolstering neoclassical or Rousseauian views about the natural equality, universal reason, and similarity of human life in the state of nature.[38] However, although neoclassical allusions continued to abound in many of the artistic and literary representations of Cook's "discoveries," the dominance of primitivist thinking was short-lived in certain circles. For the publication of the details of the voyages stimulated contending interpretations of the nature of Pacific peoples that revealed the inadequacy of classical or romantic traditions in interpreting "primitive"

37. Russell Thomas, "Contemporary Taste in the Stage Decorations of London Theaters, 1770–1800," *Modern Philology* 42 (1944): 73–74; *London Chronicle*, 25–27 December 1781; Dening, *Bligh's Bad Language*, 287–90; *The Death of Captain Cook* (London, 1790).

38. For which, see Lars E. Troide, ed., *The Early Journals and Letters of Fanny Burney*, vol. 1, (Montreal, 1988), 322–27; Burney, *Early Diary*, 320–33; and issues of the *Gentlemen's Magazine, London Magazine, Lady's Magazine, Town and Country Magazine* for 1773. See also Hoxie Sissy Fairchild, *The Noble Savage: A Study in Romantic Naturalism* (London, 1933), and Lois Whitney, *Primitivism and the Idea of Progress* (Baltimore, 1934).

cultures. As the "primitive" became subjected to empirical, scientific scrutiny and understanding, it became less a set of aesthetic standards than an ethnological category in the larger effort to assess the progress and development of human society. Indeed, the second and third voyages even had the effect of recasting a longer-held and more ferociously enacted antiprimitivism that had shaped English colonial relations for some time, not least with the Irish, Welsh, and Scots.[39]

South Sea exploration occurred at a time when natural and social scientists were under greater pressure to base the study of human society upon as firm an empirical foundation as that of the natural world. As English anthropologist and linguist William Marsden put it, in a swipe at the armchair philosophers and natural historians of the day, "the study of their own species is doubtless the most interesting and important that can claim the attention of mankind; and this science, like all others, it is impossible to improve by abstract speculation, merely. *A regular series of authenticated facts is what alone can enable us to rise towards a perfect knowledge in it.*"[40] It was precisely such "authenticated facts" that Cook's later voyages were widely heralded as providing, resulting in a profusion of theories accounting for human difference that, despite their real and apparent discrepancies, sought to contribute to a new comparative ethnology, the "natural history of man." Thanks to Cook's voyages, one typical enthusiast gushed, natural historians have been able to "eradicate former errors, and to establish permanent truths in the history of Man." As an epistemological project, this new "history" marked the beginnings of modern anthropology, reflecting not only the generalization and extension of historical time to encompass the whole world, but also its spatialization. As Johannes Fabian has noted, in the travel-as-science literature of the late eighteenth century, "relationships between parts of the world . . . [became] understood as temporal relations. Dispersal in space reflects . . . sequence in Time."[41] The application of

39. See Nicholas Canny, "The Ideology of English Colonization: From Ireland to America," *William and Mary Quarterly* 3rd ser., no. 30 (1973): 575–98; idem, "Identity Formation in Ireland: The Emergence of the Anglo-Irish," in *Colonial Identity in the Atlantic World 1500–1800*, ed. Nicholas Canny and Anthony Pagden (Princeton, 1987), 159–212; David Cairns and Shaun Ricard, *Writing Ireland: Colonialism, Nationalism, and Culture* (Manchester, Eng., 1988); and John Gillingham, "Foundations of a Disunited Kingdom," in *Uniting the Kingdom? The Making of British History*, ed. Alexander Grant and Keith J. Stringer (London, 1995). Thanks to Karl Bottigheimer and Ned Landsman for references.

40. William Marsden, *The History of Sumatra* (London, 1783), vii (emphasis mine). Adam Ferguson had made much the same point in his *Essay on the History of Civil Society* (Edinburgh, 1767), 3–4. This section on late-eighteenth-century anthropology is indebted to the careful and insightful account provided by John Gascoigne in *Joseph Banks and the English Enlightenment: Useful Knowledge and Polite Culture* (Cambridge, 1994), esp. 125–83.

41. Samuel Stanhope Smith, *An Essay on the Causes of the Variety of Complexion and Figure in the Human Species* (1788), quoted in Gascoigne, *Joseph Banks,* 147; Johannes Fabian, *Time and*

nascent anthropology to its objects—"primitive" societies—was important as a prelude to imperial control; in the shorter term, its truths were used to discern in these societies, at best, an early stage in the gradual process of human amelioration, or even less flatteringly, a nastier and less developed version of European society.

For example, natural and social scientists, including some of those who had accompanied Cook on his second and third voyages, described the island races encountered in a distinctly unromantic fashion. The Maori "massacre" and dismemberment of an entire boat-crew from the *Adventurer,* the consort vessel of the second voyage, was revealed in the separate accounts of Cook, naturalist J. R. Forster (a German émigré who believed fervently in the superiority of the British imperial project over its European competitors), Forster's son Georg, and Lieutenant James Burney, horrifying the reading public in Britain perhaps more than those who had witnessed it. Although Cook and the young Forster stressed that the Maoris probably had been provoked by the hot-tempered master's mate in charge of the boat, Burney's less measured response was more representative: "Such a shocking scene of Carnage and Barbarity as can never be mentioned or thought of, but with horror," he wrote, recalling the blood and body parts that lay strewn along the beach near the wrecked boat.[42] Similar reports of cannibalism and of human sacrifices and infanticide among the Maoris and Tahitians, respectively—pronounced by such luminaries as Joseph Banks to be "contrary to the first principles of human nature"—confirmed traditional beliefs about "savages" abroad that had titillated and horrified English and European publics for two centuries, while detailed accounts of the "shivering wretchedness," "treachery," or "stupidity" of other islanders, such as the aborigines of New Holland, also did much to qualify visions of uncorrupted noble savages.[43] Certainly Cook and many of his men made sustained efforts to assess indigenous peoples against their own rather than European standards, regarding their societies, in good relativist fashion, as having value, or even greater happiness than that obtainable in "civilized" countries.[44] But the

the Other: How Anthropology Makes Its Object (New York, 1983), 11–12. For the contending tenets within the new ethnology, see, e.g., Margaret Jolly, "'Ill-Nature Comparisons': Racism and Relativism in European Representations of ni-Vanuata from Cook's Second Voyage," *History and Anthropology* 5 (1992): 3–4, 331–64.

42. J. C. Beaglehole, ed., *Journals of Captain Cook: The Voyage of the Resolution and Adventure* (Cambridge, 1961), 744, 749–52 (the quotation is on p. 751). See also Cook, *Voyage to the South Pole,* vol. 2, 258; Georg Forster, *A Voyage Round the World,* in *Georg Forster's Werke,* ed. Robert L. Kahn (Berlin, 1968), 593–94.

43. J. C. Beaglehole, ed., *The Endeavour Journal of Joseph Banks,* vol. 1 (Sydney and London, 1962) 351.

44. See, e.g., Beaglehole, ed., *Voyage of the Endeavour,* 399, where Cook makes his famous assessment of the aborigines of New Holland as being "far happier than we Europeans; being

information gleaned from the second and third voyages also suggested to many observers that the force of climactic and developmental variations on the human, animal, and vegetable kingdoms alike had produced some unthinking and nasty brutes whose absolute difference from Europeans of any rank could not be more marked.

Accordingly, the tropics, long acknowledged to be geographic spaces of indolence, luxury, sloth, and sensuality, also began to be used to promote the idea that humankind had risen stage by stage from a lower to higher form of existence, a progression in which primitive peoples demonstrably lagged behind. This version of social evolution, although overtaken by the unlikely convergence of comparative anatomy, physical anthropology, and evangelicalism in the early 1810s and 1820s (until reconfigured in the more absolutist biological and social forms of Darwin and Spencer),[45] nonetheless marked a distinctive initiative in the late eighteenth century's efforts to understand human diversity that affected theories of natural and human history and political economy. Certainly the four-stage version of human development elaborated by Scottish social scientists, which had held that human society naturally developed over time through stages based on the mode of subsistence, was well established by Cook's time. But the current imperative for empiricism had demonstrated that Pacific peoples were prone to exhibit contradictory characteristics that were not subsumable under earlier primitivist or social science models. Hence proponents of social evolutionism following the Cook voyages tended to envision a more complex configuration of development from savagery to civilization, one that was less mechanistic, unwilling to found explanations for social differences upon a single cause such as climate or subsistence alone (although each continued to play privileged roles) and more nuanced in the understanding of history, combining spatial and progressive notions of time and simultaneity with the perception that economic and cultural growth entailed both progress and corruption. At the same time, they differed from their nineteenth-century successors in seeing cultural difference as a product of historical development and social convention, rather than inescapable natural laws, and deemed progress among primitive peoples to be possible once "discovery" had planted or nurtured the seeds of improvement or otherwise brought them into the time of History.[46]

---

wholy [*sic*] unacquainted not only with the superfluous but the necessary Conveniences so much sought after in Europe."

45. For an insightful account, see George Stocking, *Victorian Anthropology* (New York, 1992), 18–25.

46. Ronald Meek, *Social Science and the Ignoble Savage* (Cambridge, 1976); David Armitage, "The New World and British Historical Thought: From Richard Hakluyt to William Robertson," in *America in European Consciousness*, ed. Karen Kupperman (Chapel Hill, N.C., 1995),

The senior Forster, who despite his famously quarrelsome personality brought an impressive background in antiquarian and classical learning, Linnaean method, and Scottish moral philosophy to bear on his study of Pacific societies, was both indicative and constitutive of this explanatory trend. Stressing that his account was based on an intimate and empirical knowledge of the things and peoples described, a "first-hand" knowledge of the local and the particular, his assessment of the stages of civilization in which Pacific peoples existed was sustained by his equally detailed natural history. His *Observations Made During a Voyage Round the World* (1778) classified the various "nations" of the South Pacific into two "races," distinguished according to "Custom, Colour, Size, Form, Habit and natural Turn of Mind," and ranked according to manners, morals, cultivation, and religion (or the "progress towards Civilization," a rubric under which the treatment of women was accorded great significance).[47] While physical differences usually initiated Forster's discussions about what was distinctive about each island nation in the Pacific, and climate was taken to exert a strong force on their physical and mental state, it was the historical stage of their existence, identified through population size and the material base of subsistence, that "explained" the variations in culture and physiognomy: "Such are the beginnings of arts and cultivation, such is the rise of civil societies; sooner or later they cause distinctions of rank, and the various degrees of power, influence and wealth. . . . Nay, they often produce a material difference in the colour, habits and forms of the human species." Embracing the European view that primitive peoples had no history, Forster proudly undertook the task of providing a history for the islanders, who previously had had to depend upon "vague traditional [oral] reports in lieu of historical records" to account for their origins and movement. His work also tempered the implications of necessary progress inherent in earlier stage theory by arguing that South Seas peoples showed the importance of the roles of both environment and chronological degeneration in the formation of different "races."[48]

Other philosophers and social scientists used evolutionary schema to sup-

53–75; J. G. A. Pocock, "Modes of Political and Historical Time in Early 18th-Century England," in Pocock, *Virtue, Commerce, and History* (Cambridge, 1992), 95.

47. Forster, *Observations*, 418; see also 231–40, 431–35. For an extended discussion of the role of women as signs in Pacific societies' progress or degeneration, see my book *Island Race*, chaps. 2 and 6, and Harriet Guest, "'Curiously Marked': Tattooing, Masculinity, and Nationality in Eighteenth Century British Perceptions of the South Pacific," in *Painting and the Politics of Culture*, ed. John Barrell (Oxford, 1993), 118–20.

48. Forster, *Observations*, 322–26, 608. For an insightful introduction to Forster's ethnology, see the introductory chapters to the new edition of *Observations*, ed. Nicholas Thomas, Harriet Guest, and Michael Dettelbach (Honolulu, 1996). This source came to my attention after this essay was written, but it comes to similar conclusions.

port less optimistic views of Pacific peoples. In his *Origin and Progress of Language* (1773), which drew on accounts of Cook's first voyage, Lord Monboddo had been forthright in proclaiming that man's departure from his earliest state was a *progression*, not a corruption, and that the capacity for rational thought and moral improvement was not innate but acquired by toil and struggle. "There cannot be virtue, properly so called, until man is become a rational and political animal; then he shows true courage, very different from the ferocity of the brute or savage . . . the infant of our species." Despite Monboddo's notorious eccentricities, the connection he posited between the historical stage of civilization and the *capacity* for improvement was bolstered or amplified by other stars of the English and Scottish Enlightenment, as well as Continental scientists, and popularized in periodicals, fiction, and travel accounts.[49] John Millar, for example, the most celebrated proponent of stadial theory, whose second edition of the influential *Origin of the Distinction of Ranks* (1779) added a section on Pacific islanders, argued that "the lower its [i.e., savage society's] primitive condition . . . the greater the exertions of labour and activity" that must be exerted for the "seeds of improvement" to take root. And Marsden's acclaimed *History of Sumatra* (1783)—significantly, not a conventional history at all, but an account of contemporary Sumatra that placed its inhabitants in the "natural history of man"— specified a cultural evolutionary hierarchy of humankind, which placed the Europeans and Chinese at the top, Caribs, New Hollanders, Laplanders, and Hottentots at the bottom, and the South Seas peoples somewhere in the middle.[50]

On the positive side, theories of social evolution, grounded upon a view of the essentially "progressive" character of man and human society, allowed British observers to see in the customs, gender relations, or technologies of primitive societies "mirrors" of their earlier selves. "The history . . . of some of the South Sea isles, which the late voyages of discovery have tended to disclose, enables us to glance at society in some of its earlier forms," James Dunbar wrote in his *Essay on the History of Mankind in Rude and Cultivated Ages*

49. James Burnet, Lord Monboddo, *Of the Origin and Progress of Language*, vol. 1 (Edinburgh, 1773), 133, 440, quoted in Peter Marshall and Glyndwr Williams, *The Great Map of Mankind: British Perceptions of the World in the Age of Enlightenment* (London, 1982), 274. For the Continental scientists, see Londa Schiebinger, *Nature's Body: Gender in the Making of Modern Science* (Boston, 1993), 119–200. The popularization of these versions of the stage theory of human development can be seen in the journals of such diverse writers as Elizabeth Robinson Montagu and Lieutenant James Hadden, British officer during the American war, and in the assessments of Cook's biographer, Andrew Kippis. For its impact on political economy, see n. 57; for literary versions of the fierceness and coarseness of natural man, see, e.g., Cowper, *The Task*.

50. John Millar, *The Origin of the Distinction of Ranks*, 2nd ed. (London, 1779), 45–46, quoted in Meek, *Social Science*, 171–72; Marsden, *History of Sumatra*, pp. 202–3.

(1780).[51] John Marra, the seaman aboard the *Resolution* who scooped the Admiralty by two years with his published account of the voyage, exculpated the Tahitian *arioi,* the elite religious and theatrical society, from the charge of excessive sensuality by quoting esteemed antiquarian Sir William Temple on the custom of wife-sharing among the "ancient inhabitants of our own island"—a historical judgment that Gibbon himself entertained in the last volume of his *Decline and Fall* (1788).[52] The custom of tattooing, William Falconer noted, was a "custom of great antiquity, and very general" among people in a rude or savage state; "Julius Caesar mentions this practice among the ancient Britons . . . and several of the savage nations on Asiatic and African coasts follow the same practice today."[53] And others were encouraged to observe in Pacific cultures, including the Maoris, the signs of the beginnings of progress that was moving them from barbarism into the early stages of civilization. Nevertheless, in the versions of evolutionary progress being canvassed, rationality itself, as well as custom, material culture, sexual politics, and physical characteristics, became intractable parts of the progression from a lower to higher humanity. Nature becomes culture, and culture nature, in this mental universe, and mimesis fails the less advanced races as a form of knowledge production. As Cook remarked, when reflecting on Omai's lack of application on returning to his native land in 1776, "this kind of indifferency is the true character of his nation. Europeans have visited them at times for these ten years past, yet we find neither new arts nor improvements in the old, nor have they copied after us in any one thing."[54] From the perspective of explorers, social scientists, and their interlocutors, Pacific islanders existed in a temporal distance, a different historical stage, than Europeans, whose civilizations were older and hence more advanced, if also in certain respects more degenerated and corrupted.

Cook's own death at the hands of some of these islanders emotionally intensified the transformation from noble to ignoble savages. In the after-

51. James Dunbar, *Essays on the History of Mankind in Rude and Cultivated Ages* (London, 1780), quoted in Gascoigne, *Joseph Banks,* 73. The description of the Tahitian political system as "feudal" was legion in the published accounts of the voyages: see Beaglehole, *Banks's Endeavour Journal,* vol. 1, 384; *Annual Register* 16 (1773): 23.

52. [John Marra], *Journal of the Resolution's Voyage in 1772, 1773, 1774, and 1775* (London, 1775), 207–8. This account was excerpted in *Gentleman's Magazine* 45 (1775): 587–91, and 46 (1776): 15–20, 66–70, 118–22.

Gibbon noted that "disregard of conjugal honor and female chastity" was alleged by Byzantine historian Chalcondyles to have been an English custom when the Romans found them—quoted in Beaglehole, *Cook's Endeavour Journal,* clxxxvi note.

53. William Falconer, *Remarks on the Influence of Climate* (London, 1781), 172, 312.

54. Beaglehole, *Cook's Resolution Journal,* 241. It is only fair to point out that Cook was not consistent on this point: when he visited Tahiti in 1774, he had been astonished at the improved houses and canoes, which he attributed to the iron tools acquired by the islanders from English ships: *Voyage to the South Pole,* vol. 2, 346.

math of his death,[55] Hawaiians and some other more "primitive" peoples of the Pacific began to be compared to the Hottentots and Eskimos—races notorious for their cannibalism, harshness toward their women, hostility to Europeans, and disgusting personal habits, repugnantly exhibiting to British people the extreme lower boundary of humanity. Whether immature or degraded, the South Sea peoples lagged behind the Europeans in customs, progress, and initiative. They were located in an anterior historical time that, if it allowed Europeans and especially English islanders "to behold, as in a mirror, the features of our own progenitors," also ensured their place on the lower rungs of the ladder of civilization.[56] In this guise the historical differences among the "races" could serve as guides to understanding the cultural differences among the classes in Europe: in both cases human progress was contingent upon a willingness as well as capacity for self-improvement through the exertion of rationality and the reigning in of baser instinct. Such was the argument, at least, of the Anglican clergyman Thomas Malthus, who placed the South Sea peoples only just above the Tierra del Fuegans and American Indians in the "stages" of human civilization by which men learned to exercise the "moral restraint" necessary to control the sexual instinct and avert demographic disaster. Naturally, the European and especially English middle classes were seen to have excelled at liberating reason from the forces of instinct, and thus were taken to be the guarantors of future progress.[57]

ISLAND OF HISTORY

Omai, then, intervened in the scientific debates about racial and national difference that resulted from Pacific exploration. But the pantomime also contributed to the renewed interest in *history* and its role in classifying the English as a superior and distinctive people. Indeed, South Seas "discovery" bolstered contemporary efforts to recount the historical origins of British ethnicities themselves. Concomitant with the notion of "universal history" and continuous time, the period witnessed a proliferation of writing on par-

55. And indeed of other explorers, like the Frenchman La Pérouse, who lost twelve of his crew to a Samoan "massacre" in 1789; news of this did not reach Europe until 1827, however (Smith, *European Vision*, 138–41).

56. The quote is from Ferguson, *Civil Society*, quoted in Meek, *Social Science*, 150. The most famous statement of this position was by the French social scientist Joseph-Marie Degerando in *The Observation of Savage Peoples* (London, 1800).

57. See Thomas Malthus, *An Essay on the Principles of Population*, ed. Patricia James (Cambridge, 1989), vol. 1, bks. 1–3, 21, 47 and passim. Thanks to Ruth Cowan for referring me to this source. See also Stocking, *Victorian Anthropology*, 34–35. Not surprisingly, perhaps, the Abbé Raynal claimed that it was among islanders, and the ancient Britons in particular, that the custom of anthropophagy originated, a theory that Malthus strongly denied in *Principles of Population*, 46–59; he quotes Raynal's *Histoire des Indes*, vol. 2 (1795), 3.

ticularist national history, which shared a topical and epistemological propinquity with the ethnology of the day. Organized according to notions of qualitative progress in the material, scientific, and intellectual realms (themselves influenced by the comparative study of ancient, Oriental, and indigenous societies) and predicated upon the firm foundation of demonstrable "facts," this history sought to emphasize the rationality, modernity, and distinctiveness of the present through the objective presentation of specificities, antecedents, and origins.[58] "The only certain means by which nations can indulge their curiosity in researches concerning their remote origin, is to consider the language, manners and customs of their ancestors, and to compare them with those of neighbouring nations," David Hume asserted. "The fables which are commonly employed to supply the place of true history, ought entirely to be disregarded."[59] Not surprisingly, the history of England loomed large in this enterprise. Hume's disclaimer notwithstanding, a selective use of "fables" about ancient Britons and Saxons, their relationship to Britain's current ethnic groupings, and England's future place in world affairs became peculiarly charged features of cultural production in the last quarter of the century, marking the boundaries between the civilized and noncivilized while also inscribing national and ethnic particularity. As Johann Forster put it, history must be taken to be one of the "blessings of a more exalted civilization and education, which give us in every respect so great a superiority over these [primitive] nations, and assign us so high a rank in the scale of rational beings."[60] At the same time, the Pacific craze and fascination with South Sea "primitives" inspired some new perspectives on ancient Britain and its inhabitants, combining contemporary respect for empirically based scholarship with the impulse to reinvent the ancient Angles, Jutes, and Saxons as Britain's noblest savages. The central myths of Anglo-Saxonism were thus lent an "objective" coloration by association with current social science, which aided their widespread acceptance.[61]

For example, the production and popularization of multivolume national histories of England (some of which were written, with no apparent sense of irony, by Scots) abbreviated or ignored the Celtic or pre-Saxon past. Hume's *History of England,* unquestionably the most popular and influential history of the century, was arguably Anglo-Saxonist in that it painted, in

58. Hevia, *Cherishing Men from Afar,* 70–71.

59. David Hume, *History of England from the Invasion of Julius Caesar to the Revolution in 1688,* vol. 1 (London, 1802), 2.

60. Forster, *Observations,* 608. For other examples of History's role in establishing cultural difference and superiority, see Gillingham, "Foundations of a Disunited Kingdom."

61. See Hugh MacDougall, *Racial Myth in English History: Trojans, Teutons, and Anglo-Saxons* (London, 1982), and Samuel Klinger, *The Goths in England: A Study in Seventeenth and Eighteenth*

Samuel Klinger's words, "a vision of world renewal through the mass migration of the Germanic tribesmen." In the first volume, Hume notes that the conquered Romanized Britons were too "abject," "effeminate," and weak to resist the Saxons, who carried to their highest pitch the manly "virtue of valour and love of liberty," while the Irish, never conquered by the Romans, remained buried in the "most profound ignorance and barbarism" until the English took up Rome's mantle some centuries later—judgments that were later confirmed by Gibbon in his *Decline and Fall*.[62] Expanding on these themes were the "nationalist" historians of the 1760s and 1770s, such as Catherine Macaulay, Obadiah Hulme, and John Pinkerton, who despite their political differences were explicitly, even rabidly, interested in questions about ethnic national origins, the virtues of the "native stock," and the connections of both to Anglo-Saxon liberties. All agreed that the Saxons not only had provided the most perfect constitution the world had ever seen, but also that they set the standards of political liberty and civilization that other peoples, including the Celts, could only emulate. As Pinkerton asserted, the Celts "are savages, have been savages since the world began, and will be for ever savages while a separate people."[63] A less virulent acknowledgment of the blessings of the Anglo-Saxon inheritance was also commercialized in popular literature, prints, and tourism: sections on "Antiquities" in periodicals abounded with Saxon examples, while the affluent urban classes were seized with a passion for both touring "Gothic ruins" and owning prints of Gothic architecture in testimony to their collective, if barbarous, ethnic heritage.[64] And Anglo-Saxon history and political traditions were held up as a viable counter to pernicious French or foreign influences by patriotic and cultural commentators from the Anti-Gallican Society to Granville Sharp, who proposed the establishment of Anglo-Saxon com-

---

Century Thought (Cambridge, Mass., 1952). For political uses of Anglo-Saxonism under Walpole, see Christine Gerrard, *The Patriot Opposition to Walpole* (Oxford, 1994), 103–49.

62. Klinger, *Goths in England*, 92; Hume, *History of England*, 13, 15, 424; Gibbon, *The History of the Decline and Fall of the Roman Empire*, 7 vols. (London, 1926), vol. 1, 63–4. Gibbon wrote, "the Roman world was indeed peopled by a race of pygmies, when the fierce giants of the north broke in and mended the puny breed."

63. Obadiah Hulme, *An Historical Essay on the English Constitution* (London, 1771); Catherine Macaulay, *History of England* (London, 1763), vol. 11, p. 273, vol. 2, pp. 1–3, vol. 6, p. 72; John Pinkerton, *Dissertation on the Origin of the Scythians or Goths* (London, 1787). For a fuller discussion, see Thomas P. Peardon, *The Transition in English Historical Writing 1760–1830* (New York, 1933), 114–16, 162–79.

64. See, e.g., *Annual Register* 16 (1773): 137–60, which reviewed Grosse's *Antiquities of England and Wales*, Bentham's *Curious Remarks on Saxon Churches*, and *The Voyages of Ohthere and Wulfstan, from the Anglo-Saxon Version by Alfred the Great*; Ian Ousby, *The Englishman's England: Taste, Travel, and the Rise of Tourism* (Cambridge, 1990), 92–129; Timothy Clayton, *The English Print, 1688–1802* (London and New Haven, 1997), 258–59.

munities in England in order to encourage an appreciation for the pre-con-quest, Teutonic "original principles" of liberty and freedom that could then serve as a model for less fortunate peoples.[65]

The coincidence of historical (racialist) theories of the "Norman yoke" and democratic political ideas during the period 1760–90 has been ably examined elsewhere.[66] What needs to be emphasized for our purposes is that there emerged in the last quarter of the century a renewed interest in the links between ethnic and national identity that it was up to history to document. Moreover, the English were not the only Britons intent on recovering their ethnic roots. The Irish, Scots, and Welsh were similarly occupied in this period, producing a rush to document the ethnic origins of the tribes that made up ancient Britain before and after contact with Rome in order to restore the Celts to their rightful place in their own and in Britain's past and future.[67] Within these competing ethnic histories, the techniques and orientations of the ethnologists of the Pacific were drawn on to corroborate rival views. For example, the faith that philological study could discern the origins of different "races," subscribed to by ethnologists like Monboddo, J. R. Forster, and William Marsden, was also taken up by antiquarians, prompting investigations into the origins of English in order to prove the racial as well as linguistic distinctiveness of the national character. "[T]he investigation and analysis of Language conduces to point out the genius of a people," wrote Burgess in *An Essay on the Study of Antiquities* (1782). The study of old English, Cornish, and other Gaelic languages could thus demonstrate the "original" and presumably enduring differences between their speakers; as one analyst wrote, "the British, to speak plainly, has little or no resemblance to the English. . . . [T]heir idioms and genius are as rad-ically and essentially different as any two languages can possibly be."[68]

The influence of South Sea islanders on views of Britain's own ancient primitives was even more directly demonstrated in the rise of an antiquar-ian ethnography devoted to interpreting the material remains of antiquity. English naturalist George Pearson used remnants of ancient Roman and

65. Linda Colley, "Radical Patriotism in Eighteenth-Century England," in *Patriotism*, ed. Raphael Samuel, 3 vols. (London, 1989), vol. 1, 173–74; Granville Sharp, *A View of the Frankenpledge* (London, 1782).

66. See, e.g., Christopher Hill, "The Norman Yoke," in Hill, *Puritanism and Revolution* (New York, 1958); Gerald Newman, *The Rise of English Nationalism* (New York, 1987), 115–19; Léon Poliakov, *The Aryan Myth: A History of Racist and Nationalist Ideas in Europe*, trans. E. Howard (New York, 1977).

67. For which, see Peardon, *Transition*, 103–26; Stuart Piggott, *The Druids* (London, 1968), 123–55.

68. Burgess quoted in Gascoigne, *Joseph Banks*, 131; Rev. F. Drake, "Origin of the English Language," reviewed in *Annual Register* 23 (1780): 157–63; see also *Annual Register* 18 (1775): 157–65.

Saxon weapons found in Lincolnshire to make extensive comparisons between the state of British society at the time of the Roman conquest and "that in which our late discovers found the natives of the South Sea islands." Rev. Frederick Clark, a professor of mineralogy at Cambridge, reported to Joseph Banks in 1812 that diggers had found an ancient weapon "exactingly resembling the Stone Hatchets of the South Seas." Falconer's frequent parallels between the manners and customs of ancient Anglo-Saxon and present-day Pacific islanders were a standard feature of his work, although he made it clear that it was in Britain alone that the association between insularity and freedom held true over the ages. Other commentators noted the similarities between native and Oceanic arts, music, and poetry. The Oxford Prize Poem of 1791, *The Aboriginal Britons,* by George Richards, opened with an address to Cook and his South Sea navigators that exhorted them to remember, as they viewed the "wondering Savage" on those distant shores, that "a form like this, illustrious souls, of yore / Your own Britannia's sea-girt island wore."[69] The romanticization of Celtic traditions by Scots, Irish, and Welsh writers like James Macpherson and Sylvester O'Halloran, who decried the excessive Englishness of British culture, was also indebted to the interest in ethnology prompted by the South Seas "discoveries," not least since they allowed comparisons between ancient Celtic and Pacific island customs, such as the Druidical and Polynesian practices of human sacrifice, that redeemed the former from being just embarrassing. Even the evangelicals tried to exploit the identification of ancient Britons with Oceanic primitives: the Reverend Melville Horne, in his "Letters on Missions," exhorted potential supporters to remember that "Britain, Christian Britain, was once an island of idolatrous barbarians; and such it had yet remained, unless some of God's dear people in distant countries . . . had formed the benevolent plan of sending missionaries hither."[70] Through such comparisons, the Pacific present and British past mirrored each other, and Pacific peoples became imaginatively associated with the customs of English people's own ancestors. Here, if ever, we have a "past filled with the time of the now," in Benjamin's mellifluous phrase, but even further, a present filled with temporally disjunctive pasts, rendered homologous through the radical simultaneity of antithetical primitive and modern space-time.

Not surprisingly, this antiquarian ethnography could also focus on more contemporary subjects. Perhaps in a riposte to those who held out for the inventiveness and superiority of the ancient Celts, English writers turned

69. George Pearson, "Observations on some metallic arms," 402–3, and Clark to Banks, 26 January 1812, both cited in Gascoigne, *Joseph Banks,* 133; Falconer, *Remarks,* 171–72; Smith, *European Vision,* 131–32; Piggott, *Druids,* 154.

70. Piggott, *Druids,* 109, 155; Richard Lovett, *History of the London Missionary Society 1795– 1895,* vol. 1 (London, 1899), 22–23.

their ethnographic analysis on contemporary Celts as holdouts of the "primitives within." The Highlanders, for example, became the objects of much discussion in popular periodicals, travel literature, and scientific journals in these decades as atavistic survivors of an earlier age, whom the march of modernity could only extinguish. Equally indicative of the pernicious imperialist distancing involved in such views, touring enthusiast Gilbert White advocated the adoption of a plan of "exploration" of Ireland identical to that undertaken by Banks and Cook in the Pacific, in order to illumine not only the varieties of flora and fauna, but also "the manners of the wild natives, their superstitions, their prejudices, their sordid way of life."[71] Here, as above, objective "discovery" in history and science converged in the service of establishing ethnic authenticity. The anachronism of the Highlanders, Macpherson's Ossian cult, the London Welsh literary societies, and Sharp's proposals for reestablishment of the wittagemots, or Saxon parliaments, all depended upon both to produce their versions of cultural distinctiveness and ethnic particularity.[72] Hence, as the origins of Englishness as well as other British ethnicities come to seem more historically specific and authentically ascertained, they also become less naturalizable, established in and inherited from, as Edmund Burke made clear in *Reflections on the Revolution in France* (1790), a common, venerable, and *induplicable* past. History emerged, like Science, as an "art of (self) discovery" that underwrote English distinctiveness and modernity. In this context, the representation of Cook as the standard-bearer of a peculiarly national genius, and of South Seas peoples as a "mirror" of divergent British "national" pasts, demonstrated how the tangled circuitry of colonial identification, alterity exchange, and transformation could produce both an interlocution of similarity and difference, and an ineradicable otherness.

Theater conjoined these different strands of cultural production into a syncretic vision that transmuted the past and the present into the mythical, and the mythical into History. In the work of Loutherbourg in particular, the techniques of realist visual technologies made the fictive and illusory into the "exact" representation of "history as it really was." *Omai* was his last, best effort, but his earlier productions had also made evident the interplay of difference and identity in the construction of a visual regime of histori-

71. See, quoting Sir John Dalrymples, "Memoirs of Great Britain and Ireland," *Annual Register* 14 (1771): 40; Gilbert White, *The Natural History and Antiquities of Selborne*, ed. R. Bowdler Sharpe, vol. 1 (London, 1900), 178. See also "A Description of the Highlands of Scotland, and Remarks on the Second Sight of the Inhabitants," *Annual Register* 20 (1777): 83–85.

72. See Peter Womak, *Improvement and Romance: Constructing the Myth of the Highlands* (London, 1989); Gwynn Williams, *When Was Wales? A History of the Welsh* (London, 1985); Brewer, *Pleasures of the Imagination*, 658–60.

cal authenticity. Others drew upon and amplified the upsurge of interest in the sublime and picturesque within Great Britain. Loutherbourg's *The Wonders of Derbyshire* (1779) was a harlequinade that represented, with the "exactness" for which he was known, the wildness and sublimity of the northern English locality (a topography that was also believed to reflect the "savage" nature of the Peak people).[73] *Robinson Crusoe*, widely believed in the eighteenth century and after to be based on the "real" experiences of shipwrecked mariner Alexander Selkirk, had profoundly influenced voyagers' tales and travel writing as well as fiction over the century. It was produced for the stage for the first time in 1781; Loutherbourg's scenery made the pantomime's most crucial scene that which reenacted the island setting of English imperial genesis, when Crusoe secures Friday's loyalty by saving him from invading savages. As in other famous English island fictions, such as *The Tempest*, mastery over both sea and land and their various inhabitants is deemed crucial for sea-girted civilizations, and this scene was accordingly both critiqued and celebrated for its "authenticity" and likeness to the "original."[74] But this analysis will be best concluded by turning to a pantomime from Loutherbourg's earlier years, which meshed most interestingly with *Omai* and the trends discussed above.

Loutherbourg had begun his theatrical career in London by working closely with David Garrick on a number of Garrick's present-minded historical projects. Garrick had done more than perhaps any other playwright to bring the past into the present in order to bear witness to current progress, and his dramaturgical influence was felt in British theater long after his naturalistic acting style had grown passé.[75] In 1773, one year after Cook's second voyage to the South Seas had begun, Garrick produced at Drury Lane a revision of Thompson and Mallet's *Alfred, a Masque*. The story of the tribulations and ultimate triumph of Alfred the Great, Saxon king at the time of the Danish invasion, it was first produced in 1740 as part of the Patriot opposition's anti-Walpolean assault. Its refurbishment reflected the newly charged interest in Saxon history as a source of a distinctive national inheritance and character, and particularly in Alfred himself as a native symbol of Englishness that mirrored past, present, and future greatness. Yet it was Loutherbourg's elaborate new scenes that struck spectators with reflec-

73. Ralph G. Allen, "The Wonders of Derbyshire: A Spectacular Travelogue," *Theater and Drama in the Making*, ed. John Gassner and Ralph G. Allen (Boston, 1964), 1035–47; William Gilpin, *Observations . . . Made in the Year 1772, Relative to Picturesque Beauty*, vol. 2 (London, 1778), 216. See also Malcolm Andrews, *The Search for the Picturesque: Landscape, Aesthetics, and Tourism in Britain, 1760–1800* (Aldershot, 1989); Brewer, *Pleasures of the Imagination*, chap. 16.

74. *Morning Chronicle*, 30 January 1781; *London Chronicle*, 27–30 January 1781; Seidel, *Island Myths*, 36–38; Thomas, "Contemporary Taste," 73.

75. For which, see Michael Dobson, *The Making of the National Poet* (Oxford, 1993).

tion and wonder. In the prologue, Alfred is referred to as "the Godlike figure, in arms renown'd, for arts of peace ador'd. . . . the nation's father, more than lord," who ousted "Danish fury" and restored peace and freedom to his "sacred isle." In the final scene, Alfred, contemplating his victory and the future of his country, is enjoined by a hermit to "backward cast your eyes / on this unfolding scene; where pictur'd true / *As in a mirror,* rises fair to sight / Our England's genius, strength and future fame!" (Emphasis added.) With a wave of his wand, the scene changes from the "naturalistic" scenery of ancient Britain into a grand representation of the late naval review at Portsmouth, complete with an ocean in prospect, merchant ships, and men of war. Sailors jump ashore and begin to sing a specially revised version of Arne's *Rule Britannia:*

> The nations, not so blest as thee,
> Must in their turns to tyrants fall,
> While thou shalt flourish great and free
> The dread and envy of them all
> . . . .
> The Muses still, with freedom found
> Shall to thy happy coasts repair,
> Blest isle, with matchless beauty crown'd
> And manly hearts to guard the fair![76]

Liberty, the arts, and (feminine) beauty are destined to flourish, then, on the "blest isle," secured under the dual protections of topography and a paternalistic, yet ultimately coercive, masculinity, themes that would also be embellished in John Home's romantic version of *Alfred* in 1778 and in Alexander Bicknell's *Alfred, or The Patriot King* a decade later. Such panoramas provided, like *Omai,* a "mirror" of English history and futurity that reflected current English manliness, ingenuity, and achievement. The Island Race, it seems, even in its infancy, would never ever be slaves.

Omai, then, must be read as part of a larger reconfiguration in thinking about time and the "primitive" that reverberated in scientific, historical, and literary circles, which also produced an emergent theatrical style. This melded topical events, scientific reportage, and mythic histories into fable and visual spectacle in order to impart to English audiences the origins of the *difference* and *modernity* of the national character. The syncretism of the stage served perfectly as a vehicle of that historical myth- and nation-making that had become an imperative for the English in the late eighteenth century. Through the politics of performance, the arts of the theater and the

76. *Alfred, a Masque* (London, 1773); Sir Augustus Harris, *A collection of newspaper cuttings relating to London theatres,* 1704–79, British Library.

arts of discovery melded to bring into collision, and not for the last time, a past and a present "charged with the time of the now," underlining the historical specificity of the present moment in the national becoming and the possibilities for mapping its future character—a pacific modernity that whispered the destiny of imposing a Pax Britannica on the world.

The New Social History in France

Gareth Stedman Jones

If only because of the magnitude of its impact upon conceptions of history since the Second World War, a shift in the collective theoretical stance of *Annales* is an important event in the world of historians. The power of *Annales* has been both intellectual and institutional. Intellectually, its reputation was first built upon the pathbreaking methodological and historiographical innovations of its founders, Marc Bloch and Lucien Febvre; these were strongly reinforced by the achievement of its great second-generation practitioners, Fernand Braudel, Ernest Labrousse, Jacques Le Goff, Jean Meuvret, Pierre Goubert, Emmanuel Le Roy Ladurie, and others. But the power of the *Annales* has never simply depended upon that of its most gifted representatives. In the outside world, through their attachment to the Ecole des Hautes Etudes or the Maison des Sciences de l'Homme, or through their membership in one of the *laboratoires* of the state-financed C.N.R.S., its historians have generally been regarded as members of a "school." Concentrated geographically and institutionally and underpinned by a strong corporate sense of intellectual and academic lineage, they have remained the largest and most cohesive collection of publicly funded historical researchers anywhere in the world.

It is not hard to imagine the difficulties of challenging or changing the inherited emphases of such a powerful tradition, whatever the seismic shocks that have rocked the historiographic landscape during the last thirty years. During the 1990s, however, the historians of the *Annales* took a brave and timely step in confronting their past and attempting to settle accounts with it.[1] The evidence of their reassessment is to be found in the collective volume *Les Formes de l'expérience: Une autre histoire sociale*, which appeared in

1. Bernard Lepetit, ed., *Les Formes de l'expérience* (Paris, 1995).

1995 and was edited by Bernard Lepetit, an eighteenth-century urban historian and the journal's new editor, tragically killed in a motor accident shortly after the book was published. Lepetit also ably introduced and concluded the volume. The book includes the work of eleven contributors, who wrote on topics ranging from the mythical *droit de cuissage,* or the role of *lieux communs* in the Mediterranean states of medieval Islam, to professional groups in modern cities or the clothing trade in contemporary Paris. Collectively, although individual emphases differ, the essays offer the outlines of a new and alternative vision of social history at variance, it seems, with much that has been most distinctive about the *Annales'* inheritance. In the present chapter, I assess the fate of the *Annaliste* paradigm in the writing of history; as will be seen, some of the best-known and supposedly most imperishable watchwords of the *Annales* have been in effect laid to rest.

It is difficult, for example, to imagine further potential in the *annaliste* notion of *mentalité.* The term was originally an offshoot of Lévy-Bruhl's 1920s idea of a *mentalité primitive,* the mind-set of primitive peoples and the aboriginal predecessor of the rationality attained in the West from the time of the scientific revolution.[2] Until the 1980s, as Eric Brian remarks, this idea of *mentalité* still continued to be employed in studies of the history of science (p. 88), but not much elsewhere. In the 1930s and 1940s Lucien Febvre in his researches upon Rabelais and the problem of unbelief had attempted to develop the concept by linking it with the idea of *outillage mental* or the Bachelardian *blocage épistemologique.* But as Alain Boureau notes, Febvre's approach was almost completely invalidated as the evolutionary rationalism implied in the original idea of *mentalité* fell out of favor in the 1960s (p. 25).

The survival of the second connotation of *mentalité*—that of customary and unquestioned habits of thought, barely changing over centuries—is scarcely less vulnerable. When combined with ideas about the lack of any fundamental transformation of the conditions of material life in the long sweep between antiquity and the emergence of the modern economy, this notion underpinned the equally distinctive *Annales* idea of the *longue durée.* According to Braudel's recomposition of the premodern past, while traditional historians had remained deaf to all but the noise and commotion of *histoire événementielle,* the true historian could discern a counterpoint between the portentous but evanescent sound and fury of conventional narrative history and the slow, somber, and fugal sonorities of a determinantal but barely audible *longue durée.* The idea of *la longue durée* fitted easily into the structuralist constructions of the 1950s and 1960s, for instance Lévi-Strauss's long flat space between the neolithic and industrial revolutions.[3] As André Burguière points out, it reached its culmination in the early 1970s with Le

2. L. Lévy-Bruhl, *Les Fonctions mentales dans les sociétés inférieures* (Paris, 1910).
3. C. Lévi-Strauss, *Race et histoire* (Paris, 1952).

Roy Ladurie's Olympian vista of the very *longue durée,* France's eight-century agrarian and demographic cycle preceding industrialization (p. 260).

Such a position now seems unsustainable from at least two points of view. First, as the new editor of *Annales,* Jean-Yves Grenier, points out, the sophistication of economic statistics that has taken place since the 1960s has been paralleled by growing skepticism about the reality or meaning of the *longue durée* (pp. 227–28). Thus, although Grenier assures that the notion of the *longue durée* has not disappeared (p. 244), it has certainly lost any presumptive claim to statistical consistency, and thus to any uncontested quantitative existence. Second, its qualitative plausibility seems to be less assured than it was at the time of Le Roy Ladurie's *histoire immobile.* For in the crucial instance of demographic behavior, Burguière argues that although there is evidence of peasant family limitation stretching back in certain areas to the seventeenth century, this does not necessarily mean a new dating of the beginning of *the* "demographic transition," understood as the frontier between modernity and the deep structures of habit and repetition originally associated with the idea of *mentalité.* Instead, and more damagingly, he goes on to suggest that the choice of the seventeenth century as a benchmark rests upon nothing more substantial than the impossibility of reconstituting statistical series further back. Thus, far from there having been an "unthinkability" of the notion of contraception dating from time immemorial and breached at one moment in time, the supposedly age-old demographic behavior of most peasants in seventeenth-century France may have been a recent response to the energetic interference of village clergy in the post-Tridentine epoch (pp. 271–72). If such supposedly deep-seated aspects of behavior could shift in the relatively *courte durée* in response to religious change and new habits at court, conveyed to peasant households by *colporteurs,* it is hard to imagine what remains of the connection between *mentalité* and *la longue durée*—hard also to imagine what now remains to the latter, aside from glaciation, soil erosion, and other long-term physical changes in the environment.

Finally, it appears that very little remains of the obligatory social-economic framework that supported the studies of the students of Labrousse in the 1950s and 1960s. So firmly implanted were those assumptions that, as Jacques Revel notes, even when the evidence signally failed to sustain expectations about the economic logic of group or class behavior, as in the case of Albert Soboul's supposedly proletarian *sans-culottes* or the supposedly dynamic and modernizing institutional identity of Adeline Daumard's Parisian bourgeoisie of the July regime, no historian in France apparently considered questioning the general explanatory framework (pp. 68–69). Revel further reminds us that alternative approaches, like that of E. P. Thompson, were not explored (p. 70). It should also not be forgotten that the serious criticism of outsiders like Alfred Cobban or David Landes was not given a serious hearing until the whole paradigm began to collapse for internal reasons at the end of the 1970s.[4]

Once this collapse occurred and an a priori faith in the existence of "collective social actors" was lost, there were no longer any simple rules to connect social identity and political action. Nor could the complexity of social reactions now be ascribed to the impress of the convergence of economic crises of an "old" and "new" type, as suggested by Labrousse in his classic economic anatomy of the conjunctural crisis and revolution of 1847–48.[5] In the course of the last twenty years, *Annales* historians have adopted a more subtle and nuanced approach to the question of group formation and have thus discarded the simply designed political chessboard upon which Labroussian social actors made their moves at the moment of crisis. Further, much of the symmetry of the Labroussian depiction of the crisis itself, especially that on the eve of 1789, has been shown to have been the product of statistical artifice, often depending quite arbitrarily upon the choice of starting point of particular series (pp. 230 ff.).

In place of the "objectivism" and hierarchy of determinations associated with the old *Annales*, summed up in its characteristic notions of *structure, conjoncture, mentalité*, and gradations of *durée*, the new social history put forward by Bernard Lepetit and his colleagues proceeds from a renunciation of all external forms of social determination. History should follow the new paths opened up in economics, sociology, anthropology, and linguistics. Causal or structural explanations should be abandoned in favor of an approach that focuses upon situated action and restores the diachronic to its lost place in social scientific explanation by relating explanations of the ordering of phenomena to the manner of their unfolding (p. 274). Lepetit summarized what he described as the emergence of a new paradigm: "Saussurian linguistics is now opposed by situational semantics and the multiplicity of worlds of action is preferred to the causal effects of habitus. The intrinsic rationality of economic actors is challenged in the name of conventions and of procedural rationality, structural anthropology by the study of the forms and consequences of the historicised testing of cultures" (p. 14).

In this new approach, great emphasis is placed upon the freedom of individual actors. The history of social structures should no longer be seen simply or primarily as a set of deeply embedded constraints, or as Braudel liked to suggest, as the visible effects of the 'prisons of the *longue durée*' (p. 21).

4. A. Cobban, *The Social Interpretation of the French Revolution* (Cambridge, 1964); D. S. Landes, "The Statistical Studies of French Crises," *Journal of Economic History* 10 (1950): 195–211.

5. C. E. Labrousse, ed., *Aspects de la crise et de la dépression de l'économie française au milieu du XIX siècle* (La Roche-sur-Yonne, 1956).

Nor should social categories be divorced from the practices that give them meaning. Events are no longer of significance only in what they reveal about the underlying structure (p. 134). Social norms should no longer be considered—as they still are in functionalist social theory—to possess a separate and more fundamental conceptual weight than the practices and conventions from which they are formed. According to Simone Cérutti, the emphasis must be shifted away from the social responses to normative impositions (the elite culture–popular culture dichotomy so popular in the 1970s) to the ability of social actors to manipulate such norms (p. 130). Rather than proceeding from the assumption of a social whole or social totality composed of seamlessly interconnecting parts, social space should be considered irregular and "discontinuous" (pp. 76, 189). Following the practices of *microstoria* pioneered by Giovanni Levi, Cérutti states: "the biographer's task is now seen as bringing to the surface the manipulative strategies of social subjects faced with a multiplicity of normative fields whose main feature is to be mutually contradictory" (p. 131). Thus, social actors are no longer the unwitting bearers of social norms; they are knowing and consciously choosing agents whose freedom of action is the result of their location in the interstices between different normative systems (p. 130). As a result, no privilege of insight divides the participant from the social scientists: "[T]he whole ensemble of social actors is allowed access—unequal and partial, but real—to a knowledge of causation and an ability to understand their words and actions. This access is no longer reserved to the relationship between savants and the world" (p. 20).

This reflexive or recursive turn in contemporary "social science" leads to a distancing from notions of domination and social control, which characterized radical social theory in the 1970s. The historical presuppositions of Foucault's theory of representation and its connection by Louis Marin with "the classical age" are elegantly demolished by Alain Boureau (pp. 26–30). So, as Christiane Klapisch-Zuber demonstrates in the case of the supposed nobility of late medieval Florence (pp. 151–65), are the dangers of retrospectively imposing forms of social categorization that contemporaries would not have recognized. The new aim, according to Nancy Green, is to provide an analysis of social identities that does not imprison actors in reified social categories but permits us at the same time to understand the actions and representations of subjects in the context of the structures and constraints that hem them in (p. 166). Thus, the predilection of American social historians for the employment of class, race, and gender as organizing or explanatory categories is rejected in this conception of social history, except insofar as such categories possess meaning for and are deployed by the actors themselves (p. 165).

Given the emphasis upon the voluntarist aspects of social configurations and transactions, it is not surprising that the formation and re-formation of conventions, agreement, or consensus is placed at the center of this picture of social history. Thus the most interesting point about the French Revolution is seen to be the way in which the discreet and largely unseen methods of arbitrating or resolving disputes between merchants or between journeymen and masters under the ancien régime, despite their supposed abolition during the Revolution, reappear in modified form under Napoleon as the *Chambres de commerce* or the *Conseils des prud'hommes* (p. 284). Similarly, the main question addressed in a study of the twentieth-century Parisian clothing industry is the way in which apparently irreconcilable social, ethnic, and cultural differences are successfully negotiated and handled by the participants (pp. 165–87). In place of the previous emphasis upon the "constancy" of agents, whose predictable behavior patterns were driven by economic logic, the new social history draws upon a different sociology of action. This alternative approach, according to L. Boltanski and L. Thévenot, proposes to view "human actions as a series of sequences in which the individuals involved in successive moments have to mobilise within themselves different competencies so as progressively to achieve, as they confront circumstances, some form of appropriateness of response to the present situation" (p. 274).

The emphasis upon society as a collection of rules and conventions suggests a return to the perspectives of Durkheim. But structures, it is emphasized here, contain a multiplicity of voices, while a greater attention to the interaction of individuals within groups displaces the former simple treatment of groups as institutions. There can thus be no question of norms or social facts preceding or encompassing individuals, nor of any naturalization of society as an organism. The starting point, both methodological and substantive, is that of individuals, but not the individuals of neoclassical economics. The stress is upon active, self-conscious, knowing, manipulating, and ambivalent actors, preserving their freedom of maneuver at every moment of their participation in social life. Society is held together by conventional rather than juridical means. But these conventions and rules are the product of constant and arduous social labor and have never been other than provisional, ephemeral, and unstable. They are implemented by complex social actors with an ability to justify themselves by resorting simultaneously to several different and often contradictory social worlds.

This picture of social history is directed not simply against an ahistorical functionalism or an overly determinist structuralism but also against the unilinear trajectory of modernization theory. Just as there are not one but many demographic transitions, so there is no unique set of phenomena determining transitions, so there is no unique set of phenomena determining forms of social organization and their transformation. There is rather a plurality of independent phenomena of different natures coexisting in the same social space and changing not according to the imperatives of a single macrosocial process, but rather according to their own particular con-

figurational and microsocial logics (p. 189). In sum, history, if it is possible
to generalize within this schema, appears to be the process of formation and
dissolution of multiplicities of conventions holding societies together at different points in time. But how and why such shifts occur is less clear. The
historical process is a succession not of phases of objective spirit, nor of
stages in the march of mind, nor of forms of divisions of labor or modes of
production, nor of discrete episodes of *savoir-pouvoir.* While the future is
presented as bounded and finite, it is the past that is accorded a new and
paradoxical back-to-the-future freedom. For social processes are not bound
by one overarching social logic, but are presented as semidetached, kalei-
doscopic, indeterminate, and multidirectional.

It would be difficult to disagree with the substance of the critique of the
old *Annales* mounted by Bernard Lepetit and his colleagues. It is clear that,
however magnificent the historical overview established by Braudel,
Labrousse, and their followers, the particular combination of Durkheim,
Simiand, and Marx, which provided its original basis, is no longer sustain-
able. Critical attention to the often fragmentary or speculative statistics by
which its conceptions were sustained has greatly reinforced epistemological
misgivings about the naively determinist assumptions built into its models.
Among historians throughout the world over the last twenty years, a reaction has set in against all forms of unilinear grand historical narrative
depicting the advent of socioeconomic modernity, whether historical materialist or structural functionalist in inspiration. Instead, emphasis has been
placed upon the multiplicity of distinct and often contradictory paths and
directions concealed within the crude macroeconomic indices of development. Interest in trajectory and function has been replaced by interest in
context and meaning.

France has certainly experienced its own version of this shift, but the
result, as this volume testifies, is a conception of social history quite distinct
from current work in social history in the English-speaking countries. An
immediate reason for the difference may be the large impact made by
France in the 1960s via a structuralism that presented itself in part as an
extension of the methods originally pioneered by *Annales.* Such an endorsement helped to renew and prolong the life of the older paradigm, just at the
moment when analogous models of social historical development were
beginning to be challenged elsewhere. But this volume suggests a deeper
reason: the continuing prestige and weight, both intellectual and institutional, of a positivistic tradition of social scientific inquiry stretching back to
Durkheim and the pre–First World War decades of the Third Republic. No
journal comparable to *Annales* was produced in Britain or North America in
the first half of the twentieth century, mainly because before 1950 there
existed no comparable bases for interchange of ideas between historians
and social scientists. In English-speaking countries, the alliance between his-

tory and sociology was relatively late and comparatively brief. It was a product of the 1960s and 1970s and was a casualty of the move away from theories of modernization and development thereafter. In France on the other hand, as this volume confirms, the alliance between history and sociology remains deep-rooted and the rejection of structuralist, functionalist, Marxist, or neoclassical approaches to social history is not seen as incompatible with an unbroken commitment to history as a branch of social science.

To align history so unequivocally with social science is problematic, especially in light of the new emphasis that the *Annales* historians wish to place upon a conception of history built around voluntarism and convention. The editor states: "because for a long time it has fallen within the social sciences rather than the humanities, history is a technique (a craft) which is grounded in manipulation (of archives, series, contexts, scales, hypotheses, etc.) and experimentation" (p. 13). This claim is not defended at any length, but in light of the effective rejection of most of the concepts characteristic of the preceding *Annales* paradigm, it surely merits more discussion. The concentration of the original paradigm upon the problems of *durée* and *mentalité* in contrast with the traditional historian's preoccupation with *histoire événementielle* did produce a natural alignment between *Annales* and the methods and questions of the social sciences. It also made sense of Marc Bloch's ambition that history should come to be defined as "a science of change" or "a science of differences." The structuralist moment of the 1960s and 1970s reinforced this alignment, since it focused upon the unconscious mental rules of social life. Thus in addition to the contrast between structure and event, between the surface and the underlying, between *longue* and *courte durée*, there was added that between conscious and unconscious historical and social forces. In this context, the division between history as the study of the social and history as the study of politics and diplomacy, history as a branch of the humanities, possessed some justification.

With the dismantling of much of this autonomous social realm, however, it is no longer clear why the inherited distinction between social and political history should continue. In Britain, since the decline of class- and industry-inspired interpretations of modern social history from the end of the 1970s, political history has made a comeback. But it is no longer a political history bereft of social and cultural dimensions. There has been a conscious attempt to encompass terrain first uncovered by social historians. Political history no longer confines itself to the archival minutiae of *histoire événementielle;* it thinks increasingly in terms of political languages, political cultures, and the ritual aspect of political life, both at high and at popular levels.[6] Similarly, as the recent *Cambridge Social History of Britain* illustrates,

6. See for example, F. O'Gorman, *Voters, Patrons, and Parties: The Unreformed Electorate of Hanoverian England, 1734–1832* (Oxford, 1989); E. Hellmuth, ed., *The Transformation of Political*

social historians no longer refrain from interpreting material that would once have been regarded the province of the political historian.[7] Thus much that was originally valid in the social historical critique of political history is now being rectified, and to that extent the raison d'être of social history as an independent sphere has in these areas become problematic.

In France, on the other hand, it seems that the inherited *Annales* distinction between social history and *histoire événementielle* remains, although the intellectual rationale for this distinction has disappeared. The contributors to *Les Formes de l'expérience*, for example, are inspired by new approaches pioneered by the sociology of action. They propose to focus historical inquiry upon "conventions" while avoiding the Durkheimian notion of social fact. It is, therefore, clear that their concerns impinge directly upon the terrain of political history. Concern for resources of argument and justification, which accompany their investigation of conventions, also perforce occupy much of the territory studied by the history of ideas. In this area new approaches have been pioneered both in Cambridge, which has developed the historical and contextually based study of political languages, and in Germany, where Reinhart Koselleck has led the project of uniting social and intellectual history focused upon the analysis of *Geschichtliche Grundbegriffe*.[8] But in the new *Annales* perspective there is discussion neither of the boundary between social and political history nor of these alternatives in the historical study of ideas.

Additionally and strangely, the book remains virtually silent about the

Culture: England and Germany in the Late Eighteenth Century (Oxford, 1990); E. F. Biagini and A. Reid, eds., *Currents of Radicalism: Popular Radicalism, Organised Labour, and Party Politics in Britain, 1850–1914* (Cambridge, 1991); E. F. Biagini, *Liberty, Retrenchment, and Reform: Popular Liberalism in the Age of Gladstone, 1860–1880* (Cambridge, 1992); J. Parry, *The Rise and Fall of Liberal Government in Victorian Britain* (New Haven and London, 1993); P. Mandler, *Aristocratic Government in the Age of Reform: Whigs and Liberals, 1830–1852* (Oxford, 1990); M. Taylor, *The Decline of British Radicalism, 1847–1860* (Oxford, 1995); D. Feldman, *Englishmen and Jews: Social Relations and Political Culture, 1840–1914* (New Haven and London, 1994); D. Eastwood, *Governing Rural England: Tradition and Transformation in Local Government 1780–1840* (Oxford, 1994).

7. F. M. L. Thompson, ed., *The Cambridge Social History of Britain, 1750–1950*, 3 vols. (Cambridge, 1990); see also J. Harris, *Private Lives, Public Spirit: A Social History of Britain, 1870–1914* (Oxford, 1993).

8. See, especially, J. G. A. Pocock, *The Machiavellian Moment: Florentine Political Thought and the Atlantic Republican Tradition* (Princeton, 1975); idem, *Virtue, Commerce, and History* (Cambridge, 1985); J. Dunn, *Political Obligation in Its Historical Context* (Cambridge, 1990); J. H. Tully, ed., *Meaning and Context: Quentin Skinner and His Critics* (Princeton, 1984). For an explicit juxtaposition of social-historical interpretation and that starting from the analysis of political language, see G. Stedman Jones, "Rethinking Chartism," in Jones, *Languages of Class* (Cambridge, 1983), 90–179. See also O. Brunner, W. Conze, and R. Koselleck, eds., *Geschichtliche Grundbegriffe: Historisches Lexikon zur Politische-sozialen Sprache in Deutschland* (Stuttgart, 1972).

place and significance of discourse and a discursive approach to historical interpretation. It is stated that the "linguistic turn" has come and gone and that an engagement with Saussurian linguistics has been superceded by an interest in situational semantics (p. 14). But what this means is again not discussed at any length. Unfortunately, it appears to be assumed that the acceptance of a discursive approach would mean the acceptance of Foucault's discourse theory and therefore that the dismantling of the Foucauldian conception of representation or of the institution disposes of the problem of a discursive approach as such. What this ignores are other ways in which the original Saussurian insight has been developed in interpretations that are not encumbered by unacceptable structuralist, determinist assumptions or the rejection of diachrony and subjectivity. It is surely a weakness not to have engaged more directly with recent work in the history of political and other forms of discourse when, as this volume itself reveals, even peasant demographic behavior in early modern France can no longer be understood except in response to post-Reformation religious and familial discourses (Calvinist, post-Tridentine Catholic, Jansenist) and their complex impact at a village level upon contraceptive practices within families.

The danger of a view of history that not only rejects the role of the economy or other forms of structural determination, but also substitutes for the regularities of discourse the creativity of idiolects and the microscopic variety of situational semantics is that the resulting ensemble will be too boneless to fulfill the rudimentary requirements of historical explanation. Too great an emphasis upon the resources and competence of actors in the face of structures, and too insistent a focus upon the freedom offered by their liminal location between contradictory belief systems, can lead to the disappearance from view of a whole range of historical phenomena to which this voluntaristic approach offers little guidance. The articulation within various forms of political and religious discourse of a range of powerful and repetitively encountered human emotions—phobias about contamination, fears about corruption, conspiracy and the subversion of virtue, anxieties about loss or lack of sexual identity, fantasies of identification or election, anger about exclusion, obsessive fixations upon honor, insult, and betrayal—also helps to suggest why, whatever the resources and competencies of individual actors, particular patterns of practice and belief—patriarchy or anti-Semitism, for example—become dominant and long enduring.

It is also questionable whether the new way of approaching collective modes of thought and understanding current in contemporary French social science is really appropriate to the understanding of history as a whole. The methodology of this new conception of social science grew out of historical problems arising from French industrial sociology. It began as an attempt to explain the emergence and consolidation in the early twentieth century of a consensual institutional framework and a set of taxonomic devices (the adoption and measurement of the concept of unemployment, for example) whose effect was to stabilize and regulate the handling of disputes between employers, workers, and the state. In other words, it was designed to explain the emergence of a predictable system of collective practices in a country whose polity was stable, lawful, democratic, and pluralistic; whose culture was highly literate; and whose population was well versed in discriminating between multiple forms of persuasion purveyed through different types of media. It is far from clear whether this emphasis upon the conventional underpinnings of collective practices, their fragility, and their centrality in the reproduction of society would be especially useful in the understanding of other cultures and other epochs. Historically, societies based upon slavery and other forms of forced labor or upon the explicit political subordination of a subject people come to mind as only the most obvious examples of the vast array of societies in which notions of legitimacy were not connected with ideas of representativity or of reciprocal social obligation.

The evidence offered by *Les Formes de l'expérience* of the fruitfulness of this new social scientific approach to groups and collective practices when applied to the premodern era is as yet inconclusive. The effort devoted to the criticism of preceding or alternative paradigms outweighs that devoted to the construction of alternative historical interpretations. It is, for example, easier to discern the deficiency of the Labroussian approach to eighteenth-century price history than to imagine the shape of the new historical interpretation of, for example, the battle over grain deregulation in Paris in the 1760s or of the debate on the economy and crown finances on the eve of the Revolution (pp. 244–45, 276). In this volume, glimpses of these alternatives are tantalizingly brief.

During the past quarter century, educated perceptions of the importance of history have been battered to a greater or lesser extent by a series of challenges, from structuralism to postmodernism. Similarly, the popular prestige of history may have suffered from the loss of the self-assured, even complacent, evolutionary optimism that in the 1960s could still place the countries of Western Europe in the prow of a hopeful and meaningful human destiny. At the same time, however, the unraveling of the postwar settlement, the unbidden return of so much that was erased from the official memory after the Second World War, and the reemergence in new form of so many of the nationalist and racist insecurities and hatreds that had once erased the path of fascism all combine to remind us just how urgent it is that the moral and intellectual authority of history be renewed and reasserted.

The new approach to social history in France represents a welcome beginning of such a process. For it is an encouraging testimony to the collective commitment of the *Annales* to confront its past in a self-critical spirit and to renew its intellectual mandate. But it is also clear that at the moment the process still has some way further to go. There is no reason to doubt the stimulus offered to historians by new approaches in French sociology. A reassessment of the processes that enable and disable collective practices and "conventions" as the binding forces of social life may encourage important works of historical reinterpretation, just as sociologists, philosophers, and historians in Britain, for example, have recently benefited from a collaborative consideration of the importance of *trust* as an element in social life.[9] But however considerable the insights gained in particular instances, it will not be possible to rebuild history around any single category, however far reaching. Thus the emphasis of French historians over the last few years upon "convention" has generally remained rather formulaic, so far still more of a symbol of the shift away from structuralism and economic determinism than the substantive starting point of a new vision of history in its own right. The ambition of historians cannot be satisfied by discovering and multiplying confirming empirical instances of general sociological propositions. However magnificent such a division of labor may seem from a positivist vantage point, it is not history. Similarly, abstract formulations about "men and circumstances" or about "structure and agency" are of very little practical use to historians, however large they loom in manuals of social science. The only theoretical insights that matter to the historian are those that enable him or her to ask different questions, to consider or even construct new types of evidence, to uncover the importance of hitherto unconsidered or ill-considered sequences of events by constructing new contexts in which they might set or illuminate old contexts in a new way through the adoption of an unfamiliar angle of vision. Judged in this way, the process of critical reevaluation of the *Annales* tradition described in *Les Formes de l'expérience* and other programmatic statements is still far from complete. There is still too much of a gap between its proposed theoretical agenda and the substantive historical research carried out under its banner. It is only once that gap has been closed that the new generation of *Annales* historians will be able to assemble all that is necessary to construct a new vision and practice of history worthy to be compared with the achievements of the old.

9. D. Gambetta, ed., *Trust: Making and Breaking Cooperative Relations* (Oxford, 1988).

The Social Imaginary
of the French Revolution

The Third Estate, the National Guard,
and the Absent Bourgeoisie

Sarah Maza

In standard twentieth-century narratives, the late eighteenth century was the "Age of Revolutions," the crucible in which the modern class system took shape.[1] Rapid economic change in England and a sudden political convulsion in France together gave birth to the middle and working classes, whose struggle was to power Western history for decades to come. This classic story is predicated on the assumption that classes are objectively definable entities spawned naturally by certain structural preconditions. Even as, in the last decade or so, historians have challenged the tendency to take as a given just about every form of identity—gender, race, nationhood, ethnicity, and so on—the assumption that classes exist naturally "out there" has proven surprisingly resilient. Only recently, and especially in the field of British history, have scholars begun to point out that "class" is, if anything, the most imaginary of communities. The work of social scientists such as Pierre Bourdieu, Jean Baudrillard, or Zygmunt Bauman, and of historians such as Gareth Stedman Jones, Patrick Joyce, and Dror Wahrman, has shown the artificiality and contingency of standard twentieth-century assumptions about society: class is just one way, and a very recent one at that, of thinking about the social world.[2]

The rethinking of class as a historical category follows from a broader

---

1. The archetypal narrative is Eric Hobsbawm, *The Age of Revolution: Europe, 1789–1848* (London: Abacus, 1995).

2. Gareth Stedman Jones, *Languages of Class: Studies in English Working Class History, 1832–1982* (Cambridge: Cambridge University Press, 1983); Patrick Joyce, *Visions of the People: Industrial England and the Question of Class* (Cambridge: Cambridge University Press, 1991) and *Democratic Subjects: The Self and the Social in Nineteenth-Century England* (Cambridge: Cambridge University Press, 1994); Dror Wahrman, *Imagining the Middle Class: The Political Representation*

challenge to classic structural determinism and the primacy of the eco-nomic base. Many historians nowadays believe that cultural practices and representations—the ways in which people think, speak, and act—are not flimsy reflections of some deeper bedrock of reality, but rather are the stuff of which reality is made, at least in part. The social world, it follows, is at least in part created by the ways in which people think and speak about it. To say this is not to declare that other aspects of social experience are irrel-evant or to dismiss the material dimensions of the past. Rather, it is to sug-gest that we need to find new ways to think about the relationship between material experience and the discourse of the social in past societies.

In the pages that follow, I will apply some of this recent rethinking of class to the culture of the early French Revolution. For decades a standoff has opposed those—Marxists and others—who see the Revolution as fueled by social struggle, and the so-called revisionists who view it as mainly a political crisis gone awry.[3] While a good deal of this contention centers on the question of whether or not a "revolutionary bourgeoisie" can be located, there is one fundamental question that, surprisingly, nobody has asked: did the revolutionaries view themselves as a middle class or bourgeoisie? Did anyone, in the years after 1789, perceive such a group as central to the pol-itics and culture of the Revolution? I will address this problem by looking at two of the most likely places one might expect to find a "revolutionary bour-geoisie" defined in language and in practice: the pamphlets about the Third Estate published in 1788–1789, and the history of the National Guard, the urban militia created in July of 1789 whose function was pri-marily the maintenance of order in Paris. I will argue that in neither of these contexts was any sort of "middle class" as such recognized or described. What emerges instead is a refusal to draw any distinctions within the sup-posedly unanimous revolutionary *peuple,* a feature of revolutionary culture that has, I believe, important implications for the history of the Revolution and beyond. I hope with this example to raise questions—even if I cannot answer them—not only about the culture of the French Revolution, but

---

of Class in Britain, c. 1780–1840 (Cambridge: Cambridge University Press, 1995). Besides these monographs, several important collections of essays have recently evaluated the fate of orthodox and newer views of class in the wake of postmodernism: Lenard R. Berlanstein, ed., *Rethinking Labor History: Essays on Class and Discourse Analysis* (Urbana: University of Illinois Press, 1993); Patrick Joyce, ed., *Class* (Oxford: Oxford University Press, 1995); John R. Hall, ed., *Reworking Class* (Ithaca: Cornell University Press, 1997).

3. Of the many syntheses on the matter, one of the best remains William Doyle, *Origins of the French Revolution* (Oxford: Oxford University Press, 1980), 7–40. For a sampling of recent contributions to the debate, see Peter Jones, ed., *The French Revolution in Social and Political Perspective* (London: Arnold Press, 1996).

also about the challenges facing historians of "the social" at the end of the twentieth century.

Classic histories of the French Revolution equate the Third Estate with the bourgeoisie. This seems a reasonable assumption given the social identities of the 604 men who came to Versailles as deputies representing the *Tiers-État* in May of 1789. About two-thirds of the Third Estate belonged in some capacity to the legal profession (magistrates, lawyers, and notaries), and the remainder was made up of other professionals such as medical doctors, professors and writers, and merchants and manufacturers.[4] The Third Estate deputies could be described as belonging to a commoner elite or upper middle class—some indeed were squarely upper class and even of noble birth. But if one turns to writings about, or representations of, the Third Estate, it becomes difficult to equate this category with a middle class or bourgeoisie.

Circumstances produced a huge amount of commentary on the nature and composition of the "Third Estate." When the Estates-General were announced in August 1788 for the following spring, finance minister Loménie de Brienne invited public commentary on how the Estates should be constituted. Controversy soon erupted over whether the "forms of 1614," granting a single vote to each estate, should once again apply. Commoners protested that they would always be outvoted by the two privileged orders, and that the ancient forms had nothing to do with France's actual social landscape. The debate raged on, spawning hundreds of pamphlets, with the issue mostly unresolved up to and beyond the actual convening of the Estates in May of 1789.[5] Authors defending the commoners' position found it imperative to define and describe the "Third Estate" in order to assert its claims.

The most famous of these pamphlets remains the abbé Sieyes's *What Is the Third Estate?* with its familiar opening whiplash of questions and answers: "What is the Third Estate? Everything." To his own rhetorical question, Sieyes answers, "Everything"—not "the golden mean" or "the decent folks," or any other such phrase suggesting middling qualities. He writes "everything," and he means it. The pamphlet's first chapter is entitled, "The Third Estate Is a Complete Nation," and it builds on the physiocratic premise that subsistence and prosperity are the main reasons for human association. Human society is therefore "naturally" ordered on the basis of productivity, with agricultural production at the top. The Third Estate

---

4. Timothy Tackett, *Becoming a Revolutionary: The Deputies of the French National Assembly and the Emergence of a Revolutionary Culture (1789–1790)* (Princeton: Princeton University Press, 1996), 35–47.

5. Doyle, *Origins*, chapter 8.

includes, Sieyes writes, first those who work the land, then those who process matter through craft and industry, then those who ensure the circulation of goods, and finally those, ranging from intellectuals and artists to domestic servants, who provide "useful or agreeable services."[6]

Sieyes was far from alone in equating the Third Estate with the vast majority of working and productive inhabitants of the nation. The Protestant future deputy and Girondist Rabaut Saint-Étienne, for instance, published a pamphlet around the same time in which he argued that if you eliminated the clergy and nobility you would still have a full, functional, and productive nation, while if you eliminated the Third Estate the nation would not be viable.[7] And none other than Jean-Paul Marat published a pamphlet in 1789, which laid out a full enumeration: "The Third Estate of France is composed of the class of servants, laborers, artisans, merchants, businessmen, traders, cultivators, landed proprietors and nontitled rentiers; of teachers, artists, surgeons, doctors, men of letters and science, men of law, lower-court magistrates, religious ministers, of the army both of land and sea: an innumerable, invincible legion which carries in its bosom enlightenment, talent, force, and virtues."[8]

That the Third Estate was understood to include everyone except for a parasitical minority is further confirmed by another argument regularly made on its behalf, that of numerical supremacy. The nobility should not ignore our rights, said one writer, or it will find twenty-three million of us pitted against its one million members. How dare the nobility speak in our name, fumed another, when "it numbers one hundred thousand while we are twenty-five to twenty-six million strong"?[9] Sieyes himself wrote of two hundred thousand *privilégiés,* as opposed to twenty-five or twenty-six million unprivileged.[10] In short, all those who advanced numbers estimated the Third Estate at more than 95 percent of the nation and therefore as including far more than a middle class or bourgeoisie, however those are defined.

For final proof of the social capaciousness of the term *Third Estate,* one can look to the abundant imagery produced and disseminated around the time of the Estates-General, representing the three orders as human figures. In these prints, the Third Estate often embodies hard work and suffering, and thus is represented as a clog-wearing peasant crushed under the weight of a noble and a priest (the posture alludes to the unfair tax burden borne

6. Emmanuel-Joseph Sieyes, *Qu'est-ce-que le Tiers-État?* ed. Roberto Zapperi (Geneva: Droz, 1970), 119–22.

7. Jean-Paul Rabaut Saint-Étienne, *Considérations sur les intérêts du Tiers-État addressées au peuple des provinces* (Paris, 1788), 29–30.

8. Jean-Paul Marat, *Offrande à la patrie ou discours au Tiers-État de France* (Paris, 1789), 14.

9. *Mémoire du Tiers-État à présenter au roi* (n.p., 1788), 6; *Le Réveil du Tiers-État, c'est-à-dire de la Nation* (Paris, 1789), 14.

10. Sieyes, *Tiers-État,* 144.

by the *Tiers*). Other pictures show the Third Estate as an urban worker, a
tipsy cobbler raising a bottle to toast the *Tiers*, or a hardworking blacksmith
forging the Constitution.[11] Sometimes the Third Estate appears as a soldier
in uniform, sometimes as a man wearing indistinct "middling" garb (waistcoat and knee breeches), and sometimes as a respectably clad gentleman,
but one whose clothing could never be confused with the feathered and fes-
tooned costumes worn by nobles in these prints.[12] Images, like pamphlets,
make it clear that the "Third Estate" encompassed the entire working population, including the poor, and not just a middling or upper group.

This conclusion will hardly come as a surprise to anyone who has worked
on revolutionary sources, but scholars have rarely paid systematic attention
to the ways in which the social world was understood or depicted during the
Revolution, or explored the cultural and political implications of such conceptions. The pamphlets of 1788–89 contain plenty of traditional language, even under the pens of progressive authors like Rabaut, who wrote,
"The nation is the body of which the king is the head."[13] This literature also
offers plenty of instances of familial metaphors whereby the king is imagined as a good father attempting to arbitrate between the orders represented as quarreling brothers.[14]

Even as the pro–Third Estate writers rejected the old tripartite division
as irrelevant to the realities of their world, they too described society as a
series of groups differentiated by occupation and source of income. The
influence of the Physiocrats is pervasive, although many writers followed
Sieyes in emphasizing work over land as the main source of their society's
wealth.[15] As William H. Sewell points out, Sieyes countered traditional
orderings of society both by defining four groups instead of three, and by
scrambling up social hierarchies; Sieyes's class of service providers, for
instance, includes both domestic servants and members of the liberal professions.[16] But whatever the social scheme on offer, no writer in 1788–89
ever came up with a modern tripartite division of society into upper, middle,
and lower groups, or ever identified a unified middle class or invested it with
historical or political significance.

11. *French Caricature and the French Revolution, 1789–1799* (Los Angeles: Grunwald Center
for the Graphic Arts; Chicago: University of Chicago, 1988), cat. nos. 31, 34, 36, 37, 40.
12. Ibid., cat. nos. 28, 30, 33, 41, 42, 43.
13. Rabaut, *Considérations*, 32–33.
14. See, for instance, Charles, maréchal-prince de Beauveau, *Avis au Tiers-État* (London,
1788), 19–20; *Petit prosne aux roturiers* (n.p., 1788), 17–21; *Éclaircissement à l'amiable entre la
Noblesse et le Tiers-État* (n.p., 1789), 3, 16.
15. On Sieyes's differences with the Physiocrats, see Marie-France Piguet, *Classe: Histoire du
mot et genèse du concept des Physiocrates aux historiens de la Restauration* (Lyon: Presses Universitaires de Lyon, 1996), 95–100.
16. William H. Sewell, Jr., *A Rhetoric of Social Revolution: The Abbé Sieyes and* What Is the Third
Estate? (Durham, N.C., and London: Duke University Press, 1994), 57.

If no political boundary was ever acknowledged between the upper and lower segments of the Third Estate, the line separating the Third Estate, or Nation, from the group initially known as *privilégiés* and increasingly as *aristocrates* was obsessively drawn, and was the subject of much commentary. Sieyes once again serves as a useful point of departure, since he discussed the matter at length both in *What Is the Third Estate?* and in its complement, the *Essai sur les privilèges*. Like many contemporaries, Sieyes was aware of, and stressed, the original meaning of the term *privilège:* private law. The crime of the *privilégié* was less enjoyment of fiscal advantage than residence in a separate legal estate. "The *privilégié*," writes Sieyes," thinks of himself and his colleagues as forming a separate order, a chosen nation within the nation."[17]

From there it was a short step, and one regularly taken, to seeing the privileged as enemy aliens whose legal separation from the nation fully justified the nation's political rejection of them. "To be sure," Sieyes continues, "the privileged act no less as the enemies of the common order than do the English towards the French in wartime." He proceeds to even more threatening analogies, comparing the privileged to Algerians or "Barbary pirates" menacing the safety of the French coastlines.[18] This perception of the privileged or the aristocrat as an enemy alien builds upon a body of eighteenth-century historical writing, from Boulainvilliers to Mably, in which aristocratic supremacy was seen to derive, for good or evil, from the "conquest" of the realm either by Frankish warriors in the fifth century or by power-hungry lords under the Carolingians.[19] If privilege and power were based originally on violent conquest, the French people, or Third Estate, were fully justified in rejecting these usurpers beyond the pale of the nation. In sum, while no split was acknowledged within the Third Estate, the primary social division was understood to be that between a unified people and sociopolitical enemies foreign to the nation.

There is arguably nothing surprising in the rejection of "aristocracy," since for most political thinkers and actors of the early Revolution such sentiments reflected central aspects of their social experience. Revisionist arguments notwithstanding, there were striking social differences, as Timothy Tackett has shown, between noble and commoner deputies to the Estates-General. The aristocratic delegates were much richer, less educated, more devout, and in majority trained in the military; their nonnoble counterparts were typically much better educated (often in legal matters) and much less well heeled.[20] And there is evidence, in the writings of the Third Estate

---

17. Emmanuel-Joseph Sieyes, "Essai sur les privilèges," in *Oeuvres Complètes* (Paris: EDHIS, 1989), 17.

18. Sieyes, *Tiers-État,* 139–40.

19. Piguet, *Classe,* 22–30.

20. Tackett, *Becoming a Revolutionary,* chapter 1.

deputies, of considerable bitterness toward their noble colleagues on account of what was perceived as a combination of unfair social advantages and contemptuously intransigent demeanor.[21]

The emphatic drawing of lines between nobles and nonnobles in revolutionary rhetoric is therefore quite understandable. But one could argue that there were equally good reasons, both social and political, to mark off a "respectable" middle class from the lower reaches of the Third Estate. There was probably a greater social chasm between an educated lawyer-deputy and a barely literate man who worked with his hands and lived in fear of hunger than there was between the former and a nobleman, and it was clear from the beginning of the Revolution, from experiences like the Réveillon riots, that the working poor could prove dangerously volatile allies. Yet the leaders of the Revolution, in the Third Estate, the National Assembly, or the Paris city government, resisted the drawing of such a line, referring always in official discourse to an undivided "people" or "nation." A survey of discourses and practices surrounding the National Guard, the institution most likely to embody the sociopolitical claims of a Parisian middle class, illustrates the rejection of social distinctions, in practice as well as in theory, in early revolutionary culture.

From its beginnings the National Guard, created in the shadow of the storming of the Bastille, was an institution closely associated with urban government and urban elites. Calls for a militia or guard were voiced in late June as the standoff between the royal government and the new National Assembly became increasingly tense. That militia created itself in the scramble for arms of July 12–14; the new mayor Bailly and the hastily named commander of the guard, Lafayette, returning from Versailles to Paris on July 15, were faced with a fearsome crowd of men, many armed with pikes, hatchets, and scythes as well as rifles, and wearing as sole identification a blue and red badge, or *cocarde*.[22] It was imperative to prune, organize, and control this force, and this was done over the course of the following weeks. Poorer men were actually paid to give up their arms and return to work; the regulation that on July 31 organized the new National Guard of Paris, a force of some thirty-one thousand, made service in the guard a duty for all men between the ages of twenty-five and fifty, *except* for the following: workers, artisans, servants, and the nondomiciled.[23]

21. Ibid., 106–10, 132–38.

22. Louis Gottschalk and Margaret Maddox, *Lafayette in the French Revolution through the October Days* (Chicago: University of Chicago Press, 1969), chapters 6–8; George Rudé, *The Crowd in the French Revolution* (Oxford: Clarendon Press, 1959), chapter 4; R. B. Rose, *The Making of the Sans-Culottes: Democratic Ideas and Institutions in Paris, 1789–92* (Manchester: Manchester University Press, 1983), 46–50.

23. Gottschalk and Maddox, *Through the October Days*, 171–75.

The actual composition of the guard was more diverse than this regulation (and others following it) suggest:[24] in some districts of Paris and many provincial locales there simply weren't enough men of property to make up a plausible force, and in most places wealthy men were allowed to hire replacements instead of serving. But contemporary descriptions and the numbers we have still suggest that National Guard membership was skewed toward the upper reaches of urban society. Records show that the rank and file were heavily populated by the wealthier elements of the artisanal world (merchants and skilled workers such as jewelers), with a liberal sprinkling of "bourgeois de Paris" and professionals.[25] Contemporary anecdotal descriptions reinforce the numerical data. The lawyer Adrien Duquesnoy, a member of the National Assembly, wrote somewhat defensively on July 18: "It is important to note that in the Parisian militia there are a large number of very *honnêtes* [respectable] men, some of the best citizens of the city, chevaliers of Saint-Louis, chevaliers of Malta, very good bourgeois, financiers, priests, lawyers, monks, all very well disciplined and no more apt to abandon their stations than are regular troops."[26] The Marquis de Ferrières, upon learning that his brother-in-law and another nobleman had been named to head their local militias, expressed satisfaction at what he described as an alliance between the nobility and the *haut tiers*—the "higher third estate."[27]

And then there is the matter of the uniform. By August of 1789 the ragtag army of men wearing cockades had been replaced by a smartly clad militia: royal blue jackets with white facings and linings, scarlet piping, white waistcoat and breeches, not to mention the gaiters, buttons, and seasonal variations.[28] Along with a rifle, the whole getup could cost fifty livres, easily a month's salary for an unskilled worker.[29] Mayor Bailly wrote in his memoirs that he "ardently desired" that the guard be clad in uniform: "I thought that these townsmen [bourgeois] in different clothes carrying only rifles were not sufficiently imposing to our crowds of brigands. . . . The magistrate

24. The decree of 12 June 1790 limited membership in the guard to *citoyens actifs* paying taxes equivalent to three days' work for a skilled worker. The final law of 29 September / 14 October 1791, the object of heated debate, repeated the citizenship criterion, adding a one-year residence requirement. Georges Carrot, "Une Institution de la nation: La Garde Nationale, 1789–1871" (Ph.D. diss., Université de Nice, 1979), 41, 67–69.

25. Dale Clifford, "The National Guard and the Parisian Community, 1789–1790," *French Historical Studies* 16 (1990): 864–77.

26. Adrien Duquesnoy, *Journal d'Adrien Duquesnoy, député du Tiers-État de Bar-le-Duc,* ed. Robert de Crevecoeur, vol. 1 (Paris, 1894), 229.

27. Charles Elie, Marquis de Ferrières, *Correspondance inédite, 1789, 1790, 1791,* ed. Henri Carré (Paris: Armand Colin, 1932), 120.

28. Gottschalk and Maddox, *Through the October Days,* 174.

29. Clifford, "The National Guard," 850.

and the armed forces must wear distinctive signs, otherwise the people see in the magistrate or the soldier only their neighbor or their comrade."³⁰

In the summer of 1789 workers in several Parisian districts protested the decree that excluded them from membership in the guard, and the comments of one Eugène Gervais, a servant arrested for incitements to violence, suggest that in some quarters the effect of the uniform seriously backfired. Gervais had declared "[t]hat the *garde bourgeoise* and all those who wore the uniform were all j.f. [*jean-foutres*, buggers] and that 10,000 servants could take all the j.f. with their blue suits and white facings and make them dance; that all the bourgeois [in this context, bosses] were j.f., with no exceptions, . . . that there were 60,000 servants in Paris who could get together with the workers in different trades, and then you'd see all those j.f. go hide away at home with their f[ucking] uniforms."³¹ So much for impressing *le peuple*.

Matters of terminology seem to reinforce further a view of the Garde Nationale as a reflection and instrument of the urban elite. In late June and early July of 1789, the expression most commonly used in calls for and discussions of an urban militia was *garde bourgeoise*.³² Once the new force was set up it was named, on July 16, the Garde Nationale, but the older designations garde bourgeoise or *milice bourgeoise* remained in use in the following weeks, even months. The lawyer Adrien Colson, in the letters he wrote home, was slow to change terminologies; in mid-September 1789 he referred to the force as the *garde nationale bourgeoise*.³³

The early call for a "bourgeois" militia or guard to keep order was logical enough in the context of French history and institutions. Since the Middle Ages, most French towns had formed *milices bourgeoises* on a temporary or permanent basis for the defense of the community. From a real military role these troops had been reduced to internal policing and to ceremonial functions, the towns' dignitaries parading proudly in their uniforms, sashes, and plumed hats on official occasions. The bourgeois militias thus symbolized the political control of Old Regime towns by the traditional urban elite, or "bourgeoisie."³⁴ From a purely social vantage point it is tempting to label the National Guard as straightforwardly bourgeois or middle class. This was an institution modeled on Old Regime town militias, controlled and staffed

30. Jean-Sylvain Bailly, *Mémoires de Bailly*, vol. 2 (Paris, 1820; reprint, Geneva: Slatkine, 1975), 242.

31. Rudé, *The Crowd*, 65.

32. Bailly, *Mémoires*, vol. 1., 389–90.

33. Adrien Colson, *Lettres d'un bourgeois de Paris à un ami de province, 1788–1793* (Saint-Cyr-sur-Loire: Christian Pirot, 1993), 73.

34. Carrot, "Garde Nationale," vii–ix; Jean-Paul Donnadieu, " 'Bourgeois, bourgeoisie': Emploi des mots autour des cahiers de doléances des Sénéchaussées de Béziers et de Montpellier," in *Bourgeoisies de province et Révolution*, ed. Michel Vovelle (Grenoble: Presses Universitaires de Grenoble, 1987), 30–31.

by city fathers, whose function was the maintenance of law and order. But these social realities were in constant tension with the fact that the National Guard was deliberately erected into a symbol of all-inclusive citizenship, which paradoxically implied a rejection of Old Regime bourgeoisie and even of a modern middle class. The social bases and the symbolic function of this institution appear, therefore, to be at cross purposes; but this seeming contradiction should not, I believe, be explained away through recourse to the usual view of ideology as obfuscation.

In the years before 1789 a compelling new historical paradigm had come to invest special meaning in the history of urban France. Gabriel Bonnot de Mably's *Observations sur l'histoire de France,* first published in 1765, completed and republished in 1788, presented French readers with a dramatic view of their history.[35] Neither a chronicle of kings nor an argument about the competing constitutional rights of monarchs and magistrates, Mably's was a social history, and a violent one at that: the story of the rise of the feudal aristocracy and of its brutal tyranny over the populations of the French countryside. In the twelfth century, some towns purchased their freedom from the Capetian kings, becoming havens from the ravages of "feudal anarchy." "The towns," wrote Mably, "became so to speak little republics; in some the bourgeois themselves chose a number of inhabitants to manage the community's affairs. . . . The bourgeois divided themselves up into militia companies, imposed on themselves a discipline under commanders they had chosen, became masters of their town's fortifications."[36] Eventually these towns were to be the monarchy's best allies in curbing the power of the aristocracy. Mably's narrative of feudal anarchy and urban salvation became the most influential version of French history under the Revolution, providing one of the most powerful rationales for revolutionary antipathy toward the nobility. When a beleaguered deputy tried to argue in 1790 that nobility antedated feudalism, he was answered in two words: "Read Mably."[37]

The point is not, however, that historical narratives like Mably's gave the French bourgeoisie a sense of its past and historical mission. That did happen, but only in the 1820s, not the 1780s and '90s. Instead, the ideological thrust of the years after 1789 was to extend the concept of "bourgeois" citizenship to the entire nation. The overlapping meanings of bourgeoisie and citizenship are evident, even before the Revolution, in the definition of

35. On Mably see Keith Michael Baker, *Inventing the French Revolution: Essays on Political Culture in the Eighteenth Century* (Cambridge: Cambridge University Press, 1990), chapters 2 and 4, and Jean-Marie Goulemot, *Le Règne de l'histoire: Discours historiques et révolutions, XVIIe–XVIIIe siècle* (Paris: Albin Michel, 1996), chapter 10.

36. Gabriel Bonnot de Mably, *Observations sur l'histoire de France,* vol. 2 (Geneva, 1765), 98–100.

37. Baker, *Inventing,* 105.

the noun *bourgeois* in the 1786 *Dictionary of the French Academy:* "Citizen of a town. . . . As an absolute adjective one says *le bourgeois* meaning the whole body of citizens, the whole town: the bourgeois rose up, the bourgeois took up arms."[38] The Marquis de Ferrières, recounting the events of July 14, wrote, echoing the very terms of the dictionary: "The bourgeoisie has taken up arms, over thirty thousand strong."[39]

But the term *bourgeois* did not survive for very long in the revolutionary lexicon. A bourgeois in the Old Regime was a legally and fiscally privileged creature, and the status was abolished along with all other forms of privilege. A remark in the memoirs of Jean-Sylvain Bailly is, in this respect, telling. Writing of the euphoria he felt in 1788 when given his first taste of electoral politics, Bailly said: "It was amazing to be something in the political order, solely by virtue of one's status as a citizen, or rather as a bourgeois of Paris; for at that time we were still bourgeois, and not citizens."[40] A 1791 dictionary elaborated on the point in its article "Citizen": "The French were not citizens before the Revolution. . . . Citizen and bourgeois were synonymous for them; the latter title, like that of noble, evoked only the privileges enjoyed by the inhabitants of a few towns. . . . the title of citizen evokes duties and is borne now by every Frenchman."[41]

Citizenship under the Revolution was modeled, as Mably-type narratives suggest, on the example of the medieval free towns, havens of political self-determination amid an ocean of "feudal anarchy." For this reason, I believe, the Third Estate briefly called itself *les communes* in June 1789, before it became the National Assembly. Revolutionary citizenship thus derived from the example of the Old Regime right of "bourgeoisie," while necessarily repudiating it as a privileged status. During the early Revolution, full participation in the polity was always contingent on a degree of wealth. The decree of 29 October 1789 established that only men over twenty-five paying the equivalent of three days' unskilled labor in taxes could vote; about 4.3 million individuals out of a population of more than 25 million qualified as "active," or voting, citizens. And as of June 1790, membership in the National Guard was officially restricted to "active" citizens.[42] A certain

38. Michel Perronnet, "Michel Vovelle, 'Bourgeois, bourgeoisie': Les définitions du dictionnaire de l'Académie (1762–1802)," in *Bourgeoisies de province*, 13–26; the definitions appear on pp. 25–26.

39. Ferrières, *Correspondance*, 87–88.

40. Bailly, *Mémoires*, vol. 1, 9.

41. Cited in Sonia Branca-Rosoff, "Les Mots de parti-pris: *Citoyen, aristocrate,* et *insurrection* dans quelques dictionnaires (1762–1798)," in *Dictionnaire des usages socio-politiques*, vol. 3 (Paris: Institut National de la Langue Française, 1988), 71.

42. William Doyle, *The Oxford History of the French Revolution* (Oxford: Clarendon Press, 1989), 124–29; Carrot, "Garde Nationale," 41.

THE SOCIAL IMAGINARY OF THE REVOLUTION

level of wealth or property made one freer, it was assumed, to devote time and thought to political matters, and also gave one a stake in society.

But property owning was a highly contingent business, not something intrinsic to a person's being—*propriétaires* were often lauded, but were never described as having a distinct culture, identity, or tradition. Sieyes was at pains to stress the difference between the accident of wealth and the essential nature of citizenship: "The advantages whereby citizens differ lie beyond one's identity as a citizen. Inequalities of property or industry are like inequalities of age, sex, size, color, etc. In no way do they detract from the equality of citizenship."[43] Robespierre made the same point *e contrario* when he argued, in 1790, *against* property requirements for citizenship: How, he asked, could one make citizenship dependent on the vagaries of fortune? How could one deny citizenship, for instance, to the heirs of a deceased citizen if, after splitting their father's inheritance, the sons did not qualify for the vote?[44] Property was a crucial matter in the Revolution in many respects, but it never served as the basis for the cultural construction of a group identity.[45]

It would have been difficult, then, to regard the National Guard as the embodiment of a revolutionary middle class or bourgeoisie, in spite of the guardsmen's social identities and function, and of the institution's origin in the urban *milices bourgeoises*. On the contrary, the guard evolved, in the first year of the Revolution, into a central—for a while *the* central—symbol of classless sociopolitical fusion. Thousands of times, all over the realm, National Guards acted out the central political ritual of the Revolution's beginnings, the gesture that symbolized the founding of the new order: the fraternal oath. Starting in the summer of 1789, the National Guard Units that sprang up in towns of all sizes throughout the provinces made contact with one another for purposes of common defense, sealing their agreement by means of elaborate ceremonies that centered on oaths of brotherhood and loyalty.[46] In November 1789, for instance, ten thousand guards from eastern France rallied on the Plaine de l'Étoile, where they ceremonially

43. Sieyes, *Tiers-État*, 208.

44. Philippe Buchez and Philippe Roux, eds., *Histoire parlementaire de la Révolution française*, 40 vols. (Paris: Aubier, 1987), vol. 7, 323.

45. For Sieyes, property is a marker of individual identity. He posits that "liberty and property precede all else"; the purpose of government is to provide the secure setting within which men can engage in "a greater, more energetic and more gratifying development of their moral and physical faculties; thus their property, increased by all that additional industry adds onto it in the state of society is truly their own and can never be considered the gift of a power outside of themselves." Sieyes wishes to distinguish between "privilege," which is granted from outside and belongs to groups, and "property," which is self-generated and defines only the individual: Sieyes, *Essai sur les privilèges*, 4.

46. Gottschalk and Maddox, *Through the October Days*, chapter 18; Marcel David, *Fraternité et Révolution française: 1789–1799* (Paris: Aubier, 1987); Simon Schama, *Citizens: A Chronicle of the French Revolution* (New York: Knopf, 1989), 500–503.

vowed "upon their hearts and their weapons, before heaven" to defend one another as "brothers in arms."[47] Long after the brotherly euphoria of May–June '89 had given way, for the deputies and their plebeian allies, to anger, fear, and hardheaded politics, National Guardsmen rekindled the spirit of the Tennis Court Oath for audiences all over the realm.

The oath was a natural gesture for Frenchmen of this period, and not just (or not primarily) because it evoked a revolutionary tradition of contractual thought that reached back, via Rousseau, to Hobbes, Grotius, and the like. The juridical-political culture of the Old Regime was predicated upon the swearing of oaths, which the guardsmen's vows both evoked and superseded: the oaths of workers joining their "sworn trades," or *jurandes;* those of professionals such as doctors and lawyers to their *ordres;* a whole range of vows from the oldest vassal rites to the recently devised secret oaths of Freemasons.[48] Within this corporate structure the king represented the principle of unity, binding together and arbitrating among the myriad oathbound communities. With the displacement of kingship as the central principle, it made sense to redirect all of these particularistic oaths toward that more abstract unitary principle, the Nation.

But while one side of the symbolic gesture, the oath, harked back to the realm's ancient principles, the other side, fraternity, drew on more recent notions. Historians such as Lynn Hunt and Marcel David have shown that the languages of family and fraternity were ubiquitous in revolutionary culture.[49] In the pamphlets commenting on the Estates-General, for instance, the image of the king as father and of the Estates as three contentious brothers occurs repeatedly.[50] Even the monarch's representative Keeper of Seals Barentin, opening the Estates-General on May 5, 1789, spoke of family and fraternity and addressed the deputies as *enfants de la patrie.*[51] I have argued elsewhere that the prominence of family images in this period is not just another version of the ancient analogy between family and state, nor is it merely a way of acting out sociosexual anxieties about power (although it surely partakes of both). The sentimental family, I have argued, loomed

47. David, *Fraternité,* 53.

48. See William H. Sewell, Jr., *Work and Revolution in France: The Language of Labor from the Old Regime to 1848* (Cambridge: Cambridge University Press, 1980), chapters 2 and 3. For discussions of the oath in revolutionary culture, see Emmet Kennedy, *A Cultural History of the French Revolution* (New Haven: Yale University Press, 1989), 314–16, and Jean Starobinski, *1789: Les emblèmes de la raison* (Paris: Flammarion, 1979), 65–81.

49. David, *Fraternité;* Lynn Hunt, *The Family Romance of the French Revolution* (Berkeley: University of California Press, 1993).

50. See, for instance, Maréchal-Prince de Baudeau, *Avis au Tiers-État* (London, 1788); *Éclaircissement à l'amiable, Lettre des bourgeois aux gens de la campagne* (Angers, 1789); *Petit prosne aux roturiers* (n.p., 1788).

51. Buchez and Roux, *Histoire parlementaire,* vol. 1, 361–62.

large at this historically specific moment—between the demise of the language of orders and the rise of the language of class—as the *only* way of imagining a functional human community.[52]

A fraternal oath is, of course, an oxymoron. Siblings spawned by the same parents and reared in the same household are the *only* people who have no need for a covenant of loyalty. But the fraternal oath draws its strength as a symbol from this very overdetermination, the conflation of blood and law, the piling of family sentiment on top of contractual obligation. The contradiction within this gesture is arguably what makes for its riveting force: Jacques-Louis David's iconic *Oath of the Horatii* (1785) draws its power from the tension inherent to a pact whereby family members demand of each other, in the context of familial love, a loyalty that may result in the family's extinction.

I dwell upon the power and importance of the fraternal oath because this gesture was associated with the National Guard more than with any other group in the Revolution, and because it explicitly conveyed the rejection of differences within the *patrie*. The text of a March 1790 oath in western France, for instance, unambiguously repudiates all competing allegiances among participants: "Being no longer Bretons or Angevins but French and citizens of the same empire, we renounce all our local and private privileges as unconstitutional."[53]

The culmination of a year's worth of fraternal oath-taking took place on July 14, 1790, when the grandiose Festival of the Federation saw the convergence on Paris of tens of thousands of guards from the provinces, who, in the course of a rain-soaked ceremony, echoed the vow pronounced by Lafayette of fidelity to Nation, Law, and King. The same set of apparent contradictions inherent to the National Guard as symbol marked the festival itself. The presiding spirit and ideology of the festival were harmony and unity. The scene portrayed over and over again in both print and drawing was that of women and men from all walks of life helping speed up, just before the festival was to begin, the delayed preparation of the Champ de Mars, of elegant ladies with their skirts hiked up shoveling dirt or pushing wheelbarrows.[54]

Unity was tirelessly proclaimed through the iconography and symbols decorating the festival: female allegories of concord, clasped hands, triangles whose points were Law, King, and People.[55] If nationalism is indeed, as Benedict Anderson suggests, "a new way of linking fraternity, power, and

52. Sarah Maza, "Luxury, Morality, and Social Change: Why There Was No Middle-Class Consciousness in Prerevolutionary France," *Journal of Modern History* 69 (June 1997): 199–229.

53. Gottschalk and Maddox, *Through the October Days*, 435.

54. Ibid., 509–10.

55. Mona Ozouf, *La Fête révolutionnaire, 1789–1790* (Paris: Gallimard, 1976), 65.

time meaningfully together," the Festival of the Federation was a significant point of origin in the history of French nationalism.[56] Contemporaries were evidently fascinated by the idea of thousands of men converging on Paris from the provinces for the oath; much of the commentary at the time centered on this dynamic coming-together rather than on the actual static ceremony.[57] Much more than the National Assembly deputies who were, after all, chosen within the old system and convened by an absolute monarch, the National Guardsmen represented the true gathering of the national will into one time and place.

Yet the pattern of exclusions that characterized the guard as an institution marked the festival as well. As Mona Ozouf points out, there were two important parties excluded from the festival. One, named often and explicitly, was the aristocracy, the negative pole defining the "people's" unity. The other was never named, but rather defined through the topography of the festival: the common people actually stood outside the perimeter of the festival, beyond the closed ranks of armed guardsmen encircling the festival's active participants: the king, the political notables, and the National Guard. But as Ozouf points out, nobody seems to have thought anything of this: "[N]either of the two exclusions defining [the festival] was experienced as such; neither seemed to harm the national spirit celebrated by the festival."[58]

This denial of social difference might seem a shallow and transitory phenomenon, reflecting the brotherly euphoria of the Revolution's first, relatively untroubled years. But more remarkably still, the most potentially divisive event of those early years also failed to result in the clear articulation of a separation of interests between richer and poorer revolutionaries. On July 17, 1791, almost exactly one year after the Festival of the Federation, and in exactly the same place, the Champ de Mars, the National Guard opened fire on a group of petitioners who had assembled to demand the abolition of the monarchy. The guard killed about fifty people, mostly working-class members of radical popular clubs. David Andress, working on police records from the wake of the "Champ de Mars Affair," finds evidence of considerable ad hoc popular anger against the guard. Working men were heard declaring that the guardsmen were all *gueux* and *coquins* (rogues and scoundrels), and working women threatened to attack the men in blue uniforms with stones and knives. One artisan declared that "the massacre was made by the Bourgeois," another that "the National Guard were rogues who

56. Benedict Anderson, *Imagined Communities: Reflections on the Origin and Spread of Nationalism* (London: Verso, 1991), 36.

57. Ozouf, *La Fête*, 67–68.

58. Ibid., 72–74.

had fired on their own brothers."[59] Such recriminations against the guard had in fact started earlier in the summer, in June, in the wake of Louis XVI's aborted flight and arrest at Varennes; working men attacked and insulted commanders of the guard, alleging that they had helped in the royal family's attempted escape.[60]

There is plenty of evidence of anger at the guard in connection with both the Varennes episode and the massacre, but as Andress has shown, none of it translated into any statement of antagonistic social interests. Radical journalists like Gorsas and Marat wrote in their newspapers that brigands in the pay of the aristocracy had deliberately infiltrated the crowd to provoke the guard into shooting. Moderates and conservatives said that radical factions had sent in agitators to lead the people astray. Nobody saw either the crowd or the guard as having a distinct social identity or a political agenda.[61] Even in a tragic situation whose aftermath was fraught with social tension, "the people" could only be understood as a blameless and, above all, an undivided entity.

Most of us are inclined by training to explain this disjuncture by resorting to what Lynn Hunt calls the "metaphor of levels," and by reaching for images of veils or masks.[62] "Bourgeois universalism" is taken to be the deceitfully handsome cloak thrown over the ugly, hard facts of class interest.[63] Such metaphors have, I would suggest, outlived their usefulness. We may have more to gain at this stage by taking the discourses and cultural practices of the Revolution on their own terms and understanding them from the inside rather than as teleologically minded outsiders. French Revolutionary ideologies did not recognize a middle class or bourgeoisie— the sort of group to us so clearly represented by the Third Estate deputies or the National Guard—as historically or politically significant. Most of the time they saw no such group at all: just as the *garde bourgeoise* melted into the *garde nationale*, "bourgeois" became citizens—unless they went bad and turned into "aristocrats."

59. David Andress, "The Denial of Social Conflict in the French Revolution: Discourses around the Champ de Mars Massacre, 17 July 1791," *French Historical Studies* 22 (spring 1999): 183–209 (the quotes are on pp. 197, 200, 201).

60. Ibid., 190.

61. Ibid., esp. 203–7.

62. Lynn Hunt, *Politics, Culture, and Class in the French Revolution* (Berkeley: University of California Press, 1984), 12.

63. For a salient example of the interpretation of French revolutionary ideology as veiled class interest, see Patrice Higonnet's stimulating but, I believe, misconceived interpretation of antiaristocratic ideology as a self-defeating form of "bourgeois universalism": *Class, Ideology, and the Rights of Nobles during the French Revolution* (Oxford: Clarendon Press, 1981).

Most supporters of the Revolution took it as axiomatic, in stark contrast to what is generally assumed today, that freedom was best served by unanimity and despotism by diversity (the most common image of the Revolution's antithesis was the many-headed "hydra of despotism"). No lawful divisions could exist within the free French *peuple:* the aristocratic social enemy was always located *outside* the legitimate nation. As François Furet pointed out, the struggle between the high and popular politics in the Revolution was not articulated as a contest between middle and working classes, but between *representing* the people (the deputies) and *embodying* the people (the popular militants).[64]

My argument here in no way seeks to suggest that social experiences as such—hunger, fear, or envy—are unimportant. Bailly's allusion to "crowds of brigands" and Eugène Gervais's anger at the uniformed *jean-foutres* are real and do matter. But too often the language through which such experiences are apprehended has been distorted by assumptions about what was "really" going on, some parts of it magnified, others dismissed as "false" or "hegemonic." The Revolution's social vision of unanimity, predicated on the notion of an indivisible people, should be taken seriously on its own terms because it had important cultural implications. In the shorter term, it probably contributed to the Revolution's political instability—just as they could not conceive of a loyal opposition in politics, the actors of the French Revolution found it difficult to countenance the coexistence of legitimately competing social interests, hence social difference was demonized as political treason, usually under the guise of the all-purpose "aristocrat." In the longer term, the belief in a people undivided by class antagonism fed into a powerful republican tradition and various other forms of statism. This cultural tradition, as much as the data of economic and social history, explains the continued marginalization of the bourgeoisie in modern French history. Not that we can or should dispense with the data of economic or demographic history: the challenge, at the end of the twentieth century, is to find new ways of connecting the evidence about prices, population, and material culture with the ways in which people in the past have made sense of social life.[65]

By paying closer attention to language and culture, we will be better equipped to comprehend the many ways in which people perceived "the social" in the late eighteenth and early nineteenth centuries, few of which had anything to do with later understandings of "class." The attention recently bestowed on other ways of imagining human connection and com-

64. François Furet, *Penser la Révolution française* (Paris: Gallimard, 1978), 75–76.
65. For a cogent discussion of the theoretical and practical issues involved in this approach, see Wahrman, *Imagining the Middle Class,* 1–18.

munity in the eighteenth century—family, sympathy, sensibility, brother-hood, race, and nation—reflects a need to rid the past of some of the clut-ter of shopworn heuristic devices.[66] Restoring agency to actors in the past includes granting *them* the freedom to imagine and define the social world in which they lived.

66. See, for instance, David Denby, *Sentimental Narrative and the Social Order in France, 1760–1820* (Cambridge: Cambridge University Press, 1994); G. J. Barker-Benfield, *The Culture of Sensibility: Sex and Society in Eighteenth-Century Britain* (Chicago: University of Chicago Press, 1992); Hunt, *The Family Romance;* David, *Fraternité;* Linda Colley, *Britons: Forging the Nation, 1707–1837* (New Haven: Yale University Press, 1992).

Service and Servitude in the World of Labor

Servants in England, 1750–1820

Carolyn Steedman

Not so much a dissolution of boundaries as a remapping, what follows is as much about the histories of servants and service that we have been producing for the last forty years as it is about the servants themselves. Or rather, it is about the histories that *haven't* been produced, for an odd thread of paradox runs through the account that follows. In the massive and articulate effort of the postwar years to write the People into being by providing them with a history, social and labor historians actually came to define an English working class by evading discussion of its largest and most persistent component: those who undertook paid household work on behalf of employers, or resident and nonresident domestic servants.[1] One of the reasons for this—the absence of a majority of the working population from twentieth-century historians' accounts of the making of the working class—may well turn out to be connected to the perceptions bequeathed by the eighteenth century's own philosophical history, which paid much attention to servitude as one of the origins of modern (that is, eighteenth-century) bourgeois political personhood.

Since the 1960s, historians of the eighteenth and nineteenth centuries in England have been routinely accused of neglecting servants and service in giving their accounts of working-class life and experience. A typical accusation from 1976 suggests that while historians have always known that servants constituted a major group in modern European societies, their lack of

---

1. For suggestions about restorative social and labor history of the 1960s and 1970s as a feature of the postwar democratic settlement, see Carolyn Steedman, "State-Sponsored Autobiography," in *Moments of Modernity: Reconstructing Britain, 1945–1964*, ed. B. Conekin et al. (London: Rivers Oram, 1999), 41–54, and Paul Long, "The Aestheticisation of Class in Britain, 1945–1970" (Ph.D. diss., University of Warwick, 2001).

involvement in class struggle and their failure to make up a social class ensured labor history's indifference to them. Servants were isolated in middle-class households and were typically passing through a stage *of* life rather than becoming a particular type of worker *for* life. They were thus isolated from many of the cultural forms of working-class activity. Moreover, this complaint against social historians continues, not least because it is fairly certain that from the last decades of the eighteenth century, servants were increasingly women who performed work that had no economic value and that remained outside the realm of measurable industrial activity.[2] Thus, accusations about the neglect of servants merged in the 1970s and early 1980s with much louder ones having to do with the absence of women in general from the annals of the laboring poor.

For a long time, the charges against historians were well deserved. In 1963, when discussing distribution of the population by occupation as shown by the Census of 1831, Edward Thompson told his readers that after agricultural laborers, female domestic servants made up the largest occupational group in English society.[3] Yet this is the first and last mention he makes of servants in *The Making of the English Working Class,* though many of the men who made up the societies and associations he describes, or who met in secret on the moor three miles beyond Huddersfield to plant the Liberty Tree, had been servants at some point during their adolescence or, as apprentices, had been used by their masters and mistresses in the performance of domestic tasks, as a kind of household servant. Even more of them—journeymen and laborers hired by the day—probably understood the work they did as a form of unfree labor, by which for a shorter or a longer time they had leased to a master a legal right to the use and enjoyment of their energies and capacities.

Robert Steinfeld has told us that in the period dealt with by Thompson, the idea of free labor had not quite been "invented" (although such invention was in process in the former American colonies, from the 1780s onward), and that "all those who worked for others for compensation on whatever terms were in some sense 'serving' their masters." It was not just a linguistic hangover from Tudor legislation to call workers "servants," says Steinfeld, for "the broader usage of the term 'servant' [captured the] common qualities of all versions of labour relationship."[4]

Men and women of the laboring poor were told about these forms of relationship—about the property of a master or mistress in their labor, and

2. Theresa McBride, *The Domestic Revolution: The Modernisation of Household Service in England and France, 1820–1920* (London: Croom Helm, 1976), 9–17.

3. E. P. Thompson, *The Making of the English Working Class* (Harmondsworth: Penguin, 1968 [originally published 1963]), 259.

4. Robert J. Steinfeld, *The Invention of Free Labour: The Employment Relation in English and American Law and Culture, 1350–1870* (Chapel Hill and London: University of North Carolina Press, 1991), 18–21, 85–86,102, 105.

what kind of person this made him or her in law and in common understanding—every time they appeared before the magistrates in order to gain
a settlement under the Poor Law, or when their master or mistress appealed
against the duty levied on them as a household servant. (Masters and mistresses would claim that the man wasn't a servant *at all,* but really just an
apprentice who occasionally cleaned the table knives, or really just a laborer
hired by the day who happened to wait on table from time to time.)[5] These
assumptions and beliefs about labor, property, and ownership, and the
forms of relationship that derived from them, were ultimately legal ones,
and they were articulated routinely by magistrates in petty and Quarter
Sessions and other local tribunals like the one provided by the taxation system. The condition of servitude, which was an aspect of all employment
relationships, and its connection to the legal definition of domestic, or
menial, service, was much debated. Sir William Blackstone discussed it at
length in his *Commentaries on the Laws of England* (1765), and the widely read
manuals for magistrates, such as the many editions of Richard Burn's *Justice
of the Peace and Parish Officer,* offered clear statements and much-referred-to
case studies of the most commented-upon relationship in the society.[6]

Since Edward Thompson's evasion of the servant question in 1963, the
sheer weight of servant numbers has, in fact, pressed social historians to
investigate them. Only a century ago, servants of both sexes represented
one person in twenty-two of the general population of Britain, and in the
1890s one third of all women employed were domestic servants.[7] Numbers

5. In August 1778 the delightfully named James Champagne, wine merchant of Melcombe
Regis near Dorchester, complained that he had been charged for employing Thomas Peters,
who was really a porter who washed bottles and casks in the line of his business—and who was
also employed "in domestic affairs," in "waiting at table, and cleaning knives and forks; and
also in looking after [Champagne's] horse." He would not employ the man at all, Champagne
said, "was it not for the benefit of [Peters'] labour and services in [my] . . . business of a wine
merchant." (The extremely complicated system of tax exemption under this much amended
legislation was consistent in not charging those who bought others' service for the purpose of
making a living.) The King's Bench judges to whom this case went on appeal (William
Blackstone and William Mansfield among them) saw this as a clear case of trying to smuggle a
servant and upheld the decision of the local commissioners. Commissioners of Excise, *Abstract
of Cases and Decisions on Appeal Relating to the Tax on Servants* (London: Mount and Page for T.
Longman and T. Cashall, 1781). See also Thomas Caldecott, *Reports of Cases Relative to the Duty
and Office of a Justice of the Peace, from Michaelmas Term 1776, to Trinity Term 1785* (London: His
Majesty's Law Printers for P. Uriel, 1785), 11, and Richard Burn, *The Justice of the Peace and
Parish Officer: Continued to the Present Time by John Burn,* 17th ed., vol. 2 (London: A. Strahan and
W. Woodfall, 1793), 151–62.

6. Sir William Blackstone, *Commentaries on the Laws of England in Four Books* (1765), 6th ed.,
bk. 1 (Dublin: The Company of Booksellers, 1775), 422–32. Richard Burn, *The Justice of the
Peace and Parish Officer* (London: Henry Lintot for A. Millar, 1756), 622–43.

7. Leonore Davidoff, "Mastered for Life: Servant and Wife in Victorian and Edwardian
England," *Journal of Social History* 7, no. 4 (1974): 406–28.

cannot be counted in the same way for the 1790s, but estimates in the two monographs on English domestic servants that we possess—J. Jean Hecht's *The Domestic Servant Class in Eighteenth-Century England* (1956) and Bridget Hill's *Servants* (1996)—have been considered reasonably accurate. A few years ago it could be said with some certainty that at the end of the eighteenth century and in proportion to population, the servant class was twice as large as it was in the 1890s, with perhaps one person in eleven a domestic servant, perhaps as many as one in five or six in the Metropolis.[8] Further, it was claimed that perhaps 40 percent of the population of eighteenth-century England had been servants at some point between early adolescence and marriage.[9] There are now serious doubts about the demographic basis for such assertions. For example, there were simply not enough unmarried young women in the population to provide this level of residential domestic service.[10] Nevertheless, when we add to the definition of service the large amount of household work bought in, on an hourly and daily basis and almost universally performed by women, and the practice of Poor Law apprenticeship that gave adolescent girls responsibility for kitchen and household work in combination with care of domestic stock and garden, we can still speak of ubiquity of domestic service as the most common work experience of women in the society.[11]

A weight of numbers like this and a vast commonality of experience (from both sides of the borderline) must force the social historian's attention.[12] In recent years, then, serious attention has been paid to Sarah Maza's

8. J. Jean Hecht, *The Domestic Servant Class in Eighteenth-Century England* (London: Routledge Kegan Paul, 1956), 33–34. Bridget Hill, *Servants: English Domestics in the Eighteenth Century* (Oxford: Clarendon Press, 1996), 15–16.

9. Judith Laurence-Anderson, "Changing Affective Life in Eighteenth Century England and Samuel Richardson's *Pamela*," *Studies in Eighteenth-Century Culture* 10 (1981): 445–56.

10. Leonard Schwartz, "English Servants and Their Employers during the Eighteenth and Nineteenth Centuries," *Economic History Review* 52, no. 2 (1999): 236–56.

11. See Keith Snell, *Annals of the Labouring Poor: Social Change and Agrarian England, 1660–1900* (Cambridge: Cambridge University Press, 1985), 270–319, for the apprenticeship of women, including apprenticeship to housewifery. It was the work of women servants that blurred the distinction between household work and outside work. See Thomas Parkyns, *A Method Proposed, for the Recording of Servants in Husbandry, Arts, Mysteries, &etc. Offer'd by Sir Thomas Parkyns, Bart., One of His Majesty's Justices of the Peace for the Counties of Nottingham and Leicester* (London: privately printed, 1724), 40. For the permeable boundary between inside and outdoor work in Buckinghamshire in the 1750s, see G. Eland, ed., *The Purefoy Letters 1735–1753*, 2 vols. (London: Sidgwick & Jackson, 1931), vol. 1, 226–56.

12. Literary critical attention to domestic servants has produced the fruitful image of masters and servants on opposite sides of an immutable divide, showing us their massive presence in eighteenth- and nineteenth-century texts as symbolic of the working class that is absent from them. "The presence of servants indicates only the true absence of the people," writes Bruce Robbins. "Signposts left at random in the no-man's land between what can and cannot be represented, they are capable only of showing that the other side of the border is

and Cissie Fairchilds' work on service in France, and to their insistence that service was, above all else, *a relationship*.[13] It is, in fact, an emotional and affective relationship that has been investigated over the last five years, an investigation that is always accompanied, as is Amanda Vickery's brief but brilliant account of Elizabeth Shackleton's feelings about her female servants in 1780s Lancashire, by the social historian's familiar and resigned caveat that we are never likely to find out very much about how the servants felt about Elizabeth Shackleton.[14]

The discussion of these questions in provincial settings has been unusual: most recent work on domestic service has used Metropolitan sources to discover, for example, the employment of servants by relatively low strata of the artisan population of Augustan London, and above all, perhaps, to find women and women's experience.[15] In London at least, in the early part of the century, there was a dominance of female servants. These women have been seen by their most recent historians to be exercising choice, using domestic service as a way of evading marriage and maintaining independence.[16] It is clear from this recent work that English social historians can no longer be accused, as they were in 1976, of ignoring servants because they were women.[17]

We may add to this recent profusion of information about eighteenth-century servants a conceptually sophisticated understanding of the multifarious ways in which the apprenticeship system was used in order to provide households with female (and sometimes male) domestic service, particularly in the countryside.[18] And doubts about the extent of service that have been raised by reworking eighteenth-century tax records (after 1778, male servants were taxed as a "luxury" item, female servants between 1785

---

inhabited." Robbins, *The Servant's Hand: English Fiction from Below* (Durham, N.C.: Duke University Press, 1993), 27.

13. Sarah Maza, *Servants and Masters in Eighteenth-Century France: The Uses of Loyalty* (Princeton and Guilford: Princeton University Press, 1983). Cissie Fairchilds, *Domestic Enemies: Servants and Their Masters in Old Regime France* (Baltimore and London: Johns Hopkins University Press, 1984).

14. Amanda Vickery, *The Gentleman's Daughter: Women's Lives in Georgian England* (New Haven and London: Yale University Press, 1998), 134–46.

15. Peter Earle, *The Making of the English Middle Class: Business, Society, and Family Life in London, 1660–1730* (London: Methuen, 1989), 218–30.

16. D. A. Kent, "Ubiquitous but Invisible: Female Domestic Servants in Mid-Eighteenth-Century London," *History Workshop Journal* 28 (autumn 1989): 111–28. Tim Meldrum, "Domestic Service in London, 1660–1750: Training for Life or Simply 'Getting a Living,'" unpublished paper, 1994.

17. McBride, *Domestic Revolution*, 9–17.

18. Snell, *Annals of the Labouring Poor*, 257; Hill, *Servants*, 128–49; Frederic Keeling, *Child Labour in the United Kingdom* (London: P. S. King, 1914); Joan Lane, *Apprenticeship in England, 1600–1914* (London: UCL Press, 1996).

and 1792) point to the possibility that the majority of extrafamilial household work was not performed by those footboys, maids, cooks, and butlers
(all the categories of menial servant that the acts of parliament specified)
hired for the purpose, serving a year, and being paid their wages at the end;
but rather by women (and men) bought in for a couple of hours, half a day,
three mornings a week to wash the china in the china closet, to do some
ironing, to turn out a bedroom.[19] The Somerset widow Frances Hamilton,
who ran the substantial farm and quarry that was bequeathed her in the
1780s, employed two properly hired female servants, one man servant (who
did a great many things in the garden and quarry and on the farm, besides
carrying her library books into Taunton and waiting on table—she paid tax
on the powder for the wig he wore, on these rare and glamorous occasions),
and a parish apprentice—a ten-year-old boy who worked in husbandry and
in the house between 1778 and 1801. But she also frequently recorded in
her accounts such entries as the following (the first is for 1794):

> Sep 28th
> Catherine settled acct with me &
> paid me 10s6d she owed me & I paid her for working
> 30 days at washing 6
> 4 days brewg at 6
> 10 days Ironing at 4 £1 0s 4d;

and in 1799:

> January—Betty Huckleburgh
> 1 at 12 o clock
> 2 at 11 o clock
> 7 Betty sleep here
> 15 Betty Huckleburgh went Home
> to breakfast & work for herself: came at night
> 16 Betty Huckle the same
> 17 the same
> 18 the same
> 19 breakfast and sweep my room
> 20 Betty here Paid her.[20]

After about 1750, in law and in the ordinary, everyday practices of
employment, domestic, or menial, servants became more sharply distinguished from servants in husbandry. In 1765, Sir William Blackstone called
domestics "the first sort of servants acknowledged by the laws of England; so

19. Commissioners of Excise, *Abstract of Cases.* Vickery, *Gentleman's Daughter,* 139.

20. Somerset County Record Office, Bishops Lydeard Farming Accounts, DD/FS 5/8;
DD/FS 5/3. Margaret Allen, "Frances Hamilton of Bishops Lydeard," in *Notes and Queries for
Somerset and Dorset* 31, pt. 317 (March 1983): 259–72.

called from being *intra moenia*."²¹ But an inquiry into the experience of service in this period cannot restrict itself to those who dwelt "within the walls"—who were resident in households. The numbers who came and went, like Betty Huckleburgh, or Elizabeth Shackleton's servants, to clean the silver, do two hours weeding in the garden, or a morning's scrubbing must be taken into account. We need to consider the new kinds of household work and maintenance that emerged in this period, and the new forms of work that the proliferation of new household goods (carpets, china, curtains, cooking utensils) brought into the world.

None of this detail about the organization of domestic life—Sir William Blackstone called the service relationship in households "the first relation of private life"—has been told as part of the making of a working class.²² Indeed, for two hundred years now, in discussing servants and the service relationship, we have stayed very close indeed to the analytic trajectory laid out by eighteenth-century theorists of these questions. As social and labor historians, we have *perhaps* remained in thrall to Adam Smith, and to his notion of what work was and the role work played in the development of society. In his grand formulation of the relationship between the division of labor and the making of society, Smith used the servant as a figure by which to explore the idea of value, the distinction between productive and nonproductive labor, and the social relationships that emerge between people under different conditions of buying and selling labor. In *The Wealth of Nations* (1776), Smith makes it clear that fashioned and made things are labor materialized and made concrete, and that the labor fixed in these commodities is what gives them value.²³ But by way of contrast, he wrote, the "labour of the menial servant . . . does not fix or realise itself in any particular subject or vendible commodity. His services generally perish in the very instant of their performance, and seldom leave any trace or value behind them for which an equal quantity of service could afterwards be procured."²⁴ In this formulation then, the servant did work that was not work.

These questions of labor, of the location of labor in people and things, of work, service, and personhood, pushed Smith toward historical expression and historical thinking.²⁵ He had used a world history, with time arranged

21. Blackstone, *Commentaries*, bk. 1, 425.
22. Ibid., 422.
23. Adam Smith, *The Wealth of Nations* (1776; reprint, Harmondsworth: Penguin, 1997), 133–40.
24. Ibid., 430.
25. With Adam Smith, we may even ask questions about labor and subjectivity and not be anachronistic: Smith was quite clear about the role of repetitive labor in the making of intelligence and personality. See Isaac Ilych Rubin, *A History of Economic Thought* (1929; reprint, London: Ink Links, 1979), 184–85, for an account of bk. 5, chap. 1 of *The Wealth of Nations*, where Smith makes these observations.

chronologically by mode of production before 1776, in *The Theory of the Moral Sentiments* (1759) and in his *Lectures on Jurisprudence* (delivered between 1753 and 1755), but it was the questions raised by labor as an individual and social possession in *The Wealth of Nations* that brought him to the mainstream of eighteenth-century history writing. These are important origins of social history as a mode of inquiry *and* a framework within which we still operate when we discuss the service relationship in the past.

The eighteenth-century English and Scottish philosophical historians told the history of the world as a movement from barbarism to civilization: as a refinement of the laws and conventions governing the creation, possession, and exchange of property. Adam Smith, Adam Ferguson (1767), and John Millar (1771) wrote histories of civil society in which the historical account was inextricably connected to the way in which modern subjects were described as legal and social beings. Their distinction and rank, their place in the great ordering of the world, was not just an external description, but an item of their identity.[26] These were "natural histories" of humankind: a study of its evolution from a "barbarous" to a "refined" state. We should be as clear as Ferguson and Millar tried to be, that one of the meanings of *history* was "inquiry into." We should think of their work both as (speculative) historical accounts in the modern sense *and* as forms of explanation.[27]

The philosophical historians focused much of their argument on the transition from one mode of production to another; on the inauguration of private property; on "the woman question" (that is, the condition of women as a means of measuring the increase of civility and refinement); and above

26. Adam Smith, *Lectures on Jurisprudence: Glasgow Edition of the Works and Correspondence of Adam Smith*, vol. 5, ed. R. L. Meek, D. D. Raphael, P. G. Stein (Oxford: Clarendon Press, 1978), 76–78, 175–79. Adam Ferguson, *An Essay on the History of Civil Society*, ed. Duncan Forbes (1767; reprint, Edinburgh: Edinburgh University Press, 1966). John Millar, *The Origin of the Distinction of Ranks; or, An Inquiry into the Circumstances which Give Rise to Influence and Authority in the Different Members of Society*, 3rd ed. (London: John Murray, 1779). J. G. A. Pocock, "The Mobility of Property and the Rise of Eighteenth-Century Sociology," in *Theories of Property: Aristotle to the Present*, ed. Anthony Parel and Thomas Flanagan (Waterloo, Ontario: Wilfrid Laurier for the Calgary Institute for the Humanities, 1979), 141–66: "It may have been the injection into the debate [on commodities] of a concept of barbarism, that social or pre-social condition, in which there was neither ownership nor exchange—or so it was thought—which helped occasion the still imperfectly understood appearance in Western theory of the famous four-stages theory of human society."

27. Robert Wokler, "Anthropology and Conjectural History in the Enlightenment," in *Inventing Human Science: Eighteenth-Century Domains*, ed. Christopher Fox, Roy Porter, and Robert Wokler (Berkeley: University of California Press, 1995), 31–52. The century's most famous conjectural history was Rousseau's: Jean-Jacques Rousseau, *A Discourse on Inequality* (1755; reprint, Harmondsworth: Penguin, 1984), pp. 118–37; *Two Essays on the Origin of Language. Jean-Jacques Rousseau and Johann Gottfried Herder* (1781; reprint, trans. with afterwords by J. H. Morgan and Alexander Good, Chicago: University of Chicago Press, 1966), 1–74.

all else, on the question of subordination and servitude. In their pages, we may read the history of the world as a diminution of servitude. We were all servants once; civilization is a state of society in which many of us have risen from servitude.[28]

It is not clear how these formal historical statements about servitude as social condition related to more popular histories of the period, which told a national history through the servant's tale. "In the Infancy of our Constitution," said one legal guidebook of 1755,

> the Common People of England were little better than Slaves. But since the abolition of Vassalage . . . the Tyranny of Nobility is restrained; the Commonality are upon the same Footing as to Liberty and Property as the Gentry, and Servants of the Lower Class, being under the Protection of the Laws . . . have the same Remedy and Redress as their Masters.[29]

Forty years later, a quite conventional handbook for magistrates provided a routine history of service from before the Conquest as a preliminary to discussing the legislation concerning the regulation of servants then before Parliament.[30] The servant told us the story of "our ancient constitution" and of ourselves, of how we got to be the way we were. Servants were also the most illuminating means of studying the social and legal organization of society. "In the whole code of laws enacted for the benefit of preservation of social intercourse," said the author of another legal guide in 1831,

> there is not, perhaps, any branch that commands more popular interests, or that requires to be more generally known and appreciated, than that which regulates the connexion between Master and Servant,—one of the most important and universal relations of the ordinary affairs of life.[31]

There is much debate about John Locke's asking of similar questions in the 1680s and 1690s. Did he search for the actual historical origins of private property, rights, and the transferability of labor, or was the state of nature he described in *The Two Treatises of Government* (1690) a heuristic device, conjectural history amounting to no more than an explanation of how we got to be the way we are (or were, in the late seventeenth century)?[32] Locke de-

28. Millar, *Origin*, 297–362.

29. Preface to *The Laws Relating to Masters and Servants. With Brief Notes and Explanations to Render them Easy and Intelligible to the meanest Capacity. Necessary to be had in all Families* (London: Henry Lintot, 1755).

30. J. Huntingford, preface to *The Laws of Masters and Servants Considered; with observations on a Bill intended to be offered to Parliament* (London: printed for the author, 1792).

31. *A Familiar Summary of the Laws Respecting Masters and Servants, Apprentices, Journeymen, Artificers and Labourers* (London: Henry Washbourne, 1831), 1–15.

32. Pocock, "Mobility of Property," 154–55. James Tully, *A Discourse on Property: John Locke and His Adversaries* (Cambridge: Cambridge University Press, 1980), 21–25. W. M. Spellman, *John Locke* (Basingstoke and London: Macmillan, 1997), 111.

scribed how "every man has a property in his own person; this nobody has any right to but himself." The labor of his body, the work of his hands, were properly his, and he had property in them.[33] In the great abundant world that God made, people could mingle their labor with the fruits of the earth, behave like the Maker who made them, and those natural things that they mixed their labor with became theirs: their property.[34] A free person, of his own will and volition, "makes himself a servant to another by selling him, for a certain time, the service he undertakes to do in exchange for wages he is to receive." In that moment of hiring, the labor becomes the master's, not the laborer's. This moment of the transfer of labor is famously described: "the grass my horse has bit, *the turfs my servant has cut* . . . become my property. . . . The labour that was mine removing them out of that common state they were in, has fixed my property in them."[35]

At the beginning of the twenty-first century, we are right to be puzzled by the fact that this did not seem to be a problem for eighteenth-century workers (especially servants) and for their employers.[36] In the end we may have to accept what William Blackstone says so plainly and clearly: that in hiring on as a servant, in the moment of making a contract between master and servant, the problem of alienating your labor—of making things that will not belong to you when they are finished, because your labor has been leased to another—simply disappears.[37]

There is another of John Locke's assumptions that adds to the agenda for inquiry into eighteenth-century service. In all of John Locke's political writing, but particularly in *Two Treatises of Government,* man (we must add woman) is a maker, and his making makes him a person. People make things out of the material of the earth, which is provided by God; labor transforms the earthly provision into objects of use, and those who labor have a property in the product. And yet, quite conventionally, and in those everyday acts of hiring that Blackstone described, men and women acquired the labor of others: in hiring servants, men and women acquired the labor

33. Tully, *Discourse on Property,* 116–24.

34. Steinfeld, *Invention of Free Labour,* 78–81.

35. John Locke, *Two Treatises of Government,* bk. 2, chap. 5, sec. 26–28 (1690; reprint, Cambridge: Cambridge University Press, 1970), 288–89.

36. It has not been much of a dilemma for twentieth-century commentators either. But for a more troubled version of Locke's account of servants and the products of their labor, see Elizabeth Heckendorn Cook, *Epistolary Bodies: Gender and Genre in the Eighteenth-Century Republic of Letters* (Stanford: Stanford University Press, 1991), 162–63.

37. Blackstone, *Commentaries,* bk. 1, 425. See also James Barry Bird, *The Laws Respecting Masters and Servants, Articled Clerks, Apprentices, Manufacturers, Labourers, and Journeymen,* 3rd ed. (London, 1799), 5. For Bird, the foundation on which the great edifice of master and servant law—"all this doctrine"—lay could be found in Blackstone's account of "the property which every man has in his domestics, acquired by the contract of hiring, and purchased by giving them wages."

of social inferiors. The rent or lease of the servant's labor, the stacked turfs, the corn threshed (the dinner cooked? the sheets ironed? the room turned out and dusted?) became that of the master or mistress. Why, in the course of the long eighteenth century, did no one appear to find this a problem? One of the capacities that made possessive individuals in law and polity was exercised on a daily basis by those who were not persons at all, in the way "person" was coming to be defined.[38]

In discussing "The Rights of Persons" in 1755, William Blackstone called the relationship between master and servant the first of "the three great relations of private life" (the others were those pertaining between husband and wife, and between parent and child or guardian and ward).[39] When we have understood both what Blackstone meant and the dimensions of John Locke's unspoken questions, we will certainly know more than we do at present about eighteenth-century conceptualizations of society and social relations. What we can do at the moment is make the following points: that servants and service allowed the delineation of a history of civil society; that service was a component of the eighteenth century's modern labor relations, in which contract individualism only slowly replaced older forms. Service was also the legal form that governed the relationship between employers and one of the largest work groups in the population, between masters and mistresses and actual domestic (or menial) servants, whose labor (more commonly called "energies," or "service") had been purchased for a period of time.

The immense efforts of legal, political, and philosophical thinking devoted to the question of service in these years indicates great tension in this social relationship, a constant bid by the employing classes to regulate what was an ungovernable relationship. One measure of the tensions and impossibilities inherent in it was perhaps the way in which service and servitude were so often justified to servants: employers told servants why the world was the way it was, and why servants occupied their own particular place in it. This vindication of inequality and subordination is to be found in dozens of "Hints to Servants" and little tracts of "Friendly Advice to Servants." If their content and style informed the anonymous footman B. J.'s oration to a club-meeting of his fellow workers 1747, we do not yet know what ironies informed his—possibly parodic—use of them. B. J. advised his fellow servants that they were "undergoing the temporal

38. Macpherson's is the classic statement that in the seventeenth century, the whole employed labor force (including servants in husbandry, domestic servants, and day laborers) were not really persons in legal and political understanding. C. B. Macpherson, "Servants and Labourers in Seventeenth-Century England," in *Democratic Theory: Essays in Retrieval* (Oxford: Clarendon Press, 1973), 207–33.

39. Blackstone, *Commentaries*, bk. 1, 422.

Punishment inflicted upon them for Sin, and in the mean Time serving Others, as Servants. . . . any Person who has no inheritance in this lower World . . . are [sic] bound in duty to serve."[40]

The servant's subordination was part of the Great Story of the World, as we have seen in more formal and scholarly mode, in Smith and Ferguson and Millar. In the conventional complaints of the advice manuals the eighteenth-century Servant Problem was articulated. They kept breaking things; "it just came apart in my hands" was evidently a catchphrase by the 1780s.[41] They *would never shut the door,* but hung on the doorknob, saying, "But I am going out again immediately."[42] None of them would ever stay "beyond six months." Their presence in a household with children might serve as an object lesson in propriety and civility, in something of the way that animals allowed first lessons in empathy to be taught. The presence of servants showed children that there existed feeling and emotion in others—those of a different rank and who were also older than the child, and thus doubly outside its range of experience. But parents worried constantly about servants' involvement in child care and what they might *really* be teaching the children.[43]

40. B. J., *The Footman's Looking Glass: or, Proposals to the Livery Servants of London and Westminster etc., for bettering their Situations in Life, and securing their Credit in the World* (London: M. Cooper, 1747), 3–4. As B. J. used the rhetoric established by Jonathan Swift in his *Instructions to Servants* (1745) of complaining about them by issuing mock advice to servants in the voice of one of their fellow workers, the ironies of his *Proposals* are multilayered indeed. See Janet Thaddeus, "Swift's Directions to Servants," *Studies in Eighteenth-Century Culture* 16 (1986): 107–23. These instructions lasted a remarkably long time, and manual writers who used them sometimes mislaid the irony. For an apparently "straight" reproduction of them, see John Trusler, *Trusler's Domestic Management, or the Art of Conducting the Family, with Economy, Frugality and Method* (London: J. Souter, 1819), 69–70. See also Samuel Adams and Sarah Adams, *The Complete Servant; Being a Practical Guide to the Peculiar Duties and Business of all Descriptions of Servants* . . . (London: Knight and Lacey, 1825), 42–49, 227–32, who explain the instructions' "burlesque" and "sarcastic irony."

41. Sarah Trimmer, *The Servant's Friend: An Exemplary Tale, Designed to Enforce the Religious Instructions given at Sunday and other Charity Schools, by Pointing Out the Practical Implications of them, in a State of Servitude,* 2nd ed. (London: T. Longman, 1787), 66.

42. *Domestic Management, Or the Art of Conducting a Family; with Instructions to Servants in General Addressed to Young Housekeepers* (London: H. D. Symonds, 1800), 18. Late-eighteenth-century towns evidently rang with the cry of "Shut that door!" from drawing rooms after departing servants. See also Trusler, *Domestic Management,* 65, and Thaddeus, "Swift's Directions," 108–9.

43. Mitzi Myers has shown us the increased richness of representational possibilities as far as servants were concerned, and their massive and tense appearance in the genre of pedagogical texts written by and for Georgian mothers. Mitzi Myers, "Servants as They Are Now Educated," *Essays in Literature* 16, no. 1 (1989): 59–61. For their appearance in the writing of Mary Wollstonecraft, see Janet Todd and Marilyn Butler, eds., *The Collected Works of Mary Wollstonecraft,* 7 vols. (London: Pickering, 1989). Vol. 4 of the *Collected Works* contains Wollstonecraft's own *Original Stories from Real Life: with Conversations Calculated to Regulate the Affections and*

There were these ordinary, everyday complaints, and there was also the way in which the servant allowed histories to be written of the working-out of the great law of subordination, the ordering of ranks *in relation to each other* and the way in which social subjects were defined and delineated in that relationship. And so, in relation to the workforce neglected by social historians as unproductive, was consciousness of social inequality first articulated.

There was an anonymous correspondent to the *Times* in 1794 who may be our guide to this final, tentative question. His topic was the recent increase in servants' wages, much commented on in the press that October. He blamed the increase of "Luxury," the way in which every vendor of goods had increased prices, "which of course, falling on the consumer, labour consequently rises in value." He then went on to observe,

> If the master lives in dissipation or in luxury, it is not in nature to be expected, that the servant will be prudent and œconomical. Where the labourers in any great manufactory, perceive the principal owner . . . is enabled to live in a style of magnificence, *by the labour of their hands*, they then argue, "It is we who are the source from whence this happiness arises to one individual, that individual is well able to lessen his expenses and encrease our wages."[44]

He then moved on to discuss the vailing (or tipping) system, its demise, and the way in which "the encrease of [servants'] wages is easily accounted for. Formerly they were chiefly paid by guests that visited their master or mistress."[45] So he shied away from the connection between consciousness of social difference in workers in manufacture and in workers in domestic service. But though he could not make the connection, it should not stop the social historian. One day soon, we may be in a position to discuss domestic service as one of the sources of working-class consciousness, as well as of bourgeois personhood.

Form the Mind to Truth and Goodness (1788), which teaches empathy with servants; see especially p. 361. Vol. 2 of the *Works* contains her 1791 translation from the German of C. G. Salzman's *Elements of Morality for the Use of Children, with an Introductory Address to Parents*, one of her sources for the elaboration of this theme. Vol. 2 also contains her version of Maria Cambon's *Young Grandison: A Series of Letters from Young Persons to their Friends. Translated from the Dutch of Madame de Cambon. With Alterations and Improvements.* In *Young Grandison*, Emilia is able to demonstrate her civility through empathy with servants. She knows that "we ought not to give the meanest of our fellow creatures trouble when we can avoid it, if we desire to be truly great." *Works*, vol. 2, 220, 235, 237. For an example of the literature directed at children to teach them the same lessons, see Dorothy Kilner, *The Life and Perambulations of a Mouse*, 2 vols. (London: J. Marshall, n.d. [1784]), especially vol. 2, 19–27.

44. The *Times*, 24 October 1794. Emphasis in the original.

45. On vails, see Hill, *Servants*, 64–92. For a servant's (*possibly* a servant's) opinion of the vailing system, see Oliver Grey, *An Apology for the Servants: Occasioned by the Representation of the Farce called 'High Life Below Stairs' and what has been said to their Disadvantage in the Public Papers* (London: J. Newberg, 1760), 5.

Moving Accidents

The Emergence of Sentimental Probability

James Chandler

My subtitle, it will be recognized, echoes Ian Hacking's *The Emergence of Probability*, a book well known for its claim that probability achieved its distinctively modern mathematical form during the debates about casuistry among the Port-Royal Jansenists in 1662. It was just then, argued Hacking, that the statistical "case" was forged by the likes of Blaise Pascal in the fires of anti-Jesuit polemic and with it the modern sense of "opinion." I wish to intimate a certain parallel between Hacking's pivotal moment in seventeenth-century France and a conceptual-cultural transformation in Britain roughly a century later, one that we might call the creation of modern sentiment, the making of the sentimental case. While I would not seriously propose a date for the emergence of sentimental probability in Britain quite so wittily punctual as the "1662" of Hacking's account, I do have certain points of reference in view.[1]

One major reference point will be Laurence Sterne's *Sentimental Journey* (1768), a narrative that establishes or encodes many of the key features of the new probability. Behind Sterne, I will discuss what came to be called the "sentimental comedy" programmatically inaugurated earlier in the century by Richard Steele's *The Conscious Lovers* (1722). A reference point that better shows the parallel to Hacking's account, however, can be located in Smith's *Theory of Moral Sentiments* (1759), perhaps the most influential

1. Ian Hacking, *The Emergence of Probability* (Cambridge: Cambridge University Press, 1975). I would like to thank several colleagues for reading this essay in draft and offering such helpful criticism and suggestions: Homi Bhabha, Bill Brown, Sandra Macpherson, and Stuart Tave. I would also like to thank the members of the Romantic and Victorian Workshop at the University of Chicago for their responses when a version of this paper was discussed there.

account ever offered for what might be called the sentimental paradigm. Smith's analysis of moral life in a commercial society stresses a certain division within—or redoubling of—the persons who compose it. Smith outlines a form of subjectivity in which we are always at once potential spectators sympathetic with the positions of others *and* potential agents aware that we may or may not gain sympathy from those who observe what we do. The fundamental virtue to be refined or "polished" in commercial society, on this account, is a capacity for putting ourselves in the place or "case" of another.[2] This is a doctrine that we might associate with high poetic Romanticism in Britain, but it derives from Smith's account even when the Romantic version seems to occur in the context of antipathy to political economy and its basic principles.

Percy Shelley, for example, takes the sentimental frame of reference for granted when he turns against Wordsworth, a poet whose *Lyrical Ballads* he had greatly admired for having undertaken a "revolution in taste" against the poetry of Pope. It is a critique that implicitly orients Wordsworth's bold project within a larger modern transformation, one that installed imaginative sympathy at the center of moral life:

> He had as much imagination
>   As a pint-pot—he never could
> Fancy another situation
>   From which to dart his contemplation
> Than that wherein he stood. (lines 298–302)[3]

This normative ideal of imaginative sympathy belongs to a "cultural revolution" that took shape earlier in the period from 1750 to 1820 and that Shelley reaffirmed in a less ironized voice in "A Defence of Poetry": "The great secret of morals is love; or a going out of our own nature, and an identification with the beautiful which exists in thought, action or person, not our own. A man to be greatly good, must imagine intensely and comprehensively; he must put himself in the place of another and of many others."[4] This larger ideal was the guiding principle of Britain's new sentimentalism, a movement that reshaped probability because of the way in

2. This is, after all, the fundamental psychological necessity of commercial translations: two agents keen to strike a bargain must each, in order to serve his or her own interest, be able to imagine what it might be in the interest of the other to do or have done. For a helpful discussion of the commercial transformation of "virtue" in eighteenth-century Britain into a capacity for the sympathetic exchange of "interests," see J. G. A. Pocock, *Virtue, Commerce, and History* (Cambridge: Cambridge University Press, 1985), 113–15, and of course, Albert O. Hirschman, *The Passions and the Interests* (Princeton: Princeton University Press, 1976).

3. Percy Bysshe Shelley, *Poetry and Prose*, ed. Donald H. Reiman and Sharon Powers (New York: W. W. Norton, 1977), 334.

4. Shelley, *Poetry and Prose*, 487.

which it refocused the very question of what it means to "move" and be moved.

As we develop a more articulate account of the sentimental transformation in cultural norms and practices, we may be inclined to see that key aspects of Wordsworth's project, indeed of what we call Romanticism itself, are perhaps better understood in the context of a newly defined set of roles and rules for "sympathy" in human intercourse. It is true, as Stuart Tave has pointed out, that one can find references to the power and importance of "sympathy" in moral philosophy in the early eighteenth century (if not still earlier). And yet, as Tave himself goes on to insist, it was under the leadership of the Scottish enlightenment from the mid-century onward "that sympathy becomes an essential force in both ethical action and aesthetic creation."[5] Thus, even recent advocates of the originality of the Wordsworthian moral program, such as David Bromwich, tend to locate that originality in relation to the mode of sympathy outlined in the Scottish-enlightenment moral framework.[6] From Shelley's point of view, Wordsworth may have failed to achieve that mode, but what is crucial is that the sympathetic capacity remains for Shelley the measure of a poet's moral achievement.

Sentimental, it should be stressed, is a term with decidedly modern origins—indeed, a term famously associated with modernity itself by the likes of Friedrich von Schiller. Its currency was considered recent as late as 1812, when *Barclay's Dictionary* could make only a stab at definition:

> *Sentimental:* a word lately introduced into common use, but without any precise meaning. Those who use it appear to understand by it, that affecting turn of thought which is peculiar to works of fancy, or where there is a display of the pathetic, as in the graver scenes of comedy, or of novels.[7]

Barclay's is perhaps a bit behind hand in its account. This entry appeared almost two decades after Schiller's division of all poetry between the categories of the "naive" and the "sentimental" in 1795.[8] And William Cooke, looking back a quarter century from 1793 to the debut of Oliver Goldsmith's antisentimental play, *The Good Natur'd Man* (1768), already felt positioned to offer a retrospective comment: "Sentimental writing had then got possession of the stage, and nothing but morality and sententious writing lifted upon stilts, could meet the vitiated taste of the audience."[9]

---

5. Stuart M. Tave, *The Amiable Humorist* (Chicago: University of Chicago Press, 1960), 202–3.

6. David Bromwich, *Disowned by Memory: Wordsworth's Poetry of the 1790s* (Chicago: University of Chicago Press, 1999), 38–43.

7. *Barclay's Dictionary* (London: Bungay, Brightly, & Childs, 1812), 780.

8. Friedrich Schiller, *"Naïve and Sentimental Poetry" and "On the Sublime": Two Essays,* trans. Julius A. Elias (New York: F. Ungar Publishing Co., 1967).

9. Cited in *Collected Works of Oliver Goldsmith,* ed. Arthur Friedman (Oxford: Clarendon Press, 1966), 5: 5.

140   JAMES CHANDLER

Laurence Sterne's celebrated publication of that same year, *Sentimental Journey*—massively circulated, remarkably influential—marked a clear turning point in the history of the term. One German author assumed that the term *sentimental* in Sterne's title was so novel that it required an equally novel coinage in German: *Empfindsam*. In fact, the adjective *sentimental* is known to have had some currency at least since the late 1740s.[10]

The concepts of sentiment and sympathy evolved a complex mutuality over the course of the late eighteenth century. This is because the sentimental, though it emphasizes the moral sentence, typically assumes the shareable felt power of such utterances. Sympathy, by the same token, typically carries special moral overtones. But Tave's phrase about sympathy's new claim to fame in the late eighteenth century—that it becomes "an essential force" for the first time—targets the aspect of sentimentalism I wish to address here, the sense that the sentimental involves a new mode of probability. By "probability" in this context I mean codes of expectation and understandings of chance, design, and causality, especially those implicit in literary and dramatic works. True, these are terms sometimes associated with "genre" and genre theory, but what I have in view is more like a supergenre, a new institution or form of social life—not what we would now call a new sensibility so much as the development of the sensibility form itself. The sentimental movement of the late eighteenth century, concerned as it was with arrangements of sympathetic and spectatorial reciprocity, effectively developed fresh understandings of delicacy, nicety, and decorum. It reimagined "propriety"—in the construction of a story, in the aesthetic response, and indeed, in the higher-order "fit" between proprieties of story and response. If not a full-blown "revolution," "sentimental probability" certainly represented a moral and epistemological paradigm shift, one born of commercial and literary conditions specific to eighteenth-century British culture, but with an enormous and enduring impact.[11]

10. For the most detailed philological tracing of *sentimental* and its cousins, especially in relation to Sterne's impact, see Erik Erämetsä, *A Study of the Word 'Sentimental' and of Other Linguistic Characteristics of Eighteenth Century Sentimentalism in England* (Helsinki: Academia Scientiarum Fennica, 1951), 18–63. Also useful is the overview in R. F. Brissenden, *Virtue in Distress: Studies in the Novel of Sentiment from Richardson to Sade* (New York: Barnes & Noble, 1974), 11–55. A more recent overview is John Mullan, "Sentimental Novels," in *The Cambridge Companion to the Eighteenth-Century Novel*, ed. John Richetti (Cambridge: Cambridge University Press, 1996), 236–54. Janet Todd attends to the gendering of these developments in *Sensibility: An Introduction* (London: Methuen, 1986), as does G. J. Barker-Benfield in his encyclopedic *Culture of Sensibility: Sex and Society in Eighteenth-Century Britain* (Chicago: University of Chicago Press, 1992).

11. Though his focus is on what he calls "style" and on the redemption of the poetry of sensibility by a series of convincing readings that are at once "close" and "appreciative," Jerome McGann forcefully argues for the culturally revolutionary view of the sentimental movement in *The Poetics of Sensibility: A Revolution in Literary Style* (Oxford: Oxford University Press, 1996),

As if to punctuate the novelty of his moment and its methods, Smith closed his *Theory of Moral Sentiments* with a general critique of "casuistry" as a practice superannuated by the approach to ethical issues he associated with advanced commercial society, as outlined in the body of his argument. The problem with the "works of the casuists," says Smith in the final pages, is that they tried "to direct, by precise rules, what it belongs to feelings and sentiment only to judge of." On Smith's account, the effort to produce a rational and minute calibration of precept to situation must necessarily fail, and because it does fail the casuist also fails to achieve influence in the only ethical domain that matters, the one Smith calls "the heart." What ensures that the sentiments of any given heart are trustworthy is the process of open-hearted intercourse, unrestricted by such ecclesiastical institutions as auricular confession. Free commerce of sentiment allows for the dialectic of sympathy and spectatorship to do its salutary work, as "men" in society, eschewing the case of casuistry, exercise their imaginative and character-forming capacity to put themselves each in the case of the other.[12]

Such are the sentimental forms of causality and convention—the new case of the heart—that Smith brings to bear on questions about the affective psychology of commerce. The "cultural revolution" in the literary public sphere for which Smith was a primary theorist thus not only touches subsequent understandings of individual character, social cohesion, and political innovation but also the moral, social, and political practices that attend them. Much of the impact was effected by means of the so-called sentimental novel, a narrative subgenre that, thanks in some measure to Sterne, soon became the rage of Europe and America. In fact, one index to the hegemony of the sentimental in literary culture at this time can be seen in the way it held sway in the new but still British-dominated cultural centers of America after the Revolution. What is widely recognized as the first American novel, for instance, William Hill Brown's *The Power of Sympathy* (1789), is steeped in the British sentimental tradition as mediated by Goethe: Sterne's *Sentimental Journey* is approvingly discussed in an early chapter, and the protagonist dies with a copy of *The Sorrows of Young Werther* at his side.[13]

---

esp. 1–9. It will become clear as I proceed that my subject here is also allied to what Thomas Haskell twice calls "the revolutions in moral sensibility" in the century following 1750; see Haskell, "Capitalism and the Origins of Humanitarian Sensibility," parts 1 and 2, *American Historical Review* 90 (1985): 339–61 and 547–66. (The quotes appear on pp. 359 and 360.)

12. For an excellent account of the character-forming process in what she calls the British "sentimentalists," see Christine Korsgaard, *The Sources of Normativity* (Cambridge: Cambridge University Press, 1996), 55–60.

13. William Hill Brown, *The Power of Sympathy* (1789; reprint, New York: Penguin, 1996). This book is especially interesting in its deployment of the central constellation of terms. On

Call it the "power of sympathy" or a new "essential force"; the workings of this new element in the world of causes and effects, problems and explanations, merit careful analysis. How it developed, how it transformed social life and its representations, these are the problems I wish to pursue. I mean to analyze Sterne's seminal sentimental text of 1768 for a deeper sense of how the new probability structures a narrative mode. But I also mean to look at how probability in the sentimental novel bears on probability in eighteenth-century sentimental comic drama, especially in the line of Steele. Recognizing how literary narrative in the eighteenth century internalizes the conventions of the theater within the domain of a print public sphere, we will be able to see that probability has the structure it does in sentimental narrative at least partly because of a fusing of national mimesis and national mediation. I will be describing this development as a crossing of the mimetic and pragmatic axes of representation in the context of a national readership. In less schematic terms, I mean that probability arises as a problem when collective sentiment becomes the object of representation in both senses of *object*—when writers aspire to move national sympathies in the act of depicting them. The chances of success with national sentiment depend crucially, I argue, on the cross-cutting causes and effects that come into play when writers in what William Warner calls the eighteenth-century "media culture" engage in the commerce of feeling.[14]

I

The *Lyrical Ballads* volume itself can be of some help in turning the question of sentimentality toward the question of probability. The longest and arguably most ambitious of Wordsworth's contributions to the two-volume edition of 1800 was "Hart-leap Well," a poem later singled out by Hazlitt to epitomize what was best in Wordsworth's poetry. While I would not try to argue that the poem is meant to embody Schiller's point about the self-conscious reflexivity of the sentimental, it is true that "Hart-leap Well" is divided into two parts that tell the same story twice over, first in ancient ballad form and then in modern ballad form. The second part begins:

---

the one hand, it raises questions about what it would mean "to investigate the great springs by which we are actuated, or account for the operation of SYMPATHY" (p. 77). On the other, it seeks to counter a new fashion of the 1790s that takes "sentiment" to be "out of date," consistently aligning itself with "sentiment" against the risks of "sensibility" (p. 1), rather as Jane Austen will do in *Sense and Sensibility* two decades later. In Sterne's *Sentimental Journey*, the words *sentiment* and *sensibility* appear more interchangeably.

14. William B. Warner, "Formulated Fiction: Romancing the General Reader in Early Modern Britain," in *Cultural Institutions of the Novel*, ed. Deidre Lynch and William B. Warner (Durham, N.C.: Duke University Press, 1996), 302–5.

The moving accident is not my trade:
To freeze the blood I have no ready arts:
'Tis my delight, alone in summer shade,
To pipe a simple song to thinking hearts.[15]

The primary allusion in the first line is to *Othello,* and to the Moor's account of the adventurous tales with which he wooed and won Desdemona.[16] But the secondary echo in that allusion, perhaps less audible to us now than it would have been to Wordsworth's first readers, is to a prior invocation of the same Shakespearean passage in Sterne's *Sentimental Journey.*

This invocation appears in the sixteenth chapter-vignette, where Sterne's Parson Yorick offers thinly veiled satire on the travel literature of Tobias Smollett, whom he dubs the "learned Smelfungus."[17] Yorick has already produced his taxonomy of travelers, and he now identifies Smelfungus as a "splenetic traveler," one for whom even the most sublime objects encountered in a journey—the Pantheon or the Medici Venus—are "discoloured and distorted" (p. 29). Smelfungus's narrative is no more than "the account of his miserable feelings":

> I popp'd upon Smelfungus again at Turin, in his return home; and a sad tale of sorrowful adventures had he to tell, "wherein he spoke of moving accidents by flood and field, and of the cannibals which each other eat: the Anthropophagi"—he had been flea'd alive, and bedevil'd, and used worse than St. Bartholomew, at every stage he had come at— . . . (p. 29)[18]

As with Wordsworth's invocation of Othello's phrase in 1800, Sterne contrasts the tale of "moving accidents" with one that is primarily identified with thinking hearts. And Sterne's point, like Wordsworth's, is that if your heart is quick, you can find ample gratification in ordinary things.

Yorick introduces the satire on Smelfungus as part of a comic justification for his Shandean nonprogress. Indeed, at this relatively advanced point in

15. William Wordsworth, *Lyrical Ballads and Other Poems, 1797–1800,* ed. James Butler and Karen Green (Ithaca, N.Y.: Cornell University Press, 1992), lines 97–100. Subsequent references to poems in this edition will be by line number and included in the text.

16. Othello famously explains this phase of his courtship in the lines he addresses under interrogation by Desdemona's father, Brabantio: "Wherein I spoke of most disastrous chances, / Of moving accidents by flood and field" (act 1, scene 3, lines 134–35).

17. Laurence Sterne, *A Sentimental Journey through France and Italy by Mr Yorick,* ed. Ian Jack (Oxford: Oxford University Press, 1968), 28. Subsequent references are cited by page number in the text.

18. Shaftesbury, who figures in this discussion below, cites this passage in the context of debates about the improbabilities of travel narratives and the corruption of a gendered national readership. See my reply to Lorraine Daston in *Questions of Evidence: Proof, Practice, and Persuasion across the Disciplines,* ed. James Chandler, Arnold I. Davidson, and Harry Harootunian (Chicago: University of Chicago Press, 1994), 275–81.

what is supposed to be an account of his progress across the Continent, Yorick has not only failed to get himself out of Calais—he has barely gotten himself arrived there:

> Lord! said I, hearing the town clock strike four, and recollecting that I had been little more than a single hour in Calais—
> —What a large volume of adventures may be grasped within this little span of life by him who interests his heart in every thing, and who, having eyes to see, what time and chance are perpetually holding out to him as he journeyeth on his way, misses nothing he can *fairly* lay his hands on.— (p. 28)

For Wordsworth as for Sterne, the heart that interests itself in every thing is the one that is able to dilate the everyday affairs of life by means of a sympathetic imagination. It has no need of sublimities or catastrophes to make it "leap" to seize passing opportunity. Such a heart amplifies the sense of adventure in a given moment without requiring that one venture anywhere or anything in particular. Emotional amplification is a sentimental topos that bespeaks a mode of affective proliferation parallel to the economic effects of the commercial division of labor.[19]

It says something about how the sentimental movement was understood in 1821 that a writer in the new *London Magazine* produced the following observations in an article entitled "A Sentimental Journey, from Islington to Waterloo Bridge in March, 1821":

> A traveller, said I, should have all his wits about him, and so will I. He should let nothing escape him, no more will I—he should extract reflections out of a cabbage stump, like sun-beams squeezed out of cucumbers; so will I, if I can—and he should converse with every and any one, even a fish-woman. . . . Who knows but I may make a sentimental journey, as good as Sterne's but at any rate I can write it and send it to the *London Magazine*.[20]

In offering a kind of wisdom that we might call characteristically Romantic ("the meanest flower that blows . . . ," "the universe in a grain of sand"), the author of this 1821 piece, with a nod to Swift's cabbages and cucumbers, makes use of the titular phrase to frame such postures within a Sternean genealogy. And, in such a conception of things, the nature of narrative will not always be a matter of self-evidence.

Wordsworth, writing between these two Sentimental Journeys, tags one of the *Lyrical Ballads*, "Simon Lee" (later classified by Wordsworth under "Poems

19. For a good discussion of how the theory of the division of labor ramified in British writings of the period, see John Barrell, *The Birth of Pandora and the Division of Knowledge* (London: Macmillan, 1992).

20. *The London Magazine* (London: London, Cradock, and Joy, 1821), 509. The reference to sunbeams squeezed from cucumbers derives from book three of *Gulliver's Travels*, the voyage to Laputa, but the Augustan source underscores the sentimental redeployment of the topos, as explained below.

of Sentiment and Reflection"), with a caveat about narrative expectations. The narrator points out that, while the poem "is no tale," it can become one in the reader's imagination: "should you think / Perhaps a tale you'll make it" (lines 79–80). The full elaboration of this point comes in a stanza well known to readers familiar with Wordsworth's poetical experiments:

> O reader! had you in your mind
> Such stores as silent thought can bring,
> O gentle reader! you would find
> A tale in every thing. (lines 73–76)

Similarly, but on a grander scale, Wordsworth's life's project, the multipart poem he called *The Recluse*, reduces the progress of an epic narrative to "a simple produce of the common day."[21] Such productivity in the quotidian—finding tales in things—is thoroughly anticipated in Sterne's *Journey*, where the whole question of narrative *progress*, as in *Tristram Shandy* before it, had become a seriously (and comically) vexed affair. In the first fifteen chapter-vignettes of *Sentimental Journey*, almost nothing outward takes place. Several of these chapter-vignettes, for example, are given over to a narrative of what ensues when Yorick and a Mme. de L***, a lady he has just met, are left holding hands in front of the closed door of the carriage yard, when the landlord is unable to open its lock and abruptly abandons them there. In addition, as if to emblematize the narrative's stubborn refusal to move forward, Yorick narrates two ensuing experiences in *stationary* carriages, once by himself in a carriage-for-one, or *desobligeant* (in which we are to imagine him writing the "Preface"), and once in a two-person coach with that same lady of his new acquaintance. In such instances, as we shall see, internal motion is generated by external immobilization.

Sterne's "travel" in his immobile coach prepares the way for Wordsworth's travel on his immobile couch—his "wandering lonely as a cloud" while "on [his] couch [he] lie[s]," in the famous lyric about the daffodils.[22] In both cases, "sentimental journey" becomes something more (or less) than a journey to affecting places, though that is how Sterne's famous phrase often signifies for us nowadays. Rather, it becomes travel in and by sentiment. This is why the narrator of the 1821 "Sentimental Journey" can suggest that, while he may or may not make a sentimental journey as good as Sterne's, he "at any rate . . . can write it, and send it to the *London Magazine*" (p. 509). This is also why this narrator can launch his narrative in the very next sentence, with the studiedly ambiguous opening: "I had hardly

21. William Wordsworth, *Home at Grasmere*, ed. Beth Darlington (Ithaca, N.Y.: Cornell University Press, 1977), 102.

22. William Wordsworth, *Poems in Two Volumes, and Other Poems*, ed. Jared Curtis (Ithaca, N.Y.: Cornell University Press, 1983).

left the threshold of my door, ere I met, as I thought, with an adventure."
And let it be noted that such narratives reproduce the structures of sentimentality even when they pretend to be contesting sentimental attitudes:
"These reflections [it is later explained], and the incidents which gave rise
to them, I resolved to treasure up, for they would perhaps have their use in
some part of my journey. They will warn me against being too sentimental,
said I" (pp. 509–10). If such a pattern (resistance in participation) is more
like a rule than an exception for sentimental writings, it is worth recalling
that what Schiller described as the modernizing reflexivity of the sentimental mode tends precisely to foster proleptic gestures acknowledging or deny-
ing the sentimentality of the sentimental performance itself.

My point, however, is that with all three writers—Sterne, Wordsworth, and
the contributor to the *London Magazine*—the issue of *narrative* movement
(how the story goes from point A to point B) is closely related to that of *affective* movement (what a reader spectator might be expected to feel about the
story). Indeed, so closely are these two kinds of movement related that at
times they seem to merge or change roles. Thus, one of Wordsworth's most
famous formulations of his innovative understanding of narrative is a claim
he makes for his poetic experiments in the 1800 preface to *Lyrical Ballads:*
"the feeling therein developed gives importance to the action and situation,
and not the action and situation to the feeling."[23] The reason why this relation of a story's motion and emotion is so complicated in Wordsworth, and
why it is hard to identify the *site* wherein "the feeling" is "developed," is that
his poetic is so thoroughly associationist in its principles. It means to show,
he says, "the manner in which our feelings and ideas are associated in a state
of excitement" as a way of helping to exemplify a sympathetic response "without the application of gross and violent stimulants"[24]—without, that is, "moving accidents." Such a remark suggests that the "accidents" of these poetic
stories were *without* location, at large in a medium of associative affect and
affective communication (even when they insist on a compensatory
specificity: "There is a thorn . . ."). The displacement of action into medium
or mediation is a problem to which I will return shortly.

Rhetorically considered, this shift of emphasis in Wordsworth's poetry
involves the extended sense of the trope known as "hypallage," the trope of
"exchange." In Greek poetics it referred to the practice of switching
modifiers, but was later broadened to suggest causal inversion. It is defined
in the OED, for example, as "an interchange of two elements of a proposition, the natural relations of these being reversed." It becomes the trope of
preposterousness, of explanatory ambiguity, and one apposite to a period

23. Preface to *Lyrical Ballads* (1800), in *Prose Works of William Wordsworth*, ed. W. J. B. Owen
and J. W. Smyser, vol. 1 (Oxford: Clarendon Press, 1974), 128.
24. Ibid. 126, 128.

that produced Hume's associationist critique of causal assumptions. We see a good example of such a reversal when, in a poem such as "The Thorn," we understand that the narrative gives us a map to the Old Sea Captain's affective psychology. Does the thorn tree appear so threatening to him because it is the place where something terrible has happened, or does he imagine that something terrible has happened there because it looks so terrible to him? Sterne himself used the term, as Jonathan Lamb has astutely shown, and already in an avowedly associationist context.[25] Though the question of the hypallage has resonance throughout *Sentimental Journey,* the most explicit formulation of its relevance to Sterne's practice is to be found late in *Tristram Shandy:*

> As my father told my uncle Toby upon the close of a long discussion—"You can scarce," said he, "combine two ideas together upon it, brother Toby, without an hypallage"— "What's that? cried my uncle Toby.
> The cart before the horse, replied my father—
> —And what has he to do there? cried my uncle—
> Nothing, quoth my father, but get in—or let it alone.
> Now widow Wadman, as I told you before, would do neither the one or the other.
> She stood however ready harnessed and caparisoned at all points to watch accidents.[26]

Lamb suggests that Walter actually produces an example of hypallage for Uncle Toby with his observation (apropos Toby's regard for the Widow Wadman) that love is "not so much a SENTIMENT as a SITUATION" (p. 589).[27] This formula, interestingly, closely echoes the terms of Wordsworth's claim to novelty in the preface to *Lyrical Ballads.*

The point is not that Walter's proverb could stand as the moral to Wordsworth's poems. Rather, it is that the grammatical opposition that structures it also structures them. Clearly, such distinctions as feeling/action, or sentiment/situation, were already undergoing a major transformation some decades before Wordsworth came forward with his claim to a bold new cultural initiative. This transformation, as I'll show, is to be explained partly in terms of the divided subject of commercial society—the notion that a subject could be defined by its capacity to be in two places, or operate in two modes, at the same time.[28] The commercial subject, subject

25. Jonathan Lamb, *Sterne's Fiction and the Double Principle* (Cambridge: Cambridge University Press, 1989), 76–79.
26. Laurence Sterne, *The Life and Opinions of Tristram Shandy, Gentleman* (New York: The Odyssey Press, 1940), 552.
27. See Lamb, *Double Principle,* 77.
28. In a trial run for his own famous theory of imaginative sympathy, which so influenced Keats, the young William Hazlitt would argue that this sense of being in two places at the same

to mediation by the print-cultural theatricality of the sentimental public sphere, came to be understood as decidedly constituted in this dual modality. This is the crux of the new "case of sentimentality."

II

Since Sterne's *Sentimental Journey* had such major impact not only on novel writing but also on magazine culture for more than a half century after its publication, it is worth looking more closely to see how the issues of sentiment and situation—"movement" and "accident"—achieve such richness of implication in its pages. In fact, we need look no further than those opening chapter-vignettes that tell of Yorick's "hour" in Calais, which focus primarily on Yorick's choice of a "vehicle" for his "sentimental journey," on his negotiation of various financial rituals, such as alms-giving and bargaining, and on his flirtation with Mme. de L***. Although all of Yorick's affairs during his long hour in Calais seem to center on an inscrutable character not accidentally named "M. Dessein," (the "master of the hotel"), almost every event in the sequence seems to occur by happenstance. We are left to ponder the question of what it means for Yorick to "put [himself] into motion" (p. 28).

An early sequence of vignettes—"The Monk: Calais," and "The Desobligeant: Calais"—relates how he begins his career in France by rudely refusing alms to a monk on his way to looking into the purchase of a vehicle for his voyage. His treatment of the monk in a sense becomes the vehicle he seeks, as he launches a reflection on his own motives and on the cultural translatability of charity. But then, in the coach yard, the vehicle seems to become literal again when he finds and mounts a one-passenger carriage (a "desobligeant"). While waiting for Monsieur Dessein to return from vespers, Yorick writes the "Preface: In the Desobligeant," which, though a preface, appears well into the narrative sequence. In the ensuing vignette, entitled simply "Calais," as though beginning the journey anew, Yorick describes his initial encounter with "Monsieur *Dessein*" and his subsequent negotiations with him over the sale of the desobligeant. Yorick is badly outmaneuvered in the encounter, and after Dessein's successful thwarting of Yorick's best ploy, Yorick has to concede: "The dose was made up exactly after my own prescription; so I could not help taking it—and returning Mons. Dessein his bow, without more casuistry we walk'd together towards his Remise [or, coach house], to take a view of his magazine of chaises." But as

---

time was tantamount to a person's being at two times in the same place. See his *Essay on the Principles of Human Action*, vol. 1 of *Collected Works*, ed. P. P. Howe (London and Toronto: J. M. Dent & Sons, 1931).

the defensive ratiocination of the casuistry ceases, Yorick's heart becomes active, and more than ever we become aware that we are being carried along by a new kind of narrative vehicle, one in which all this stopping and starting and starting over counts as movement.[29] Subsequent vignettes in the comically extended Calais episode—from this moment through to Yorick's consummation of a deal for a carriage and his realization that he has been in Calais for just over an hour—amount to a tour de force of sentimental narrative, in which Sterne treats the key issues of movement and accident with dizzyingly self-conscious playfulness.

A good sample of this kind of writing appears in the opening paragraphs of the next chapter-vignette, "In the Street: Calais," where we open with Yorick's reflection on his feelings:

> It must needs be a hostile kind of a world, when the buyer (if it be but of a sorry post-chaise) cannot go further with the seller thereof into the street to terminate the difference betwixt them, but he instantly falls into the same frame of mind and views his conventionist with the same sort of eye, as if he was going along with them to Hyde-park corner to fight a duel. For my own part, being but a poor sword's man, and no way a match for Monsieur *Dessein*, I felt the rotation of all the movements within me, to which the situation is incident—I looked at Monsieur *Dessein* through and through—ey'd him as he walked along in profile—then, *en face*—he look'd like a Jew—then a Turk— disliked his wig—cursed him by my gods—wished him at the devil—
>
> —And is all this to be lighted up in the heart for a beggarly account of three or four louis d'ors, which is the most I be over-reach'd in? Base passion, said I, turning myself about, as a man naturally does upon a sudden reverse of sentiment—base, ungentle passion! thy hand is against every man, and every man's hand against thee—heaven forbid! said she, raising her hand up to her forehead, for I had turned full in front upon the lady whom I had seen in conference with the monk—she had followed us unperceived—heaven forbid indeed! said I offering her my own—she had a black pair of silk gloves open only at the thumb and two fore-fingers, so accepted it without reserve—and I led her up to the door of the Remise. (p. 15)

The peripety, or reversal, here occurs in a passage from "base passion" to something gentler, something more polished, in which the commercial proliferation of possibilities and positions becomes a key to the process. The movement of this passage leads Yorick from commercial conflict, back through the sentiments of a precommercial mode of conflict resolution (the duel), and around again to the commercial reckoning of the worth of

---

29. In a chapter on *Sentimental Journey* in his book *Laurence Sterne and the Argument about Design* (Totowa, N.J.: Barnes & Noble, 1982), Mark Loveridge includes some interesting remarks about Sterne and Shaftesbury but, strangely, nothing about M. Dessein and his role in the text. Cf. Hacking's chapter "Design" in *Emergence of Probability*, 166–75.

the anger thus kindled as against its costs and its risks. From the deal, to the duel, and back, Yorick "moves" in a full rotation. Yorick is enabled to feel *all* the "movements" to which the situation is incident. We are left unclear as to whether the emotion registered here is to be understood as located in the *rotation* of these movements or in the various *feelings* through which he moves.[30] Moreover, having illustrated the sentiments to which the situation is incident, the narrative proceeds by creating the situation to which the sentiments are incident. Not only does Yorick's rotation in space mimic his last "sudden reverse of sentiment," but his exclamation about passion's hand and every man's hand being against each other is answered in a clasp of hands between himself and Mme. de L***, upon whom he had unwittingly turned "full in front."

What's crucial to see here is how the narrative's complication of the question of what counts as "moving" goes hand in hand with a complication of the question of what counts as an accident, or indeed as an "event"—a complication not only in the sense of a confusion about actions "inside" and "outside" the represented characters, but more radically, in the sense of a "hypallage" about what is motivating what. With what kind of "coincidence" are we faced in the moment when, performing his sudden softening reverse of sentiment as a physical turn, accompanied by a remark about a hand, Yorick turns flat into the hand of the woman for whom he has a soft spot in his heart?[31] Is this a case of a situation bringing about a sentiment, or a sentiment bringing about a situation? How does causality run in this sequence, and what might "probability" mean for it?

Thus begun, Yorick's narrative game is extended with remarkable inventiveness by means of yet another of what might be called the book's "literal figures." Monsieur Dessein discovers that he has come with the wrong key to the door of the remise, leaving Yorick and the lady comically still facing the door and still holding hands while he goes off to find the right one. "Movement" is thus suspended in the face of a blank space blocking the way to a passage yet to be unlocked by a "master" character named "Design." (It is not until the beginning of the sixth chapter to follow this one that we are informed: "Mons. Dessein came up with the key of the Remise in his hand, and forthwith let us into his magazine of chaises.") The obvious point, again, is that we are allowed to witness how much can happen in a moment of suspended action, but what is less obvious is how we are to understand its intentionality.

30. For an account of some related issues of what might be called "moral mechanics" in *Tristram Shandy,* see Sigurd Burckhardt, "*Tristram Shandy*'s Law of Gravity," *ELH* 28 (1961): 70–88.

31. The kind of confusion inscribed here is well known to beginning students of literature when they first pass from talking about characters and their motives to talking about authors and *their* motives.

During the five-chapter suspension of outward narrative progress, the topic of "dessein" intrudes itself in at least two ways. The first is by way of "drawing," as we learn in Yorick's immediately ensuing flashback to his initial view of the lady, just moments prior, as he explains that though he initially "had not yet seen her face" this was "not material," "for the drawing was instantly set about, and long before we had got to the door of the Remise, *Fancy* had finished the whole head."[32] So the "dessein" of the woman's head, completed in the company of Monsieur Dessein, is also completed before it is seen. Does "dessein" inhere in incidents or only create an illusion of projected intelligibility after the fact? Does it come from within or without? A similar kind of question brings a second sense of *dessein* into play. As soon as Monsieur Dessein departs, Yorick reflects on his and the lady's extraordinary situation:

> Now a colloquy of five minutes, in such a situation, is worth one of as many ages, with your faces turned towards the street: in the latter case, 'tis drawn from the objects and occurrences without—when your eyes are fixed upon a dead blank—you draw purely from yourselves. A silence of a single moment upon Monsieur *Dessein's* leaving us, had been fatal to the situation—she had infallibly turned about—so I began the conversation instantly. (p. 16)[33]

Thus, the second chapter to follow this one (the one after the flashback on the drawing of Madame's face) opens with Yorick's attempt to break the ice without losing his grip on the situation:

> This certainly, fair lady! said I, raising her hand up a little lightly as I began, must be one of Fortune's whimsical doings: to take two utter strangers by their hands—of different sexes, and perhaps from different corners of the globe, and in one moment place them together in such a cordial situation, as Friendship herself could scarce have atchieved for them, had she projected it for a month. (p. 18)

Mme. de L***'s rejoinder—that Yorick's reflection on Fortune's doings reveals his embarrassment—establishes a contrapuntal movement in which fortune and propriety vie for the position of ruling principle in the narrative. A few minutes later, when, once finally inside the remise, Monsieur Dessein shuts them together in a chaise and leaves again, Yorick as narrator reports the "reflection that this was the second time we had been left together by a parcel of nonsensical contingencies" (p. 26). And again his fatalism is parried. The puzzle, then, is how we take this playful treatment of

---

32. See Lamb's perceptive discussion of this kind of moment in *Double Principle*, 29–30.
33. A further bilingual pun can be found here in the notion of things "drawn" or taken from a source.

accident and "design" in the context of a narrative where "movement" seems repeatedly displaced from outside to inside and back again.

Throughout the novel, such issues are correlated with what Lamb, following Jina Politi, identifies as the trope of *syllepsis* in Sterne: the condition of textual uncertainty as between the literal and figurative levels.[34] The sylleptic troping is nowhere more insistent than in Sterne's treatment of the main "object" of the opening chapters, the search for a "vehicle." Insofar as we take Sterne's narrative to be an account of *literal* travel across the Continent—however *fictionalized* it might be—to that same extent we may take literally the references to vehicles of various sorts: *desobligeant, vis à vis,* and *chaise.* Historically, however, the sense of "vehicle" as a carrier or medium actually predates its more specific reference to wheeled instruments of transportation. It thus becomes very difficult not to read certain references to the vehicle as a metaphor for a means of travel that is, precisely, "sentimental"—in other words, as the "movement" of or through sentiment itself. It is not that the travel of a "sentimental journey" is merely "figurative"; it is that the distinction between the literal and the figurative is impossible to maintain with confidence. All this becomes nearly a matter of explicitness when, in the taxonomy of various kinds of travels in "Preface: In the Desobligeant," Yorick worries that, as a sentimental traveler, he may have no "better grounds" for "draw[ing] attention" to himself "than the mere *Novelty of my Vehicle*" (p. 11). In one sense, Yorick's vehicle at this point is the stationary desobligeant, but in another it is the literary medium—call it the popular sentimental novel—in which design and accident, internal and external movement, the literal and the figurative, are joined under a given conceit.

III

I have been arguing for what might be called the "syllepsis of the vehicle" in early sentimental writing—the way in which the figural dimension of the medium is made literal in the work and play of language on the printed page. This is in fact a trope self-consciously developed under the heading of "The Vehicle" in the feature narrative series for the initial number of *The Sentimental Magazine,* launched five years after Sterne's novel, in 1773, and which bears the markedly Sternean title "A Sentimental Journey Through Life."[35] The trope is later reworked by more considerable admirers of Sterne such as Sir Walter Scott. In the novel that gave its name to the Waverley series, Scott introduced his tale of 1745 and the end of antique manners in

34. Jina Politi, *The Novel and Its Presuppositions* (Amsterdam: A. M. Hakkert, 1976), 144.
35. *The Sentimental Magazine* 1 (March, 1773): 6.

Scotland with an apology for having provided so much explanatory background for the story:

> The truth is, I cannot promise . . . that this story shall be intelligible, not to say probable, without it. My plan requires that I should explain the motives on which its action proceeded; and these motives necessarily arose from the feelings, prejudices, and parties of the times. I do not invite my fair readers, whose sex and impatience give them the greatest right to complain of these circumstances, into a flying chariot drawn by hyppogriffs, or moved by enchantment. Mine is a humble English post-chaise, drawn upon four wheels, and keeping his majesty's highway. Those who dislike the vehicle may leave it at the next halt, and wait for the conveyance of Prince Hussein's tapestry, or Malek the Weaver's flying sentry-box.[36]

Each vehicular medium is associated with a mode of probability, a style of world-making. Broadly speaking there are two kinds of vehicles in Scott and two modes of probability. For shorthand we can call them romantic and novelistic, and they are associated with different stages of society (the precommercial and the commercial). And just as England's commercial order, epitomized in the movement of people and information by means of the post system, evolved its own set of motives and their interpretation (as Smith explained them in *The Theory of Moral Sentiments*), so the novel of this period offers a new realism defined in these same motivational terms. Scott spells out the point in *Ivanhoe*, his next extended attempt to explain his practice as a novelist, when he writes that just as Galland had had to render the "wildness of Eastern fiction" in a probabilistic mode that would render it "interesting and intelligible" to the "feelings and habits of the Western reader," so he, too, had to perform a similar act of vehicular translation with his medieval materials in *Ivanhoe*: "I have so far explained the ancient manners in modern language, and so far detailed the characters and sentiments of my persons," that the modern reader will remain engaged.[37]

Scott's vehicle, the widely circulating printed novel, depended on the very means of transportation by which it is metaphorized, the humble

36. Sir Walter Scott, *Waverley*, ed. Andrew Hook (Harmondsworth: Penguin, 1972), 63. On issues of gender and probability in this period, see n. 18, above.

37. Sir Walter Scott, *Ivanhoe*, ed. Clair Lamont (Edinburgh: Edinburgh University Press, 1998). There are other variations on this theme. Wordsworth's sylleptic representation of walking and writing as conflated activities, so deftly analyzed by Celeste Langan, might be rethought in terms of Wordsworth's implicit claim to be working without a vehicle, without a medium—to be working out, that is, what Geoffrey Hartman long ago called "the unmediated vision." See Langan, *Romantic Vagrancy: Wordsworth and the Simulation of Freedom* (Cambridge: Cambridge University Press, 1995), esp. 161–75, and Geoffrey Hartman, *The Unmediated Vision: An Interpretation of Wordsworth, Hopkins, Rilke, and Valéry* (New Haven: Yale University Press, 1954).

English post-chaise. The metaphor suggests that, like the post-chaise itself, the novel stays close to the ground, makes no explanatory leaps. You have the sense that you understand how you are getting to where you are going, or at least how you got there after the fact. The motion, the progress, of the narrative is explicable; it can be made "intelligible." This intelligibility of motion in the English novelistic vehicle might perhaps itself be explained by way of Barbara Shapiro's account of how the new mathematical form of probability affected English literary theory and practice, how it helped to forge a new literary norm defined by enhanced precision.[38]

In his discussion of "sentimental communion and probable inference" in the fiction of Mackenzie and Sterne, Douglas Lane Patey discriminates between two kinds of probability in the eighteenth-century novel, two kinds of "conditions of knowing." The first kind is what Patey ascribes to the didactic manner of *Joseph Andrews* and *Tom Jones*, where the point is to teach probable judgment and to rectify expectation. This is the sort of probability that governs the relation of external signs to their causes and possible effects, and it informs the work of prudential judgment. "Judgment of [this] sort . . . is what Fielding's victimized innocents—Adams, Joseph, and Fanny—must learn in order to survive in a world full of Roasting Squires and partial Justices; it is also what in *Tom Jones* Fielding warns us he expects of his reader."[39] This first kind of probability belongs to the practice of prudential calculation. The second kind of probability is explicitly associated by Patey with "the sentimental novel as it is practiced in England in the last third of the eighteenth century." On this account, the sentimental novel tends to associate the first kind of prudential calculation, the kind taught in the fiction of Fielding, with villainy rather than virtue: the facility in "calculating probabilities" of this sort is just the sort of thing "that the sentimental hero typically eschews." Thus, in Mackenzie's *Man of Feeling* (1771), a novel written very much in the wake of the Sterne craze, the titular hero Mr. Harley can declare: "To calculate the chances of deception is too tedious a business for the life of man."[40] In lieu of prudential calculation, the sentimental novel as Patey sees it "celebrates the spiritual and social advantages of a quasi-intuitive communion with the thoughts and feelings of others." This is what we have been calling "sympathy," which Patey distinguishes from

38. Barbara J. Shapiro, *Probability and Certainty in Seventeenth-Century England: A Study of the Relationships between Natural Science, Religion, History, Law, and Literature* (Princeton: Princeton University Press, 1983), 228–32.

39. Douglas Lane Patey, *Probability and Literary Form: Philosophic Theory and Literary Practice in the Augustan Age* (Cambridge: Cambridge University Press, 1984), 222.

40. Henry Mackenzie, *The Man of Feeling* (1771; reprint, London: Oxford University Press, 1967), 53. Among the many genealogies for the "man of feeling," one must not forget the traditions of Christian folly. But see R. S. Crane, "Suggestions Towards a Genealogy of the 'Man of Feeling,'" *ELH* 1 (1934): 205–30.

"judgment" in a way that suggests something of the early Victorian problematic of sympathy and judgment in the dramatic monologue. The sentimental novel of "anti-prudence and anti-probability" thus provides a testing ground for a new probabilistic mode, one based in a special intuitive facility in reading "probable signs," especially those signs that betray the subjective state—or, we might better say, the "case"—of another person."[41]

Having supplemented Shapiro's thesis with Patey's notion of a specifically sentimental form of probability, one associated with the sympathy of the face-to-face encounter, we nonetheless run afoul of a second key point made by Shapiro. Her further claim is that the new mathematical probability in England not only enhanced precision but also drastically reduced ambiguity of reference.[42] Sterne's sentimental probability, as we have begun to analyze it, would seem to depend on a comparatively high degree of ambiguity. If the sentimental novel did indeed offer a new mode of probabilistic intelligibility—a kind of transparency that trades in the mutual legibility of persons—then whence all the "opacity," all the destabilizing verbal play, that seems to be so characteristic of the sentimental novel as practiced by Sterne?

I believe that the key to this problem can unlock other matters as well, and I suggest that the best way to begin with it is to identify the paradox of sentimental fiction, whereby the dynamics of the face-to-face encounter come to govern a cultural form (the novel) that is defined by action at a distance in Britain's literary public sphere. The problem gains resonance in relation to the ongoing debate about the question of, in Thomas Haskell's phrase, "Capitalism and the Origins of the Humanitarian Sensibility." For this debate centers not only on a "revolution in moral sensibility" in just these decades of English culture, but also, at least for Haskell himself, on "the power of market discipline to inculcate altered perceptions of causation in human affairs" and "new habits of causal attribution that set the stage for humanitarianism."[43] And what Haskell means by "altered percep-

41. In a passage from *Sentimental Journey* noted by Patey, Sterne famously describes a kind of "short hand," which, though produced in a printed text, seeks to go beyond words of any kind to a more natural form of the exchange of human expression. It is a point that might remind us of Smith on the importance of "open-hearted commerce" as the key to a well-formed moral sensibility:

> There is not a secret so aiding to the progress of sociality, as to get master of this *short hand,* and be quick in rendering the several turns of looks and limbs, with all their inflections and delineations, into plain words. For my own part, by long habitude, I do it so mechanically, that when I walk the streets of London, I go translating all the way; and have more then once stood behind in the circle, where not three words have been said, and have brought off twenty different dialogues with me, which I could have fairly wrote down and sworn to. (p. 57)

42. Shapiro, *Probability and Certainty,* 256–57.

43. Haskell, "Origins," part 2, 548.

tions of causation" and "new habits of causal attribution" has to do precisely with the capacity of the new market society to establish a sense of action at a distance. With the new promise-keeping "form of life" of the eighteenth-century market came "the teaching of the virtues of reflection and close attention to the distant consequences of their actions."[44] The question we have posed about the sentimental novel can help to address the literary implementation of this new form of life.[45] And success in that exploration will eventually depend on twinned, or at least entwined, recognitions.

The first is that the novel gradually took the place of theater as the dominant popular genre in Britain in the course of the eighteenth century, and the second is that the novel gradually began to assimilate certain theatrical features and functions into itself. Thus David Marshall has studied the "figure of theater" in this period as "a cultural paradigm for eighteenth-century English culture" more generally. He is interested in the "theater that lies outside the playhouse."[46] Marshall is particularly concerned with the "novel" as a genre or (in our terms) "vehicle" in which this paradigm is especially visible, in part just because of the novel's centrality to that culture. And hence, too, Jean-Christophe Agnew has expanded this argument to show how the eighteenth century transformed the age-old trope of the *theatrum mundi* from its status as a figure of philosophical resignation to a way of giving representation to the new "placeless" market of commercial relations, especially literary-commercial relations.[47] It was the novel, Agnew argues, that "remained one of the few cultural forms in which the spectacle of the market was formally, as well as substantively, explored."[48] The arguments of Marshall and Agnew are crucial to any understanding of how "face-to-faceness" is managed sylleptically in the sentimental novel, transforming codes of expectation and probability in the process.[49] There is, of course, one particularly apposite development within the institution of British theater during the years before its "figure" was absorbed into the sentimental

44. Ibid., 561.

45. For an approach to Haskell's thesis in relation to the novel that emphasizes the function of descriptive particularity in the new modes of fiction, see Thomas Laqueur, "Bodies, Details, and the Humanitarian Narrative," in *The New Cultural History*, ed. Lynn Hunt (Berkeley and Los Angeles: University of California Press, 1989), 176–204.

46. David Marshall, *The Figure of Theater: Shaftesbury, Defoe, Adam Smith, and George Eliot* (New York: Columbia University Press, 1986), 1.

47. Jean-Christophe Agnew, *Worlds Apart: The Market and the Theater in Anglo-American Thought, 1550–1750* (Cambridge: Cambridge University Press, 1986), 18–56.

48. Ibid., p. 190.

49. Hazlitt, writing at the other end of the long century, is not wrong to call his own an essentially undramatic age, since his was indeed an age dominated by print; but the burden of Marshall's and Agnew's arguments is, in effect, to call attention to the absorption or displacement of theatricality back into the print-cultural public sphere. See Hazlitt's "General Reporter" column "The Drama" for *The London Magazine* 1, no. 2 (April 1820): 432.

novel. I mean the development we call "sentimental comedy." For this is a genre that, every bit as much as the sentimental novel, has long posed major problems of probability for audiences and commentators alike. Understanding the workings of "sentimental comedy" is the last piece necessary to solving the puzzle of ambiguity and intelligibility in the sentimental novel and to unpacking the paradoxical commitment to face-to-faceness in a literary institution defined by action at a distance.

IV

Sentimental comedy is generally thought to have had its programmatic inauguration in Richard Steele's *The Conscious Lovers* (1722), a play staged on hundreds of occasions through the eighteenth century and published in at least forty-seven printed editions over that same period.[50] Probability is an issue in the sentimental comedy crafted after Steele's model in part because of its handling of resolution—in this case the "coincidence" that young Indiana, hitherto objectionable lover to Bevil Junior, turns out to be the lost daughter of his father's best friend. Thus Tave, taking *The Conscious Lovers* as representative of the sentimental in his more recent book on comic structure, points to Steele's questionable use of the term *Providence* to explain "what is in fact another species of thing, that convenient solution of Act V— which is such a statistically astonishing connection that it seems to defy the laws of natural probability and therefore must be credited to a heavenly intervention and reward."[51] Another commentator on the issue, John Traugott, though willing to concede that "all comedy is a fantasy of triumph . . . and improbability, its proper mode," nonetheless argues for an especially egregious form of "violence done to probability" in sentimental comedy, which he describes as "a degraded genre that bestows happy denouements on distressing situations in order to give a disingenuous and parochial moral instruction, often that a sentimental disposition will get you a pot of money and the best looking women in the cast."[52] (Traugott does not say what a sentimental disposition will get you if "you" happen to *be*, say, the best looking woman in the cast.)

50. See Richard Steele, *The Conscious Lovers*, ed. Shirley Strum Kenney (Lincoln: University of Nebraska Press, 1968), xii, xvi. Kenney notes that this play is acknowledged the "first thoroughly sentimental English comedy" (p. xlv). All references to the play are to this edition. Although Steele's drama was announced and received as an innovation in its time, the word *sentimental* was not applied to this dramatic mode for some years after the first production. As we have seen, the word itself does not come into currency until the 1740s.

51. Stuart M. Tave, *Lovers, Clowns, and Fairies: An Essay on Comedies* (Chicago: University of Chicago Press, 1993), 132.

52. John Traugott, "Heart and Mask and Genre in Sentimental Comedy," *Eighteenth-Century Life* 10 (October 1986): 143.

While it is clear enough that the two primary literary forms taken by the sentimental can be characterized in relation to crucial issues of probability, there has been little or no attempt by commentators to understand how these respective issues of probability might be linked. We can note first that, formally, the connection between the issues of probability in the sentimental comedy and in the sentimental novel, as defined by Patey, has to do with how the sentimental plot transcends "plotting," or what Patey, in the context of the novel, describes as the probability of prudential calculation. In Steele's sentimental comedy it is the scheme of the protagonists that must be foiled before the sentimental solution can unfold. Tave points out that Steele's plot resolution in *The Conscious Lovers* forms a variation within a larger class of productions with improbable resolutions. In such plays, "the participants in the action work madly at their job of reaching their desires by whatever, often wildly ingenious, means they can invent; and, when they've done their exhausted best to deserve success, fortunate chance steps in with the last and best trick of all."[53] When Tave describes the alternative to scheming calculation in the sentimental comedy it is called "fortunate chance." When Patey describes the alternative to scheming calculation in the sentimental novel, it is called "sentimental communion." But how is it that sentimental communion can function as fortunate chance and vice versa?

Just as face-to-face encounters dramatized in the theater are mediated by a sense of a new commerce in print, so the action at a distance enabled by print culture returns to theatrical face-to-faceness for its basic paradigms. These two developments prove to be two sides of the same coin, or at least two moments in the same process. We must recall, on the one hand, that sentimental comedy involves a very self-conscious "reform" of the more licentious mode of comedy that had been in play for several decades. This reform is launched very much from within the mode of the print culture whose burgeoning power and influence would support the great ambitions of the sentimentalized public sphere of the post-Sternean novel. On the other hand, however, we must also recall the Marshall-Agnew thesis that the novel achieves a distinctive form in the eighteenth century by virtue of its internalization of "the figure of theater." Thus, while what becomes crucial to the novel is the figure of theatrical spectatorship, as Marshall and others have argued, it is no less noteworthy that Steele reformed the drama into a sentimental mode after having established himself as the author of the innovative print-cultural organ he called *The Spectator,* or indeed that he discussed the dramatic reform in its pages, and linked that reform to the emergence of precisely the kind of *reading* public that *The Spectator* innovatively catered to.

53. Tave, *Lovers, Clowns, and Fairies,* 131.

The "violence done to probability" in Steele's comedy derives from changes associated with the newly expanded domain of literary commerce, and the "sympathetic communion" of the sentimental novel is a function of the wider "theater" of British literate society in the latter eighteenth century. But how, exactly, does knowing this connection help us to understand the way in which "the power of sympathy" becomes an "essential force" in the new form of life characterized by sentimentalized probability? We can better answer this question if we clarify what it is that the severest critics of sentimentality find most objectionable in it. For Traugott, the violent improbability of sentimental comedy lies in what he calls the "unlikely oxymoron" of "worldliness and sentiment, the two darlings of the age."[54] These "opposites," he suggests, "seem to feed on each other" in this genre: "If the world is composed of nothing but masks, the pretended desire of sentiment to penetrate the mask and spy out the naked heart is just another mask."[55] Tave's critique, as it happens, is grounded in related observation. What distinguishes *The Conscious Lovers* as sentimental is what Tave calls a certain "slipping of levels."[56] In *The Conscious Lovers*, the trick ending is not an artifice to be admired, a wonder to be marveled at, but rather a confusion of actual and normative orders: "the trick is a pretense that heaven is earth." The point is driven home, for Tave, when the play's hero, young Bevil Junior, defends his impressive benevolence toward his would-be lover, Indiana, whom he rescued from dire circumstances, as if it were ordinary conduct in his society: "no more than what every gentleman ought to be, and I believe very many are," as Bevil himself puts it. And just as the concluding trick of *The Conscious Lovers* is that heaven is earth, so, writes Tave, "Bevil Junior as modest hero is both the gentleman that ought to be and the gentleman that is."[57]

I think Tave is quite right to suggest that problems of probability in the sentimental tradition spawned by Steele's play turn exactly on a problem about a "slipping of levels"—levels that might well be called the actual and the normative. After all, the most philosophically searching account of the sentimental mode in its own time—Schiller's *Essay on Naive and Sentimental Poetry*—identified the sentimental as a form of poesis in which the work of affective representation aimed at the ideal order.[58] To gain a better purchase on the emergence of sentimental probability at this time, I now undertake

54. Traugott, "Sentimental Comedy," 143.
55. Ibid.
56. Tave, *Lovers, Clowns, and Fairies*, 132.
57. Ibid.
58. Thus Brissenden ends his strenuous "attempt at definition" for *Sentimentalism* by concluding that what "sentiment" ultimately comes to mean is "a reasonable feeling" (*Virtue in Distress*, p. 54). The connection of sentiment, so understood, to "sympathy" lies in the fact that sympathy allows for feelings to be mutually coordinated in the theater of everyday life.

to redescribe how these two levels function and thus to explain the "slippage" between them in slightly different terms. This means returning one last time to Steele's *Conscious Lovers*.

Although the play's resolution depends on the coincidence that Bevil Junior's lover turns out to be the long lost daughter of his father's friend, it has long been recognized that the decisive point in the plot actually occurs in act 4. Indeed, in the preface to the printed edition of his drama, Steele himself openly acknowledged "that the whole was writ for the sake of the scene in the fourth act, wherein Mr. Bevil evades the quarrel with his friend." This scene, to set it up briefly, involves Bevil and another man, Mr. Myrtle, who seeks the hand of the woman, Lucinda, whom Bevil's father has in mind for his own son. Bevil Junior has been helping Myrtle undo the comic tangle of lovers, so that the two men can marry Indiana and Lucinda, respectively. But now Myrtle has become suspicious of Bevil, and begins to provoke him with insults. The more coolness Bevil shows in the face of these insults, the more angry grow Myrtle's provocations. Finally, himself in a rage he is eager to have Bevil join, Myrtle adds an insult to Bevil's beloved Indiana: "Your marriage [i.e., to Lucinda, as Myrtle thinks] goes on like common business, and in the interim you have your rambling captive, your Indian princess, for your soft moments of dalliance—your convenient, your ready Indiana" (act 4, scene 1, lines 146–49). At this final insult, Bevil's anger is finally sparked, and he agrees to a duel with Myrtle.

But in the act of summoning his servant to call a coach to carry him away from Myrtle, Bevil pauses to notice the act of social discipline required to speak to his servant civilly in spite of his rage toward Myrtle. At this moment we have the following aside. Here Bevil "recollect[s] [him]self" and in lieu of going through with the duel decides to show Myrtle the proof (a letter) that all that Myrtle has alleged is false. On reading the letter, Myrtle is mortified by his rashness and begins to ask forgiveness, but Bevil cuts him off: "You have o'erpaid the inquietude you gave me in the change I see in you towards me. Alas, what machines are we! Thy face is altered to that of another man, to that of my companion, my friend" (act 4, scene 1, lines 195–98). This is a necessary, though not a sufficient, condition for the comic resolution that follows. A duel in this case would spell a tragic outcome, just as the violent conflict between Mercutio and Tybalt turns the comic potential of *Romeo and Juliet* (a plot much like that of *The Conscious Lovers* for the first three acts) toward its tragic conclusion. To understand the question of "levels" in Steele-inspired sentimental probability, we must examine the decisive moment when Bevil "recollects himself." We must see by what principle of causality or motivation we can account for this moment. And we must note, straightaway, that although it is perhaps the most important "event" in the play, this moment takes place in a space of nonaction: a long pause of the sort that enables reflection. The occasion of this reflection is the most ordinary behavior imaginable—the request to a servant to call a coach. And yet the manners—the sense of "polish"—that enable Bevil to temper his anger for that act prove to him his resources for self-control. He is allowed to recognize that, though he has been provoked, control is available to him—that his "anger" is an artifice of his circumstances and his "resentment" a decision in which he must weigh a lifetime of obligations. Steele presents a transformation of the "face-to-face" encounter: the face of the man Bevil might have killed changes in an instant to the face "of another man," his friend.

In Steele's programmatic comments about this new-mode comedy, even as he insisted that this scene in act 4 was the very raison d'être for the play, he allowed that such incidents "are esteemed by some people no subjects of comedy." To these people his reply is that "any thing that has its foundation in happiness and success, must be allowed to be the object of comedy," and it must have seemed obvious enough to Steele that such a "recovery" as was effected by Mr. Bevil implied a foundation in happiness and success. But such an answer does not address Tave's objection that Steele's play involves a deliberate and characteristically sentimental confusion of norms and facts. And indeed, Steele's comment about the point of the key scene in act 4 is instructive in this regard: "I . . . hope it may have some effect on the Goths and Vandals that frequent the theaters, or a more polite audience may supply their absence."[59] The disparity between the behavior of the fine gentleman Bevil, offered as at once exemplary *and* typical, and the characterization of the audience as barbarians, suggests the Traugott-Tave problem for Steele's representation—how can the gentleman Bevil typify barbarism? Presumably Bevil stands for a virtual audience. But who constitutes this more polite virtual audience that might supplant the Goths and Vandals who have held sway to this point? How does that more polite audience come to figure in the scene of the theater?

The preface from which I am quoting is in fact no part of the theatrical production itself but rather a printed text. Steele himself calls attention to the difference in media: "the greatest effect of a play in reading is to excite the reader to go see it; and when he does so, it is then a play has the effect of example and precept." The "more polite" audience that might come to supplant the barbarians in the theater will be drawn from readers whose interest is excited by their confrontation with the text of the play. This, I believe, is where the strangely actionless quality of the key moment in *The Conscious Lovers* must be revisited in a new light. The consciousness that is aroused in Bevil in that long pause—his reflection on his own ability to temper himself for so trivial a cause as the calling of a coach but not to avoid death or murder—is a mediated awareness, a thought aroused as if in the

59. Steele, *The Conscious Lovers*, 5.

mind of a reader pausing over a printed text. (Myrtle's counterpart conversion actually depends on his reading of a letter.) Bevil's soliloquy on the stage, in other words, is the reverse mirror of Shaftesbury's soliloquy on the page (as the latter has been explicated by Marshall and Agnew). For Shaftesbury's *Soliloquy* (1710) argues for the place of the soliloquy as a "dramatic method" by virtue of which an author can divide in two for "the work of introspection." On such an account, as Agnew shrewdly summarizes it, conscience emerges as "less the cause than the product of reflection."[60] And "reflection" is itself produced by a dramatic method in print, which turns out to be the flip side of the "print method" of sentimental drama. There is in this sense less distance than one might have imagined between the Steele of *The Spectator* papers and the Steele of *The Conscious Lovers*. Indeed, *The Conscious Lovers* was written according to a blueprint first sketched out in *The Spectator*, for a kind of anti-Etheregean comedy, a mode counter to that of *The Man of Mode*. The mode of *The Spectator* itself is defined in relation to the soliloquy. It refunctions this Elizabethan dramatic principle for eighteenth-century print culture after a manner articulated by Shaftesbury.[61]

For Steele, it would seem, the wider audience that surrounds the one physically present at any given performance is the new polite reading public composed of those new gentlemen and ladies who composed the readership of Shaftesbury's *Letters* and the *Spectator* papers themselves. Steele's verse prologue to *The Conscious Lovers* seems to gesture toward just this wider audience of "Britons":

> Your aid, most humbly sought, then, Britons lend,
> And liberal mirth, like liberal men, defend,
> Nor more let ribaldry, with licence writ,
> Usurp the name of eloquence or wit;
> Nor more let lawless farce uncensored go,
> The lewd dull gleanings of a Smithfield show.
> 'Tis yours, with breeding to refine the age,
> Tho chasten wit, and moralize the stage. (lines 21–28)

Here the programmatic aspects of Steele's dramaturgy become clear. And the stakes in the campaign are spelled out in the ensuing lines, which conclude with an exhortation to "judge politely for your country's fame." This capacity to judge "politely" had to do with the extension of trade—the commerce that sweetens as it polishes—and the expansion of the mercantile class.[62]

---

60. Agnew, *Worlds Apart*, 164.

61. Anthony, Earl of Shaftesbury, *Characteristics of Men, Manners, Opinions, Times,* vol. 1, ed. John M. Robertson (Indianapolis: Bobbs-Merrill, 1964), 103–234.

62. Agnew points out that this language of polish and politeness is already linked with the revised theatricality of commerce in Shaftesbury, in *Worlds Apart,* 164. See also J. G. A. Pocock's

While the new reach of commerce and consciousness registered in Steele's drama had its primary development in print, print narrative depended on the conventions of drama for its virtual effects. The crossing of these crucial developments is anticipated in Shaftesbury's analysis of the incorporation of the soliloquy form into modern authorship and the production of "conscience" as an impartial spectator internalized within the writer's mind. As the century proceeded, the sentimental campaign would be waged increasingly on the grounds of literary narrative and expository publications. If Sterne's Yorick, whose name marks his descent from Hamlet, soliloquizes in print the triumph of commercial sympathies over the impulse to violent resolution of conflict (with Monsieur Dessein), this moment is the converse of that in which Bevil, on the stage, depends on the reflective capacities of a national readership to manage something like the same feat.

V

Another way to put the point I have been arguing for is to say that, in sentimental narrative, the probabilities of these story lines are orthogonally crossed by the probabilities involved in the affective rhetorical aims and situations made possible within the development of the sentimental public sphere. This point depends for its force on our seeing how the subject of representation in the sentimental narrative can coincide with its object: the national humanitarian sensibility taking shape in the new commercial order. As Liz Bellamy points out: "the economic system is not analyzed in the abstract, but presented through the creation of fictional characters who epitomise the values of commercial society."[63] The mimetic task of the sen-

---

analysis of the commercial redefinition of *virtue* in *Virtue, Commerce, and History* (Cambridge: Cambridge University Press, 1986), 37–50. Within the play itself, the merchant class is represented by the aptly named man of commerce, Mr. Sealand, father to Lucinda, who explains his position to Sir John Bevil:

Sir, as much a cit as you take me for, I know the town and the world; and give me leave to say that we merchants are a species of gentry that have grown into the world this last century and are as honorable and almost as useful as you landed folks that have always thought yourselves so much above us; for your trading, forsooth, is extended no farther than a load of hay or a fat ox. (act 4, scene 2, lines 45–54)

Both the landed gentry and the cits (citizen merchants) are involved in trade. The difference is in "extent." But this question of extent, of quantitative spread, soon becomes a question of qualitative changes. Indeed, this shift from a quantitative spread to a qualitative change is the history told by Agnew as the story of the transformation of the market from a place to a placeless process, and by Haskell as the story of the emergence of a new humanitarian sensibility in the extended markets of eighteenth-century British capitalism.

63. Liz Bellamy, *Commerce, Morality, and the Eighteenth-Century Novel* (Cambridge: Cambridge University Press, 1998).

timental narrative is to make a representation of the "sensibility" of Britain's commercial society to itself, but, as it seeks to epitomize or allegorize this sensibility, it also means to *activate* it by affective movement, and thus to shape it amelioratively—to help it to realize its full capacity.

This rhetorical aim is explicitly avowed, in fact, in the long subtitle of *The Sentimental Magazine* as it appears on the title page: "Or, General Assemblage of Science, Taste, and Entertainment. Calculated to Amuse the mind, to improve the understanding, and To amend the Heart." What I have termed the pragmatic consideration—defined here as the rhetorical project not only to display the motivations of a sensibility but to better them[64]—involves its own probabilistic dimension, its own issues of likelihood and chance. In *The Sentimental Magazine*'s announcement, for example, the apparently innocuous term *calculated* is of special relevance, since it suggests that the desired moral effects of amusement, edification, and emotional repair all require a reckoning of cases in their own right. If, for example, the heart is amended by being affected, moved, then part of the "calculation" in a sentimental narrative has to do with the question of what is likely to interest and to move the heart of the audience.[65]

By the same token, however, if the heart of the audience is to be understood as a collective (national) sensibility, and if the characters of the story are to be understood as part of a collective national allegory, then the probabilities calculated to amend the sensibility and the probabilities on which one bases a representation of its performance can be mapped as orthogonal coordinates. That is, the mimetic axis of probability (how the epitomized members of commercial society are likely to respond within the frame of the action) is crossed by the pragmatic axis of probability (how the addressed members of commercial society are likely to respond to the action as framed). For a literary culture self-conceived in the advanced commercial state of society and caught up in a certain fiction of a general participation in a print-culture public sphere, the relation between the society represented and the society addressed can be imagined as one of full identity. The point can be illustrated in that moment early in "The Miser Convinced of His Error," another serial narrative from the opening numbers of *The Sentimental Magazine,* when the narrator underscores the "miraculous" character of the transformation that will have to take place in the miser Doriman, a Scrooge prototype: "Who will take compassion on his youth? Who will undertake the task of convincing him of his error? By whom is this mir-

---

64. This problem of how to weigh the "realism" of a work against its capacities for moral elevation is, of course, a celebrated critical crux in Samuel Johnson's *Preface to Shakespeare,* published just seven years earlier.

65. This line of thought would logically lead to a revision of Patey's first-level distinction between the two kinds of probability, prudential and sentimental, discussed previously.

acle to be performed?"[66] There is a strong sense, I want to suggest, that the miracle is performed in a "person" defined at the juncture between the mimetic and pragmatic axes of this plot: the Briton who is at once the audience and the referent (object and subject) of the representation. The split in the author of Shaftesbury's printed soliloquy and the split in the protagonist of Steele's dramatic comedy may each be seen as a refraction of this miraculous "person."

Of course, any plot might be said to have both a mimetic and a rhetorical axis. Any plot can be seen as rule-governed both in its diegesis (the line of action) and in its practical operation on the emotions of readers (the line of affect). And surely there is a long tradition—from *The Winter's Tale* to *Peter Pan*—of invoking audience credibility or generosity in the realization of some bit of action on the stage or page. But in the case of the sentimental as I am describing it, these two axes become unhinged from each other. This, I believe, is what accounts for the "slippage" identified by Tave. The improbability of the plot is a projection of the anticipated effect of the sentimental text on the collective sensibility of its readers. In a scheme of (strictly speaking) sentimental progress, such as that outlined by Steele—an age in which the expanse of trade promotes a higher and higher degree of polish in manners and softened sentiments in daily life—the represented national subject is one that, to have its case truly captured, must improve on what it represents.[67]

Sentimental probability, then, involves a public system of self-representation in which the case of the nation can be reinvented in the process of its being represented, because it can be improved in the process of its being moved. Sterne's Abdera "Fragment" in *Sentimental Journey* nicely illustrates the logic of the point in the context of early Greek theater, a reverse projection from his own moment.[68] To illustrate how this plays out for narrative hypallage, the "syllepsis of the vehicle," and thus for probability in the sense with which we began, we can consider the denouement of "The Preface Written in the Desobligeant." This denouement unfolds with a marvelous witticism in Sterne's sentimental mode, when, in a fashion Sterne's readers would recognize from *Tristram Shandy*, a discourse is interrupted by, but at the same time takes account of, events contingent to its composition. It is

66. "The Miser Convinced of His Error," in *The Sentimental Magazine* 1 (March, 1773): 21.

67. This point becomes explicit in Shelley's later account of the difference between the American and British systems of representation in poetry *and* politics, and his discussion of the "sentiment of the necessity of change" in *A Philosophical View of Reform*, as I attempt to show in *England in 1819: The Politics of Literary Culture and the Case of Romantic Historicism* (Chicago: University of Chicago Press, 1998), 477–80 and 515–16.

68. When Euripides' *Andromeda* is performed in the vile and profligate town of Abdera, Sterne relates, Perseus' address to Cupid so enchants the city that it reforms itself: "The fire caught—and the whole city, like the heart of one man, open'd itself to Love" (p. 35).

also a moment of the materialization of a figurative or general reference, much like the later materialization of Mme. de L***'s hand in the act of turning into her which is (in turn) a concretization of a sentimental turn in the thought. In the case of the Preface, what is interrupted is a discourse on England and the English, in which Yorick has been questioning the need for "literal" travel to the Continent in the first place on the grounds that England now has all that one might need:

> . . . there is no nation under heaven abounding with more variety of learning—where the sciences may be more fitly woo'd, or more surely won than here—where art is encouraged, and will so soon rise high—where Nature (take her all together) has so little to answer for—and, to close all, where there is more wit and variety of character to feed the mind with—Where then, my dear country men, are you going— (p. 13)

The interrupted question appears to be rhetorical in mode and general in scope, an address to the English readership who participate in the rich and rapidly developing public sphere of science and art that Yorick has described. But the reason for the dash that interrupts Yorick's question before its question mark proves surprising:

> —We are only looking at this chaise, said they—Your most obedient servant, said I, skipping out of it, and pulling off my hat—We were wondering, said one of them . . . what could occasion its motion.—'Twas the agitation, said I coolly, of writing a preface—I never heard, said the other . . . of a Preface wrote in a Desobligeant.—It would have been better, said I, in *Vis à Vis.*
> —*As an English man does not travel to see English men,* I retired to my room. (p. 13)

Sternean hypallage (causal exchange) and syllepsis (literal-figurative confusion) reinforce each other in such moments. The literalization of the "country men" to whom Yorick as writer of the Preface addresses his rhetorical question ("Where then are you going?") pointedly raises the question of where they are, certainly of where he is. On the one hand, the "here" of Yorick's comment is the England where Sterne writes and his readers read. On the other, "here" is the coach yard in Calais where Yorick begins his journey. But "here" is also the vehicle he inhabits—now momentarily the one-passenger job—which is moved but not budged by a masturbatory "agitation" that would (presumably) have been better in a vehicle defined by the structure of the *vis à vis,* or "face-to-face."

Face-to-face, of course, is the structure that Sterne can achieve only figuratively in the sylleptic materialization of his readers / countrymen as the interlocutors who inquire about his solitary agitation in the first place. Much the same sort of literalization of the reader occurs frequently and famously in those hilarious asides from *Tristram Shandy* that take the form "No, Madame, when I said a nose I meant a nose and nothing other than a nose." Completing a "rotation of movements," this little episode in *A Sentimental Journey* rounds out with a return to the generalized discourse of the proverb, in which the "literal figures" of the countrymen alongside the carriage are returned to their status as generalities: *An English man does not travel to see English men.*

VI

I mentioned at the start that while I would be paying some attention, perforce, to Sterne's *Sentimental Journey*, it was Adam Smith's *Theory of Moral Sentiments* that made more evident the sense of a sentimental transformation parallel to Hacking's "emergence of probability." There is a moment in Sterne's narrative, however, where the issue of probability is quite directly articulated in a self-consciously sentimental context, and what makes it an especially good passage with which to close is that it articulates sentimental probability in a pointedly national frame of reference. It is the famous vignette, involving (like so many) an impediment to movement, in which Yorick's servant, La Fleur, riding a bidet beside Yorick's post-chaise, encounters an obstacle in the middle of the road. Here, in slightly abridged form, is the vignette:

> A dead ass, before we had got a league, put a sudden stop to La Fleur's career—his bidet would not pass by it—a contention arose betwixt them, and the poor fellow was kick'd out of his jack-boots the very first kick.
>
> La Fleur bore his fall like a French christian, saying neither more or less upon it, than Diable! so presently got up and came to the charge again astride his bidet. . . .
>
> The bidet flew from one side of the road to the other, then back again—then this way—then that way, and in short every way but by the dead ass—La Fleur insisted upon the thing—and the bidet threw him. . . . and away he [the bidet] scamper'd back to Montriul—*Peste!* said La Fleur.
>
> It is not *mal a propos* to take notice here, that tho' La Fleur availed himself but of two different terms of exclamation in this encounter—namely, *Diable!* and *Peste!* that there are nevertheless three, in the French language; like the positive, comparative, and superlative, one or the other of which serve for every unexpected throw of the dice in life.
>
> *Le Diable!* which is the first and positive degree, is generally used upon ordinary emotions of the mind, where small things only fall out contrary to your expectations—such as—the throwing once doublets—La Fleur's being kick'd of his horse, and so forth—cuckoldom, for the same reason, is always—*Le Diable!*
>
> But in cases where the cast has something provoking in it, as in that of the bidet's running away after, and leaving La Fleur aground in jack-boots—'tis the second degree.
>
> 'Tis then *Peste!*

And for the third—

But here my heart is wrung with pity and fellow-feeling, when I reflect what miseries must have been their lot, and how bitterly so refined a people must have smarted, to have forced them upon the use of it.—

Grant me, O ye powers which touch the tongue with eloquence in distress!—whatever is thy *cast*, Grant me but decent words to exclaim in, and I will give my nature way.

—But as these were not to be had in France, I resolved to take every evil just as it befell me without any exclamation at all.

La Fleur, who had made no such covenant with himself, followed the bidet with his eyes till it was got out of sight—and then, you may imagine, if you please, with what word he closed the whole affair.

As there was no hunting down a frighten'd horse in jack-boots, there remained no alternative but taking La Fleur either behind the chaise, or into it—

I preferred the later, and in half an hour we got to the post-house at Nampont. (pp. 38–39)

It is an episode with far-reaching resonance in the history of sentimentality. Wordsworth's *Peter Bell*, the ostensible object of Shelley's parody, reprises the spectacle of the peasant man beating and cursing a stubborn animal in the middle of a road (this time it is the ass itself), and the 1821 "Sentimental Journey, from Islington to Waterloo Bridge" makes pointed reference to the obsession of "sentimentalists" with encounters of this sort ("the first dead dog . . . they might meet with").[69]

Of signal interest to a discussion of probability in Sterne is the governing conceit of the dice game. Merely at the level of pun or paronomasia, for example, we can notice that, beyond the wordplay on *movement, motion, emotion, accident, turn,* and *design* in the earlier passages (many of which terms remain in play here), this passage extends the paronomasia to *cast, case, throw* (coup), *fall,* and *befall.* Ian Hacking has shown how, at an earlier moment, the language of the "equal probability of cases" merged with the language of the equal probability of chances: "chances" understood paradigmatically as possible outcomes in a game of chance such as dice.[70] Sterne frames his story as a series of "cases" in which the chance outcome (the cast) can be graded in the triadic grammar of positive, comparative, and superlative. The basis of the grading system is the degree of "provocation" registered in the sensibility of the subject who suffers the "cast." Fortune or misfortune acquires a kind of measure in the marked levels of expressive exchange between agents. The assumption that "accidents" move us is elaborated by way of the conceit that, in some "casts" of the dice, Fortune "provokes" us—calls forth an emotional response. The person who becomes the

69. *The London Magazine,* 508.
70. On this usage, see Hacking, *Emergence of Probability,* 122–33.

object of Fortune's call or "cast" responds with the grammatically appropriate "invocation": *Diable, Peste,* or (one suspects) *Nom de Dieu.* Emotion can be thus closely keyed to degrees of improbability. The odds of "throwing once doublets," as the standard handbooks of games of chance would have suggested for games played with two dice, are 6 / 36, or one in six. One in six is an ordinary enough "case" or "befalling" of improbability to call for no more than an "ordinary emotion of the mind."

It is a crucial part of the theory of sentiments that, while a provoking case of misfortune calls forth a response from the sufferer, this response in turn will affect the response of witnesses to the entire spectacle. As a third party in or to the scene, one may or may not have fellow feeling with such suffering. Adam Smith explains that restraint in response to unlucky chance, as recommended in the disciplines of Stoicism, will, along another axis of probability, increase the likelihood of a spectator's active sympathy with the victim. Sterne tacitly relies on Smith's theory here when he prays for decent words and when he resolves, in the absence of decent words in France, to accept what befalls him "without any exclamation at all." But on a level of national sentiment, Sterne wittily suggests, one can also—as a Stoical Englishman—have fellow feeling with the case of a nation whose long-term fortunes (provocations) have been such as to "force" them to resort to such an expression as the offensive superlative.

Implicit in this articulation of sentiment and probability are many of the emergent forms and structures I have been describing. The slippage between the literal and figural levels, for example, can be seen in the connection between the governing metaphor of the "casting of the dice" and La Fleur's being kicked by and thrown from his horse. This connection cleverly intimated in the punning use of "fall" (German for "case") as a link or zeugma between "cast" and "case." Earlier, we saw the literalization of the rhetorical "countrymen" and the materialization of the "hand" of fate at the end of the arm of Mme. de L***. Now, the slide of the syllepsis goes the other way. After we are told that "La Fleur bore his fall like a French christian" we find that this "literal" fall becomes the more metaphorical or abstract sense of how "things fall out" in relation to expectations. The "fall" becomes a "case." We may even perhaps note the appearance of that most provocative of all dice "doublets"—snake eyes—in the image of the two empty jack-boots left on the bare road after Sterne's casting of this scene on the page.

My final speculation about this extraordinary passage concerns its relation to the figure of "hypallage": the trope of the preposterous, strictly speaking, in which the before and after of related ideas, even those of causal relations, are reversed. We have seen that this trope is rhetorically crucial to sentimental probability. Is there not, I wonder, an allusion to Sterne's own account of this trope in the concluding sentences of the "Dead Ass" vignette, in which the choices confronting Yorick are reduced to "taking La Fleur either behind the chaise, or into it"? We must recall that when Sterne has Walter Shandy explain the trope of hypallage to Uncle Toby, a strikingly similar phrasing is involved: "What's that? cried my uncle Toby. The cart before the horse, replied my father——And what has he to do there? cried my uncle—Nothing, quoth my father, but get in—or let it alone." Sentimental probability depends on this reversibility of the driving force and the driven object, vested interest and vehicle, motive and medium, norm and fact.

There are many directions in which to take the argument from here. One direction is to the final vignette of *Sentimental Journey,* where the "Case of Delicacy" offers a reworking of the "Case of Conscience" chapter from the novel's first volume. Another is toward the nineteenth-century novel, to Scott, that great admirer of Sterne and Mackenzie, or to Dickens, whom Anthony Trollope satirized with the tag "Mr. Popular Sentiment." The case of Dickens' Scrooge, our culture's most famous "miser convinced of his error," nicely illustrates the later development of the form of probability I have been outlining here, in that his "transformation" is at once an allegory and an effect of projected readerly sympathy. Another direction would be toward France, and the nationalization of the principle of "dessein" suggested in Sterne's *Journey.* In America, it would be worth attempting a redescription of Ann Douglas' thesis about the sentimentalization of American culture, trying to show the problems with her key distinction between "romanticism" and "sentimentalism." Indeed, twentieth-century mass culture, her destination in the three-part project, is very much what I have in view in undertaking this analysis of eighteenth-century proto-mass-cultural forms. It may be evident that my analysis of sentimental mediation here owes much to recent work in film and media studies. The other side of that coin, however, is that a better understanding of the emergence of sentimental probability in eighteenth-century print culture can help reframe the notorious problem of sentimentality in classical Hollywood cinema. Dickens would appear as the Janus-faced figure in such an account. Even Serge Eisenstein, who long ago insisted that Dickens was a key to the world made by D. W. Griffith, failed to address the question of how early cinema translated print sentiment into a new medium.[71] That story is yet to be told.

71. Sergei Eisenstein, "Dickens, Griffith, and the Film Today," in *Film Form*, ed. and trans. Jay Leyda (New York: Harcourt Brace, 1949), 195–255.

The Secret History of Domesticity

Private, Public, and the Division of Knowledge

Michael McKeon

In recent years, one of the most productive theses in the study of early modern culture has been that of the eighteenth-century rise of "domesticity." The thesis posits, by definition, a specifically modern understanding of a much larger phenomenon—the separation between the private and the public spheres—and it has enabled us to see modern culture with a new illumination. Yet the distinction between the private and the public has been with us for a great deal longer than this modern understanding of it, and we may be justified in wondering what the modern separation replaces.

Too often, the rise of domesticity—and more generally, the rise of modern privacy—is invoked as though it were *sui generis,* so coextensive with the emergent present of modernity as to be utterly unrooted in the past. This view has an inevitable tendency to simplify the nature of the thing itself, so that domesticity takes on a monolithic homogeneity whose structure and meaning are relatively simple and can, in each individual instance, be posited from the outset. My question—What does the modern separation replace?—may become more tractable if we reformulate it by narrowing our attention to specifically literary history: What does domestic *fiction* replace? Of course, various answers to this question have already been advanced: romance; the conduct book; a more "public" adventure narrative, like epic, or, more proximately, like *Robinson Crusoe* (1719). Does domestic fiction, as has lately and influentially been argued, suddenly appear in 1740 with the publication of *Pamela?*

In the following essay I propose to begin with the narrower literary question and then proceed to the broader cultural issue. The virtue of narrowing our focus from sociocultural behavior in general to discursive forms in particular is that it obliges us to attend to the concrete specificity of literary structure. What is the "shape" of domestic fiction in comparison with that of the forms it replaced? How might this formal comparison enhance our understanding of the sociocultural change that is our larger concern? If we're to go beyond the implausible hypothesis of a sudden rupture, historical break must be reconceived as historical emergence. By attending to the "secret histories" of discursive forms we may gain access to the incremental phenomenon of historical emergence. I'm using the term *secret history* because this is the name contemporaries often gave to one type of text with which I'll be concerned, the political roman à clef. But I also mean it to allude to what might be called the "prehistory" of domestic fiction, its crucial existence before it attains its identifiable status as such. Only by some such recourse can we deploy the notion of a "cultural revolution" in a fully historical fashion—without succumbing, that is, to the peculiarly modern belief that revolution consists in pure innovation.

I

Although diverse in their thematic concerns, the narrative forms that participate in the emergence of domestic fiction share a basic allegorical structure in which meaning, the realm of the signified, is adduced by postulating as its signifier the realm of the domestic. Yet although some of these allegorical narratives may have a religious concern, none uses its domestic figures to accommodate or signify the immaterial realm of the spirit. The aim of these secular allegories is rather to signify one material domain by another—typically, public history or politics by a private, domestic counterpart.

The basic mechanism can be seen in Swift's *Tale of a Tub* (1704, 1710), whose allegory of the public history of the Christian Church is figured by the domestic story of three brothers at large in London and bent upon turning their dead father's will to their own advantage.[1] Swift's aim in signifying the public by the domestic was no doubt at least in part pedagogical. Seventeen centuries of intricate church history are compressed and concentrated here with a polemical ingenuity that casts Anglicanism in the brilliantly normative light of moderation. This may seem to confirm the efficacy of the little in representing the great. However, hostile readers of his allegory accused Swift of mocking Christian belief, of trivializing sacred history and doctrine by reducing them to a ludicrously profane tale of estate settlement.[2] Can the profane really accommodate the sacred in this fashion?

1. Jonathan Swift, *A Tale of a Tub. To which is added the Battle of the Books and the Mechanical Operation of the Spirit*, 2nd ed., ed. A. C. Guthkelch and D. Nichol Smith (Oxford: Oxford University Press, 1958).

2. See William Wotton, *A Defense of the Reflections upon Ancient and Modern Learning* (1705), excerpted in Swift, *Tale*, 312–28.

More central to my present purpose, can a domestic story effectively encompass those ends that great public narrative exists to serve?

One of Swift's less celebrated "concentration narratives," because it is devoid of religious argument, may throw the crucial formal mechanism more clearly into relief. *The Story of the Injured Lady* was written around 1707 in anticipation of, and in complaint against, the English union with Scotland.[3] The eponymous "injured lady" is Ireland, mistress of a good estate, who, having been seduced by England with a promise of marriage, is now distressed to see her suitor engross her estate and propose marriage instead to her rival, Scotland. In this concentration narrative, domestic crisis figures sociopolitical crisis. Swift seems to operate on the conviction that the narrative "domestication" of colonial rule, its micro-depiction as a private and gendered perfidy, will make it more legible and odious to his readers.

A similar assumption underlies Defoe's concentration narrative *Seldom Comes a Better* (1710).[4] Here the political crisis involves Queen Anne's replacement of the Whig by a Tory ministry that threatens to end the Whig-led war against France. The crisis is signified by—or domesticated as—the story of a powerful landowner's aggression against the estate and manor of a neighboring "Wise Lady." Defoe may have mixed motives here for pursuing the allegorical mode. No doubt he, too, believes the domestication of the story will render it more immediate and intelligible. But Queen Anne is by no means blameless in Defoe's account of the change in ministry, and allegory, like the tract's anonymity, may also have seemed a necessary safeguard against prosecution.

Needless to say, the emergence of domestic fiction cannot be explained by any single factor. In any case, my purpose here, less explanatory than descriptive, is rather to suggest that in observing the construction of these concentration narratives, we can watch domestic fiction emerge as a well-shaped but ostentatiously instrumental signifier, not a self-sufficient story but one in service to public and extradomestic ends. It's in this sense that domestic fiction is "emergent" in the concentration narrative, recognizable as something like "itself" yet part of another form entirely. In structural terms, the concentration narrative is therefore related to the roman à clef, or "secret history," which tells scandalous stories about real public figures under the guise of romance fictions. In England the form was established by such political allegories as Sir Philip Sidney's *Arcadia* (1593), Lady Mary Wroth's *Countess of Montgomeries Urania* (1621), and John Barclay's *Argenis*

---

3. "The Story of the Injured Lady. In a Letter to her Friend, with his Answer" (1746), in Jonathan Swift, *Irish Tracts 1720–23 and Sermons,* ed. Louis Landa, vol. 9 of *The Prose Writings of Jonathan Swift,* ed. H. Davis (Oxford: Blackwell, 1948), 3–12.

4. [Daniel Defoe], *Seldom Comes a Better: Or, a Tale of a Lady and her Servants* (London, 1710).

(1628–29). For contemporaries its most notorious practitioner was Delarivier Manley.

In a series of anonymous publications, Manley told stories of sexual and monetary corruption among noble courtiers who, veiled only by their Italianate names, transparently signified English personages. Like Defoe, she had strong prudential motives for shielding her political scandal behind private intrigue. But she also practiced a mode of political allegory in which the deep analogy between private and public is unusually clear owing to the fact that putatively private, "domestic" matters of sexual dalliance play a vital role even on the level of the public signified.

The reason for this is not far to seek. It is a commonplace that traditional English politics posited a profound connection between the family and the state. The connection was double. First, patriarchalist principles, conceiving the authority of the magistrate to be that of the father, propounded a metaphorical relation between the family and the state. Second, royal authority was passed on metonymically by familial inheritance. In this way, politics as traditionally conceived were always "sexual" politics, a matter of paternal authority and dynastic succession. This is one register of the way traditional culture tacitly acknowledged a distinction between the private and the public realms while still deferring to a dominant view of them as analogous parts of a larger whole.

Yet the whole was only as vital as its parts. The history of the royal house of Stuart must have appeared to many a century-long allegory of familial crisis: the desertion and murder of the husband-father, Charles I; the widowhood of the wife-mother, England; the belated return of the eldest son, Charles II; the rivalry of fatally defective heirs (the imperious younger son the Duke of York, his bastard nephew the Duke of Monmouth); the futile effort to extend the line through James II; and the conveyance of the estate to Hanoverian interlopers. As this account makes clear, it was still possible to conceive even this most troubled history of the state in familial terms. However, the transition from premodern to modern attitudes toward politics is largely the work of the seventeenth and eighteenth centuries. Hence the history of the royal house of Stuart also correlates with an emergent conviction that the private and the public, the family and the state, are not only distinct, but also fully separable, spheres.

I want to suggest that the political allegories and secret histories of this period are experimental attempts to inquire into the relations between the public and the private at the ambiguous historical moment of a transition— a transition (we now see with hindsight) from one system of belief to the other. The popularity of such narratives at this time attests to the popularity neither of the traditional nor of the modern view of the relation between the private and the public, but rather, to the popularity of the problem of that relation. The generic institutionalization of domestic fiction as such marks a culmination of this experimental investigation, no more a historical innovation than a historical remainder, already prefigured in partial form.

The experimental nature of these narratives may be seen in the fact that their formal inquiry into the problem of the private / public relation is often self-consciously thematized on the level of content. For example, Manley's autobiographical *Rivella* (1714)[5] comes to a head when the heroine is threatened with prosecution for having written her most famous roman à clef, the *New Atalantis* (1709). Throughout *Rivella*, Manley has impersonated, as narrator, a male suitor who is convinced that Rivella's best policy would be to retrieve her damaged honor by retiring from the world of politics and publication under male protection, preferably his own. Having resisted this domestication for a number of years, Rivella now seems, in court, to accede to it. Admitting her authorship of the offensive work, she claims nonetheless that her design was not political but personal, that her romance characters signify nothing beyond themselves. The charges are dropped, and the narrator informs us that Rivella "now agrees with me, that Politicks is not the Business of a Woman, especially of one that can so well delight and entertain her Readers with more gentle pleasing Theams . . ." (p. 117).

Of course, her narrator is quite wrong. Manley's "political business" persists in the ongoing publication of her secret histories: not only in their political reference, but also in the way their publication retrieves her honor more effectively than male protection might have done. As Rivella, Manley is thus content to let her narrator speak for her because she knows that his denial of a political signified in her current and future work is no more persuasive than hers concerning her previous work. The drastic separation of the public from the private, the male from the female, politics from more "gentle, pleasing themes," is affirmed as official doctrine even as it is denied in the very structure and publication of Manley's allegory.

And yet the structure of the roman à clef, the signification of public events by domestic intrigue, is far from straightforward in what it implies about the problem of the private/public relation. In traditional narrative, the distinction between the two spheres is real but tacit enough to make their full separability unthinkable. In these transitional works, however, the unification of the spheres is explicitly premised on their prior (if still only instrumental) separation. The most profound narrative inquiry into this paradox—and into the problem of the private/public relation that it

---

5. [Delarivier Manley], *The Adventures of Rivella; or, the History of the Author of the Atalantis. With Secret Memoirs and Characters of Several Considerable Persons her Co[n]temporaries . . .* (London, 1714). Citations appearing parenthetically in the text refer to this edition.

evokes—is Aphra Behn's *Love-Letters Between a Noble-Man and his Sister* (1684–87).[6] Behn's narrative appears to its readers as, simultaneously, a complex web of private amatory intrigue; a translation of a French roman à clef about the persecution of the Huguenots; and an English roman à clef about the politics of the Exclusion Crisis, whose aftershocks were still being felt at the time of publication. Because of this double detachment from the political signified, the exoticism of Behn's romance names may seem to support her repeated claim that " 'tis not my business here to mix the rough relation of a War with the soft affairs of Love . . ." (p. 10; cf. p. 426).

Throughout the story, Behn both sustains and discredits her ostensible self-confinement to the domestic sphere. It is not only that, even on the level of the signifier, her story often is about war, not love. More important, the narrative is saturated with the sociocultural politics of its historical moment. Even in their private capacities as lovers, Behn's protagonists are politically coded as Tory or Whig, pro- or anti-patriarchalist, respectful or contemptuous of the father's authority in the marriage choice. The putative boundaries between love and war are constantly being tested. On the one hand, Behn pushes so far the extravagant Petrarchan figuration of embattled love that her story seems to affirm the sober, Clausewitzian maxim that love is war by other means. On the other hand, war may really be love. Behn goes some distance in imputing to love and the sphere of domesticity a central role in the generation of political ambition and war. To read the *Love-Letters* is to experience an uncanny and quite unrationalizable oscillation between the public and the private, a movement that both reduces and reinforces our sense of their difference. The domestic politics of family and sexual relations both mirrors a distinct politics of the public realm and affords that realm its essential engine. To signify the one by the other is also to redescribe a singular entity.

Read in this fashion, Behn's *Love-Letters* becomes intelligible as both a political allegory and a proto-domestic fiction. Historical continuity may be established also from the other direction. Encountered in a vacuum, the unremitting domesticity of *Pamela* (1740) seems a decisive break with past narrative practice. Placed in the context of the *Love-Letters*, however, *Pamela* becomes instead a decisive stage in the ongoing process whereby "private" narrative learns to intimate so efficiently its "public" significance that the allegorical structure of signification itself becomes expendable. What remains is not a radically different sort of politics—a "new" sexual politics that conceals, contains, or transforms the "old" politics of social hierarchy and state domination. After all, the metaphorical language of state politics—of "tyranny," "liberty," "enslavement," "rebellion," "treachery,"

---

6. Aphra Behn, *Love-Letters Between a Noble-Man and his Sister,* ed. Janet Todd (Harmondsworth: Penguin, 1996). Parenthetical citations in the text refer to this edition.

"submission," "obedience"—is explicit and everywhere in *Pamela*. The difference is rather that state politics has ceased to constitute a distinctly public realm of the signified, because Richardson is experimenting with the capacity of the private realm of domesticity to stand on its own by internalizing, as metaphor, its public reference.

Nor is it only by metaphor that we are made to see the public significance of Pamela's private drama. At the heart of this drama is the problematic relationship between domestic marriage and domestic service. In asking whether and how the servant can become a wife, Richardson internalizes and thematizes the problematic relation of the public and the private within the realm of the domestic. A useful parallel may be found in the relationship between *Robinson Crusoe* (1719) and the religious allegory that precedes it. In dispensing with the allegorical structure of, say, *The Pilgrim's Progress* (1678, 1682), Defoe's first novel does not dispense with its explicitly spiritual concerns. Rather, it internalizes and thematizes the struggle for salvation that in Bunyan occurs only in the realm of the signified. Seen in this light, in fact, *Pamela,* putatively the first domestic novel, is no more strictly "domestic" than *Robinson Crusoe* is strictly secular. Rather, it takes on the form of a private story by incorporating its public concern within a literal narrative.

II

I will turn now from specifically literary questions of separation, internalization, and emergence to the broader historical context. And in the absence of pristine beginnings, I will take as my starting point the early modern separation of "state" from "civil society." "Civil society" may be seen as the Enlightenment consolidation of the Renaissance category "society."[7] As both idea and institution, "society" obviously predates the Renaissance; yet it also comes into being over against the Renaissance "state," which in its own emergence is both the antithesis of "society" and the very condition of its being. This is at once a conceptual and an objective process, customarily associated with the epoch of absolutism and its centralization of political power in royal hands. Historians of the absolutist state have been willing to associate it with the emergence of state power as such because absolutism entails an unprecedented essay in separation—that is, in easing the traditional dependence of political power on metaphysical and moral sanctions. This is a well-known story, especially in its paradigmatic Italian develop-

7. For contemporary and modern overviews, see Adam Ferguson, *An Essay on the History of Civil Society* (Edinburgh, 1767), and Marvin B. Becker, *The Emergence of Civil Society in the Eighteenth Century: A Privileged Moment in the History of England, Scotland, and France* (Bloomington: Indiana University Press, 1994).

ment.[8] The absolute prince or monarch is he who practices the "art of the state": who exercises his dominion according not to overarching principles of nature, justice, or reason, but to an autonomous "reason of state," the "mysteries" of rule or *arcana imperii* whose autotelic end is the maintenance of state power itself. In the figures of speech that organize more traditional political theory, the state is distinguishable but not separable from the estates of the realm; "reason of state" defines precisely the grounds of its separability.

The autonomization of state power gave to the Renaissance state a compelling coherence over against other institutions. Once postulated, however, the conception of absolute, self-justified authority could be detached from the "body natural" of the absolute monarch and embodied elsewhere: in the courtier; in parliament; even in the common people. Over the long term, the indefinite transferability of royal absolutism fed the notion that even—perhaps only— the individual is endowed with an absolute authority. At the same time, it encouraged the depersonalization of state authority, which manifestly persisted even when the head was forcibly detached from the rest of the body politic.

One consequence of this depersonalization was the rise of alternative theories of state sovereignty. In Locke's famous analysis, political government, or the state, originates through a "compact" by which individuals agree to relinquish some of the liberties enjoyed in the state of nature in order to secure and preserve their properties. Accordingly, those rights that are inseparable in the state of nature are, to the end of security, parceled out to a legislative, a judicial, and an executive branch of government. Contract theory rationalized the state's impersonality as the effect not of the magistrate's, but of the proto-citizen's, depersonalization. By this way of thinking, the institutions that compose the state, never embodied in the magistrate, are instead created by an act of collective disembodiment or detachment. The devolution of absolutism from magistrate to citizen that is evident in contract theory depends on a parallel devolution of attitudes toward property. English common law conceived all property to be held in fee from one's lord—which early on meant, ultimately, from the king. The property of commoners was seen customarily as a use-right that might under different circumstances be both inclusive and exclusive, both shared with others and conditionally "privatized" to some or one. The quintessential mark of private property, on the other hand, is its unconditional alienability: to own something absolutely is to be able to disown it.[9] The theory of royal absolutism held that property was

8. See M. Viroli, *From Politics to Reason of State: The Acquisition and Transformation of the Language of Politics 1251–1600* (Cambridge: Cambridge University Press, 1992).

9. See C. B. Macpherson, "The Meaning of Property," in *Property: Mainstream and Critical Positions,* ed. C. B. Macpherson (Toronto: University of Toronto Press, 1978), 1–13.

an unconditionally exclusive, or absolute, possession of the monarch. When Charles I was deposed, so was the presumption that all property was his property. In 1646, parliament abolished feudal tenures, formally freeing major landholders of their feudal ties to the king. Thanks to the abolition of feudal tenures, Defoe wrote, the English gentry hold and inherit "their land *in capite,* absolutely and by entail. . . . All the knight's service and vassalage is abolish'd, they are as absolutely possess'd of their mannours and freehold as a prince is of his crown."[10] The abolition of feudal tenures enabled an unprecedented degree of long-term estate planning, experiment, and investment, a wholesale "improvement" of land. Observing this process from the other direction, Locke took the demonstrable fact of land improvement as the crucial legitimation of property as an absolute possession: "[E]very Man has a *Property* in his own *Person.* . . . The *Labour* of his Body, and the *Work* of his Hands, we may say, are properly his. Whatsoever that he removes out of the State that Nature hath provided, and left it in, he hath mixed his *Labour* with, and joyned to it something that is his own, and thereby makes it his *Property.*"[11]

By detaching the title to property from allegiance to one's sovereign, these developments depoliticized property, transforming it from a political into an economic category. The pursuit and fulfillment of one's own economic interest came to be conceived as a negative freedom, a freedom from state control. In this way, the ground was laid for the modern association of the public sector with state "politics," and of the private sector with "economics"—that is, with the market behavior of private individuals. Of course, the association between the political state and the "public" is already present in classical antiquity: in the Greek separation of the *polis* from the *oikos;* in the Roman republic and its concern with *res publica.* "Private things," by contrast, are defined by the condition of privation. They are things pertaining to the obscure material necessities of the household—to women, children, and slaves—a realm of under-theorized social practice that was properly hidden from public view. The most fundamental difference between the ancient and the modern arrangements involves the theorization of the private realm in two contrary but compatible directions. On the one hand, the ancient management of the *oikos,* of the household economy, was transformed into a model for the management of the greater household—that is, for "political economy." On the other hand, the residue of this transformation—the household divested of its economic function—

10. Daniel Defoe, *The Compleat English Gentleman* (written 1728–29), ed. K. D. Bülbring (London, 1890), 62–63.
11. John Locke, *An Essay Concerning the True Original, Extent, and End of Civil Government (The Second Treatise of Government),* ch. 5, sec. 27 (1690), in *Two Treatises on Government,* 2nd ed., ed. P. Laslett (Cambridge, 1967), 305–6. Parenthetical citations in the text refer to this edition.

became the model for the "domestic sphere." Both of these emergent categories—political economy and the domestic sphere—retain in the modern world their ancient associations with privacy, even as each stands in oppositional relation to the other.

Several factors are involved in this historical process. At least through the sixteenth century, economic production in England was dominated by what's been called a "domestic economy," a system that is the direct heir of the ancient *oikos* and in which the household is the major unit of production. Energized by the abolition of feudal tenures, the capitalist improvement of the land precipitated the breakdown of the domestic economy and the concomitant withdrawal of women from work deemed economically productive. The flexibility of traditional work relations depended on customary arrangements that capitalist improvement rendered unprofitable. Productive labor became an activity increasingly undertaken only by men and only outside the household, whereas domestic labor slowly acquired the status of "housework," the exclusive domain of women and increasingly denigrated as unproductive.[12] So the private work of economic reproduction was gradually separated out from the household and undertaken for the market. Yet it did not lose thereby its ancient association with privacy. Rather, the "privacy" of economy shed the connotation of "privation" that colored the traditional household economy and took on the sense of "negative liberty" that undergirds modern political economy. The household, deprived of its (private) economic function, gradually assumed the (private) status of the modern family, also valued for its negative liberty from public control.

Both the modern family and the modern economy are therefore conceived as private sanctuaries from state political interference. Moreover both have crucial, if stealthy, public functions. Market activity takes over and obviates the positive law of the state by enacting what is conceived as an absolute law of human nature—indeed, as an objective and natural "law of the market" itself.[13] Family behavior takes over not only domestic financial management, but also the tasks of primary socialization—of moral governance, spiritual pedagogy, and personal authentication—once performed by public institutions of state and church but now defined and valued precisely in opposition to what are conceived as dangerously corrupting "public" values. Indeed, from the perspective of family values, even economic values are seen as partaking of public corruption. The modern family, divested

12. See S. Cahn, *Industry of Devotion: The Transformation of Women's Work in England, 1500–1660* (New York: Columbia University Press, 1987); B. Hill, *Women, Work, and Sexual Politics in Eighteenth-Century England* (Oxford: Blackwell, 1989).

13. See J. O. Appleby, *Economic Thought and Ideology in Seventeenth-Century England* (Princeton: Princeton University Press, 1978).

of economic productivity, is thus consoled and distinguished by its status as the absolute domain of private efficiency and ethical authenticity. In aristocratic households, these developments were reinforced by long-term changes in the way inheritance patterns shaped ideas of family integrity. At the risk of over-schematization: marriage and child rearing among the nobility traditionally served the dominant "public" function of ensuring the diachronic transmission and preservation of patrilineage; like wives and mothers, individual families were finally no more than instrumental means to this overarching end. The continuity of the patriline did not lose its importance in modern noble households, but it was complicated by a very different, more "private" view of the family as synchronically rooted in its own current identity. Responsibility came to be felt less for the familial past or future and more for the socioethical coherence of the household in its present subsistence.

III

One advantage of this kind of analysis is that it ensures against the illusion that cultural revolution can occur discontinuously, by a sudden break with past practices. For something new to emerge, something old must persist. In fact domesticity, like political economy, owes its innovative power precisely to its capacity to extend traditionality in other terms. Let me pause for a moment to name two principles, one of discontinuity and one of continuity, that together may capture the complexity of the historical process I am trying to describe.

The first principle, that of *explicitness,* consists in the way the tacit habit of differentiating between the public and the private gradually becomes concentrated into an explicit motive to separate them, a motive reflected also in the ongoing sexual division of labor. This is not an absolute principle, however—the sexual division of labor being a case in point. If domestic labor was broadly reconceived as economically unproductive, *Rivella*'s plot proposes that female honor is better satisfied by a productive career in publication than by the privacy of married domesticity—a proposition that many women besides Manley took to heart as the century wore on. The agrarian decline of the domestic economy was coextensive with a process of urbanization that opened up a range of female employments ideologically at odds, but experientially compatible, with emergent domesticity.

The second principle, that of *dialectical recapitulation,* consists in the way the initial separation of state from civil society also establishes a momentum (I have called it the devolution of absolutism) that carries absolute authority from greater to lesser spheres—from the political to the economic, from the economic to the domestic, from the domestic to the personal—relativizing distinctions between public and private activity by successively discovering within the latter a new outpost of the former. Of course, my summary account does not begin to exhaust this process, which is not limited to domestic (or hence to programmatically heterosexual) contexts. In a fuller inquiry I would want to consider how print culture authorized private personality by a depersonalizing act of publication; how Protestant conscience revealed in the soul the immanent interiority of the subject, of individual choice; how psychology disclosed within subjectivity itself the mechanism by which a manifest and "public" agency controls—that is, "displaces," "censors," "revises," "represses"—its latent and "private" counterpart. For the present, however, it is enough to ask what is gained by juxtaposing my brief account of the formal emergence of domestic fiction with this brief account of the dialectical relation between the modern realms of the private and the public.

Unlike political sovereignty, marriage had always demonstrably been based on some form of consent; hence it was always plausible to conceive it in contractual terms. Locke ratified this view when he described "*Conjugal Society*" as "a voluntary Compact between Man and Woman . . . , [t]he *Power of the Husband* being so far from that of an absolute Monarch, that the *Wife* has, in many cases, a Liberty to *separate* from him . . ." (bk. 2, ch. 7, secs. 78, 82, pp. 337, 339). Mary Astell, however, pondering not the theory but the practice of conjugal life, was unimpressed by Locke's assurances:

> The Domestic Sovereign is without Dispute Elected, and the Stipulations and Contract are mutual; is it not then partial in Men to the last degree to contend for and practice that Arbitrary Dominion in their Families which they abhor and exclaim against in the State? . . . For whatever may be said against Passive-Obedience[14] in another case, I suppose there's no Man but likes it very well in this; how much soever Arbitrary Power may be disliked on a Throne, [no one] would cry up Liberty to poor *Female Slaves,* or plead for the Lawfulness of Resisting a Private Tyranny.[15]

Astell's argument capitalizes on the devolution of absolutism, which she proposes to extend, if to male political subjects, then also to what she calls the "rational and free agency" of married women. Yet she knew that in reality, married women were "absolute Monarchs" only (as she put it) "in our own Bosoms."[16]

As Astell's critique suggests, the very disentanglement of the state and the family achieved by the critique of patriarchalism permitted the theories of political and conjugal obligation the illumination that comes with explicit

14. Royal absolutism required passive obedience of dissenting subjects.
15. [Mary Astell], *Reflections upon Marriage,* 3rd ed. (1706), in *The First English Feminist,* ed. B. Hill (Aldershot: Gower, 1986), 76, 102.
16. [Mary Astell], *A Serious Proposal to the Ladies,* pt. 2 (1697), in *First English Feminist,* p. 179.

and reciprocal reflection. I have already noted that this can be seen in the proto-domestic fiction of Behn and Richardson. It is also more broadly evident in the way Enlightenment discourse on marriage obsessively returns to the competition between two kinds of marriage: the "arranged" marriage of "alliance" or "convenience," and marriage for love. Defoe's treatment of this commonplace is as clear as any. He labels "Matrimonial Whoredom" that marriage which is motivated by the financial demands of a patriarchalist absolutism that turns fathers into tyrants and their marriageable children into "slaves": "As Matrimony should be the Effect of a free and previous Choice in the Persons marrying, so the breaking in by Violence upon the Choice and Affection of the Parties, I take to be the worst kind of Rape; whether the Violence be the Violence of Perswasion or of Authority; I mean, such as that of Paternal Authority . . ."[17] In this fashion, the conflict between the couple's choice and the parents' constraints is figured by the conflict between the subject's liberty and the sovereign's absolute will.

At the same time that Mary Pierrepont's noble father was making arrangements for her marriage to a wealthy but unloved aristocrat, Mary herself was involved in a secret correspondence with her future husband that is suffused with the aura and apprehensions of absolutist politics:

> My present Duty is to obey my Father. . . . [He] may do some things disagreeable to my Inclinations, but passive Obedience[18] is a doctrine [that] should allwaies be receivd among wives and daughters. . . . [I] do not think I have any hand in makeing [marriage] Settlements. People in my way are sold like slaves, and I cannot tell what price my Master will put on me. . . . My Family is resolv'd to dispose of me where I hate.[19]

We need not embrace the notion that marriage for love was an invention of the early modern period to appreciate the extraordinary and unprecedented currency it gains during that period. Indeed, the conflict between marriage for love and marriage for money may be the most profound and pervasive legacy of absolutist politics to the sexual politics of domesticity. So thoroughly familiarized as to have lost its original aura of the public realm of state politics, the battle between love and money saturates the private marriage plots of the late-eighteenth- and nineteenth-century domestic novel. Thus the early modern separation of the public from the private, decisive as it is for modern culture, is nonetheless also the necessary pre-

17. [Daniel Defoe], *Conjugal Lewdness; or, Matrimonial Whoredom* (London, 1727), 37, 166.

18. At this moment (Aug. 20, 1710) Henry Sacheverell, passionate proponent of absolutist doctrines of passive obedience and nonresistance, was at the height of his celebrity.

19. *Complete Letters of Lady Mary Wortley Montagu*, vol. 1, ed. R. Halsband (Oxford: Oxford University Press, 1965), 54, 64, 123 (Aug. 20, 1710–June 11, 1712).

condition for the internalization and thematization of public politics within the domestic realm.

Some of the most telling evidence of this development is found, as we have already seen, in extra-novelistic sources. Although Astell's critique of marriage is generally indisputable, the growth of absolute private property was aided in her period not only by the abolition of feudal tenures, but also by the liberalization of the laws of marriage settlement. This provided for, among other things, the institution of married women's separate property: principally, jointure (for use in the event of widowhood) and pin money (for use during the marriage itself). To Mary Pierrepont, the legal possibility of married women's separate property had little to do with the realities of married life. To others, however—and no doubt especially to men— these legal innovations seemed to set in motion the devolution of absolute private property from "public" husbands to "private" wives. To Richard Steele it seemed excessive that a wife might possess her own property—as well as the absolute liberty to alienate it as she would. Like the parental marriage of convenience, this threatened to transform an affective into a crassly monetary association. The problem with pin money and jointures was that they rendered the state of matrimony "terrible," making young people distrustful and intimating "that they are very soon to be in a State of War with each other."[20]

Two years later, Joseph Addison imagined such an eventuality. Hoping to marry "a young Woman of a good Family," a correspondent of Mr. Spectator complains that he was obliged to enter "into a Treaty with her longer than that of the Grand Alliance."[21] Taxed by this marital obligation, the correspondent sardonically invokes the language of international politics and warfare to inquire of Mr. Spectator "whether you find any mention of *Pin-money* in *Grotius, Puffendorf,* or any other" authors (that is, theorists of natural law). In his response, Mr. Spectator agrees that "the supplying a Man's Wife with Pin-money, is furnishing her with Arms against himself." That is, the wife's desire for a modicum of financial autonomy transforms the matrimonial state of nature into a state of war. So for men like Addison, the devolution of absolutism, commendable enough in its passage from magistrate to parliament to male property owner, must come to a halt at married women. If the husband cannot be absolute sovereign in his own house, then he must be a slave and his wife absolute mistress.[22]

20. Sir Richard Steele, *Tatler,* no. 199 (July 18, 1710), in *The Tatler,* vol. 3, ed. D. F. Bond (Oxford: Oxford University Press, 1987), 66.
21. The Grand Alliance was concluded between England, Holland, and the Emperor Joseph I at The Hague in 1701.
22. Joseph Addison, *Spectator,* no. 295 (Feb. 7, 1712), in *The Spectator,* vol. 3, ed. D. F. Bond (Oxford: Oxford University Press, 1965), 51–52. On international relations as constituting a state of nature, see Locke, *Second Treatise of Government,* ch. 2, sec. 14 (pp. 294–95).

In these commentaries, the analogy between the family and the state has acquired the self-conscious detachment of parody. Like the mock-heroic literary forms with which it is contemporary, such discourse seems delicately balanced between approval and critique of the comparison, which sheds a public light on private matters even as it appears to disdain that illumination. As in much mock-heroic, moreover, the signifying relationship has become reversed. The little, no longer a means of reflecting on the great, has become instead an uncertain end in itself—that which political metaphor is itself invoked to disclose. In some mock-heroics, the two crucial questions converge. "What's the relation between the heroic and the trivial?" is made to seem a slightly different way of asking the question "What's the relation between the public and the domestic?" Self-consciously "domesticating" classical epic as modern boudoir escapades—and ultimately, as modern marriage—Alexander Pope prefaces *The Rape of the Lock* (1712, 1714) with the observation: "For the ancient Poets are in one respect like many modern Ladies; Let an Action be never so trivial in itself, they always make it appear of the utmost Importance." Like Behn (and, he implies, like Homer himself), Pope finds it no easy task to disentangle love and war, private and public; he begins his poem in allusion to the *Iliad:*

What dire Offence from am'rous Causes springs,
What mighty Contests rise from trivial Things . . . [23]

And yet despite their evident resistance, men like Steele and Addison were also able to conceive modern marriage in the emergent terms of domesticity, and the modern wife in the more positive (if patronizing) terms of ethical governance and financial management. Addison imagines Aurelia, whose "Family is under so regular an Œconomy, in its Hours of Devotion and Repast, Employment and Diversion, that it looks like a little Common-Wealth within itself."[24] In this fashion, the modern wife internalizes as private virtues some of the public functions of the magistrate. Steele writes that "the Soul of a Man and that of a Woman are made very unlike, according to the employments for which they are designed. The Ladies will please to observe, I say, our Minds have different, not superior Qualities to theirs. . . . To manage well a great Family, is as worthy an Instance of Capacity, as to execute a great Employment. . . ."[25]

Steele's words suggest that if modern sexual difference is structured as a comprehensive separation of the public from the private, this structure also

23. Alexander Pope, *The Rape of the Lock,* in *The Twickenham Edition of the Poems of Alexander Pope,* ed. J. Butt, vol. 2, ed. G. Tillotson (London, 1940), "Dedication" and canto 1, lines 1–2 (pp. 142, 144). For the conjugal moral, see canto 5, lines 9–34.
24. Addison, *Spectator,* no. 15 (March 17, 1711), in Bond, *The Spectator,* vol. 1, 68.
25. Steele, *Tatler,* no. 172 (May 16, 1710), in Bond, *The Tatler,* vol. 2, 444.

mobilizes the discovery of a "public" authority within the province of the private. Thus one of Steele's correspondents wonders at the rarity of the man wise enough to seek a wife "who will manage that Share of his Estate he intrusts to her Conduct with Prudence and Frugality, [and] govern his House with Oeconomy and Discretion."[26] As we have seen, the traditional household or domestic economy has the complex modern destiny of aiding in the institutionalization not only of domesticity, but also of political economy. Modernity conceives both domesticity and political economy as components of the private realm, coexisting over against the public realm of state politics. And yet within the private realm, the passage of the typically male breadwinner between home and economy is persuasively experienced as a shuttling back and forth between the private and the public. By the same token, however, the fixity of the typically female homemaker within the private home entails a practice that bears a persuasive resemblance to the public employment of the minister and the magistrate. The ideology of domesticity, in other words, provides a disarmingly simple model—the model of "separate spheres"—of how activities and identities are definitively separated out in the modern world. For the explicit separation of public from private also facilitates a flexible system of correlation, whereby the categories of public and private, and those of male and female, may be compared and even conflated.

IV

I will conclude this essay by drawing attention to one feature of an emergent domesticity to which I have already alluded, and that is especially suggestive for the assessment of its broadest historical meaning. This is the element of allegorical signification. Sixteenth- and seventeenth-century proponents of the patriarchalist analogy between the state and the family often stress its pedagogical utility. To cite only one formulation, John Cheke observed in 1549 that "dissension we see in small houses, and thereby may take example to great commonwealths. . . . and thereby learn to judge of great things unknown, by small things perceived."[27] Cheke's commonplace formulation suggests that the pedagogical utility of the patriarchalist analogy has a specifically hermeneutic character. By closely observing what is proximate and known, we learn how to interpret what is inaccessible and unknown. In this form, the maxim bears a close relation to a basic principle of Christian hermeneutics, the doctrine of accommodation. In Defoe's words, "we can

---

26. *Spectator,* no. 268 (Jan. 7, 1712), in Bond, *The Spectator,* vol. 2, 546.
27. John Cheke, *Hurt of Sedition* (1549), sig. K3r, quoted in L. C. Orlin, *Private Matters and Public Culture in Post-Reformation England* (Ithaca, N.Y.: Cornell University Press, 1994), 88.

Form no Idea of any Thing that we know not and have not seen, but in the Form of something that we have seen."[28]

But if patriarchalist hermeneutics is thus formally comparable to Christian hermeneutics, it also differs in (at least) one important respect. For in the allegorical relationship of family and state, the hermeneutic form of the relationship is also recapitulated on the level of content. One common figurative meaning of the verb *to domesticate* is, after all, to accommodate: to "naturalize" or to "familiarize" the great, the distant, the worldly, the strange, or the foreign by "bringing it home"—through the medium of the little, the proximate, the local, the familiar, or the native. This insight may aid us in a deeper understanding of the historical phenomenon of domesticity, which is evidently not only a social, but simultaneously an epistemological, practice. That is, the sociopolitical authority of the familial is confirmed by the epistemological authority of the familiar. Yet if the hermeneutic power of the domestic is traditional, modernity transvalues the domestic beyond hermeneutics, from a means to an end, from an instrumental signifier to a self-sufficient signified.

In Book 5 of *Paradise Lost* John Milton provides an instance of Christian hermeneutics that is remarkable in the way it thematizes its epistemological concerns within, and through, an explicitly domestic setting. Anticipating a visit from the seraph Raphael, Eve gathers from the Garden a wealth of "savoury fruits" and "nectarous draughts" with which to prepare "Dinner" in their "Silvan Lodge" for

> our Angel guest, as hee
> Beholding shall confess that here on Earth
> God hath dispenst his bounties as in Heav'n.
>   (bk. 5, lines 304, 306, 377, 396, 328–30)[29]

Eve's hopeful comparison becomes the topic of dinner-table conversation. This is "unsavory food perhaps/To spiritual Natures," Adam remarks doubtfully. Raphael replies that "Intelligential" creatures can happily eat the food of "Rational" creatures because they are able to "transubstantiate" it, "[a]nd corporeal to incorporeal turn" (lines 401–2, 408, 409, 438, 413).

Having eaten his fill, Adam now seeks to satisfy his hunger "to know/Of things above his World . . . ," and the angel proceeds to describe how creation is a vast scale of steps "[d]iffering but in degree, of kind the same." Food and knowledge, matter and spirit cohere in a gradual but integral process of transubstantiation:

28. Daniel Defoe, *Serious Reflections during the Life and Surprising Adventures of Robinson Crusoe* . . . (London, 1720), p. 46 (new pagination).

29. John Milton, *Paradise Lost* (1667), ed. M. Y. Hughes (New York: Odyssey Press, 1962); parenthetical citations in the text refer to this edition.

> . . . time may come when men
> With Angels may participate, and find
> No inconvenient Diet, nor too light Fare:
> And from these corporal nutriments perhaps
> Your bodies may at last turn all to spirit . . .
>
> (lines 454–55, 490, 493–97)

This is a simultaneous act of ontological modulation and hermeneutic accommodation, and it echoes other ways in which the great may be domesticated by the little—spirit by matter, knowing by eating, ontology by domesticity, theology by poetry. Forty years later, Steele undertook to accommodate the already arduous language of Milton's instant classic to the urbane idiom of emergent middle-class culture. Adam and Eve's quarrel after the Fall, Steele writes, "to a Modern will appear but a very faint Piece of Conjugal Enmity." Translated "out of Heroicks, and put into Domestick Stile," Milton's verse undergoes in turn its own parodic domestication, into the novelistic prose that will replace and extend—that is, accommodate—epic poetry in the modern world.[30]

I have suggested that the ultimate rebuke to royal absolutism is the radically devolutionary conviction that only the individual has absolute authority. If this is so, domesticity both sustains and socializes that rebuke by insisting that the site of absolute authority in the modern world is better seen to be the family, which anchors the mobile individual within the ethical collective that is overseen by the authority of the individual who stays at home. This is of course an ideology, not a blueprint for equality in the gendered distribution of power. One achievement of domestic ideology is to justify an emergent system of sexual difference by appearing to mitigate or annul the condition of inequality that the traditional system of sexual hierarchy ostentatiously proclaims.[31] At the same time, it is worth confronting what is manifestly liberating in the feminist maxim "the personal is political" with what is evidently patronizing in the domestic view of the housewife as a magistrate in miniature. The question is, at least in part, what do we mean by "power"?

To a striking degree, the logic of modernity is the logic of progressive privatization and interiorization, the implacable movement inward that initially finds there a more legible version of an authoritative exteriority—the trivial signifier of a greater signified—but ultimately discloses a nearer approach to the interior domain of authenticity "as such." Domesticity domesticates publicity; but it also transvalues the erstwhile triviality of privacy and obscurity by reconceiving that triviality as the seriousness of what

---

30. Steele, *Tatler*, no. 217 (Aug. 29, 1710), in Bond, *The Tatler*, vol. 3, 137–38.
31. See Michael McKeon, "Historicizing Patriarchy: The Emergence of Gender Difference in England, 1660–1760," *Eighteenth-Century Studies* 28, no. 3 (spring 1995): 295–322.

is authentically interior and subjective. Keep a journal of your life, said Johnson to Boswell. "It is by studying little things that we attain the great knowledge of having as little misery and as much happiness as possible."[32] But if the logic of modernity is that of the journey inward, the coherence of this journey depends entirely on the dialectical rediscovery, at each successive stage, of a new outpost of exteriority. The modern relation between the private and the public is finally not a mutual exclusion, but a tool to think with.

32. James Boswell, *Life of Johnson*, ed. R. W. Chapman (Oxford: Oxford University Press, 1980), July 14, 1763, p. 307.

The Cultural Contradictions of Feminism in the French Revolution

Carla Hesse

L'existence des femmes en société est encore incertaine.
MME. DE STAËL, *De la littérature*, P. 132

THE CULTURAL CONSEQUENCES
OF THE COMMERCIALIZATION OF PRINT

The progressive exclusion of women from public life during the decade of the French Revolution has become almost a commonplace in recent feminist historiography.[1] It is now widely argued that the patriarchalist cultural institutions of the Old Regime—mostly notably the court, the theater, and the salon—were more open to women, and more inherently mixed than the commercialized world of print, the cafés, and the universities inaugurated by the revolutionary Republic. This recent generation of research has been based almost entirely on the study of discursive constructions of modern gender norms, produced almost exclusively by men. The results of a statistical study I have conducted charting the history of female publishing practices between 1750 and 1800, however, has led me to a contrary conclusion—one that, I want to suggest in this essay, puts the development of normative gender claims in a distinctly different historical light. The study of female literary practices may reveal a different trajectory for women into the modern era.[2]

The collapse of the cultural institutions of the Old Regime after 1789—

---

1. See, most notably, Joan Landes, *Women and the Public Sphere in the Era of the French Revolution* (Ithaca, N.Y.: Cornell University Press, 1987); Lynn Hunt, *The Family Romance of the French Revolution* (Berkeley: University of California Press, 1992); Dena Goodman, *The Republic of Letters: A Cultural History* (Ithaca, N.Y.: Cornell University Press, 1994); Joan DeJean, *Tender Geographies: Women and the Origins of the Novel in France* (New York: Columbia University Press, 1991); Elizabeth C. Goldsmith and Dena Goodman, eds., *Going Public: Women and Publishing in Early Modern France* (Ithaca, N.Y.: Cornell University Press, 1995).

2. Carla Hesse, "French Women in Print, 1750–1800: An Essay in Historical Bibliography," in *The Darnton Debate: Books and Revolution in the Eighteenth Century,* Studies on Voltaire and the Eighteenth Century, vol. 359 (Oxford, 1998), 65–82.

most notably court patronage, the salons, the academies, and the system of royal guilds, privileges, and censorship that had organized the publishing world—resulted in a total restructuring of literary commerce along free-market lines, at least until 1810.[3] This dramatic deregulation of publishing led to an unprecedented expansion in the participation of women in public life through the venue of the printed word. Although there is not time for full exposition here, let me just briefly point to some of the results of my recent statistical research. After decades of stasis (1750–1789), the number of women in print more than trebled in the decade after 1789—from 78 to 330. Moreover, analysis of the annual incidence of publication during the revolutionary decade makes clear that this increase in female participation in print culture was no mere side effect of the vicissitudes of the early years of revolutionary mobilization, nor was it linked to the political logic of tolerance and repression over the course of the Revolution as a whole. Rather, it formed part of a long-term structural change linked to commercial trends in the publishing world. The most significant years of female literary production were thus those after Thermidor, when the French book trade began to recover from the revolutionary upheaval.[4] The laissez-faire economic policies of revolutionary legislators thus unwittingly made possible a dramatic entry of women into print. So dramatic, in fact, that Isabelle de Charrière would write to Benjamin Constant in August of 1798, "It seems to me that women are writing more than men these days."[5]

Statistical investigation of female participation in print culture from the Old Regime through the Revolution thus tells a radically different story than the one offered by recent historians of gender ideology and politics during the period. It suggests first of all that female participation in the public cultural life of the Old Regime was not only relatively marginal, it was also relatively static. The period of the high Enlightenment, despite the prominence of a few women novelists and a few *salonnières*, was not a period of significant inclusion of women in the public life of letters. Nor was it followed by their increasing exclusion during the closing years of the Old Regime and the revolutionary decade. To the contrary, the revolutionary decade witnessed a dramatic expansion of female participation in public cultural life and even in political debate. The single most frequent form of publication by women during the revolutionary decade was the political pamphlet.[6] It turns out, then, that the cultural institutions of the monarchy and the aristocracy were far less hospitable to female participation—at least

---

3. Carla Hesse, *Publishing and Cultural Politics in Revolutionary Paris, 1789–1810* (Berkeley: University of California Press, 1991), 359.

4. See Hesse, "French Women in Print," 70.

5. Letter from Isabelle de Charrière to Benjamin Constant, August 3, 1798, in *Oeuvres Complètes,* ed. Daniel Caudaux et al., vol. 5 (Geneva: Slatkine, 1981), 466.

6. Hesse, "French Women in Print," 79.

as measured by access to print—than was the liberalized commercial publishing world that the Revolution instituted. In contrast to the princes, courtiers, censors, and wealthy patrons of the Old Regime, the commercial publishers of the revolutionary period cared less about who was qualified to write and what they put into print—even when the political risks were extremely high—than whether or not it sold. The Revolution created unprecedented opportunities for women to enter into the public arena.

This is not to deny that the late eighteenth century and revolutionary period also witnessed the increasing elaboration of scientific and philosophical discourses aimed at maintaining sexual hierarchy and the subordination of women to men after the collapse of Aristotelian and biblical justifications.[7] Nor is it to deny that the successive regimes of the revolutionary period deployed this misogynist gender ideology to legislate laws in order to ensure the political and civic subordination of women.

But science, philosophy, and even law and politics are not mirrors of the social world, and the evidence concerning female literary production puts these developments in a somewhat different light. The data on women writers suggests that the economic and commercial vision of the Enlightenment and Revolution opened up possibilities for female participation in public life that may have been at odds with the dominant male conception of appropriate relations between the sexes. And it suggests that the elaboration of these philosophical, cultural, and ultimately juridical and political gender norms were not so much a reflection of the sociopolitical or cultural realities of the revolutionary period as they were a reactionary response to a sociocultural world that was rapidly exploding the normative boundaries of gender that these men held dear. It is the nature of this cultural contradiction that I want to examine in the remainder of this essay.

THE CULTURAL CONTRADICTIONS OF LITERARY WOMEN

Genevieve Fraisse and Lynn Hunt, among others, have rightly identified the period of the Thermidorian reaction (1795–1800) as a critical moment in the elaboration, and more important, the popularization of biological theories of gender difference as a means of justifying the continued civil and political subordination of women.[8] Early in the Revolution the Marquis de Condorcet and others had put the lie to the traditional biological argument that man was destined to rule woman in modern political affairs simply

---

7. See, in particular, Thomas Laqueur and Catherine Gallagher, eds., *The Making of the Modern Body* (Berkeley: University of California Press, 1987), and Thomas Laqueur, *Making Sex: Body and Gender from the Greeks to Freud* (Cambridge: Harvard University Press, 1990).

8. Genevieve Fraisse has charted the trajectory of this discourse from Pierre Roussel, *Système physique et moral de la femme* (1775), to Pierre-Jean-Georges Cabanis, *Rapport du physique et du moral de l'homme* (1802), and Julien-Joseph Virey, *De la femme sous ses rapports physiologique, moral,*

because of his superior physical strength. Advocates of women's political rights argued, following Locke, that the capacity for self-government resided not in physical force, but in the ability to reason—a capacity shared equally by both sexes.

The new biological science of the Thermidorian period was aimed directly against this position. Pierre Cabanis, most notably, argued that the capacity for independent reasoning was an attribute of the male sex alone. While the male sexual organ functioned independently from the brain, female sexuality was not specific to an organ. Rather, female sexuality permeated the entire body, including the brain, which it linked to the particular aims of reproduction. In this new biology women were seen as unsuited to govern not because of physical weakness, but rather because of mental incapacity.[9]

From these new theories a full-blown assault not upon women in general, but specifically upon *women writers,* emerged under the Directory. And this new mode of argumentation had consequences far beyond the debates about civil and political equality. It went right to the heart of cultural life itself, questioning the suitability of women to the production of knowledge through reading and writing and advocating a limited education for women, tailored narrowly to their maternal role. Drawing upon the theories of Cabanis, certain men of letters at the turn of the century began to elaborate a full-scale reaction to the increasing prominence of women in the world of print. They began to argue publicly that women were born to be objects rather than subjects of knowledge, to be represented by men because they were incapable of adequately representing themselves. And, thus by extrapolation, women who wrote were to be deemed not only anti-social, but also unnatural. Here are a few lines from Écouchard-Lebrun's "Aux belles qui veulent devenir poètes" [To the beauties who would be poets], published in 1796: "Voulez-vous ressembler aux Muses? Inspirez, mais n'écrivez pas" [If you wish to be muses, inspire, but don't write].[10] Sylvain Maréchal went further still, arguing against female literacy in his

---

et littéraire (1823), and *De la physiologie dans ses rapports avec la philosophie* (1844): See Genevieve Fraisse, *Muse de la raison: Democratie et exclusion des femmes en France* (Paris: Gallimard, 1995). See also Lynn Hunt, *The Family Romance,* esp. ch. 6; Anne Vila, "Sex and Sensibility," *Representations* 52 (1996): 76–93; and Michel Feher, "La retraite des femmes aimables," *Critique* (June 1997): 1–25. For the definitive treatment of the subject, see Laqueur, *Making Sex.*

9. See Fraisse, *Muse de la raison,* and Feher, "La retraite des femmes aimables," esp. p. 7. Feher quotes, for example, the following passage from Cabanis, *Rapport du physique*: "Les fibres charnues sont plus faibles et le tissu plus abondant chez les femmes que chez les hommes. . . . [O]n ne peut douter que ce soit la présence et l'influence de l'uterus et des ovaires qui produisent cette différence."

10. Ponce Denis Écouchard-Lebrun, "Aux belles qui veulent devenir poètes" (1796), in *Oeuvres,* vol. 1, bk. 6, Ode 3 (Paris: Berquet, 1827), 368–69, cited in Fraisse, *Muse de la raison,* 77.

notorious *Projet d'une loi portant défense d'apprendre à lire aux femmes* [Proposal for a law prohibiting women from learning to read], published in 1801.[11] This proposal was clearly satirical in nature, but coming as it did upon the heels of the new sex-specific curriculum for the primary schools and the denial of higher public education to women, the threats of further restrictions upon the cultural skills and power deemed suitable to women seemed real enough.[12]

The new chauvinism of the Thermidorian period met with criticism from both men and women.[13] I want to focus here on the female responses because, I will argue, they crystallized the parameters of a modern female poetics in the nineteenth and twentieth centuries, and indeed even formed the basis, I will suggest, for what has become a feminist poetics since World War II.

The most prominent women writers of the revolutionary period responded vociferously to this assault on female cultural equality and moral autonomy, and they mobilized a formidable arsenal of historical and linguistic erudition to their cause. Constance Pipelet, the Princess of Salm, launched a poetic counterassault on Lebrun in her *Épître aux Femmes* (1797):

> Mais déjà mille voix ont blâmé notre audace;
> On s'étonne, on murmure, on s'agite, on menace;
> On veut nous arracher la plume et les pinceaux;
> Chacun a contre nous sa chanson, ses bon mots.[14]

> [But already thousands condemn our courage;
> They are shocked, they whisper, they are unnerved, they heckle;
> They want to take our pens and our paintbrushes away;
> Each has against us song or a bon mot.]

11. Sylvain Maréchal, *Projet d'une loi portant défense d'apprendre à lire aux femmes* (Paris: Masse, 1801).

12. For an account of the retrenchment of democratic educational policies in the primary schools after Thermidor, see Isser Woloch, *The New Regime: Transformations of the French Civic Order, 1789–1820* (New York: Norton, 1994), 208–39. For the gender differences in curriculum and the exclusion of women from higher education after Thermidor, see Robert R. Palmer, *The Improvement of Humanity: Education and the French Revolution* (Princeton: Princeton University Press, 1985), esp. p. 316. See also Françoise Mayeur, "The Secular Model of Girls' Education," in *A History of Women,* vol. 4, ed. Georges Duby and Michelle Perrot (Cambridge: Harvard University Press, Belknap Press, 1993), 228–45.

13. Two of the most eloquent male defenders of female intellectual equality were Gabriel Legouve, in *Le mérite des femmes* (Paris: 1801), and Charles-Guillaume Thérémin, in *De la condition des femmes dans les républiques* (Paris: Laran, an VII [1799]).

14. Constance Pipelet, the Princess of Salm, *Épître aux Femmes* (1797), reedited in *Opinions des femmes de la veille au lendemain de la Révolution française,* ed. Geneviève Fraisse (Paris: Cotesfemmes, 1989), 69. On Constance Pipelet's self-fashioning as a writer, see Elizabeth Colwill, "Laws of Nature / Rights of Genius: The *Drame* of Constance de Salm," in *Going Public: Women and Publishing in Early Modern France,* ed. Elizabeth C. Goldsmith and Dena Goodman (Ithaca, N.Y.: Cornell University Press, 1995), 224–42.

Isabelle de Charrière's novel *Trois femmes* (1796) directly spoofed the sex-specific curriculum of the new French higher schools and, more generally, the assertion of female intellectual inferiority.[15] Mme. de Staël devoted an entire chapter of *De la littérature* (1800) to "Women who cultivate letters."[16] These three were followed by Fanny Raoul's *Opinion d'une femme sur les femmes* (1801), Albertine Clément-Hémery's *Les femmes vengées de la sottise d'un philosophe du jour, ou réponse au projet de loi de M. S**.M***, portant défense d'appendre à lire aux femmes* (1801), Mme. Garçon-Dufour's *De la nécessité de l'instruction pour les femmes* (1805), Mme. Dufrenoy's two-volume novel *La femme auteur ou les inconvénients de la célébrité* (1812), and not least, Mme. de Genlis' 1811 treatise, *De l'influence des femmes sur la littérature française,* where, in an extraordinary opening passage, she openly acknowledges that in the face of recent attempts to prohibit women from writing and publishing she has decided to break her silence on these matters and come to the defense of literary women.[17]

None of these women asserted the physical equality of women and men, nor did many of them demand equal civil or political rights (indeed they held an extraordinary range of views on these matters). All of them, however, from Genlis to Pipelet, insisted upon the intellectual equality of women and their right to moral autonomy, even from their husbands. All of them found specious and degrading the argument that women's intellectual capacities were biologically determined. All of them insisted upon the right of women to self-representation through writing and the visual arts and to self-constitution through an independent moral and intellectual life. All of them defended, as Albertine Clément-Hémery put it, "le besoin qu'elles éprouvent . . . de peindre leurs maux et leur félicité" [the need (women) have to depict their woes and their happiness].[18] And all would have no doubt concurred with Pipelet that "pour nous comme les hommes, l'oubli est le plus grand des maux, l'espoir d'y échapper place nos esprits dans une autre sphere d'idées" [for us as for men, being forgotten is the greatest of ill-fates, and it is the hope of escaping it that sends our thoughts to higher spheres].[19] In a fundamental sense, then, the feminist politics that

15. Isabelle de Charrière, *Trois femmes* (1796), in *Oeuvres Complètes*, vol. 9.

16. Mme. de Staël, *De la littérature considérée dans ses rapports avec les institutions sociales*, pt. 2, ch. 6 (1800; reprint, Paris: Garnier-Flammarion, 1991), 332–41.

17. Mme. de Genlis, *De l'influence des femmes sur la littérature française, comme protectrices des lettres et comme auteurs; ou Précis de l'histoire des femmes françaises les plus célèbres* (Paris: Maradan, 1811), xxxiii.

18. Albertine Clément-Hémery, *Les femmes vengées de la sottise d'un philosophe du jour* (Paris: Benoist, 1801), 124.

19. Constance Pipelet, the Princess of Salm, "Lettre CLXIII: Femmes auteurs," in *Ouvrages divers en prose, suivis de mes soixantes ans, par Mme la Princesse, Constance de Salm*, vol. 1 (Paris: Firmin Didot, 1835), 243–44.

emerged in response to the new biology of Thermidor was centrally preoccupied with the literary.

TOWARD A FEMININE POETICS OF ENLIGHTENMENT

Two of the greatest contributions to French literary theory made by women, Mme. de Staël's *De la littérature* (1800) and Mme. de Genlis' *De l'influence des femmes sur la littérature* (1811) were written in the context of, and indeed, in large part in response to, this debate. Both were written to establish the achievements and claims of women to the literary. These two postrevolutionary texts departed from earlier works on women writers, such as Louise de Kéralio's *Collection des meilleurs ouvrages français composés par des femmes* (1786–88), in that they were not celebrations of women who wrote, but rather critical histories of the literature itself. As Genlis put it:

> Il y avait beaucoup d'ouvrages volumineux, contenant l'histoire des femmes auteurs, mais la plus grand partie de ces auteurs sont médiocres. On a fait cet ouvrage sur un plan différent: on n'y parlera que des femmes qui ont eu quelque influence sur la littérature françoise.[20]
>
> [There have been many voluminous works, treating the history of women authors, but the greater part of these authors are mediocre. This work has a different goal: it will discuss only those women who have had some impact on French literature.]

Indeed, it would not be an exaggeration to say that these two texts represented attempts to recover the right to the literary for women in the face of what appeared to each of these very different women as attempts by science to reduce women to their objective corporeal essence.

The central theme of Mme. de Staël's chapter on women in *De la littérature* is precisely that of the problem of the overexposure of women, and especially women who publish:

> On peut remarquer que dès qu'un homme s'aperçoit que vous avez éminemment besoin de lui, presque toujours il se refroidit pour vous. Quand une femme publie un livre, elle se met tellement dans la dépendance de l'opinion que les dispensateurs de cette opinion lui font sentir durement leur empire.[21]
>
> [It is worth remarking, that as soon as a man realizes that you desire him, he almost always cools towards you. When a woman publishes a book, she has put herself so much at the mercy of opinion that the dispensers of that opinion make her feel their power over her.]

In publishing, Staël suggests, one puts oneself up for public scrutiny, and

---

20. Mme. de Genlis, *De l'influence des femmes*, vii.
21. Mme. de Staël, *De la littérature*, 334.

women are especially vulnerable to this because they are always at greater
risk of being read transparently, as though their words are a window into
their natures. The Republican cultural politics of the revolutionary moment
aggravated this tendency, because though it sought to encourage greater
simplicity and openness in public discourse, this frankness in reality ended
up in an unbearable coarseness of expression:

> . . . [D]epuis la Révolution, les hommes ont pensé qu'il était politiquement et
> moralement utile de réduire les femmes à la . . . plus absurde médiocrité. . . .
> [O]n n'a pu rendre la simplicité des premiers âges; il en est seulement résulté
> que moins d'esprit a conduit à moins de délicatesse, à moins de respect pour
> l'estime public.[22]
>
> [Since the Revolution, men have thought it politically and morally useful to
> reduce women to the most absurd mediocrity. . . . It wasn't possible to recover
> the simplicity of manners of earlier ages; rather, the result has been a coars-
> ening of manners, less *délicatesse,* and less deference to public esteem.]

This loss of "délicatesse" and of respect for the distinction between public
and private, between life and its representation, person and author, formed
part of the same tendency to render women's nature transparently readable. In reaction to this, she speculates, women who write under republics
will perhaps find themselves turning from philosophy to literature. They will
need to recivilize public discourse by insisting on the opacity rather than the
transparency of language, on the differences among particular lives rather
than the universal characteristics of mankind. Indeed, women may become,
under republics, the sign of the literary itself:

> Peut-être serait-il naturel que . . . la littérature proprement dite devint le
> partage des femmes, et que les hommes se consacrassent uniquement à la
> haute philosophie.[23]
>
> [Perhaps it is natural that . . . literature, in the narrow sense, will become the
> domain of women, and that men will devote themselves exclusively to formal
> philosophy.]

The literary, that is, an insistence on the opacity of language rather than its
transparency, its fictive powers, could provide women with a means to engage
in public discourse without overexposing their persons to critical male
scrutiny. In response to the Republican movement to naturalize woman's
identity, women would insist upon their capacity to invent themselves.

Two years after the publication of *De la littérature,* Staël's novel *Delphine*
appeared. Here she developed in fictional form a tragic account of the risks
of feminine transparency that she cautioned against in *De la littérature.*

22. Ibid.
23. Ibid.

Delphine's life story exemplifies the dilemmas of a woman who refuses to dissimulate in society—a woman who overexposes herself to public scrutiny. The irony, of course, is that in a society characterized by the art of dissimulation, transparent actions result only in misapprehensions. Purity of motives cannot protect virtuous women from the public assumption that women dissimulate. The only hope for women is either to play the game of social dissimulation—willfully taking public opinion into consideration—or to renounce social life altogether. Transparency, for women, leads to tragedy.

Mme. de Genlis took these themes even further in the preliminary discourse to *De l'influence des femmes sur la littérature.* She writes:

> On prétend que les femmes par leur organisation sont douées d'une délicatesse que les hommes ne peuvent avoir; ce jugement favorable ne me paraît pas plus fondé que tous ceux qui leur sont avantageux: plusieurs ouvrages faits par des gens de lettres prouvent que ce mérite n'est nullement exclusif chez les femmes; mais il est vrai que c'est un des caractères distinctifs de presques tous leurs écrits.[24]

> [It is claimed that women, by constitution, are gifted with a refinement that men are not capable of; this favorable judgment seems to me no better founded than the less flattering ones: several works composed by men of letters are proof that this quality is not exclusive to women; but it is true that it is one of the distinctive characteristics of almost all of their writings.]

Genlis thus takes the trait of "délicatesse" attributed to female biology and denaturalizes it, exposing it as an effect of literary artifice. Indeed, she exposes the purported biological attributes of the "feminine" to be, rather, as series of representational tactics, that work precisely to produce a gap between the object and its representation:

> Cela doit être parce que l'éducation et la bienséance leur imposent la loi de contenir, de concentrer presque tous leurs sentiments et d'adoucir toujours l'expression: de là ces tournures délicates, cette finesse excercée à faire entendre ce que l'on n'ose expliquer.[25]

> [This must be because education and proper comportment requires them to contain and to constrain practically all of their feelings and to always soften their expression: the result is those delicate turns of phrase, that acute refinement of making oneself understood without daring to explicate.]

The withholding of an explicit betrayal of one's inner feelings is not, she continues, a form of dissimulation or an attempt to hide one's feelings; "au contraire, sa perfection est de le faire bien connaître sans expliquer, sans

---

24. Mme de Genlis, *De l'influence des femmes,* xx–xxi.
25. Ibid.

employer des paroles qu'on puisse citer comme un aveu positif"[26] [to the contrary, when perfectly achieved it makes known with explaining, without employing words that could be quoted as a positive avowal]. This is not simply the essence of women's art, she continues, but of all great art:

> Quel mauvais goût il faut avoir pour dévoiler tout ce mystère, pour anéantir toutes les grâces, en présentant dans un roman, ou dans un ouvrage dramatique, une héroïne sans pudeur, s'exprimant avec tout emportement.[27]
>
> [What bad taste one must have to disclose all the mysteries of the soul, to extinguish all the traits of grace, by presenting—be it in a novel or a dramatic work—a heroine lacking modesty who expresses herself without reserve.]

The great effects of all fictional works are, she writes, the result of reticence and the constraint of sentiment.[28] All great works produce their dramatic effect by revealing the gap between inner feeling and its external representation. These moments of constrained expression are not moments of repression but, to the contrary, moments of extraordinary self-possession, in which the self can be seen to exist independently from, and in a determining relation to, its external representations. This doubling of the self, this gap between inner and outer, is precisely the essence and the sign of moral autonomy.

Indeed, one of the most striking features of women's writing of the revolutionary, and especially the post-Thermidorian, era is the abundance of feminine figures of a doubled self. Early on in the Revolution they emerge as embattled gestures of capitulation or resistance to misogynist attacks upon politically active women—for example Louise de Kéralio writing to Brissot de Warville, in the face of virulent public criticism of her activism, recants her life of letters, but only by referring to herself in the third person.[29] Or, alternatively, Olympe de Gouges defiantly signs the *Prognostic sur Maximilien Robespierre*—the poster-pamphlet that precipitated her arrest and ultimate execution for treason—with the pseudonym of "an amphibious animal."[30] These, to be sure, were desperate rhetorical maneuvers, attempts to resurrect a separation between their private persons and their public representations in moments of extreme public conflict.

After Thermidor, with the advent of the new biology, the figuration of the

26. Ibid.

27. Ibid., pp. xxiii–xxiv.

28. Ibid.

29. *Archives Nationales:* (Papiers Brissot) series 446 AP 7, doc188: Letter from Louise de Kéralio to Brissot de Warville, 10 October [1789?].

30. Olympe de Gouges: *Prognostic sur Maximilien Robespierre, par un animal amphibie* (N.p., n.d. [Paris, 1793]): She opens with a "portrait exact de cet animal" in the following terms: "Je suis un animal sans pareil, je ne suis ni homme, ni femme. J'ai tout le courage de l'un, et quelquefois les faiblesses de l'autre."

woman writer as a doubled self was developed as a self-conscious and systematic motif in women's writing—both theoretical and fictional. Constance Pipelet, following the work of Charles-Guillaume Thérémin, responded to the new biology through a reprise of the line of Enlightenment argumentation begun by John Locke and developed by the Marquis de Condorcet. She writes:

> . . . [I]l y a deux êtres dans la femme, aussi bien que dans l'homme; le premier est un être moral, libre par essence, ne connaissant des lois que celles de sa moralité, et n'ayant point de sexe; et le second, un être physique, dépendant de l'homme de la même manière que l'homme en est dépendant. . . . Cette distinction ingénieuse jette une vive clarté sur les contradictions perpétuelles.[31]

> [There are two beings in a woman, as there are in a man; the first is a moral being, free in essence, knowing no law except its own morality, and having no sex; the second is a physical being, dependent on man in the same way that man is dependent upon woman. . . . This ingenious distinction throws a clear light upon perpetual contradictions.]

Unlike Condorcet, however, Pipelet did not view the existence of this independent moral self as the basis for equal female participation in civil and political society. Subscribing instead to the theory of virtual representation through the "head of the household," she argued that women were dependent upon men in civil and political life, but nonetheless retained an independent moral voice. In short, Pipelet advanced an argument identical to that of Immanuel Kant in his famous essay of 1784, "What Is Enlightenment?": women were to be at once public individuals—that is, juridically subservient to the sovereign—and yet at the same time private individuals—that is free moral participants in a critical public sphere.

The motif of the women writer as a doubled self, at once public and private, circulated in fictional forms as well after Thermidor. The most explicit example is Mme. Dufrenoy's 1812 novel, *La femme auteur, ou les inconvénients de la célébrité*, a thinly allegorized recounting of the struggles between Mme. de Staël and Napoleon. But in this fictionalized version, the young widowed woman writer, Mme. Simiane, is able to triumph over the chauvinist prejudices of the military hero she adores by wooing him first under an assumed name, which permits him to see her virtues independently of her fame and ultimately to overcome his aversion to literary women.[32] It is only by pro-

---

31. Constance Pipelet, the Princess of Salm, "Rapport sur un ouvrage intitule 'De la Condition des Femmes dans la République'" (1799), in *Ouvrages divers en prose, suivis de mes soixantes ans, par Mme la Princesse, Constance de Salm*, vol. 2 (Paris: Firmin Didot, 1835), 149–50.

32. Anne Dufrenoy, *La femme auteur, ou les inconvénients de la célébrité*, 2 vols. (Paris: Bechet, 1812).

ducing a second self, as it were, that she can be seen for what she is. Dissimulation makes the recognition of feminine virtue possible.

From these women's writings at the beginning of the new century a set of poetic tropes of female literary invention were thus set in motion—the proliferation of pseudonymous publications, or repudiation of the family name in public signatures, from the St. Simonians to Colette to the practices of literary transvestism à la George Sand—all of which aimed not to hide the female identities of their authors, but rather to insist upon the fictive nature of their elective public identities.[33] This feminine poetics of antitransparency that emerged from the cultural contradictions of the revolutionary decade would ultimately form the point of departure for feminist philosophical reflection in our own times. At a minimum it suggests that Simone de Beauvoir's assertion in *The Second Sex,* that "Woman is not born, she is made," drew upon very deep roots in the literary engagements of the women of the revolutionary era.

CONCLUSION

The French Revolution did not result in a structural exclusion of women from the public sphere. To the contrary, the deregulation of print commerce permitted a dramatic expansion of their presence in public discourse of all forms. However, the postrevolutionary period saw the advent of regulatory and disciplinary mechanisms of the state and neo-corporatist professional associations which, in effect, made it possible to sustain gender hierarchies in the face of the ever corrosive and democratizing possibilities of the market (for example, restrictions of access to higher public education and exclusion from the professions). The modern French woman writer emerged from the French Revolution as a Kantian, rather than a Lockean, subject: a doubled self, at once public and private, at once subservient and independent. The long nineteenth century (actually, the period from 1789 to 1945), I suggest, was for women essentially a century of enlightened absolutism. The structural position of women as at once morally autonomous and political subservient was given expression through an aesthetics of antitransparency, and this would put women's writings in opposition to the realist aesthetic dominant among the male writers who emerged from the revolutionary era. Modern French women writers thus forged an alternative aesthetic trajectory to that of their male counterparts.

33. See Carla Hesse, "Reading Signatures: Women and Literary Property in Revolutionary France," *Eighteenth-Century Studies* (winter 1989): 469–87; on the specific question of female pseudonymity, see Roger Bellet, "Masculin et féminin dans les pseudonymes des femmes de lettres aux XIXe siècle," in *Femmes de lettres au XIXe siècle: Autour de Louise Collet,* ed. Roger Bellet (Lyon: Presse Universitaire de Lyon, 1982); on literary transvestism, see Leyla Ezdinli, "George Sand's Literary Transvestism: Pretexts and Contexts" (Ph.D. diss., Princeton University, 1988).

The new biology of the Thermidorian period sought to put female intellectual activity into total subservience to her reproductive role, and hence to restrict her access to public modes of intellectual exchange. Literary women responded to these challenges to their newfound cultural authority by asserting a special relationship to the literary and to fictional writing. Faced with the constant pressure to denaturalize their identities in reaction to the era's scientific and philosophical attempt to determine their nature, women writers had to assert themselves continuously against discourses of naturalization, and to insist upon the opacity of language as well as the fictive and indeterminate nature of female identity. The trajectory I have traced is admittedly an odd one, running as it does from Mme. de Genlis to Simone de Beauvoir, but it is precisely the incommensurablity of their identities that attests to the success of their literary tactics in inventing and sustaining a space for feminine self-representation in the modern era.

Misogyny and Feminism

The Case of Mary Wollstonecraft

Barbara Taylor

Misogyny and feminism: a provocative pairing. And to attach the misogynist label to Mary Wollstonecraft, heroine of western feminism, seems provocation indeed. In 1994 Susan Gubar published an article on Wollstonecraft offering precisely these provocations. In her essay "Feminist Misogyny: Mary Wollstonecraft and the Paradoxes of 'It Takes One to Know One,'" published in *Feminist Studies*, Gubar took a coolly irreverent look at Wollstonecraft and the western feminist tradition that succeeded her, and concluded that for the last two hundred years, "the histories of feminism and misogyny have been (sometimes shockingly) dialogic."[1] From 1792 on, feminists, fondly believing they were marching to their own political drum, have in fact all too often been engaged in an elaborate pas de deux with women-hating contemporaries, matching idea to idea in an "uncanny mirror dancing that repeatedly link[ed] feminist polemicists to their rivals and antagonists."[2] Hence the "takes one to know one" of Gubar's subtitle: the feminist knows at whom to hurl the charge of woman-hater because his visage is so shockingly similar to her own; the adversarial hailing is a repudiated self-recognition. Accuser and accused are one.

This article begins from Gubar's provocations. If Mary Wollstonecraft can be described, as Gubar emphatically does, as a misogynist, how are we—as inheritors of Wollstonecraft's project—to understand the origins and implications of this antiwomanism for her emancipationist aspirations? What kind of heretical historical writing is capable of addressing such difficult issues? Heroic versions of the feminist past of the sort popular during the

1. Susan Gubar, "Feminist Misogyny: Mary Wollstonecraft and the Paradoxes of 'It Takes One to Know One,'" *Feminist Studies* 29, no. 30 (1994): 454.

2. Ibid., 462.

heyday of the women's liberation movement clearly will not do; but integrating a misogynist element into the feminist story will require more than just abandoning these earlier idealizations. If Gubar's argument is even partly right—as I think it partly is—a radical revision of approach is needed.

The necessary revision, I'm proposing here, is toward a method that combines traditional modes of historical inquiry—the intensive scrutiny of sources and context—with an interpretative theory capable of tackling what I'll call the deep agenda of feminism, by which I mean the unconscious fantasies as well as the conscious intentions fueling feminist ideals. Every political agenda is driven by unacknowledged and unacknowledgeable wishes, as well as by more or less realistic ambitions: desire in the social/political sphere is no more reason-governed than desire in any other area of life. This may seem so obvious as to hardly be worth saying, except that its implications have barely begun to register in histories of political thinkers and movements. In my own research I explore how fantasies of gender shaped Wollstonecraft's ideas about women, and here I draw on some of this work to probe the issues raised by Gubar's provocative essay.

Gubar's discussion of Wollstonecraft begins with the question "What images of women emerge from *A Vindication of the Rights of Woman?*" to which she replies:

> Repeatedly and disconcertingly, Wollstonecraft associates the feminine with weakness, childishness, deceitfulness, cunning, superficiality, an overvaluation of love, frivolity, dilettantism, irrationality, flattery, servility, prostitution, coquetry, sentimentality, ignorance, indolence, intolerance, slavish conformity, fickle passion, despotism, bigotry, and a "spaniel-like affection." The feminine principle, so defined, threatens—like a virus—to contaminate and destroy men and their culture. For, as Wollstonecraft explains, "Weak, artificial beings, raised above the common wants and affections of their race, in a premature, unnatural manner, undermine the very foundation of virtue, and spread corruption through the whole mass of society."[3]

She goes on to give additional examples in the same mode, and I could add plenty more: denunciations of women's fanatical piety and superstition; contemptuous dismissals of their passions for shopping, lap-dogs, and romantic novels; fierce tirades against their exploitation of sexual charm to trap and tyrannize men in private life, and to obtain illicit influence over public affairs; and so on and so forth. The tone, as Gubar indicates, is so severe as to be strongly reminiscent of male misogynist satire. Gubar

---

3. Ibid., 456. The sentence of Wollstonecraft's quoted by Gubar here is not a description of women, but of "the great": it is this symbolic equation between women and the ruling elite that I go on to discuss in this article (Mary Wollstonecraft, *A Vindication of the Rights of Woman* [1792; reprint, New York: Penguin Books, 1992], 81).

acknowledges that these "derogations of the feminine . . . are framed in terms of [Wollstonecraft's] breakthrough analysis of the social construction of gender," which emphasized "the powerful impact of culture on subjectivity"; but she goes on to point out that "although . . . *A Vindication of the Rights of Woman* sets out to liberate society from a hated subject constructed to be subservient and called 'woman' it illuminates how such animosity can spill over into antipathy of those human beings most constrained by that construction."[4]

The aim, then, of the feminist enterprise as Wollstonecraft inaugurated it (as Gubar might have said, but doesn't) was less to free women than to abolish them: an aspiration certainly suggested at various points in *A Vindication of the Rights of Woman*. It is the "desire of being always women" that is the "very consciousness which degrades the sex," Wollstonecraft writes, while again: "Men are not always men in the company of women; nor would women always remember that they are women, if they were allowed to acquire more understanding."[5] The woman of wisdom and virtue, she tells her readers at one point, is the one who can "forget her sex" even at that time of life when sexual consciousness is most insistent, promoting in herself instead those capacities common to all humanity, "regardless of the distinction of sex."[6]

Being able to forget one's sex may not seem a very life-enhancing ambition. It is, however, one with serious staying power in the feminist tradition. Ann Snitow, another American literary critic, some years ago wrote a splendid personal reflection on the paradoxes of female identity in second-wave feminism. Recalling her first experience of attending a consciousness-raising group in the early 1970s, Snitow remembered thinking exultantly, "Now I don't have to be a woman anymore. . . . 'Woman' is my slave name; feminism will give me freedom to seek some other identity altogether." Another woman asked Snitow, "How can someone who doesn't like being a woman be a feminist?" to which Snitow replied, "Why would anyone who likes being a woman *need* to be a feminist?"[7]

Gubar cites this, along with a catalogue of similarly complex antiwoman comments from feminists as diverse as Olive Schreiner, Kate Millett, Denise Riley, and Germaine Greer, to make the general case that "as a genre, feminist expository prose inevitably embeds itself in the misogynist tradition it seeks to address and redress."[8] In Cora Kaplan's words, which Gubar quotes, "There is no feminism that can stand wholly outside femininity as it is posed

4. Gubar, "Feminist Misogyny," 457.
5. Wollstonecraft, *Rights of Woman*, 202, 234.
6. Ibid., 140.
7. Ann Snitow, "A Gender Diary," in *Conflicts in Feminism*, ed. M. Hirsch and E. Fox Keller (London: Routledge: 1990), 9, 33.
8. Gubar, "Feminist Misogyny," 462.

in a given historical moment. All feminisms give some hostage to feminini-
ties and are constructed through the gender sexuality of their day as well as
standing in opposition to them."[9]

Kaplan's point is clearly right. Yet in the rest of her essay Gubar (unlike
Kaplan) makes little attempt to look at the historical moment in which
Wollstonecraft was writing. She has little to say about early modern misogynist traditions, or why such rhetoric might have appealed to eighteenth-century feminists. The word *inevitably*—as in "feminist . . . prose inevitably
embeds itself in the misogynist tradition"—simply closes an explanatory
door that must be prized open if we're to explore these difficult issues.

So what kind of history of feminism can grapple with such matters?
Three levels of historical inquiry are required to illuminate Wollstonecraft's
antiwoman rhetoric. First: the study of intellectual and cultural context.
This is presumably uncontroversial, but worth emphasizing since the kind
of detailed investigations necessary for a properly historical account of feminist thinkers are still, in most cases, at a fairly early stage. Second: individual and (in appropriate cases) collective biographies, which in turn cannot
be separated from . . . Third: the exploration of feminist mentalities, or
what I would call a psychic history of feminism. This is, I need hardly say, a
much more contentious area of inquiry, particularly when it is linked, as I
think it must be, to a psychic history of femininity—that is, to an account of
the unconscious fantasies as well as conscious aspirations that go into the
making of feminine identity, and how these fantasies and aspirations are in
turn reflected in feminist politics.

Once we begin to think in terms of the third dimension of historical
method—that is, in terms of feminism's motivating fantasies—we can begin
to explore a question that Gubar strikingly fails to ask: what is misogyny?
Using this term to describe Wollstonecraft's invective is perfectly accurate if
what is meant by misogyny is any expression of hostility to women as a sex;
but is this really adequate? After all, just who is being hated when something
called Woman is hated? The mother, the lover, the wife, the whore, the cas-
trating bitch, or the Amazon man-woman (as Wollstonecraft herself was so
often represented)? In the case of men, misogyny is now generally understood as a phobic response to feared and repudiated aspects of the male
personality that are designated as feminine in order to be consigned to others (women or other men, notably male homosexuals). What is hated is a
fantasy, or fantasies, of the feminine that is a projection of whatever is most
frightening or unsettling in the male psyche, particularly feelings of disor-
der, helplessness, humiliation. As one interpreter of early modern satire
observes, the satirist "hopes, almost prays, that whatever out there threatens

9. Cora Kaplan, "Wild Nights: Pleasure/Sexuality/Feminism," in F. Jameson et al., eds.,
Formations of Pleasure (London: Routledge, 1983); quoted in Gubar, "Feminist Misogyny," 459.

him does not by a stretch of his own imagination absorb him," and that fearful hope, it has been argued, is what can generally be detected behind male hatred of women.[10]

But what about misogyny in women, if such a thing can be allowed to exist? Who or what is hated when a woman hates women? Experiencing oneself as being "woman," I want to propose, is not a natural fact but an act of the imagination that draws on fantasies of femininity that are not necessarily more welcome to women than they are to men. I develop this point further on; let me turn first to the world in which Wollstonecraft's philippics against her sex were formulated and received.

"Is it possible," Gubar asks, "to view Wollstonecraft's description of femininity in *A Vindication of the Rights of Woman* as a portrait of any middle-class woman of her age?"[11] The answer is clearly meant to be yes, but in fact must be no, it isn't. The portrait of femininity that Wollstonecraft draws is, by and large, a depiction *not* of ordinary women of her own class but those of the wealthy landed elite. Wollstonecraft was *addressing* women and men of the middle class, but representing women of a higher strata—"ladies," as she scornfully dubs them—partly as a way of flattering the cultural sensibilities of men and women of her own background, but more importantly because elite women played a central symbolic role in eighteenth-century political thought. Viewing Wollstonecraft's writings on women as documents in early democratic radicalism (which is partly how they must be viewed) we can see in them metaphorical usages of Woman common to virtually all oppositionist political rhetoric. The figure of the idle lady of fashion, her languorous days passed in a "hot-bed of luxurious indolence," wallowing in the sybaritic pleasures of the table, the body, and steamy French novels, was a favorite symbol of aristocratic decadence not only for Wollstonecraft but for writers as varied as the Country polemicist John Brown, the radical James Burgh, the Evangelical Hannah More, and feminists such as Catherine Macaulay and Mary Hays.[12] "[S]poiled by prosperity and goaded on by

10. Michael Seidel, *The Satiric Inheritance: Rabelais to Sterne* (Princeton: Princeton University Press, 1979), 12, quoted in Felicity Nussbaum, *The Brink of All We Hate: English Satires on Women, 1660-1750* (Lexington: University Press of Kentucky, 1984), 4.

11. Gubar, "Feminist Misogyny," 460.

12. The quote is from Wollstonecraft, *Rights of Woman*, 162. "Estimate" Brown—as the Reverend John Brown was known after the title of his famous jeremiad against the evils of the times, *An Estimate of the Manners and Principles of the Times* (London, 1757)—fulminated against the "vain, luxurious and selfish effeminacy of the age," which eroded the "peculiar and characteristic" differences between the sexes: "the one Sex having advanced into Boldness, as the other has sunk into Effeminacy."

See James Burgh, *The Dignity of Human Nature* (London, 1754), for denunciations of the spread of female fashionable manners—frivolity, idleness, self-indulgence, etc.—downward from elite women to those of the rising middle class: "The ladies of our times give themselves up too generally to an idle and expensive manner of life, to the great detriment of œconomy,

temptation and the allurements of pleasure, [women of fashion] give a loose rein to their passions, and plunge headlong into folly and dissipation . . . to the utter extinction of thought, moderation, or strict morality," Mary Hays wrote sternly, adding that "[i]f this sentence, which I presume to pronounce on a considerable portion of my own sex, be deemed severe; let me be permitted to appeal to the votaries of fashion themselves; and let their own hearts tell, whether or not I judge harshly of their conduct."[13]

As in this quotation, what was particularly denigrated in such polemics was the erotic engrossment of fashionable women, which Wollstonecraft attacked at length and with a severity that has led many commentators to describe her as a sexual puritan. As in the writings of other political moralists, however, Wollstonecraft's target here was not women only; rather, the image of a corrupt, eroticized femininity was extended to all parasitic groups in society, most notably the professional military and the male rich. Throughout the late eighteenth century, political reformers had equated elite culture with what was dubbed "effeminacy," a polysemous term whose meanings all circulated around a feminized sexual subjectivity—weak, passive, penetrable rather than penetrating—to be found in women and the sexually incontinent, foppish, Francophile, and possibly homosexual men of the ruling class.[14] Political virtue and vice were sexualized through a series of symbolic connections in which heterosexual manliness was identified with a life of public duty and set against the luxuriously self-involved lives of the effete idle rich.[15] At one point in *A Vindication of the Rights of Men*, for

---

and the vexation of prudent masters of families" (p. 51). Burgh was an influential advocate of parliamentary reform; his widow, Hannah Burgh, was Wollstonecraft's neighbor and friend in Stoke Newington in the 1780s.

Hannah More, *Strictures on the Modern System of Female Education* (London, 1799), was a fierce opponent of Wollstonecraft's "Jacobinical" radicalism, but she was also—like many Evangelicals—a sharp critic of elite impiety and immorality. See also Catherine Macaulay, *Letters on Education* (1790).

13. Mary Hays, *Appeal to the Men of Great Britain on Behalf of Women* (London, 1798), 82–83.

14. I use the term *political reformer* loosely here, to refer both to "Country" opponents of the Whig establishment and to more liberal-minded radicals. Both attacked elite effeminacy, although the specifics of the attack differed somewhat. Foremost in the minds of most oppositionist politicians when they condemned "ladies of fashion" were the wives and mistresses of the Whig nobility. An important factor behind hostility to these women was the "illicit" influence they were seen to wield over their lovers and husbands. It is this notion of the "power behind the throne" that Wollstonecraft refers to when she repeatedly attacks women who, "not taught to respect public good . . . intermeddle with . . . weighty affairs, neglecting private duties only to disturb, by cunning tricks, the orderly plans of reason which rise above their comprehension" (*Rights of Woman*, 88).

15. For the importance of "effeminacy" in eighteenth-century political discourse, see Kathleen Wilson, *The Sense of the People* (Cambridge: Cambridge University Press, 1995), and Philip Carter, "An 'Effeminate' or 'Efficient' Nation? Masculinity and Eighteenth Century Social Documentary," in *Textual Practice* 11, no. 3 (1997).

example, Wollstonecraft describes the French nobility as "the profligates of rank, emasculated by hereditary effeminacy," while in a 1794 text she condemns the entire ancien régime as a "nation of women."[16] The English ruling class and all its various hangers-on—politicians, clergy, the professional army—have all been unmanned by rank and fortune, she writes; "supinely exist[ing] without exercising mind or body, they have ceased to be men."[17]

The derogation of femininity involved in such rhetoric of course demands explanation, as does Wollstonecraft's perpetuation of it in a text dedicated to the promotion of female status. Hostility to the sexual woman, as Gubar indicates, is the dominant motif, and it's here that Wollstonecraft reads most like earlier misogynist satirists. But again, when this issue of satire is examined more closely, matters appear more complex than Gubar indicates. As Alice Browne has noted, misogynist satire was seen by some women as an inspiration to self-improvement: the moralist and educator Sarah Trimmer, for example, claimed to have been set on the right moral track in her youth by reading Young's satires against women.[18] Further, these satirical traditions need to be set alongside the alternative literary tradition of chivalry or gallantry, in which women were praised for those qualities in which they were deemed superior to men: wit, beauty, compassion. If satire was the language of disgust, as Browne observes, gallantry was the language of desire;[19] yet feminists tended to be much more impatient with gallantry than misogyny, viewing it—as Wollstonecraft certainly did—as more patronizing toward women in its sentimental idealizations than the language of sex-war insult to be found in satire. "Why are girls to be told that they resemble angels; but to sink them below women?" Wollstonecraft demanded.[20] Listening to her rebut the sexual attitudes of her male contemporaries—particularly those of Edmund Burke, Drs. Gregory and Fordyce, and of course Rousseau—we hear very clearly the stern feminist voice, harshly condemnatory of the demerits of her sex, taking on those chivalric sentimentalists whose praise of female beauty and frailty barely masked an anxious revulsion. The *Rights of Woman* opens with the hopeful declaration, "My own sex . . . will excuse me, if I treat them like rational creatures, instead of flattering their *fascinating* graces, and viewing them as

16. Mary Wollstonecraft, *A Vindication of the Rights of Men* (1790; reprint, London: Pickering and Chatto, 1989), 40; Wollstonecraft, *An Historical and Moral View of the French Revolution* (1794; reprint, London: Pickering and Chatto, 1989), 121.

17. Wollstonecraft, *Rights of Men*, 10.

18. Alice Browne, *The Eighteenth Century Feminist Mind* (Brighton: Harvester Press, 1987), 22. Browne's brief but well-informed and subtle remarks on the relationship between misogynist satire and feminism are typical of this excellent book.

19. Ibid., 23.

20. Wollstonecraft, *Rights of Woman*, 197. See Nussbaum, *Brink of All We Hate,* chap. 9, for a good discussion of the shift from satire to idealization in the mid- to late eighteenth century.

if they were in a state of perpetual childhood," since such "soft phrases" of praise "are almost synonymous with epithets of weakness . . . and those beings who are [its] objects . . . will soon become objects of contempt." And further on: "If women be ever allowed to walk without leading-strings, why must they be cajoled into virtue by artful flattery and sexual compliments? Speak to them the language of truth and soberness, and away with the lullaby strains of condescending endearment!"[21]

As objects of desire and derogation, women are denied any independent intellectual or moral existence: they are merely, to use Wollstonecraft's word, "chimeras" of the male erotic imagination, manufactured into social existence through romantic conventions and cultural codes ("manners," in her eighteenth-century vocabulary). Against this objectified, eroticized version of femininity Wollstonecraft set the ideal of a rational womanhood dedicated to knowledge of truth and performance of duty. Love in such women would exist not as a fever of the appetites or as romantic sentiment but as a higher passion for all that is beautiful and good—in other words, as a devotion to God. The tradition on which this ideal drew, as I've shown elsewhere, was Christian Platonism[22]—and here again Wollstonecraft's thought was marked by a legacy of androcentric assumptions. Milton and Rousseau were the primary sources of her Platonism; yet in *Paradise Lost* it is of course Adam who is enjoined by the archangel to redirect his earthly passion for Eve toward heavenly love, while in *Emile* it is the eponymous hero who must learn to sublimate his desire for Sophie into divine ardor—never the other way around. Male spirit transcending the temptations of female flesh is an awkward paradigm of moral redemption for a feminist to work with. But in seizing on such ideas Wollstonecraft also—often very effectively—reworked them, designing a program for female moral emancipation that was genuinely, in some respects breathtakingly, new.

This achievement on Wollstonecraft's part highlights a problem with Gubar's notion of what she calls a "patrilineal literary inheritance."[23] This concept, which serves as her main explanation of feminist misogyny, describes a tradition of antiwoman writings by men to which feminist theorists become hostage: in Wollstonecraft's case, the chief culprit is of course Rousseau. This is a very big topic on which much needs to be said, but suffice to note here that the positions of men and women writers in the eighteenth century were much less fixed than this idea of "an alien and alienating aesthetic patrilineage" implies. Both Rousseau and Milton, for example, were

21. Wollstonecraft, *Rights of Woman,* 81, 82, 196.

22. Barbara Taylor, "For the Love of God: Religion and the Erotic Imagination in Wollstonecraft's Feminism," in *Mary Wollstonecraft and 200 Years of Feminisms,* ed. Eileen Yeo (London: Rivers Oram, 1997).

23. Gubar, "Feminist Misogyny," 462.

seen as friends to women because they attacked the sexual double standard, promoted companionate marriage, and—in Rousseau's case particularly—celebrated women's maternal role as moral educators. Rousseau's ideas about gender were far more complex and ambiguous than Gubar's presentation of them suggests, which is why they proved so important to Wollstonecraft. And the notion of women writers in this period being supinely indoctrinated by men is merely risible when one considers the numbers of these women, the range of genres in which they worked, and the cultural authority they were capable of wielding. Wollstonecraft spoke from the intellectual century of Pope and Swift and Rousseau but also from that of Johnson and Richardson—both strong supporters of women writers—and of Catherine Macaulay, Elizabeth Carter, Fanny Burney, Hester Thrale, Elizabeth Montagu, Anna Barbauld, Elizabeth Inchbald, Anna Seward, Mary Hays, Charlotte Lennox, Maria Edgeworth, Joanna Baillie, and Hannah More, all of whom, by the way, shared her stringent views on the need for a "revolution in female manners" to eradicate the vices of modern women.

That women have often been women's sternest critics is probably no news to most women reading this article; but the specific issue of Wollstonecraft's misogyny is clearer now that we see that it was the eroticized lady of fashion at whom her hostility was largely directed, as it was in the writings of most bourgeois moralists, male and female. Along with the ideological mileage to be gained by such sentiments, there were important social factors contributing to them. The first chapter of the *Rights of Woman* denounced the spread of "false refinement" from the aristocracy to the middle class, and particularly to newly affluent women who now, Wollstonecraft writes, "all want to be ladies"—that is, to ape the leisured lifestyle of the rich in place of the modest, work- and home-oriented lives of the traditional middling orders. Wollstonecraft's book is redolent with nostalgia for an idealized petit bourgeois world of craft manufactories, small shops, and independent businesses in which women could fully participate both as workers and wives, rather than living as the "voluptuous parasites" they now aspired to be. The reality behind this ideal was much more complex than Wollstonecraft's rhetoric allowed, but the impact of commercialism and consumerism on the lives of English women was clearly evident in her views, as were the attendant changes in women's position in a highly competitive marriage market.[24] Women's increased dependence on marriage, and the

24. For illuminating discussions of these changes, see Harriet Guest, "The Dream of a Common Language: Hannah More and Mary Wollstonecraft," *Textual Practice* 9, no. 2 (1995): 429–43; Elizabeth Kowaleski-Wallace, *Consuming Subjects: Women, Shopping, and Business in the 18th Century* (New York: Columbia University Press, 1997); Amanda Vickery, *The Gentleman's Daughter* (London: Yale University Press, 1998); John Brewer, *The Pleasures of the Imagination: English Culture in the 18th Century* (London: HarperCollins, 1997).

miserable fate suffered by many single or widowed women without independent sources of income, was a major stimulus behind Wollstonecraft's feminism—as it had been central to her own life experience.[25] Poised between the gentry to which her parents aspired and the poverty of self-supporting spinsterhood, Wollstonecraft knew all too well the degradation of a life spent in the respectable grind of teaching, governessing, seamstressing, companioning: those badly paid, disregarded employments that were often all that were available to genteel women of small means. Bitter at her parents' overt preference for her elder brother (who was educated to the law), and yet determined not to marry for economic support, Wollstonecraft was typical of that small army of bright, undereducated women who found their way into the eighteenth-century world of letters and then began to raise a protest against the social and economic conditions that had taken them there. It is worth remembering that *A Vindication of the Rights of Woman* was, among other things, a potboiler—written to satisfy Wollstonecraft's commitments to her employer (the radical publisher Joseph Johnson) and to keep the wolf from her family's door.

Wollstonecraft's resentment of women whose lives were easier, sexier, happier than her own is evident in her early writings and correspondence, particularly when she was working as a governess to the aristocratic Kingsborough family in Ireland. Her caricatures of elite women clearly drew on the Kingsborough women, particularly the beautiful Lady Kingsborough. Letters to her sister Everina written at the time speak disparagingly of the silly ways of pretty women who use their looks to attract potential husbands, something to which Wollstonecraft herself, she made clear, would never ever stoop. Her disapproval, as well as her insistent tone of cultural superiority, reek with envious unhappiness, occasionally mixed with rueful self-mockery. "I am like a *lilly* [*sic*] drooping—Is it not a sad pity that so sweet a flower should waste its sweetness on the *Desart* [*sic*] Air. . . . Yours an Old Maid. . . . Alas!!!!!!!!!" she wrote to Everina in 1787.[26] Five years later, at the time she wrote the *Rights of Woman*, she was probably still a virgin, and there can be little doubt that some of the hate directed at sexy women in that book originated in a sense of sexual exclusion. Gubar refers to the self-hate revealed by Wollstonecraft in her personal writings and speculates that her debased portrait of womanhood was partly self-representation: "the misogyny of Wollstonecraft's work," she proposes, "dramatises the self-revulsion of a woman who knew *herself* to be constructed as feminine, and

25. Amy Erickson, *Women and Property in Early Modern England* (London: Routledge, 1993); Ruth Perry, "Women in Families: The Great Disinheritance," in *Women and Literature in Britain, 1700–1800*, ed. Vivien Jones (Cambridge: Cambridge University Press, 1999).

26. Mary Wollstonecraft to Everina Wollstonecraft, 24 March 1787, *Collected Letters of Mary Wollstonecraft*, ed. Ralph Wardle (Ithaca, N.Y.: Cornell University Press, 1979), 145.

thus it proposes a kind of 'anti-narcissism.'" Knowing herself to be as prone as any woman to the vicissitudes of female emotional life, Gubar seems to be suggesting, Wollstonecraft projected these feelings onto other women, in order to retrieve for herself an image of rational self-control. Her misogyny, as Gubar puts it, was a desperate attempt to "negotiate the distance between desire and dread."[27]

This argument seems to me partly right. Certainly Wollstonecraft experienced savage self-dislike, enough to try to murder herself twice over. The reasons for this would fill another essay, but her feelings for her parents— a drunken, abusive father and cold, ineffectual mother—must have been a major factor. Being a woman wasn't something for which Wollstonecraft had been given any happy preparation.[28] But to suggest, as Gubar does, that she *knew* herself to be Woman, whether by nature or culture, and then turned against her womanhood, is a difficult position to adopt. For what kind of knowledge is this, this knowledge of one's sex? Whatever it is, Gubar is assuming that all women, including all feminists, possess it, and that feminist politics reflects it. The object of feminism is this Woman, and the correct feminist stance is pro-Woman. These are all assumptions that, at the very least, deserve to be questioned.

As a politics with Woman as both its agent and object, feminism has always been beleaguered by uncertainty about who Woman is, can be, should be. Actually existing women are either seen as too-much Woman, as Wollstonecraft is accusing her maligned ladies of fashion of being, or too little, as Gubar's charge of misogyny implies in the case of Wollstonecraft herself.[29] Ann Snitow, whose autobiographical account of the women's movement I referred to earlier, argues that these difficulties reflect the paradox at the heart of feminism: that is, the paradoxical drive to seek emancipation as women while at the same time experiencing powerful wishes not to be women at all. This is a paradox, Snitow claims, that "will only change

27. Gubar, "Feminist Misogyny," 461.

28. Her personal correspondence reveals many instances of intense self-loathing. See, for example, Wardle, *Collected Letters,* 189, 221. For more on Wollstonecraft's attempted suicides and unhappy childhood, see her most recent biography, Janet Todd's *Mary Wollstonecraft: A Revolutionary Life* (London: Weidenfeld and Nicholson, 2000). See also Claire Tomalin, *The Life and Death of Mary Wollstonecraft* (Weidenfeld and Nicholson, 1974).

29. For an influential discussion of the problem of too-little "Woman" vs. too-much "Woman" in feminist discourse, see Denise Riley, *Am I That Name? Feminism and the Category of 'Women' in History* (Macmillan Press, 1988), esp. chap. 1. My approach differs substantially from the one offered in Riley's important book. See also Sally Alexander, *Becoming a Woman* (Virago Press, 1994), for illuminating explorations into the psychic life of feminism. And—on a highly provocative note—Donald Winnicott, "This Feminism," in his book *Home Is Where We Start From* (W. W. Norton, 1986), contains an infuriating but fascinating discussion of what he regards as the roots of misogyny in both sexes and its impact on feminism.

through a historical process."[30] I want to suggest, however, that this is one area of human difficulty that is, in certain respects, beyond history; that the tensions Snitow describes are in fact the inevitable, insuperable dilemmas intrinsic to having a sexual subjectivity at all. "Only the concept of a subjectivity at odds with itself," Jacqueline Rose has written, "gives back to women the right to an impasse at the point of sexual identity"—the impasse that can be heard throughout the feminist tradition.[31]

In my own work, like Rose and other psychoanalytic theorists, I have used the concept of unconscious fantasy to understand how this impasse occurs. The process of becoming a woman is a trajectory not only through biology but also through fantasies of masculinity and femininity that shape every child's selfhood. Each individual occupies a body that is biologically sexed, but the psychological gender with which mind and body are invested is not inborn but acquired: a trickier business altogether. The fantasies that give birth to the ego are a conflux of masculine/feminine identifications—derived in the first instance from parental figures—whose outcome is never Man or Woman in some absolute sense but a sexual identity that is always partial, defensive, wishful. We feel ourselves to belong to one sex because of our fantasies about what it would feel like to belong to the other: imaginings that pull us to and fro along the gender axis.[32]

Such fantasies, to return to Snitow's point, are certainly open to historical change at the level of *content:* that is, what constitutes imaginary maleness or femaleness will differ in important respects between periods and cultures. The presence of a soul within the human subject, for example, or changing views of bodily sexual difference, or shifting boundaries between the animal and the human, all transfigure inner maps of gender. What does not change, however, is the mapping process itself—those deep mechanisms of fantasy formation, particularly identification, that are the precondition to having *any* sexed subjectivity, and indeed to becoming human at all.

The politics of gender, I'm arguing, is inevitably embedded in these phantasmic identifications and the conflicting emotional postures—love/hate, acceptance/repudiation, idealization/denigration—to which they give rise. Fantasy belongs to individuals, but within cultural communities it can take related forms and produce shared effects. The love and hate that women feel for the varieties of femininity inscribed on our imaginations have shaped our political visions and the radical projects generated by them. In Wollstonecraft's case, we obviously know far more of her political project than the deeper wishes behind it. But her husband, William

30. Snitow, "Gender Diary," 19.

31. Jacqueline Rose, *Sexuality in the Field of Vision* (Verso Books, 1986), 15.

32. "To fully appreciate being a woman one has to be a man, and to fully appreciate being a man one has to be a woman" (Winnicott, "This Feminism"), 132.

Godwin, referring to her feelings for her father, described her as a "very good hater,"[33] and I suspect the description applied just as well to her feelings for her mother, whose unloving figure surely hovers behind the savage caricatures of the *Rights of Woman*. All her life Wollstonecraft displayed ambivalent attitudes toward female acquaintances, particularly her intimates. The pattern of her friendship with her beloved Fanny Blood, beginning in adoration and ending in disappointment, may have extended into other relationships (her depiction of this relationship, in her first novel, *Mary, a Fiction*, setting it within a wider picture of romantic losses and disenchantments, hints at this).

On the other hand, Wollstonecraft frequently imagined herself into an idealized male position—a stance that is most obvious in *A Vindication of the Rights of Men*, where she pits her manly democratic voice against Burke's effete elite apologetics, but is also clearly audible in the *Rights of Woman*, where manly courage is seen as a prerequisite to women's emancipation, and those "few extraordinary women who have rushed in eccentrical directions out of the orbit prescribed to their sex" are viewed as "*male* spirits, confined by mistake in female frames."[34] A central hope for women in the *Rights of Woman*, that they should achieve an authentic moral subjectivity through amorous identification with God, evoked a female selfhood molded in the image of a sacralized paternalism. At other times, however, she spoke from the position of the mother, describing maternal sentiments as true womanhood and setting the good mother—particularly the breast-feeder—against the sexualized woman whose body is for pleasure rather than reproduction. But in her final writings, in the years when Wollstonecraft herself had found sexual happiness, the erotic woman—the woman who can both acknowledge and act on her sexual feelings—is at last allowed to speak out on behalf of female desire.[35] What Wollstonecraft discovered in the course of her lifetime is that there is no single way of being Woman, and it is this understanding—intuited rather than explicated—that motivates the most radical impulse in her feminism: the wild wish, in her own words, to see the "distinction of sex confounded in society" in order that women may experience all their varieties of being.[36] It is only with the death of Woman, in other words, that real women come to life, in their own minds

33. William Godwin, *A Memoir of the Author of "A Vindication of the Rights of Woman"* (1798; reprint, New York: Penguin Books, 1987), 207.

34. Wollstonecraft, *Rights of Woman*, 120.

35. See *The Wrongs of Woman, or Maria* (1798; reprint, London: Pickering and Chatto, 1989), Wollstonecraft's final, unfinished novel, for a passionate, if highly ambiguous, endorsement of female desire.

36. The full quotation is: "A wild wish has just flown from my heart to my head, and I will not stifle it, though it may excite a horse-laugh. I do earnestly wish to see the distinction of sex confounded in society, unless where love animates the behaviour" (*Rights of Woman*, 148–49).

as well as in the wider culture. That the wish for this transformation was often driven as much by hate as by hope seems to me simply to underline what we already know: that the feelings that fuel political visions are no purer or sweeter than any other, and that the feminist personality—no matter how charismatic or visionary—is never more than vitally, ordinarily human.

It's worth concluding on this point, because the figure of Wollstonecraft herself has been so mythologized that her mere humanity is frequently forgotten. The palpable sense of betrayal detectable in Gubar's essay is a good indication of this. For two hundred years Mary Wollstonecraft has been *the* iconic figure of early western feminism, a central symbol of Woman in revolt. Yet as the feminist pioneer par excellence, she has elicited a very divided response from her successors, ranging from the anxiously repudiatory attitude of Victorian feminists—fearful of her reputation for political extremism and sexual license—through to the madly idealized portrayals of her produced by early-twentieth-century feminists such as Virginia Woolf, Emma Goldman, and Ruth Benedict.[37] Since the 1980s both her importance and her ambiguity have continued to increase, as feminist scholars scrutinize her work and life for the secret of our ancestry, the true meaning of our collective history. Writings pour out; conferences are held; debates erupt over her class attitudes, her view of Empire, her sexual philosophy, her Enlightenment perspectives. Critics of present-day feminism evoke her white middle-class background as indicative of the narrowness of the western feminist tradition, while others accuse her of complicity in the patriarchal attitudes she ostensibly opposed. And now Gubar has charged her with the darkest treachery of all—hating those whose cause she is seen to represent. No pedestal is capable of bearing the weight of this, but the passion with which Wollstonecraft's heroic stature has been attacked, defended, attacked, and so on surely reveals more about the fantasies with which she has been invested than the woman herself. As a symbol of dissident womanhood Wollstonecraft has been freighted with the ambivalent visions of femaleness that haunt the feminist imagination, and then idolized and punished for them—an inevitable fate for a heroine.[38]

"Why would anyone who likes being a woman *need* to be a feminist?" the young Ann Snitow wanted to know, and the question still deserves consideration—not only because *being* a woman is so tough in many respects but

37. For Virginia Woolf, see "Mary Wollstonecraft," (1929) reprinted in Woolf, *Women and Writing* (Women's Press, 1979); for Emma Goldman, see Alice Wexler, "Emma Goldman on Mary Wollstonecraft," *Feminist Studies* no. 1 (1981): 132; for Ruth Benedict's view, see her essay "Mary Wollstonecraft" in *An Anthropologist at Work: Writings of Ruth Benedict*, ed. Margaret Mead (1959).

38. Barbara Taylor, "An Impossible Heroine? Mary Wollstonecraft and Female Heroism," *Soundings* 3 (1996): 119–35.

because *becoming* a woman is a process fraught with ambivalence, with hostility and repudiation as well as with affirmation and love. To say that part of Wollstonecraft loathed being a woman is perhaps to say no more than that she *was* a woman: that her so-called misogyny, while probably more extreme than in happier women, was as inevitable a feature of her female selfhood as it has been of the feminist tradition as a whole. Gubar thinks there's a case to answer here, but surely this isn't a matter of culpability but rather of self-recognitions essential to the maturity of a politics whose heroines can never be more or other than the complex fantasies they embody, the "wild wishes" and troubled aspirations that have fashioned the modern feminist imagination.

Parallel Stages

Theatrical and Political Representation
in Early Modern and Revolutionary France

Paul Friedland

From the very beginning of the French Revolution, contemporary observers were struck by the overwhelming theatricality of political events. Pamphlets were written in which the entire National Assembly was unmasked as a troupe of actors in disguise, and election results were printed in the form of a cast list. Edmund Burke's *Reflections on the Revolution in France* is only the most enduring of countless works in which France's new politicians were denounced as second-rate hams. And, while politicians were being unmasked as actors, dramatic actors were conversely being denounced by both the political left and the right as secret agents of the other, a suspicion that would ultimately lead to the large-scale imprisonment of actors in several of France's larger cities during the Terror.

Indeed, there is much to lend credence to the perception that the political and theatrical stages were merging during the revolutionary years: Dramatic actors, who only a few months before had been social and political outcasts in an old regime that officially regarded their craft as profane, were elected to powerful political and military positions. There were reports that deputies to the National Assembly were taking acting lessons, and that paid "claqueurs" were being planted in the audience to applaud the speeches of representatives who, in Burke's view, were "act[ing] like the comedians of a fair before a riotous audience."[1] And a mock National Assembly was erected

This article was written while I was a member of the School of Social Science at the Institute for Advanced Study, and I would like to express my gratitude to the institute and to the National Endowment for the Humanities, which funded my membership. I would also like to acknowledge the helpful suggestions and comments given to me by the faculty and members of the School of Social Science when I presented an early version of this paper at one of the regular Thursday Lunch Seminars.

1. Edmund Burke, *Reflections on the Revolution in France,* ed. Conor Cruise O'Brien (New York: Penguin, 1981), 161.

under a circus tent in the middle of the Palais-Royal, charging admission to spectators who wanted to act the part of political representatives.

Although the events of the Revolution have long been portrayed as *dramatic,* only recently have historians begun to focus explicitly on the *theatricality* that seemed so striking to the Revolution's contemporaries.[2] But the very existence—one might even say ubiquity—of this theatricality raises a fundamental question that, I think, has yet to be asked: How, when, and why did politics and theater become so intimately intertwined?

In the following pages, I argue that the reason why politics and theater became virtually indistinguishable during the revolutionary period is the parallel evolution of theories of theatrical and political representation: Prior to the mid-eighteenth century, actors on both stages believed their fundamental task to be the re-presentation[3] or embodiment of a fictional body (a character in a play, or the *corpus mysticum* of the French nation) that had no visible or tangible presence of its own. In the decades after 1750, however, the task of actors on both stages was redefined: theatrical actors were prevailed upon to represent their characters abstractly, in a manner that *seemed realistic* to the audience, rather than in a manner that the actors

2. As I use the terms, the quality of *theatricality* is as different from *drama* as artifice is different from truth, as representation is different from reality, and as orchestration is different from spontaneity. *Drama,* for example, might refer to the inherent pathos or historical import of an event: the spontaneous scene in which the king and queen were forced from Versailles to Paris by a mob of their subjects, accompanied all the way by the heads of the royal guards, impaled on pikes—this is clearly a dramatic event in every sense of the word. *Theatricality,* in contrast, describes the conscious staging of an event for the purposes of producing a particular effect, the intentional grafting of theatrical elements onto "real" life: the speeches of Mirabeau, for example, or the festivals of the Terror are *theatrical* in the sense that they are carefully scripted, choreographed, and performed, leaving little to spontaneity.

For works that have explored the theatricality of the Revolution, see Angelica Goodden, *Action and Persuasion: Dramatic Performance in Eighteenth-Century France* (Oxford: Clarendon Press, 1986), and Susan Maslan, "Resisting Representation: Theater and Democracy in Revolutionary France," in *Representations,* vol. 52 (fall 1995): 27–51. Most important, see the following works by Marie Hélène Huet: *Rehearsing the Revolution: The Staging of Marat's Death, 1793–1797,* trans. Robert Hurley (Berkeley: University of California Press, 1982); "Performing Arts: Theatricality and the Terror," in *Representing the French Revolution: Literature, Historiography, and Art,* ed. James A. W. Heffernan (Hanover, N.H.: Dartmouth College, University Press of New England, 1992), 135–49; and *Mourning Glory: The Will of the French Revolution* (Philadelphia: University of Pennsylvania Press, 1997).

3. Throughout this essay, I use the hyphenated form of the word *re-presentation* to refer to the act by which an intangible body is presented in concrete form; this form of re-presentation is analogous to the Catholic conception of transubstantiation, in which the body and the blood of Christ are materially re-presented, or incarnated, within the bread and the wine of the Eucharist. I use the non-hyphenated form of the word *representation* to refer to the process by which an intangible body is abstractly represented in spirit rather than in substance; this form is analogous to the various Protestant conceptions of the Eucharist in which the body and blood of Christ are symbolically referred to by the bread and the wine.

experienced *as real*. And with respect to political representation, the invention in 1789 of a revolutionary political body known as the National Assembly marked the sudden triumph of abstract representation on the political stage: unlike previous political bodies that had claimed to *be* the French nation, the National Assembly merely claimed to speak on its behalf. Implicit within the new theory of representation (on both stages) was a clear demarcation between actors and spectators that had never existed before, and which had as its most profound consequence the relegation of the audience to the role of passive observers to a spectacle performed on their behalf.

THE REVOLUTION IN THEATRICAL REPRESENTATION

Before 1750, the unchallenged rule of French acting theory might very well be summed up by the following maxim, credited to the playwright Boileau: "If you want me to cry, you must cry yourself."[4] Acting textbooks of the period repeatedly stressed the importance of the verity of the actor's emotions because it was taken for granted that only real feelings could be perceived as real by spectators. Largely derivative of classical Greek rhetorical theory,[5] French acting textbooks uniformly insisted that a successful performance depended upon the actor's experiencing the passions of the character, on the actor's literally becoming the character for the duration of the play. Writing in 1657, the Abbé d'Aubignac maintained that a character could be made present on the stage only if the actor "believed in [the character's feelings] even as he expressed them. . . . [I]t would be ridiculous to see him deliver a long speech either of lamentation or of joy, on a matter which he considered to be false."[6] And almost a century later, a poem entitled "L'art du théâtre, ou le parfait comédien" expressed an identical conception of dramatic re-presentation:

I wish that an actor, whether he screams [in anger] or he jests,
be in truth that which he represents.[7]

As late as 1747, acting textbooks were warning prospective actors that acting was a difficult process of metamorphosis, a process in which actors

4. Cited in [Alex Tournon de la Chapelle], *L'art du comédien vu dans ses principes* (Amsterdam and Paris, 1782), 21.
5. See Joseph R. Roach, *The Player's Passion: Studies in the Science of Acting* (Newark: University of Delaware Press, 1985), 26.
6. François-Hédelin, abbé d'Aubignac, *La pratique du théâtre* (Amsterdam, 1715; reprint, Munich: W. Fink, 1971), 299.
7. [De Brize], *L'art du théâtre, ou le parfait comédien. Poëme en deux chants* (n.p., [1744]), 9. See also [Pierre-Alexandre Lévesque de la Ravallière], *Essay de comparaison entre la déclamation et la poésie dramatique* (Paris, 1729), 43–44, which expresses a similar conception of acting.

had to suspend their sense of self and become the characters they presented on the stage: "If you cannot lend yourself to these metamorphoses, do not venture upon the stage. In the theater, when one does not feel that which one wishes to make appear, one presents us with only an imperfect image."[8]

Perhaps the best way to gauge the extent to which this process of metamorphosis was perceived to be literal rather than figurative is to consider the arguments contained in the numerous antitheatrical texts of the period. Religious pamphlets, in particular, were often rather explicit in their identification of the problem: It lay at the very heart of a process in which intangible spirit became flesh in the body of the actor; theater, in short, was a profanation of the incarnation of Christ. As an *abbé* from Auxerre declared, justifying that city's strict ordinances against theater, "Theater . . . leads to nothing less than rendering the suffering and death of J. C. useless; in one word, it directly attacks the point of the Incarnation."[9] The problem was not that theater was false or that the actor was lying; rather, the problem lay precisely in the *reality* of the character's incarnation: "These are not lifeless characteristics and colorless complexions which are in operation; these are living characters *[personnages]*, real eyes animated with passion, real tears in the Actors who make flow real [tears] as well within those who listen to them."[10] Whether one approved of it or deplored it, theatrical representation, prior to the mid-eighteenth century, was perceived as a literal process of bodily metamorphosis.

In 1750, the first crack in the monolith of French theatrical theory appeared in the form of François Riccoboni's *L'art du théâtre*. Riccoboni, a well-known actor in Paris, espoused a radically new conception of theatrical representation that directly challenged centuries of French theatrical tradition. Riccoboni called into question the cardinal rule that the representation of a character necessarily entailed the actor's actual physical experience of the character's emotions:

> I am far from ever having shared this opinion, which is almost universally held, and it has always seemed evident to me that if one is unfortunate enough actually to feel that which one is trying to express, then one is not acting *[hors d'état de jouer]*.[11]

Instead of insisting that actors present the real passions of the characters,

8. Rémond de Sainte Albine, *Le comédien* (Paris, 1747), 32.

9. [L'Abbé Mahy], *La comédie contraire aux principes de la morale chrétienne* . . . (Auxerre, 1754), 4. See also Jean Savaron, *Traitté contre les masques* (Paris, 1611), for a seventeenth-century indictment of the wearing of masks as a profanation of the incarnation.

10. Mahy, *La comédie contraire*, 34. This is taken almost word for word from Bossuet. See Bossuet's letter to Caffaro, as well as his "Maximes et réflexions sur la comédie," in Ch. Urbain and E. Levesque, *L'église et le théâtre* (Paris, 1930), 125, 178.

11. François Riccoboni, *L'art du théâtre* (Paris, 1750), 37.

Riccoboni called upon actors to present passions that seemed real—a performance that was not *vrai* (true), but rather *vraisemblable* (literally: resembling the true).

The fundamental novelty of Riccoboni's conception of representation cannot be overemphasized. Instead of a process in which the intangible body of the character was made incarnate within the body of the actor, Riccoboni's conception of theatrical representation involved abstract appearances, and the bifurcation of the actor's body into believable exteriors and false interiors; instead of transubstantiation, Riccoboni called for imitation. Over the next several decades, this new conception of theatrical representation would sweep the French stage. By the 1770s, a decidedly defensive tone had crept into the writings of those who still clung to the old belief of theatrical representation as metamorphosis. In 1772, for example, the playwright Cailhava criticized the "crowd of actors who reduce to a purely mechanical state, an art which can be sublime, & which [they] bring down to the [level] of a monkey's or a parrot's talent."[12] And the celebrated playwright and author Levacher de Charnois was even more straightforward when, in 1788, he offered the following observation on Boileau's famous maxim: "If you want me to cry, you must cry yourself. Boileau did not say: pretend to cry."[13]

Riccoboni was by no means the lone progenitor of a revolution. His new method of acting, although undoubtedly revolutionary in itself, would ultimately form the core of a much more extensive project to transform the theory and practice of theater as a whole—a project whose most complete articulation is to be found in the works of Denis Diderot. At the heart of the *Paradoxe sur le comédien,* a text written some twenty years after Riccoboni's *L'art du théâtre,* Diderot offered a definition of acting virtually identical to Riccoboni's: "[The actor's] entire talent consists not in feeling, as you [the spectator] suppose, but in rendering the outward signs of feeling so scrupulously that you [the spectator] mistake them [for real] *[que vous vous y trompiez]*."[14] Much like Riccoboni, then, Diderot maintained that acting had nothing to do with the presentation of true passions, but rather with the abstract or figurative representation of those passions in outward manner-

12. Cailhava, *De l'art de la comédie, ou détail raisonné des diverses parties de la comédie, et des différents genres* (Paris, 1772), 16.

13. [Levacher de Charnois], *Conseils à une jeune actrice, avec des notes nécessaires pour l'intelligence du texte. Par un coopérateur du "Journal des théâtres"* (n.p., 1788), 21. See also [Tournon de la Chapelle], *L'art du comédien,* 21–36, for similar criticisms of the new theories of theatrical representation.

14. Denis Diderot, *Paradoxe sur le comédien* (Paris: Garnier-Flammarion, 1967), 132. Although the *Paradoxe* was not actually published until 1830, Diderot circulated various drafts of the work as early as 1769, and several of its most important concepts can be found in earlier works, such as the *Discours sur la poésie dramatique* (1758). See Roach, *Player's Passion,* 117–69.

isms, or what Diderot called "signs." Diderot reasoned that there were two ways to produce such signs: One method, the one employed for generations in the French theater, was the authentic production of external appearances as the natural by-product of real emotions by actors who subjected themselves to the grueling process of metamorphosis. Another method, clearly the one that Diderot preferred, might be termed the artificial method: external appearances could be manufactured by actors who, after spending some time in front of a mirror, could imitate the outward signs of passions with none of the inner turmoil: "The cries of his sorrow are recorded in his ears. The gestures of his despair are from his memory, and were prepared in front of a mirror. . . . The actor is weary, and you are sad; he has thrashed about without feeling a thing, and you have felt without thrashing about."[15]

Diderot's vision of the actor as an unfeeling automaton, who somewhat paradoxically elicits a torrent of emotions from spectators, helps to explain the negative connotations associated with the actor's craft even after the actor could no longer be accused of profaning the Incarnation. If actors prior to 1750 were profane because they *were* what they re-presented on the stage, actors who were devotees of the new method were not profane but rather duplicitous precisely because they *were not* that which they pretended to represent. In the following passage, Diderot compared the "great" actor with the stock figures of duplicity in the eighteenth century:

> [The actor] cries like an unbelieving priest who preaches the Passion; like a seducer on his knees before a woman whom he does not love, but whom he wishes to deceive; like a beggar in the street or at the door of a church, who insults you when he loses hope of moving you; or like a courtesan who feels nothing, but who swoons in your arms.[16]

Although Diderot's conception of the actor's craft differed little from Riccoboni's reconceptualization, Diderot pursued the logical ramifications far beyond Riccoboni's initial vision, grasping a key component of the new method of acting that his predecessor had only dimly understood: The old system of metamorphosis had been entirely dependent on the actor's ability to believe himself transformed. But this new, artificial system depended not on the actor's belief (it actually precluded the actor's belief), but rather on the *spectator's* belief—or, as we tend to refer to it today, on the spectator's suspension of disbelief. This fundamental shift in the burden of belief was the cornerstone of an entirely new conception of representation.

I would be tempted to say that the onus of belief was simply transferred from the actor to the spectator, but such a statement implies a simple shift-

15. Diderot, *Paradoxe*, 132–33.
16. Ibid., 133–34.

ing of burdens between two already existent entities, and this is not the case. It would be more accurate to say that after redefining the role of the actor, the new theater set about *inventing* the modern spectator, to whom it then transferred the burden of belief. For it is crucial to understand that the passive and silent individual, seated in the darkness, obsessed with the action on the lighted stage, did not exist in the middle of eighteenth century; that willing and pliant spectator had to be manufactured in theory, and then meticulously sculpted in practice over a period of several decades.

Prior to the middle of the eighteenth century, the rigid differentiation of actors and spectators, a concept that would later become one of the fundamental principles of the modern theatrical space, was virtually unknown in the French theater. Instead, the relationship between actors and spectators was decidedly more carnivalesque, and permitted a great deal of fluidity between the representative space and the audience.[17] On the stage itself, spectators who had paid for the privilege sat virtually in the middle of the actors who were attempting to perform. Down below in the lighted parterre, audience members wandered about, greeting one another, chatting, and occasionally commenting on the play, out loud, whenever they saw fit. Indeed, certain theatergoers seem to have made a part-time career out of intentionally upstaging the actors with performances of their own.[18]

We might think that the chaotic atmosphere of the premodern theater made it difficult for spectators to pay attention to the play, and this was undoubtedly the case. But the spectators of the eighteenth century hardly seemed to mind the numerous offstage distractions vying for their attention. Perhaps we are even mistaken in labeling them "distractions," for as many observers of the French theater prior to the 1760s pointed out, spectators often behaved as if it were the *actors* who were distracting them. The real spectacle was the spectators themselves; the action on the stage was merely a sideshow.[19] In the *Persian Letters*, for example, Montesquieu cleverly

---

17. I use the term *carnivalesque* here in the specific sense in which Bakhtin uses it in contradistinction to the pre-scripted, orderly nature of the modern theater. See Mikhail Bakhtin, *Rabelais and His World,* trans. Hélène Iswolsky (Bloomington: Indiana University Press, 1984), 7: "In fact, carnival does not know footlights, in the sense that it does not acknowledge any distinction between actors and spectators. Footlights would destroy a carnival, as the absence of footlights would destroy a theatrical performance. Carnival is not a spectacle seen by the people; they live in it, and everyone participates because its very idea embraces all the people."

18. Barbara G. Mittman, *Spectators on the Paris Stage in the Seventeenth and Eighteenth Centuries* (Ann Arbor: University of Michigan Research Press, 1984), 29–32. See also John Lough, *Paris Theater Audiences in the Seventeenth and Eighteenth Centuries* (London: Oxford University Press, 1965), 115–18.

19. James Johnson provides wonderful details about spectator inattentiveness at the Opéra in the chapter "Opera as Social Duty" in his book *Listening in Paris: A Cultural History* (Berkeley: University of California Press, 1995). See also the recent book by Jeffrey Ravel that is sure to become the classic text on the eighteenth-century French parterre: *The Contested*

satirized the inattention of French theatergoers by having his foreign visitors assume, in their first visit to the theater, that they were *supposed* to be watching the "actors" in the spectator boxes and the parterre, taking no notice of the professional actors on the stage.[20]

For those who hoped to revolutionize the nature of theatrical representation, the problem was clear: The burden of belief could hardly be transferred from the actor to the spectator if the latter only occasionally glanced at the stage. The new theories of acting called for rapt attention on the part of the spectator, and in order for this to be achieved, something had to be done to force the spectators to pay attention, to stop chatting among themselves and instead turn their (silent) attention to the professional actors on the stage. But how was this to be accomplished? How could these active and unruly individuals who seemed to think of themselves as participants in the theatrical spectacle be transformed into passive and attentive spectators? The answer lay in a series of practical innovations, each one of which was intended to remove spectators from the stage, and to isolate spectators visibly and audibly from one another; as a result of these innovations, theatrical spectators in France were exiled and cordoned off from a newly delineated representative space and forced into the role of nonparticipatory observers. As I will discuss in the second part of this essay, these revolutionary transformations in the theatrical space would soon be paralleled by events on the political stage.

The first task of the theatrical revolutionaries was to remove the most obvious intrusion into the representative space: the spectators seated on the stage itself. The reign of the carnivalesque stage came to an end, beginning in 1759, when theatrical companies began removing spectator benches from the Parisian stages.[21] This act was immediately hailed by many theater critics and playwrights, who praised the remarkable effects of this simple innovation. In the following passage, the playwright Collé describes his

---

Parterre: Public Theater and French Political Culture, 1680–1791 (Ithaca, N.Y.: Cornell University Press, 1999).

20. Montesquieu, *Lettres persanes* [Letter xxviii].

21. Perhaps the most extensive account of the existence and subsequent removal of spectator benches on the theatrical stage can be found in Adolphe Jullien, *Les spectateurs sur le théâtre, établissement et suppression des bancs sur les scènes de la Comédie-Française et de l'Opéra . . .* (Paris, 1875). See also Pierre Peyronnet, *La mise en scène au XVIIIe siècle* (Paris: A.-G. Nizet, 1974), 59; Mittman, *Spectators on the Paris Stage*, 97; Jules Bonnassies, *Comédie française. Notice historique sur les anciens bâtiments* (Paris: Aug. Aubry, 1868), 21–22; and *Le théâtre à Paris au XVIIIe siècle. Conférences du musée Carnavalet* (Paris: Musée Carnavalet, 1929), 121. It should be noted that Voltaire had suggested the removal of spectator seating on the stage as early as 1730 in his *Discours sur la tragédie*. Apparently, however, no theaters were willing to put his ideas into practice, no doubt reluctant to forgo the comparatively high revenues for stage seating (see Jullien, *Les spectateurs*, 16).

impressions upon first witnessing a performance on a stage cleared of spectators:

> I went to see the theater of the Comédie-Française, [where] people are no longer allowed upon the stage. God willing this will last! This produces the best effect in the world; I even think you could hear the actors' voices better. The theatrical illusion is actually whole; no longer does one see Caesar [accidentally] about to remove all the powder [from the wig] of some jackass seated in the front row of the stage seats, or Mithradates expiring in the midst of all of one's acquaintances.[22]

To sharpen the distinction between the stage, newly cleared of spectators, and the audience down below, in 1759 (the very same year that spectator seats began to disappear from the stages of Paris) theater technicians began to experiment with ways of improving the chandeliers that up until then had bathed both actors and spectators indiscriminately in bright light.[23] By 1778, a device had been perfected that made it possible to illuminate the stage while hiding the sources of light and casting a shadow of relative darkness upon the audience.[24] Audience members who had always been so fond of looking at and displaying themselves to one another could now perceive each other only dimly, in contrast to the now brilliantly illuminated figures of the actors on the stage.

Perhaps the last tangible vestige of the undifferentiated theatrical space was the existence of spectator boxes above and on both sides of the stage. In 1793, these began to disappear as well. And the rationale for this aesthetic reform was once again the enhancement of the illusion: an even clearer differentiation between the representative space and spectators could be achieved if spectators were not only cleared from the stage, but cleared from the sight lines of the audience as well. The *Moniteur* reported the rationale for this architectural innovation as follows:

> The theater owners felt that, in order to render the theatrical illusion more complete, there was need for a line of clear demarcation between the spectators and the action which was represented; and, if it is necessary for the enchantment of the public that all of their senses focus entirely on the play, then the actor must, so to speak, be alone with his character upon the stage.[25]

I have mentioned only practical reforms to the theatrical space. But per-

22. Cited in Jullien, *Les spectateurs*, 23. See also Richard Sennet, *The Fall of Public Man* (New York: Knopf, 1977), 80.

23. Bonnassies, *Comédie française*, 24. Bonnassies cites de Mouhy as his source. See also Peyronnet, *La mise en scène*, 67.

24. Peyronnet, *La mise en scène*, 67.

25. *Réimpression de l'Ancien Moniteur*, vol. 17 (Paris, 1860), 372. I owe this reference to Beatrice Hyslop's article "The Parisian Theater during the Reign of Terror," *Journal of Modern*

haps the innovation that was most fundamental to the creation of the realistic representative space was not a practical element of stage design, but rather a theoretical concept that has come to be known as the "fourth wall." The fourth wall was a concept predicated on the conviction that no action on the stage would ever have the appearance of plausible reality (*vraisemblance*) if the actors betrayed any hint that they were aware of being watched. Instead of directing their performances toward the audience, actors should pretend that the open space between the stage and the audience was a fourth wall. Actors should behave, in short, just like real people enclosed in a defined space, without observers: they should direct their lines to one another, and respond appropriately.

That the concept of the fourth wall seems so elementary today is testimony to the complete victory achieved by the practitioners of the new theater: until their ideas took hold, in the 1760s and 1770s, it was customary for French actors to direct their performances to the audience, comparatively ignoring those who shared the stage with them. Diderot, who more than anyone else was responsible for the rapid proliferation of fourth walls in theaters throughout France, can be credited with redirecting the attention of the actors toward one another; it was he who instructed actors to "think no more of the spectator than if he did not exist. Imagine, at the edge of the stage, a high wall that separates you from the parterre. Act as if the curtain never rose."[26]

And so, in the newly created void made possible by the physical separation of actor and spectator, an imaginary wall arose, conceptually separating the world inhabited by the actors from that inhabited by the spectators. This wall was opaque on one side, translucent on the other, and permitted nothing to pass through it but the gaze of the spectator, a gaze that now focused on something that had never existed before: an entirely self-contained artificial reality. Before, there had been nothing but scattered performances in the midst of a crowd of spectators who could choose to devote their attention either to the performances on the stage or to one another. Now, there existed two completely separate worlds: Down below in the darkness were isolated spectators who could no longer communicate with one another,

---

History 17, no. 4 (December 1945): 332–55. See also the review of the first play to be produced on the newly cleared stage: "What is most remarkable, is the proscenium, which, instead of being filled with little spectator boxes and benches, as at all the other theaters, is an area which is decorated with statues and bas-reliefs, which form a very pronounced line of demarcation between the stage and the spectators. . . . The illusion is maintained by not seeing the characters in the spectator boxes mixed up with those in the play" (*Réimpression de l'Ancien Moniteur*, vol. 17, p. 515. Again, I owe this citation to Hyslop).

26. *Discours de la poésie dramatique*, cited in Michael Fried, *Absorption and Theatricality: Painting and Beholder in the Age of Diderot* (Chicago: University of Chicago Press, 1980), 95. I have modified his translation somewhat.

and who formed a cohesive body *only* through their common experience of watching the action on the stage, rather than through their interactions with one another. And up above, the separate performances of the actors had been fused into a believable whole. As I quoted Collé above, upon witnessing his first performance on a stage cleared of spectators, "The theatrical illusion is actually whole."

The fourth wall, therefore, made possible something greater than the sum of individual illusions produced by each actor's performance. A stage devoid of spectators suddenly made possible the creation of something that could never have existed before: a new world, purged of mundane reality, and made up entirely of realistic fictions; a universe physically and conceptually set apart from the world inhabited by spectators; a world existing in its own time and place, which took no notice of anyone or anything beyond its borders, and which to the spectators seemed somehow more interesting, more believable, more intoxicating than their own fragmented reality. This was the theoretical premise of the modern theater; it was also, as we shall see, the theoretical premise of modern representative politics.

The creation of this new self-contained artificial reality necessitated that all of the various practical aspects of the French stage be brought into line with the dictates of *vraisemblance*. Whereas such things as costume and scenery had always been tangential to the dramatic process, now such trappings became the centerpiece of theater, and theater critics applauded the fact that "All the Heroes of Rome no longer show up in white gloves, and with *coiffures à la Française*."[27] Each innovation in the movement to create a more *vraisemblable* theater seemingly spawned a new idea, as if once a blatantly unrealistic aspect of the stage was removed, other vestiges of the old theater suddenly became glaringly apparent. One critic, for example, insisted that the stiff tableaux of characters be replaced by more realistic domestic scenes: "Why ... not ... have the actors chat with one another around a fireplace. This would at the very least have an air of truth. Because I do not see anything as ridiculous as never letting people who are [supposed to be] in their own homes sit down."[28] Other implausibilities that

27. [Cl. Jos. Dorat], *La déclamation théâtrale, poëme didactique en trois chants, précédé d'un discours* (Paris, 1766), 23–24. For additional statements on the importance of realistic costumes, see La Harpe, "Eloge de Lekain," in *Oeuvres de la Harpe . . . accompagnées d'une notice sur sa vie et sur ses ouvrages*, vol. 4, ed. Saint-Surin (Paris, 1821), 453. On the actor Talma's obsession with costumes, see C. G. Etienne and A. Martainville, *Histoire du théâtre français, depuis le commencement de la révolution jusqu'à la réunion générale*, vol. 2 (Paris, [1802]), 114–16.

28. Charles-Joseph, prince de Ligne, *Lettres à Eugénie* (Paris, 1774), 99–100. On the rise of bourgeois dramas that seemed to fulfill this vision, see Scott Stewart Bryson, *The Chastised Stage: Bourgeois Drama and the Exercise of Power*, Stanford French and Italian Studies, vol. 70 (Saratoga, Calif.: Anma Libri, 1991). See also Sarah Maza, *Private Lives and Public Affairs: The Causes Célèbres of Prerevolutionary France* (Berkeley: University of California Press, 1993), 61–63.

drew the fire of theatrical critics included the "aside" (the widespread convention according to which it was somehow possible for characters to deliver lines directly to the audience without any of the other characters noticing) and the practice of writing plays in verse, both of which became increasingly rare, if not extinct, toward the end of the eighteenth century.[29]

By the time of the French Revolution, the theater that had existed in France until 1750, replete with individual metamorphic performances and a carnivalesque mixing of spectators and actors, was almost nowhere to be found. In less than four decades, it had ceased to exist. In its place, two different worlds had come into existence: One, a world of artificial reality, where actors basked in the stage lights, seemingly oblivious to anything or anyone that lay beyond the representative space. The other world, on the opposite side of the fourth wall, was made up of individuals seated in the darkness. Unable to see one another, the spectators' only function as an audience was to gaze in rapt attention at the actors, who ignored them. Active participants in the representative process had been transformed into passive observers of the new realistic, representative spectacle. The following pages trace how this process was paralleled on the contemporary political stage.

THE REVOLUTION IN POLITICAL REPRESENTATION

If we were to look for the political parallel to theatrical re-presentation as it was understood prior to 1750, we might be tempted to compare the king's bodily re-presentation with that of the actor's. As Ernst Kantorowicz's classic study, *The King's Two Bodies,* has shown, medieval English and French political theorists drew a distinction between the *king* as body natural (the mortal, individual and human body of the king) and the *King* as body politic (the intangible, eternal office of king, re-presented successively by the nat-

---

29. See de Ligne, *Lettres à Eugénie,* 100. See also Cailhava, *De l'art de la comédie,* 425–48. Although Cailhava remarks on p. 446 that "everyone is lashing out against asides," he himself allowed for certain conditions under which they could plausibly be done. See also Dorat, *La déclamation théâtrale,* 54. As far as ridding the French theater of verse was concerned, the classics presented something of a problem for the practitioners of the realistic theater. An acting textbook from 1782 simply advised actors to do their best to deemphasize the rhyme: "Speak in a tone which most approaches ordinary conversation. . . . As there is in reality and in nature, and above all in theater, [no practice] of speaking in cadenced words, the Actor must take as much care in making rhyme and measure disappear as an author may have taken in making [them] appear" (Du Fresnel, *Essai sur la perfection du jeu théâtral . . .* [Liège, 1782], 4–5). One might almost credit the decline of opera as a popular art form to this new obsession with *vraisemblance.* As an anonymous author declared, also in the year 1782, "I have never been able to get used to the idea of seeing a man die while singing. This is such an affront to *vraisemblance,* that unless you have no taste you should blush for the author as well as for the actor" (*Lettres d'un solitaire sur le théâtre, ou réflexions sur le tableau du spectacle français* [n.p., 1782], 23).

ural bodies of individual monarchs).[30] We might say, then, that the king as a political actor (body natural) re-presented the King (body politic) in much the same way that a dramatic actor re-presented a fictional character: both were presumed to *be* the character they portrayed; both incarnated the content of their re-presentations.

Upon closer inspection, however, the comparison does not hold up: whereas the fictional character is the ultimate objective of the theatrical actor's re-presentation,[31] the political body of the King cannot properly be called the ultimate objective of the king's re-presentation. As far as early modern and medieval theorists were concerned, political bodies were themselves re-presentations, and therefore the political body of the King was itself a re-presentation of the head of the mystical body of the nation, or the *corpus mysticum.*

The concept of the *corpus mysticum* was the fundamental organizing principle of premodern political re-presentation, and, for the purposes of the analogy being drawn here, constitutes the "fictional character" that was re-presented on the political stage. If, in other words, we are looking for an intangible body that was made present within the body of a political actor (or actors), then the *corpus mysticum* was clearly that body. Originally, according to Kantorowicz and his student Ralph Giesey, the term *corpus mysticum* was a religious concept, referring to the body of the Christian community as well as to the body of Christ, intangible except when it was made present or re-presented in the visible form of the Eucharist.[32] By the early fifteenth century, however, the mystical body had found its way into political discourse and had come to be defined in relatively precise terms as a body of which the three estates of France (together referred to as the Estates General) constituted the members, and the King, the head.

Although political theorists uniformly held that the King re-presented the head of the mystical body of the nation, there seems to have been a fair amount of poetic license in describing which of the different Estates made up which of the organs and members of the mystical body underneath the

30. Ernst H. Kantorowicz, *The King's Two Bodies: A Study in Medieval Political Theology* (Princeton: Princeton University Press, 1957), 18.

31. One might argue, as Rousseau did in an essay entitled "De l'imitation théâtrale," that the character is itself a re-presentation of the image in the author's mind; such a three-stage conception of theatrical re-presentation would offer perhaps an even neater parallel to the conception of political re-presentation that I describe here.

32. Kantorowicz, *Two Bodies,* 209. Ralph E. Giesey, "The French Estates and the Corpus Mysticum Regni," in *Album Helen Maud Cam, Studies Presented to the International Commission for the History of Representative and Parliamentary Institutions,* vol. 23 (Louvain and Paris, 1960), 157. See also Ernst H. Kantorowicz, "Mysteries of State: An Absolutist Concept and Its Late Mediaeval Origins," *Harvard Theological Review* 48 (1955): 65–91.

head.[33] But if the exact makeup of the mystical body seems to have been open to question, the purpose in invoking the *corpus mysticum* as a political concept was relatively constant. As the various peoples and territories in the French kingdom were being slowly forged into a modern nation-state, the concept of the *corpus mysticum* was instrumental to the expression of the ideal of the seemingly different and unrelated parts of the kingdom being united in a living whole under the leadership of one King. Jean de Terre Rouge, who wrote in the early fifteenth century and was perhaps the first political theorist in France to evoke the *corpus mysticum* with regularity, maintained that the very essence of a mystical body was the unity of wills, without which there would be only a conglomeration of individual members: "[A] mystical body is united alone by the union of its will."[34] This simple statement should signal to us one of the most important legacies of the *corpus mysticum:* long after the term itself had fallen by the wayside, generations of French political theorists still assumed that the very concept of nationhood necessarily implied the existence of a solitary (general) will.

The *corpus mysticum* was not merely a metaphor for social organization. Terre Rouge did not claim, in other words, that society functioned *like* a body; rather, he claimed that society *was* a body and therefore ought to function like one. The mere mention of the *corpus mysticum* was tantamount to an injunction to the various groups who composed the French nation to

33. Jean Gerson, for example, writing in the early fifteenth century, characterized the knighthood as the chest and arms ("for their vigor and strength") of the *corpus mysticum;* the clergy as the stomach ("the stomach does not labor but it nourishes the other members"); and the bourgeoisie, merchants, and laborers as the legs and feet ("for their labor and humility in serving and obeying"). See Jean Gerson, "Pour la réforme du royaume (vivat rex, vivat rex, vivat rex) [7 Nov. 1405]," in *Oeuvres complètes*, vol. 8, with an introduction, text, and notes by Mgr. Glorieux (Paris: Desclée & Cie, 1968), 1013. Gerson is here offering an interpretation of Nebuchadnezzar's dream of a statue with a head of gold, finding a contemporary political parallel to each part of the statue.

Writing almost two centuries later, Guy Coquille offered a somewhat different breakdown: The nobility was the heart of the mystical body ("the vivacity and vigor of the whole body"); the clergy was the brain ("the understanding and exercise of reason"); and the third estate was the liver ("the nourishment of the body"). See Guy Coquille, "Discours des estats de France, et du droit que le Duché de Nivernois a en iceux. Par Maitre Guy Coquille sieur de Romenay, Procureur General audit Duché," in *Les oeuvres de Maistre Guy Coquille, Sieur de Romenoy . . .* , vol. 1 (Paris, 1666), 328.

34. Giesey argues, "The *corpus mysticum* was the chief element [of Terre Rouge's political writings], and more than any other writer known to us Terre Rouge tested—or taxed—its mettle as a concept of the state" (Giesey, "The French Estates," 157). According to Giesey, Terre Rouge refers to "the mystical body of the realm of which the subjects are the mystical members and the king is the mystical head" a hundred or so times in the third tract of his *Tractatus de iure futuri successoris legitimi in regiis hereditatibus* (ibid., 163). Terre Rouge's "union of its will" quote is in ibid., 164.

behave with respect to the head as if they constituted a single body; it was very literally a way of "organizing" the confusing mass of rivalries and allegiances that made up the French nation. And although the mystical body was intangible, it was somehow more concrete, more comprehensible than the disorganized chaos of the visible world, and the inhabitants of premodern France tended to see themselves as members of the mystical body rather than as individual citizens of the nation.

Moreover, the mystical body was not *always* invisible and intangible. Under certain circumstances, the entire mystical body of the French nation could be made visible, could be literally re-presented in a tangible, visible form. Like the Eucharistic *corpus mysticum* upon which the political *corpus mysticum* was based, the mystical body of France could be made present through a process of transubstantiation: At the King's summons, ordinary individuals from the farthest reaches of the Kingdom would gather at an appointed place and time to take part in the political spectacle of the re-presentation of the mystical body. With the King at their head (or literally *as* their head), these separate individuals would become, together with the King, the mystical body of France. This political spectacle, in which spirit took on flesh, in which political actors re-presented with their own bodies a fictional body that had no substance of its own, was the convocation of the Estates General.

Unlike modern representative assemblies, the Estates General were not routinely convened, but rather convened only under such extraordinary circumstances in which the King was bound to consult the entirety of his people.[35] To the modern mind, of course, there is an essential difference between a representative assembly and the entirety of a nation assembled in one place, between the government and the people. But to the inhabitants

---

35. Opinions differed as to precisely which circumstances necessitated the calling of the Estates General, but most agreed that the following situations constituted events in which the King was required to consult with the entire nation: the imposition of any kind of tax or subsidy; the alienation of any part of the realm; any unusual event in the reign of succession, such as rival claimants or the necessity of establishing a regency; and the undertaking of any fundamental legal or religious reforms. See [Pierre Matthieu], *Histoire des derniers troubles de France. Soubs les regnes des Rois Tres-Chrestiens Henry III. Roy de France & de Pologne; & Henry IIII. Roy de France & de Navarre* . . . 2nd ed. (n.p., 1600), 111a–112b; Coquille, "Discours des estats," 333; *De la puissance des roys* . . . (Paris, 1593), 30–31; "La Forme, et Ordre de l'assemblée des Estats tenus à Blois, sous le Tres Chrestien Roy de France & de Pologne, Henry III, du nom, és années 1576 & 1577" in *Ordre de l'assemblée des Estats tenus*, in Theodore Godefroy, *Le cérémonial françois* . . . , vol. 2 (Paris, 1649), 299–301; and L'Hospital, "Harrangue prononcée à l'ouverture de la session des états généraux assemblées à Orléans le 13 décembre 1560," in *Oeuvres complètes de Michel L'Hospital, chancelier de France, ornées de portraits et de vues dessinées et gravées par A. Tardieu, et précédées d'un essai sur sa vie et ses ouvrages Par P. J. S. Dufëy, de l'Yonne,* vol. 1 (Paris: Chez A. Boulland et Cie, Libraire, 1824), 379. Several of these texts also suggest that civil and foreign wars constitute another situation in which the convocation of the Estates General is necessary.

of premodern France, the political body of the Estates General was synonymous with the entirety of the French mystical body. Such an "absorptive" representation was possible not because prerevolutionary French people
failed in some way to differentiate between reality and representation; it was
possible because they re-presented differently.[36] Unlike modern representation, which attempts an approximation of a general majority consensus
and, in theory, reflects the proportional breakdown of constituents' opinions, premodern re-presentation sought a holistic re-creation of the entire
object that could not present itself. Just as the Eucharist gave material form
to the body of Christ, which was not capable of showing itself; just as the dramatic actor gave flesh to the fictional character that otherwise had no form;
so the political body of the Estates General made visible and tangible the
mystical body of France that was visible nowhere else.

A political body that absorbed the entirety of the mystical body within its
own body was not—and could not have been—the result of simple political
elections. The process of forming the political body of France was costly and
time consuming. It began with the word of the King, the head summoning
forth its own body, and in response, each of the estates would begin the
arduous process of forming themselves: Members of the third estate who
lived in urban areas would gather into preliminary assemblies, admission to
which was often limited by wealth. By contrast, members of the third estate
who were inhabitants of the countryside would hold comparatively open
assemblies composed of "heads of families" from the surrounding communities. In general, women, children, and servants were deemed re-presented
by the male head of the household.[37] And Jews, actors, executioners, and
foreign nationals, all of whom were not considered to be members of the
corpus mysticum, were excluded from all aspects of the formation of the representative body.

Unlike modern electoral assemblies, whose primary purpose is the delegation of sovereign authority itself, these local assemblies were convened
with the express purpose of delegating merely the expression of sovereign
will. Consequently, the selection of delegates was almost incidental to the
process of re-presentation; infinitely more important was the task of articu-
lating, in tangible, written form, the unified will of the members of the community. To that end, in all of these preliminary assemblies of the third

36. I borrow the term absorptive from Otto von Gierke, Political Theories of the Middle Age,
trans. F. W. Maitland (Cambridge, 1927), 65.

37. Although in certain areas, the term head of family was applied only to the most prominent individuals, in other areas all heads of families would attend, a rubric that occasionally
included women and minors, in the absence or death of the adult male head of the household. See J. Russel Major, The Deputies to the Estates General in Renaissance France, Studies Presented
to the International Commission for the History of Representative and Parliamentary Institutions, vol. 21
(Madison: University of Wisconsin Press, 1960), p. 11.

estate, whether they were the relatively restricted assemblies of the cities or the comparatively open assemblies of the villages and parishes, the same fundamental task was undertaken: those assembled painstakingly drafted a *cahier de doléance*. The various individuals composing the assembly would attempt to fuse their separate complaints and opinions into one coherent document that ideally contained every idea worth recording. Redundancies and inanities were weeded out, and the final product would be a *cahier* containing a distillation of their ideas. Participants would then select a delegate or delegates to carry (literally) this *cahier* to the regional assembly in the district capital.

Deputies from the various local assemblies would then gather in a regional assembly of the third estate, where they would essentially reproduce the activities already undertaken at the lower level: they would consolidate their *cahiers*, crossing out redundancies and occasionally attempting to remove articles that were deemed too specific or insignificant for the ears of the King. Ideally, the personal opinions of the deputies were deemed irrelevant; the will of the people expressed in the *cahiers* held precedence. And there is no better evidence of this fundamental difference between premodern and modern political representation than the fact that in the former regions occasionally deputized several individuals to transport the *cahier* to the national assembly; it was the *quality* of the single *cahier* and not the *quantity* of deputies that mattered.[38]

Members of the first two estates, given their comparatively small numbers, usually proceeded directly to the district capitals to form their respective assemblies.[39] And the activities of all of the estates at the regional level were identical: each estate fused its various grievances and opinions into one regional *cahier* (one for each estate) and named a delegate or delegates to carry the regional *cahier* to a higher convention, in this case the national assembly of the Estates General.

From local, to regional, to national assemblies, the various *cahiers* were

38. The letter of convocation for the Estates General of 1560 was vague in stipulating the number of deputies to be sent, declaring that "at least one deputy" be sent from each estate in every region of France (*Recueil des monuments inédits de l'histoire du tiers état*, vol. 2 [Paris, 1853], 670). At the Estates General of Pontoise in 1561, by contrast, the crown stipulated that only one delegate be sent from each estate, but only about half of the thirteen *gouvernements* of France seem to have respected this directive (J. Russell Major, "The Third Estate in the Estates General of Pontoise, 1561," in *The Monarchy, the Estates, and the Aristocracy in Renaissance France* [London: Variorum Reprints, 1988], sec. 4, 466). See also Georges Picot, *Histoire des Etats Généraux*, vol. 5 (Paris, 1888), 248, and Major, *Deputies to the Estates General*, 5. See also Godefroy, *Le cérémonial françois*, vol. 2, 303, for a listing of the varying number of deputies sent by each of the estates to the Estates General of 1576.

39. On the changing manner in which deputies of the first two estates were selected before and after the fifteenth century, see J. Russell Major, "Royal Initiative and Estates General in France," in *The Monarchy, the Estates, and the Aristocracy*, sec. 8, 254–55.

transported by delegates who had sworn a binding oath, known as the *mandat impératif* (imperative, or binding mandate); each delegate swore that he would in no way alter the contents of the *cahier* or misrepresent the *cahier* in any way. Because the King's original letter of convocation had enumerated the specific items that would be on the agenda at the Estates General, every opinion to be expressed by the delegate was contained in his *cahier;* the task of a delegate was therefore more analogous to a modern-day proxy than to a modern political representative.[40] Whereas modern representatives who violate the will of constituents (if indeed that will is ever concretely known) might be voted out of office, delegates in premodern France who strayed beyond the bounds of their *cahiers* could be immediately disavowed and even sentenced to a fine or imprisonment.[41]

When the regional delegates arrived at the city where the Estates General was to be held, they would begin the crucial process of the co-verification of powers. The delegates would examine one another's papers, ensuring that they were the rightful possessors of duly executed powers, and that the *cahier* that each delegate carried had been properly confided to his care.[42] Only when this initial verification of powers had been completed could the official opening of the Estates General take place. The raw stuff of re-presentation was present, and now the process had come full circle: The word had gone forth from the King to his subjects, and his subjects had assembled in their entirety, at the appointed time, to present their *cahiers,* or as one witness to the events put it, "to bring the word" to the King.[43] The head had summoned, and the body had appeared. As a witness to the Estates General that met in Blois in 1588 reported, delegates from throughout France transformed that city into "a condensation *[abrégé]* of all France."[44] Duly assembled and verified, it only remained for this assemblage of individual

40. Carré de Malberg gave an apt description of the task of a delegate to the Estates General when he wrote, "[The delegates] are ambassadors, sent to the King so that he might hear the voice of the nation; [they are] plenipotentiaries. . . . In all of this, the idea of representation is quite clear: the manner in which the Estates General represents the diverse elements of the nation before the King, resembles, in a sense, the manner in which a diplomatic agent represents his country before a foreign sovereign" (Carré de Malberg, *Contribution à la théorie générale de l'état* [Paris, 1922], 239).

41. Major, *Deputies to the Estates General,* 8–9; see also Major, *The Estates General of 1560,* 73.

42. See, for example, Major, "Pontoise, 1561," sec. 4, 467, where he describes an instance during the verification of powers in which one of the deputies was initially refused the right to sit in the assembly because of irregularities in both his powers (mandate) and his *cahier.*

43. "Ordre et séance gardés en la convocation et assemblée des trois états du royaume de France . . ." [1560], in Lalourcé and Duval, eds., *Recueil de Pièces originales et authentiques, concernant la tenue des États-généraux d'Orléans en 1560, sous Charles IX; de Blois en 1576, de Blois en 1588, sous Henri III, de Paris en 1614, sous Louis XIII,* vol. 1 (Paris, 1784), 32.

44. [Matthieu], *Histoire des derniers troubles,* 114.

political actors to be transformed into the political body of the Estates General.

On the official opening day of the Estates General, the King and the royal court would march as part of a carefully orchestrated procession (whose body was made up of the three estates), which culminated in a ceremonial communion at the main cathedral. The opening ceremonies, both the procession itself and the taking of communion, constituted nothing less than the incarnation of the *corpus mysticum* in its entirety. With this coming together of the head and the body, the *corpus mysticum*—a body that had existed only in the mystical realm since the last meeting of the Estates General—re-presented itself in the visible form of a political body. A brief glance at the seating arrangements of the Estates General of 1588, for example, reveals the correspondence between the *corpus mysticum* and its re-presentation: the King was seated at the head of the assembly; below him, to his right and left respectively, were seated the first and second estates, arranged like organs of the mystical body; and on the sides and along the bottom, like so many hands and feet, were arranged the members of the third estate.[45] Seated in this manner, and partaking in the act of communion, the deputies to the Estates General simultaneously participated in the transubstantiation of the Eucharist and the transubstantiation of their own bodies into the *corpus mysticum* of the French nation.

In Estates Generals prior to 1560, the symbolic re-presentation of the mystical body of the nation in the opening ceremonies was immediately followed by a corresponding practical condensation of the nation's will in which delegates condensed their regional *cahiers* into one general *cahier* for each of the estates. And then, in an act by which the wills of millions of inhabitants of France were theoretically fused into one body, the three estates met together to form one *cahier*, containing the condensed will of the entire nation, which they then presented to the King. The transparency between political body and the mystical body of the nation was such that it could be said that, through the body of the Estates General, all the people of France met with their King. As Chancellor L'Hospital declared in his opening remarks to the Estates General in 1560, "It is without doubt that the people receive great benefit from these estates [general]; because at this hour [the people] approaches the person of its king, makes its complaints, presents its requests, and obtains necessary remedies and provisions."[46]

By the act of receiving this final *cahier*, and determining how to answer and ultimately act upon it, the King essentially merged his own will with that of the nation, and the *corpus mysticum* in its entirety could speak as one body

45. Godefroy, *Le cérémonial françois*, vol. 2, p. 321. Diagrams of the seating arrangements of various assemblies can also be found in Lalourcé and Duval, *Recueil*.
46. L'Hospital, "Harrangue prononcée," 379–80.

with one will. Once the King had responded to the *cahier* of the nation, the will of the nation had been formed, and the Estates General could disband. One final ceremony would take place, during which the King would once again assemble with his court and the deputies of the three estates, exactly as they had done in the opening ceremony. After this final act of re-presentation, the political body would disband into its constituent parts, and the King would once again take on his role as the sole re-presentation of the *corpus mysticum:* the visible head of a mystical body.

Beginning with the Estates General of 1560, however, the re-presentation of the *corpus mysticum* seems to have encountered difficulties. Unlike the Estates General of 1484, in which the mystical communion of wills still seemed within the grasp of those assembled, the Estates General of 1560 was marked by grave religious and social cleavages that produced an irreducibility of wills.[47] One important consequence of this spirit of disunity was the fact that the three estates, rather than combining their three *cahiers* into one, eventually chose instead to submit three separate *cahiers* to the King, a precedent that would be followed by later assemblies. Frictions between the estates were compounded by tensions between the various estates and the King. And, tellingly enough, although Chancellor L'Hospital had begun his opening speech to the deputies of the Estates General in 1560 with the traditional exhortation to harmony, he concluded the speech with a hint at more radical methods of achieving unity, broaching the idea of a kind of emergency surgery to save the *corpus mysticum:* "Because if we are all like a body, of which the king is the head *[chief]*, it is much better to cut off the rotten member than to allow it to ruin and corrupt the [other] members, and force them to die."[48]

In this statement, L'Hospital abandons the presupposition that the people of France formed a cohesive body whose single will could be formed by the condensation of the parts. Instead, reminding the deputies that "the King does not receive his crown from us, but from God,"[49] L'Hospital posits the will of the body to be already present in the head. As for those whose will did not conform, they were by definition not a vital part of the body, but rather a "rotten member" which posed a threat to the health of the whole.

In this bold assertion of the sovereign authority of the head, L'Hospital was attempting to effect a mutation in the theory and practice of re-presentation that essentially substituted the will of the King for the painstakingly distilled will of the people. As a direct response to L'Hospital, several political theorists of the late sixteenth century began to articulate a notion

47. For a discussion of the religious, economic, social, and intellectual context in which the Estates General of 1560 was convened, see Major, *The Estates General of 1560*, 16–41.

48. L'Hospital, "Harrangue prononcée," 404.

49. Ibid., 389.

of sovereign will that was body-centered, and these individuals consequently (and, from an organological point of view, somewhat illogically) declared the head to be a mere appendage of the body.[50] Their explicit intention was to prove not only that the people, not God, had created Kings, but also that the people, in giving themselves a king, had merely intended to delegate the *exercise* of sovereignty rather than sovereignty itself; in the case of an interregnum—or even when the will of the King was at odds with the will of the nation—sovereignty always devolved back to the people.

It would be difficult to imagine a clearer contrast between those who argued that the will of the King was primary and the advocates of popular sovereignty who maintained that the will of the people was primary. And yet, the apparent opposition between these two positions masks a fundamental shared assumption that was rather new: advocates of royal sovereignty and popular sovereignty unanimously rejected the notion that had been current before the latter half of the sixteenth century that the will of the *corpus mysticum* could be produced through a coming together of the deputies with the King. For both these groups, sovereignty was indivisible: it resided *either* in the head *or* in the body, but it could not reside in both. The almost universal acceptance of the idea of the indivisibility of sovereignty by the late sixteenth century left only two possible paths for France's political future: the tyranny of the head or the tyranny of the body. By the last decades of the sixteenth century, France's path had been narrowed to a choice between absolutism and revolution.

Nowhere is the principle of the indivisibility of sovereignty articulated more clearly than in the writings of the late-sixteenth-century political theorist Jean Bodin. By maintaining that the indivisibility of sovereign will could be assured only if the political body were composed of one individual,[51]

---

50. Hotman and others conducted extensive historical research in an attempt to locate the original act by which the sovereign people had given themselves a King—research that, as the historian J. G. A. Pocock has written, "forced [them] into a kind of historical obscurantism [and] compelled [them] to attribute their liberties to more and more remote and mythical periods in the effort to prove them independent of the will of the king" (J. G. A. Pocock, *The Ancient Constitution and the Feudal Law: A Study of English Historical Thought in the Seventeenth Century* [Cambridge: Cambridge University Press, 1957], 17). On Hotman's historically based argument, see Ralph E. Giesey, "The Juristic Basis of Dynastic Right to the French Throne," in *Transactions of the American Philosophical Society*, new series, vol. 51, pt. 5 (1961), 30, and André Lemaire, *Les lois fondamentales de la monarchie française, d'après les théoriciens de l'ancien régime* (Paris, 1907), 92–101.

51. In his earlier writings, Bodin had suggested that the principle of indivisibility did not necessarily mandate one particular form of government over another: as long as the political body possessed sovereignty absolutely, that body could be an assembly of the people, an aristocratic senate, or a King. Eventually, however, the deteriorating political situation in France, and the St. Bartholomew's Day Massacre of 1572 in particular, seem to have persuaded Bodin that absolute and indivisible sovereignty could truly exist only in a monarchy. Only a political

Bodin and other advocates of royal sovereignty[52] espoused a political theory that, in effect, reversed the traditional "flow" of the will of the *corpus mysticum*. Instead of a process in which the will would be gathered from the many and condensed into a single whole, absolute royal sovereignty presupposed the will to be already present in the body of the monarch. Instead of *condensation* from the periphery to the center, therefore, absolutism necessarily implied a *radiation* of sovereign will from the center to the periphery. Absolutist theorists, in effect, relieved the French people of the cumbersome process of drafting *cahiers* and selecting proxies; there was no need to condense the will of the nation or to form a political body when that will and that body were already present in the body of the King. And, although Bodin initially argued that assemblies of the Estates General might be retained as a purely ceremonial spectacle of homage to the monarch,[53] in the end the iconographic role in the process of re-presentation would also be arrogated by the monarch. After all, an individual human body is in many ways better suited to the re-presentation of a unified mystical body than is an assemblage of several hundred deputies. After 1614, spectacles of royal entry and public appearances by the King would fulfill the function formerly performed by the Estates General: the King himself had become not only the repository of sovereign will, but also the iconographic re-presentation of the mystical body.

So, if the Estates General never met again from 1614 until the eve of the Revolution in 1789, does absolutism mark a break in the conception of political re-presentation? Yes and no. Unquestionably, absolutism changed the process of re-presentation in a variety of important ways. In addition to the transformation of political re-presentation from a process of condensation to one of radiation (a transformation that gave rise to a plethora of solar metaphors), absolutism transformed the act of political re-presentation from a rare into a continuous function. Whereas the *corpus mysticum* had previously been re-presented in its entirety only when the King met with his Estates, now the entire mystical body of the nation was held to be permanently re-

---

body composed of one natural (i.e., human) body could, by its very nature, guarantee a unitary will. And, as his firsthand experience as a deputy to the Estates General had proved to Bodin, political bodies composed of more than one individual inevitably tended toward factiousness rather than the coherent expression of a unitary will. See Julian H. Franklin, *Jean Bodin and the Rise of Absolutist Theory* (London and New York: Cambridge University Press, 1973), 26, 41, 49.

52. See Lemaire's discussion of the views of Jean du Tillet, Grégoire de Toulouse, and Loyseau in Lemaire, *Les lois fondamentales*, 82–86, 128–33, 153–54.

53. Jean Bodin, *Les six livres de la république* (Paris, 1583; reprint, Aalen: Scientia, 1961), 141. Although Bodin did not challenge the right of the Estates General to assemble, or indeed challenge the essential equation of the Estates General in assembly with the nation in its entirety, he did very clearly state that it was not particularly "necessary to pay much attention to their opinion" (ibid., 137–38).

presented in the political body of the King alone. Like a Eucharist that no longer needed to be transubstantiated, and was in a state of continuous re-presentation, the process of political re-presentation became a function of permanent display rather than extraordinary metamorphosis.

In addition, absolutism altered the traditional relationship between the king's two bodies: Because the king now re-presented the political body in its entirety (rather than its head alone), there was no longer any practical reason to differentiate formally between the king's body natural and the King as body politic. For all intents and purposes, the king's body natural was the nation itself, a concept so elegantly summed up by the phrase that Louis XIV may or may not have uttered: *l'état c'est moi.* The theoretical relationship between the body of the king and the body of the nation seemed so perfectly transparent that, at least in the eyes of absolutist theorists, the king merely needed to *be,* in order for the nation to be re-presented. As the historian Carré de Malberg characterized this view, "The king is, according to the claims of the absolutist monarchy, the State itself. He is not a representative of the state; he is the direct organ of the state."[54]

Despite the practical changes that did result from absolutism, however, one cannot say that the fundamental conception of re-presentation itself was markedly transformed. The essential purpose of political re-presentation remained the visible and tangible incarnation of a mystical body. France remained a mystical body with one head and three estates, and although the King now performed the incarnation of the mystical body entirely with his own body (whereas previously he had formed only the head of the re-presentative body), the form of re-presentation was still embodied and concrete. The play of political re-presentation therefore remained relatively unchanged, even if the number of actors on the political stage had been reduced to one.

The most important innovations in the theory of political representation— those that paralleled the revolution in theatrical representation—would not occur until the middle of the eighteenth century, when the absolutist model of re-presentation came under attack by rival theories of political representation. Particularly in the 1750s, and culminating in the *patriote* discourse surrounding the Maupeou coup of the 1770s, political theorists began to challenge the royal monopoly on representation. Although *patriote* authors claimed to want nothing more than the restoration of France's traditional bodily constitution, in which the King and the Estates General together constituted the political body, theoretical novelties began to work their way into the political discourse concerning representation, novelties

---

54. Carré de Malberg, *La théorie générale,* 239.

that were to prefigure many of the practical innovations of the revolutionaries some fifteen years later.

Perhaps the clearest expression of such theoretical novelties can be found in the Remonstrances of the Cour des Aides of 1775, drafted by Chrétien-Guillaume de Lamoignon de Malesherbes. Written soon after Louis XVI had restored the parlements, Malesherbes' remonstrances reminded the young King of the days when his ancestors had personally dispensed justice before the entire nation assembled on the Champ de Mars. Although painting a picture of the day when Louis might too "reign at the head of a Nation which will, in all its entirety, be your Council,"[55] Malesherbes and his fellow magistrates were proposing something very different from a restoration of the original Champ de Mars, something whose very conception would have been unthinkable only a few years earlier: they were proposing the creation of what we might today call a "virtual" Champ de Mars.

No one debated the fact that the French nation was simply too large to assemble all in one place, as they were supposed to have done in the days when Charlemagne met with the entire nation assembled. And the remonstrances clearly regarded the traditional Estates General as an acceptable representation of an assembly of the entire nation, declaring the restoration of the Estates to be the "unanimous wish of the Nation."[56] But alongside this—by that date—conventional position, the remonstrances broached new conceptual territory. If France was clearly too large for the entirety of the nation to assemble in one place, then the age of printing, combined with the increasing literacy and enlightenment of the French people, could usher in an era in which politics might approach—in the abstract, if not in actual practice—the publicness and the immediacy of the assemblies under Charlemagne: "The Art of Printing has therefore imparted to writing the same publicity that the [spoken] word had in earlier times, in the midst of the assemblies of the Nation."[57]

What Malesherbes and his colleagues were proposing was a national assembly that would resemble the assemblies on the Champ de Mars in their "publicity," but also an assembly that would be relieved of the burdensome task of actually assembling: this was a national assembly that existed on a purely abstract plane, a political public based upon the educated reading public and the theatrical public that had developed in France at mid-century. Government, far from being the *secret du roi,* could play to the audience of public opinion, a scenario that, Malesherbes suggested, had certain advantages over an actual assembly of the people:

55. Malesherbes, "Remontrances relatives aux impôts, 6 mai 1775," in Elizabeth Badinter, *Les 'Remontrances' de Malesherbes, 1771–1775* (Paris: Union generale d'éditions, 1978), 275.
56. Ibid., 265.
57. Ibid., 273.

Knowledge having spread as a result of printing, written Laws are today known by all the world; each individual can understand his own affairs. . . . Judges can themselves be judged by an informed public; and this censure is much more severe and more just when it can be exercised in a dispassionate *[froide]* and thoughtful reading, than when voting is swept up in a tumultuous assembly.[58]

We should pause for a moment to consider Malesherbes' use of the phrase "dispassionate and thoughtful reading," which he contrasts to a "tumultuous assembly." Malesherbes implicitly assumes here that the sum of numerous dispassionate readings will somehow result in a coherent public opinion, one that is more studied and more reasonable than a decision produced by a "tumultuous assembly." As Roger Chartier has suggested, "Malesherbes converted the congeries of particular opinions that emerge from solitary reading into a collective and anonymous conceptual entity that is both abstract and homogenous."[59]

Precisely how the solitary experiences of individual citizens/readers/ spectators would be formed into a collective and presumably unified opinion was a somewhat thorny issue, and Malesherbes seems to have resolved it in a manner that is extraordinarily suggestive for our purposes here. Explaining why so many years had passed between the invention of the printing press and the possibility of constructing a new, public-minded political order, Malesherbes maintained that it had been necessary for the French people to become more literate, and for there to have developed a cadre of "gifted" individuals capable of expressing public opinion on behalf of the public:

But several centuries were necessary before the discovery of this Art [i.e., printing] had had its full effect on mankind. It was necessary for the entire Nation to form the taste and the habit of instructing itself through reading, and that enough individuals gifted in the art of writing had been formed who could lend their abilities to the Public, and could take the place of those who, gifted with a natural eloquence, let themselves be heard by our forefathers on the Champ de Mars or in public proceedings.[60]

Here, in this concise passage, is the crux of Malesherbes' conception of how abstract political opinion finds expression: The gifted few write, lending their abilities to the public, whose task is presumably restricted to the act of reading. Although the Remonstrances clearly demanded greater "publicity"

58. Ibid., 272–73. My comparison of Malesherbes' political public opinion to prepolitical forms of public opinion owes much to Roger Chartier's discussion of Malesherbes' remonstrances in general, and his interpretation of this passage in particular. See Roger Chartier, *The Cultural Origins of the French Revolution,* trans. Lydia G. Cochrane (Durham, N.C.: Duke University Press, 1991), 30–32.
59. Chartier, *Cultural Origins,* 31.
60. Malesherbes, "Remontrances," 273.

in government, Malesherbes and his colleagues were not in any way proposing that the public assume control of political affairs; rather, they were proposing that political representation ought to regard the public as its primary audience. Far from transforming the public into political actors, Malesherbes was proposing the creation of a nation of political spectators— a nation in which the public would relinquish active participation to expert representatives, uniquely gifted in the art of expressing themselves.

In this early vision of a dawning political age, Malesherbes envisioned a politics that, although it catered to the public in the abstract, would nevertheless exclude the public in reality as active participants. As in the world of the theater, the spectator was posited as the raison d'être of representation, while at the very same time the collective audience was on the verge of being declared a meaningless abstraction.[61] The lone, quietly attentive spectator would replace the vocal audience; the silent, reasoning citizen, would replace the nation that voiced one will.

Malesherbes did not stop at the level of theory, however. Inserted almost parenthetically into the remonstrances is a curious sketch for a political system that Malesherbes is quick to minimize as a temporary expedient that could function "while waiting [for the moment when] it pleases the King to convene [the Estates]."[62] Nevertheless, despite Malesherbes' assurances to the contrary, one wonders whether he did not believe his own system to have certain advantages over the traditional re-presentation by Estates General. Indeed, Malesherbes repeatedly stresses the cost-efficiency of his system: it would make use of two noncompensated representatives, one who was already in the capital on personal business (and would therefore not have to be compensated by the home district for traveling expenses), and another back home who would serve for no recompense other than the honor of doing so.

Here, in rather rudimentary form, is an abstract system of political representation. The constituency would be spared the expense and inconvenience of gathering together its tangible will in the form of a *cahier* and paying for a deputy to travel to some distant assembly in order to re-present the *cahier*. Instead, a representative who lived semipermanently in the capital would represent the interests of those back home. But Malesherbes was not yet ready to cut the cord completely between the representative and the rep-

61. For the theatrical version of this, see Mona Ozouf's discussion of Beaumarchais' *Essai sur le genre dramatique sérieux*, in which, according to Ozouf, "Beaumarchais held the [theatrical] public to be a fiction that did not hold up under examination and a collective being permanently threatened with dissolution and dispersion, constrained to give way to 'the judgment of the smaller number'—to intrigue and to influence" (Mona Ozouf, " 'Public Opinion' at the End of the Old Regime," *The Journal of Modern History* 60, Supplement [September 1988]: s17).

62. Malesherbes, "Remonstrances," 282.

resented, and he therefore stressed the "constant contact" (by means of letters) between the representative in the capital and the representative back home, who would "know more about the true interests" of the province.[63] We should note, however, that the will of the people would be inferred, rather than scrupulously ascertained. And, in Malesherbes system, there is of course no talk of a binding mandate: after all, one can hardly bind a representative to a will that does not exist in any tangible form.

In Malesherbes' political system, the representative plays a much greater role in determining the content of the representation than did traditional deputies to the Estates General. And the role of the constituency is comparatively diminished; indeed, the constituency would seem to have no practical role in the representative process, apart from the act of voting, an act that constituents undertake as individuals, rather than as a collective. In such a system, the will of the people verges on an abstraction, while the will of the representative becomes paramount.

The traditional form of re-presentation had been based upon the premise that the re-presentative body, taken as a whole, reincarnated the entirety of the mystical body, rendering that body visible. The older system had presupposed that the nation was capable of forming its own will, and that it made use of deputies to carry that will from one assembly to the next. Malesherbes' deputies, by contrast, would not claim to reincarnate their constituencies, but would merely, in Malesherbes' words, "stipulate the interests of their Provinces."[64] And Malesherbes' vision of the national body is not a collective whole, but rather an amorphous, abstract body, composed of fragmented individuals who, even if they are capable of forming their own opinions, are incapable of forming, much less expressing, a national will except through their representatives. Like the spectators in the newly reconfigured theaters of France, Malesherbes' constituents would cease communicating with one another and turn their (silent) attention to the professional representatives who performed for their benefit. In these Remonstrances of the Cour des Aides of 1775, many of the theoretical building blocks were put in place that the National Assembly would eventually use to craft its political legitimacy in 1789: the concepts of an abstract social body, united virtually by the written word, and represented in reality by professional representatives who spoke on behalf of constituents without deeming it necessary to gather their will in any tangible form and were therefore free to act without any specific mandate from these constituents— all of these concepts were present in Malesherbes' remonstrances.

Seventeen seventy-five was something of a banner year for representative schemes. That same year, Anne-Robert-Jacques Turgot, who had recently

63. Ibid., 233.
64. Ibid.

been named controller general, drafted his *Mémoire sur les municipalités,* a document that contains a rather detailed plan for a new representative system. Although loosely based on the Estates General, complete with a "whittling down" of deputies from the local to the national level, Turgot's scheme was decidedly within the framework of abstract representation. One of the cornerstones of Turgot's system was to stratify the local and national assemblies by wealth rather than by order, an innovation that would not only eliminate the inequities of the past, but would have the added advantage of ensuring dignified assemblies that "would take place without tumult; reason could be spoken there. For it is an important matter, in all deliberations in which a large number of persons have interests and rights, to get rid of the chaos of the multitude, while ensuring the rights and interests of each of its members."[65]

Turgot's system was therefore designed to manufacture rational public opinion (as opposed to the popular opinion of the multitude). In contrast to Malesherbes, however, who was careful to describe his system as a temporary expedient in lieu of the Estates General, Turgot proudly boasted of the superiority of his municipal assemblies, whether local, regional, or national: "They would have all the advantages of the assemblies of the Estates & none of the disadvantages: neither confusion, intrigues, nor corporatism or the animosities and prejudices of one order against another."[66]

If Turgot's assemblies lacked the "confusion" and the "corporatism" of the assemblies of the Estates, they also lacked other characteristics of the Estates General: namely, *cahiers,* binding mandates, and a system of re-presentation intended to condense the will of the nation without divesting it of its sovereignty. Instead of a *cahier* detailing the will of his constituents, each of Turgot's deputies would arrive at the assembly bearing a "statement" detailing "the number of parishes forming the district from which he was sent, & the number of citizens' votes [determined by wealth] included within them."[67] The stuff of representation, the document that assured the legitimacy of the representation, was not the concrete will of a locality being re-presented, but rather the number and wealth of inhabitants it possessed (a factor that would be used to determine the relative rank of the deputy). If, as Turgot claimed, the aim of his system was "to establish a chain by which the most remote places might communicate with Your Majesty,"[68] it was a chain of elections, each link of which further removed the representative from the will of his constituents. In short, the effect of Turgot's system was

65. [Anne-Robert-Jacques Turgot], *Des administrations provinciales, mémoire présenté au roi, par feu M. Turgot* (Lausanne, 1788), 62. (The work is commonly known as *Mémoire sur les municipalités.*)

66. Ibid., 95.
67. Ibid., 78.
68. Ibid., 69.

the progressive delegation of sovereign authority, as opposed to the unadulterated transmission of the sovereign will of the nation.

Turgot's system was one in which the representatives reigned supreme. Rather than whittling down the opinions of their constituents into one coherent document, their task was to vote among themselves, with the majority of their votes substituting for the will of the nation. And, in contrast to the traditional Estates General, in which the quantity of representatives was inconsequential in comparison to the quality of the *cahier,* Turgot's system very clearly stipulated that each region should be represented by a single deputy. Although each deputy would be allowed an assistant who could "attend the assemblies as spectators," they were expressly deprived of the right to participate or vote.[69] The role of the assistant, like that of the constituents back home, was to observe without participating. Here, very simply, was a system of representation in which professional representatives alone were entitled to act, while all others were relegated—as Turgot so aptly termed it—to the role of "spectators."

If individuals like Malesherbes and Turgot laid the theoretical foundation for abstract representation, it remained for the revolutionaries of 1789 to effect a revolution in the practice of representation—a revolution that they accomplished virtually instantaneously, in June of 1789, when the deputies to the third estate seceded from the *corpus mysticum* and created their own assembly. By this act, the representatives to the third estate not only created a new political body, they also brought into existence a new species of representation: declaring themselves to be independent from the will of their constituents expressed in the *cahiers,* the representatives of the third estate transformed themselves into the abstract representatives of the nation's will. Forsaking any claim to re-present the mystical body of the nation, the representatives to the National Assembly instead spoke on behalf of a newly fragmented collection of individuals who were nevertheless still deemed to posses a unified will—a will that could be voiced only through its representatives. Like its theatrical counterpart, the role of the political audience was theoretically limited to passive observation. And the new political actors, like *their* theatrical counterparts, would be less concerned with their own material legitimacy than with the outward perception of the appearance of legitimacy. A politics of concrete embodiment was being replaced by a politics of *vraisemblance.*

The transition between these two forms of legitimacy was not effected without difficulty. Even among the representatives who composed the renegade assembly, there was a great deal of hesitation before they could bring themselves to define the form and content of their representation; they were painfully aware of the fact that—if they represented *anyone* apart from

69. Ibid., 81.

themselves—they represented only a majority of the nation rather than the nation in its entirety. The representatives to the new National Assembly therefore paused on the threshold of the new political era. For several days, they struggled to find an *accurate* name for themselves that might help to lend them an aura of legitimacy. To the modern ear, the names that they considered seem hopelessly awkward. Such names as "Legitimate Assembly of the Representatives of the Major Portion of the Nation, Acting in the Absence of the Minor Portion" or "The Assembly Comprising the Majority in the Absence of the Minority,"[70] testify to the reluctance on the part of these political actors to pretend to represent something that, in truth, they were not.

Only Mirabeau, the most dynamic speaker among them, and arguably the most politically astute, seemed to grasp the subtleties of the new political order. Referring to a somewhat awkward, if accurate, name suggested by one of his colleagues, Mirabeau declared, "Is [this name] really intelligible? Will it jolt your constituents who are used to [the name] 'Estates General'?" Instead, Mirabeau urged his colleagues to worry less about accuracy, and to chose a name that might prove more palatable to the French people: "Do not take a name that is jarring. Find one that no one can challenge, which [is] more smooth *[doux]*."[71] When the representatives finally voted to christen themselves the "National Assembly," France's new political actors signified that they understood legitimacy in the new regime would be staked on the believability rather than the actual legitimacy of the representation.

Nine days after formally coming into existence on 17 June 1789, the National Assembly took up the question of binding mandates, and by 8 July decided to abolish them. As far as the overwhelming majority of the representatives was concerned, the concept of the binding mandate effectively *prevented* the representation of the general will rather than ensuring it: if all the individuals composing the nation were incapable of assembling except through its representatives, and if the general will could be expressed only by the totality of the nation, then it stood to reason that the general will could be expressed only by the nation's representatives. As Lally-Tollendal declared to the Assembly,

> Each portion of society is a subject; sovereignty resides only in the whole assembled *[réuni];* I say "the whole" because legislative power does not belong to a portion of the whole; I say "assembled" because the nation cannot exercise legislative power when it is divided. [But the nation] cannot deliberate as a whole *[en commun]*. This deliberation of the whole can take place only through representatives; where I see the representatives of twenty-five million men is where I see the whole in which resides the plenitude of sovereignty;

70. *Archives parlementaires de 1787 à 1860*, vol. 8 (Paris, 1875), 113, 123 [15 June 1789].
71. Mirabeau (15 June 1789) in ibid., 111.

and if [this whole] should encounter a portion of the whole which wishes to oppose the nation, I see only a subject who would claim to be more important than the whole.[72]

Thus the National Assembly had become the sole voice of the general will. By contrast, the French people, because they were incapable of assembling or deliberating in one place, were regarded as incapable of expressing anything but particularizations of the general will. Much like the practitioners of the new theater who believed that a more realistic representation necessitated a stage free of spectators, the representatives to the new National Assembly, by rejecting the *mandat impératif*, effectively cleared the stage of political spectators. Only in so doing could they offer a representation that seemed *vraisemblable*—a representation more real than the real people for whose benefit they performed. And the constituents who had elected them were now declared an abstract particularization of the general will, and consequently relegated to the political parterre to watch in silence.

From that moment forward, critics of the National Assembly would refer time and again to the rejection of the *mandat impératif* as the moment when the foundation for a new tyranny had been laid. For those who had hoped for a different kind of revolution, a revolution that would have "revolved" France back to its pre-absolutist system of re-presentation in which the political body had been composed of bound representatives who transparently reflected the will of their constituents, the actions of the National Assembly were an assault upon the newly reclaimed sovereignty of the French people. As the frontispiece to an anonymous counterrevolutionary pamphlet declared, there simply was no middle ground between an assembly of bound *mandataires* and an assembly of tyrants: "Either the Deputies who sit in the riding hall [of the Tuileries] are the *mandataires* of the Capital and of the Provinces, or they are the usurpers and the tyrants of the nation."[73]

Such allegations of tyranny were increasingly leveled against the National Assembly by the political opposition of both the right and the left during the years 1790–1793. These characterizations often implied that the Revolution had been co-opted by political actors, and that the true beneficiaries of the new regime were not the French people, but rather the people's "so-called *[prétendus]*"[74] representatives. Counterrevolutionary pamphlets in particular spoke of despotism and tyranny under the guise of

72. Lally-Tollendal (7 July 1789) in ibid., 204.

73. *L'Assemblée nationale, traitée comme elle le mérite* (n.p., [1789?]), 1.

74. Critics of the National Assembly often referred to it as the *Assemblée prétendue nationale* [the so-called National Assembly] in order to highlight its illegitimate and nonrepresentative nature. Antoine Ferrand was particularly fond of doing this in the titles to his pamphlets: *Le dénouement de l'Assemblée prétendue nationale* (Paris, 1790); *Tableau de la conduite de l'Assemblée*

representative democracy, of political actors free to do as they pleased on a stage from which the French people had been excluded. As one such pamphlet put it:

> [T]o the [National Assembly], and to it alone belongs the [right] to interpret and to present the general will of the nation; . . . [T]he nation itself has ended up deprived of [the right] to express its wishes, its will, since its representatives have arrogated that exclusive right unto themselves.[75]

Apart from the rejection of the *mandat impératif* and the clearing of the political audience from the representative space, transformations on the political stage mirrored those on the theatrical stage in another important aspect: in what might very well be seen as the political version of Diderot's theatrical fourth wall, representatives to the National Assembly declared themselves inviolable on 23 June 1789. Although ostensibly the principle of inviolability was intended to protect the fledgling assembly from the forces of reaction, the Assembly's critics were quick to assert that the principle of inviolability was less a defense against royal troops than against the French people themselves. And so, like theatrical actors alone upon the stage, who ignored spectators on the other side of the fourth wall, political representatives freed from their mandate, and safe behind a wall of inviolability, could act as if their constituents did not exist. As one counterrevolutionary author complained:

> They have foreseen everything; their persons and their possessions are inviolable. What does anything else matter to them; it is in vain that you might scream to them that they have made out of society an assemblage of lunatics . . . ; they are deaf to such complaints; they listen only to their own ambition.[76]

On the other side of the political spectrum, the prominent radical Camille Desmoulins urged the French people to resist their removal from the political stage. Declaring the crowds of people who gathered every day in the Palais-Royal to be the exemplars of active, direct democracy, Desmoulins

---

prétendue nationale, adressé à elle-même, par l'auteur d'un ouvrage intitulé: Nullité et despotisme, &c (Paris, 1790); and *Nullité et despotisme de l'Assemblée prétendue nationale* (n.p., 1790). See also the anonymous pamphlet *Grands tableaux magiques des fameuses supressions faites par la très-grande et très-infaillible assemblée prétendue nationale. Par l'auteur de la trahison contre l'état ou les jacobins dévoilés, de la joyeuses semaine; &c., &c.* (Paris, n.d.). It is interesting to note that critics of the Théâtre Français, once it had changed its name to the Théâtre National, also referred to it as the Théâtre Prétendu National in order to imply that it was engaged in nonpatriotic, counterrevolutionary activities.

75. [Le Comte Murat de Montferrand], *Qu'est-ce que l'Assemblée nationale? Grande thèse en présence de l'auteur anonyme de Qu'est-ce que le tiers? Et dédiée au très-honorable Edmund Burke, comme à un véritable ami de la vraie liberté* (n.p., 1791), 10.

76. [Antoine Ferrand], *Ambition et égoïsme de l'Assemblée nationale* (Paris, 1790), 9.

praised those who had resisted being "idle spectators" to the "spectacle" of Revolution:

> [The Palais-Royal] is the seat of patriotism, the rendez-vous of the finest patriots who have left their homes and their provinces in order to take part *[assister]* in the magnificent spectacle of the revolution of 1789, & not to be idle spectators to it.[77]

CONCLUSION

On both the political and the theatrical stages, a concrete material re-presentation had given way to a more metaphoric, more abstract representation. On both stages, the representatives had become clearly differentiated from the spectators. And on both stages, the public was exiled from the representative space, and in its own best interest, for the purposes of more effective representation, ignored. The theatricality of politics in revolutionary France is undoubtedly a consequence of the parallel trajectories of theatrical and political representation. That these parallel paths converged is therefore less surprising than the fact that they should have been separate in the first place, a consequence of the divisions drawn by the old regime between sacred and profane incarnations. But once representation ceased to be a function of embodiment and became a function of *vraisemblance,* there was no longer any practical reason to keep theater and politics in separate, parallel realms. The French Revolution therefore stands at the threshold of an era in which theatrical and political forms became virtually indistinguishable.

77. [Camille Desmoulins], *Discours de la lanterne aux Parisiens* (Paris, 1789), 49.

On Queen Bees and Being Queens

A Late-Eighteenth-Century "Cultural Revolution"?

Dror Wahrman

Shortly after the Glorious Revolution, a physician from Croydon published a tract that went through no less than nine editions in the next half-century; a tract that sang the praises of a particular matriarchal society headed by a "glorious" queen. This queen was "one Terrible to her Enemies, who will maintain War with any State that dares Assault her, or invade even the Borders of her Territories." "As to her Power," his description continued with appropriate awe, "the Grand Seignior with all his janizaries about him . . . is not half so absolute." The second edition of 1713 was dedicated, rather inevitably, to Queen Anne: "I here present Your Majesty with a true State of these *Amazons,* or rather, a State of the true *Amazons;* and tho' there be Male as well as Female amongst them, 'tis not for nothing, nor by chance, that He who is Wisdom itself, should thus place the Government of their famous Monarchy in a Queen." In many ways, the author contended, this was the perfect polity. Not least, in contrast to the still painful memories of the "sacrilegious" rebellion in England, the extraordinary loyalty of this queen's subjects had our provincial physician waxing lyrical:

No *Amazonian* Dame, nor *Indian* more,
With [such] Loyal Awe their Idol Queen Adore.
Whilst she survives, in Concord and Content
The Commons live, by no Divisions rent.

This perfect polity was, of course, the beehive. Long serving as a continuing source of fascination, investigation, and speculation, the beehive was famously seen by early modern people as a parable—indeed, a divine

For comments and criticisms I am grateful to Donna Andrew, David Armitage, Eitan Bar-Yosef, David Bell, Rebecca Earle, Sarah Knott, Mary Catherine Moran, and Jonathan Sheehan.

allegory—on human society. And key to the understanding of the beehive, always heavily anthropomorphized, was its perceived gender relations: from the seventeenth century onward, bee society was increasingly recognized as a society whose warring and governance were wholly female. Discussions of bees can therefore serve us, too, as a parable, an allegorical window into bigger questions of eighteenth-century society, particularly in relation to gender.

The apiary manual from which the above lines have been quoted had the evocative title *The True Amazons: Or, the Monarchy of Bees*.[1] The point of view it represented was far from unusual: at least two other early modern apiarian texts carried the title "The Feminine/Female Monarchy." One made again the analogy between the valorous and magnanimous bees and "the warlike Nation of Women called *Amazons*." The other characterized the bees as "such bold, daring, intrepid Animals, that nothing can intimidate them"; by which the author—one John Thorley—meant of course the worker bees, those that he labeled "imperious Dames" even as he admitted (wrongly, of course) that "in Truth, they are of neither Sex." The queen bee at their helm, moreover, was a "noble, beautiful Creature," "strong and vigorous," commanding the absolute and unswerving loyalty of the community. A famous mid-eighteenth-century poetic tribute to the bees (again, as a model for national emulation) summed up this view in referring to the queen bee as "the martial Dame" heading "the Female State."[2]

Compare now these late-seventeenth- and eighteenth-century portraits of bee society with another, no less anthropomorphic, in 1800. "The queen is, literally, the mother of her people"; "the sole office of the queen, the importance of which is known to her subjects, and which makes this mother so valuable, is to produce a numerous progeny; it is this to which she seems entirely destined, and the only title by which she lays claim to royalty." The

---

1. Joseph Warder, *The True Amazons: Or, the Monarchy of Bees. Being a New Discovery and Improvement of Those Wonderful Creatures* . . . , 3rd ed., with additions (1st ed., 1693; 2nd ed., 1713; London: 1716), ix, 42–44, 66. And note Robert Maxwell, *The Practical Bee-Master* . . . (Edinburgh, 1747), which actually disagreed with Warder's depiction of the sexes in the beehive (especially regarding the sex of the monarch), but not because he found such gender reversal offensive or difficult to stomach; on the contrary, Maxwell assured his readers that it was "of small, if any Consequence, whether this Sovereign is Male or Female" (p. 10).

2. Charles Butler, *The Feminine Monarchy; Or the History of Bees* . . . (London, 1704), 12, 61. [John Thorley], *The Female Monarchy: Or, the Natural History of Bees* . . . (London, 1745), 3–4, 6. (Thorley, however, was uneasy about admitting the defenseless drones as full-fledged males.) Joshua Dinsdale, *The Modern Art of Breeding Bees, a Poem* (London, 1740), 18–19. See also Samuel Purchas' "Amazonian Commonwealth" in *A Theatre of Politicall Flying-Insects. Wherein Especially the Nature, the Worth, the Work, the Wonder, and the Manner of Right-ordering of the Bee, is Discovered and Described* . . . (London, 1657), 33, 40. The use of "Amazons" to denote bees was common enough to make it into contemporary reference works, including the first edition of the *Encyclopaedia Britannica* (London, 1771).

implications of this image were radically different. The queen was no longer a fierce ruling Amazon: in fact, this text assured its readers, she was of "extremely pacific" nature. Rather, the queen was a perfect female—indeed "the only person of her sex"—and that on account of her being *a mother.* And crucially, her motherhood was now singled out as her only claim to the position of ruler and to the natural loyalty of her subjects. These subjects, moreover, were also realigned to meet new gender expectations: the laborers, this writer asserted, were "of no sex." Thus, *tout court:* there was no added qualification that might have allowed the laborer bees to be represented at the same time as "imperious Dames" in the manner of John Thorley half a century earlier. On the contrary, in the 1800 text the default pronoun for the laborer bee turned out to be *him.* And as for the short-lived drones at the bottom of the pecking order, they turned out to be not straightforward males, but rather effeminate, degenerate males ("leading a life so soft and delicate," "slothful and voluptuous"), who thus merited through their loss of manliness everything that befell them (they "would disgrace arms, and [thus] they wear them not"). Once again, against all odds, this writer succeeded in turning the seeming subversion of expected gender norms in the beehive into a critique that *reaffirmed* those very gender norms. Nor did the text stop there; it actually made a further unexpected move, shifting the distinction between worker bees and drones from a gender to a *class* axis, along the comfortably familiar line of gentry versus laborers ("these lazy gentry are never seen with a basket, of which each laborer carries two"). One can only marvel at the resourcefulness of the multiple strategies for circumventing what this author of 1800 presumably saw as the potentially subversive gender implications of the earlier depictions of the hive.[3]

Once again, this apiary work of 1800 was also far from atypical for its times. Quite the contrary: by the closing decades of the eighteenth century, the common language of bee-texts changed unmistakably, doing away as much as was possible with the female state, distinguished for its feminine warring and governance and its Amazonian, daring monarch.[4] Hanging its

3. *A Short History of Bees. In Two Parts* (London, 1800), 80–85, 90–91.

4. These observations are based on a survey of thirty-six texts about bees between the late seventeenth and the early nineteenth centuries; this encompasses the lion's share of full-text discussions of bees and a considerable proportion of shorter discussions during that period. For a different perspective on transformations in bee-texts, focusing primarily on the bees' political structure, see P. Burke, "Fables of the Bees: A Case-Study in Views of Nature and Society," in *Nature and Society in Historical Context,* ed. M. Teich et al. (Cambridge, 1997), 112–23. J. Merrick's pioneering "Royal Bees: The Gender Politics of the Beehive in Early Modern Europe," *Studies in Eighteenth-Century Culture* 18 (1988): 7–37, discusses the often disturbing political consequences of the earlier seventeenth-century discovery that the queen bee was indeed a female. However, Merrick's conviction that bee-texts throughout this period consistently provided "ample evidence of the persistence of patriarchalism" (p. 26) has led him to

words on the authority of the naturalist William Smellie, the *Historical Magazine* told its readers in 1790, "The queen-bee is the only perfect female, and is the mother of her subjects." Indeed, another explained, though she seemed analogous to an Amazon queen, the essence of the matter was different. In truth the queen "boasts no military pride": without a sting, she is "unfit by nature for th'embattled fray." Nature made her unfit to be an Amazon; instead, the queen, distinguished by her "modesty," was surrounded by "the body-guard, a brave, a faithful band, [who] Round the QUEEN-MOTHER close embodied stand." The image conjured up here was that of a demure female surrounded by valiant protective males.[5]

But if so, how can one explain the males' ignominious end? One work of 1815 had little doubts: "Although by their make the drones appear to possess a superiority over the Bees," this writer affirmed knowingly, "yet they do not appear to offer any resistance to the attack." In other words, the males, "by their make," are really superior to the females, however invisible this superiority might be; and their annihilation in "the most cruel massacre" by the worker bees can be nothing but an altruistic act of self-sacrifice.[6] This move surely competed in its far-fetched mental agility with that made by John Evans, M.D., a few years earlier, when he suddenly reinvented the drones as the epitome of caring fatherhood. Although they are reputed to be "lazy Fathers," he versed, the truth is that "these seeming idlers share / The pleasing duties of parental care," as they stand in constant, loving watch over the embryo hive cells, becoming manly counterparts to "the MOTHER-BEE," a.k.a. "the pregnant Queen." In 1821, an anonymous poem even turned the worker bees themselves into benevolent males (in contrast to the idle, aristocratic drones), extending their manly protection to their graceful feminine queen as well as to their tender offspring. The fully domesticated, properly gender-distinct and gender-defined image of the

---

underestimate the varied and often contradictory attitudes they manifested toward the gender peculiarities of the hive.

5. *Historical Magazine* 2 (1790): 287, adapted from William Smellie, *The Philosophy of Natural History*, vol. 1 (Edinburgh, 1790), 344–49. Arthur Murphy, *The Bees. A Poem. From the Fourteenth Book of Vaniere's Praedium Rusticum* (London, 1799), 20–23, 37. Compare also the maternal queen bee in J[acob] Isaac, *The General Apiarian* (Exeter, 1799), 39–41 (especially the pathetic poetic address from the Queen Bee to the Ladies of Britain on behalf of her progeny), and in George Strutt, *The Practical Apiarian: Or, a Treatise on the Improved Management of Bees* (Clare, 1825), 92.

6. Robert Huish, *A Treatise on the Nature, Economy, and Practical Management of Bees . . .* (London, 1815), 17, 40. Defining "the Queen, or Mother Bee" as "the mother of . . . the whole family," Huish further emphasized that she "is both virgin and mother" (p. 28), thus cleansing her of sexuality. This move, reproduced also by Thomas Nutt, *Humanity to Honey Bees: Or, Practical Directions for the Management of Honey Bees . . .* (Wisbech, 1832), 14, may augur a further development of this story as our authors turned Victorian.

beehive was now as complete as was conceivable by the most exerting stretches of the imagination.[7]

But lest this foray into apiary texts appear to have strayed too far from natural history into playful flights of fancy, let us return in its conclusion to learned discourse, in the form of John Hunter's contribution to the *Philosophical Transactions of the Royal Society* in 1792. Announcing his intent to counteract those "unnatural" accounts of bees that previous authors "have filled up from their imagination," Hunter introduced the queen as "the female breeder," who "is to be considered in no other light than as a layer of eggs." No longer an Amazon, his scientifically characterized queen— once again—was solely a mother. Referring to the bees' famous attachment to their queen, without whom the whole community falls apart, Hunter rejected previous explanations in terms of loyalty of subjects to their powerful monarch, and suggested instead: "May we not suppose that the offspring of the queen have an attachment to the mother, somewhat similar to the attachment of young birds to the female that brings them up? . . . it is the dependence which each has on its mother, that constitutes the bond; for bees have none without her." Rather than political attachment of subjects to ruler, it was the instinctive bonds naturally generated by feminine motherhood that were revealed to be the glue that held the beehive together.[8]

In the end, Hunter found it impossible to disregard common usage, admitting that "this standard of influence, which is the breeder, is [commonly] called the queen." But he then hastened to add: "and I shall keep to the name, although I do not allow her voluntary influence or power." This was the key to the late-eighteenth-century position—the same consideration for inadequate common usage was conceded in almost the same words by John Keys in 1780 and James Bonner in 1789—but here it slipped out with unusual, if unwitting, candor: "I do not allow her voluntary influence or power."[9] How far have we moved from those Amazonian bees of the previous hundred years, completely in control of the fate of their matriarchal polity: whereas the earlier writers had drawn attention to—and were fasci-

7. John Evans, M.D., *The Bees: A Poem, in Four Books. With Notes, Moral, Political, and Philosophical*, bk. 1 (Shrewsbury, 1806), 17, 29, 31; this description of the queen was unable to maintain its stability, however, slipping on p. 32 into a simile of a *male* warrior, and a "manly" one at that. *The Monarchy of the Bees; A Poem* . . . (London, 1821). For more on the drones as caring fathers, see Robert Sydserff, *Sydserff's Treatise on Bees; Being the Result of Upwards of Thirty Years Experience* (Salisbury, 1792), 15.

8. John Hunter, "Observations on Bees," *Philosophical Transactions of the Royal Society of London*, pt. 1 (1792), 132, 139, also reproduced in *Historical Magazine* 4 (1792): 266. Cf. Merrick, "Royal Bees," 24, on "the dethronement of the queen" by Abbé della Rocca in 1790.

9. Hunter, "Observations on Bees," 140. John Keys, *The Practical Bee-Master* . . . (London, 1780), 1–4 (this tract in fact bears close resemblance on all these points to Hunter's lecture). James Bonner, *The Bee-Master's Companion, and Assistant* (Berwick, 1789), 23–24.

nated by—the gender reversals suggested by the bees, the latter ones (in Hunter's formulation) could not "allow" an image of powerful female governance over a community embodying apparently reversed gender roles, and thus made the bees conform as much as possible to predetermined, rigid gender boundaries and expectations. And none of them was more radically affected than the queen bee, who, having been disallowed the role of Amazon queen, was now safely recast as the queen mother.

We have seen what appears to be a repeated pattern in depictions of the beehive: namely, an increasing difficulty at the turn of the eighteenth century with allowing for a gender-reversed picture of female governance, and consequently the recourse—at times unselfconsciously, at times comically—to a variety of strategies to circumvent or suppress those aspects of bee society that had previously proven to be such a continuing source of interest. But what can we make of such an observation? I would like to suggest that this pattern was neither a coincidence nor a phenomenon peculiar to natural historians and other dedicated apiologists. Instead, it was an unusually revealing indication of a much wider transformation; a late-eighteenth-century transformation, perhaps, precisely of the kind that may be identified as a "cultural revolution." In the limited space at my disposal here, I would like to focus on the one aspect of the beehive that can best signal this transformation—the changing representations of the queen bee; for it was the queen that evoked distilled and magnified images of a female in key roles, whether the quintessential public role of political and military leadership or the quintessential private role of the bounteous mother.

The following pages will thus draw the contours of the broader "cultural revolution" that drove the Amazon queen out of the beehive by the late eighteenth century, and that rendered the queen mother her most likely replacement. We need, therefore, to trace the evolution of both sides in this balance—the image of the Amazon on the one hand, and that of the mother on the other. Both, it will be suggested, went through parallel shifts during this period—shifts from understandings capacious enough to allow for individual deviation from dominant gender norms to more essentialized and gender-rigidified ones. The consequence was the foreclosure of the space for particular individuals to circumvent the normative gender expectations that these understandings entailed; a shift that rendered "Amazon" as unacceptable a characterization for a female—be she bee or human—as maternity was to become an inescapable one for her very essence. Finally, after suggesting how this contextualization can render the transformation in the representations of the beehive not only comprehensible but perhaps even predictable, the last section of this essay will elevate its viewpoint to encompass—however briefly—broader and broader swathes of eighteenth-century culture, in order to hypothesize how far this "cultural revolution" may have reached, not only in other realms of perceptions of gender, but also in the widest sense of the categorization of identity itself. This last section will also cast a concluding look back at other contributions to this volume, to see how some of their observations may fare within the framework of such a putative "cultural revolution."

To begin, then, with the Amazon. In looking at the cultural position of the figure of the Amazon, some scholars have asserted—or rather assumed—that the Amazonian image has always presented a constant threat to patriarchy. Therefore, this assumption continues, Amazons became the inevitable target of continuous repression and vilification throughout the history of Western society—what one such work summed up as "The War against the Amazons."[10] But this can readily be shown not to have been the case: in fact, Amazons could get—and did get—a good or bad reputation depending on historical circumstances.

Throughout most of the eighteenth century, in fact, the lot of the human Amazons, like the Amazonian bees, was overall a rather good one.[11] This for instance was how Ephraim Chambers began the relevant entry in his famous *Cyclopædia* of 1728: "Amazon, in Antiquity, a Term signifying a bold, courageous Woman: capable of daring, hardy Atchievements. See VIRAGO, HEROINE, &c." Thus *tout court:* a heroic bundle of extraordinary qualities. These qualities of the Amazons—their "greatest Valour and Heroism" (1758)—were often commented upon: "Have we not read of *Amazons* of Old," versed another mid-century writer, "How great in *War,* how resolute and bold?" In Oliver Goldsmith's *Vicar of Wakefield,* Olivia was to be "drawn as an Amazon, sitting upon a bank of flowers . . . and a whip in her hand" as part of an idyllic, flattering family portrait. Contemporary art critics would have approved: Goldsmith perhaps got the idea from Joseph Spence's learned treatise on the imagery of classical mythology, published a few years earlier, according to which the ancients had represented Virtue as a manly, armed Amazon in order to highlight her "firmness and resolution, not to be conquered by any

---

10. A. Wettan Kleinbaum, *The War against the Amazons* (New York, 1983).

11. The following observations are based on a survey of more than two hundred texts (of widely varying genres) written between the seventeenth and the early nineteenth centuries that made explicit references to literal or figurative Amazons. See also J. Pearson, *The Prostituted Muse: Images of Women and Women Dramatists, 1642–1737* (New York, 1988), 87–92, which begrudgingly admits (despite the author's obvious presuppositions to the contrary) that Amazons in Restoration drama tended to be "sympathetic figures"; G. J. Barker-Benfield, *The Culture of Sensibility: Sex and Society in Eighteenth-Century Britain* (Chicago, 1992), 351–59, which reminds us that *Amazon* was the "Augustan code-word for female pride and gender crossing" (p. 359); and G. Kates, *Monsieur d'Eon Is a Woman: A Tale of Political Intrigue and Sexual Masquerade* (New York, 1995), 157–58, 203–4. A compressed version of the argument in the next few paragraphs is included in D. Wahrman, "*Percy's* Prologue: From Gender Play to Gender Panic in Eighteenth-Century England," *Past and Present* 159 (May 1998): 132–36.

difficulties or dangers." Spence evidently endorsed this iconographic choice, except in cases where Virtue-as-Amazon was not given enough refinement: when he criticized one particular image for appearing "rude; and entirely with the look of a common soldier," it was less a critique of gender than of status reversal. Earlier in the century the Earl of Shaftesbury had likewise suggested that the firmness and manliness of Virtue—"a martial Dame"— could be well conveyed by clothing her like an Amazon. An allegory of 1729, similarly, had Minerva as a benevolent Amazon—again, in line with ancient practice as described, for instance, by Spence.[12]

Moreover, throughout most of the eighteenth century one can readily find representations of actual Amazon queens—be they avowedly mythical or supposedly historical—as noble, honorable, and unreservedly heroic.[13] Nor were these only the bygone Amazon queens of antiquity: Joseph Warder, after all, believed he was being genuinely flattering when he dedicated his account of the "glorious" Amazonian queen bee and her entourage to his own monarch, Queen Anne. Warder's effort resonated with other contemporary attempts to portray the queen as a martial Amazon, beginning with Anne's inaugural medal, which showed her as the warrior goddess Pallas actively engaged in warfare. (These attempts, it is also true, did not go very far—but that was because of their incongruity with Anne's personal inclinations, not because the Amazonian image itself was unacceptable.)[14] Perhaps the best testimony, however, to the meaning of

12. Ephraim Chambers, *Cyclopædia: Or, an Universal Dictionary of Arts and Sciences*, vol. 1 (London, 1728), 74. James Eyre Weeks, *The Amazon: Or Female Courage Vindicated* . . . (Dublin, 1745), 3. *Female Rights Vindicated; Or the Equality of the Sexes Morally and Physically Proved. By a Lady* (London, 1758), preface. Oliver Goldsmith, *The Vicar of Wakefield* (1766), in *Collected Works of Oliver Goldsmith*, vol. 4, ed. A. Friedman (Oxford, 1966), 83. Rev. [Joseph] Spence, *Polymetis: Or, An Enquiry Concerning the Agreement between the Works of the Roman Poets, and the Remains of the Antient Artists*, 2nd ed., corrected (London, 1755), 59, 140–41. Anthony Ashley Cooper, Earl of Shaftesbury, *Characteristicks of Men, Manners, Opinions, Times*, 4th ed., 3 vols. ([London], 1727), vol. 3, 362–63, 386. J. B., *Henry and Minerva. A Poem* (London, 1729), 10.

13. A few examples include: Philip Frowde, *The Fall of Saguntum: A Tragedy* (London, 1727), 14–15. *The Famous History of Hector, Prince of Troy* . . . *together with the Noble Actions of Hector, Achilles, the Amazon Queen, and Divers Other Princes* (London, [c. 1750–1770]), 22. Even the mildly mocking letter by "Thalestris" (the Amazon queen) in Frances Brooke's *Old Maid* 15 (February 21, 1756): 87–88 is critical of contemporary men, but is not at all anti-Amazonian.

14. T. Bowers, *The Politics of Motherhood: British Writing and Culture, 1680–1760* (Cambridge, 1996), 77–79. Bowers points out the increasing sense of incongruity of such images for this home-sitting monarch, but also wants to see it at the same time as a change in understandings of femininity more generally. However, the continuing juxtaposition of Anne with Queen Elizabeth—as in Richard Blackmore's *Eliza: An Epick Poem* (London, 1705), esp. pp. 219–21—suggests that even for those who emphasized Anne's domestic side, the Amazonian queen remained no less a positive image. For Elizabeth as Amazonian queen in the eighteenth century, see below, n. 24. Also note the obviously celebratory parade of virgins dressed "like Amazons, with Bows and Arrows" in Anne's ceremonial entry into Bath in 1702, as cited in

Warder's Amazonian tribute came from an adversary in the buzzing debate on bees, Robert Maxwell, explaining why he thought Warder got the sex of the monarch bee all wrong. Warder, he wrote, "found a Conveniency in maintaining that this Sovereign [of the beehive] was a Female": wishing to dedicate his book to Queen Anne, he had molded the head of the beehive to be a female, "and taken her Assistance to make out these fine Compliments." Even as his own natural-historical observations made him skeptical of the Amazonianism of the queen bee, Maxwell did not for a moment doubt the flattery involved in associating this Amazonianism with the reigning queen.[15]

So the Amazon—whether literally or figuratively—was doing rather well until the last two decades of the eighteenth century, commonly seen as an example of ancient glory, more transcendent than transgressive. This is not to say, of course, that there were no pejorative invocations of the Amazons during this period—of course there were—but rather that such negative characterizations sat side by side with more positive ones, allowing for a wide range of possible evaluations of the Amazon in which the former did not impart the dominant tone.[16] But then the fortunes of the Amazons changed rapidly and dramatically. One would be hard-pressed to find many writers in the 1780s and 1790s who would have used the epithet *Amazonian* in anything but a loaded pejorative sense. When the *Historical Magazine* carried in 1792 a putative eyewitness report of a matrilineal and matriarchal society in Lesbos, the closest to "an Amazonian commonwealth" that had ever been found, it turned out that these "lordly ladies" were distinguished "by a haughty, disdainful, and supercilious air"; their dress was "singular and disadvantageous"; and, most important, their usurpation of male prerogatives had led to the disintegration of the natural social fabric. "Nothing is more common," the report asserted, "than to see the old father and mother reduced to the utmost indigence, and even begging about the streets, while their unnatural daughters are in affluence": these were the dire consequences of "unnatural" Amazon rule. Elsewhere it became commonplace to

---

R. O. Bucholz, " 'Nothing but Ceremony': Queen Anne and the Limitations of Royal Ritual," *Journal of British Studies* 30 (July 1991): 295–96 (I am grateful to Seth Denbo for this reference). The open-ended meanings of representations of Anne as female monarch are also discussed in R. J. Weil, *Political Passions: Gender, the Family, and Political Argument in England 1680–1714* (Manchester, 2000), chap. 7. And see further below, p. 264.

15. Maxwell, *The Practical Bee-Master,* 10–11 (and for Maxwell's own nonchalance about this question, see above, n. 1).

16. When Amazons *were* portrayed negatively during this period, moreover, it was more often as sexually loose than as gender transgressive: cf. James Sterling's 1731 epilogue to *Richard the Third* in *The Prologues and Epilogues of the Eighteenth Century,* pt. 2, 1721–1737, vol. 4, ed. P. Danchin (Nancy, 1992), 423; [William Combe], *The Diabo-Lady: Or, a Match in Hell . . .* (London, 1777), 13.

invoke, in the context of the critique of modern times, the "modern Amazon's" "*folly*, as a reward for her manhood" (1787), or "the unpleasing airs of an Amazon, or a virago" (1789)—words used with rather different connotations than those they had had, say, in Chambers's *Cyclopædia* of 1728. "I am no Amazon," declared the milkwoman poet Ann Yearsley in 1796, endowing her portrait as a bare-breasted figure of liberty with a sorrowfully imploring feminine expression as a clear repudiation of the Amazonianism that "profanes [the] heart by nature made." By contrast, when Yearsley's predecessor of half a century, the washerwoman poet Mary Collier, had published *her* poems, she proudly imagined herself at the head of "an Army of Amazons."[17]

By the 1790s, this change—which had begun already in the 1780s—became much easier to dress in a more explicit political garb. But this renunciation of the Amazon was true not only of 1790s conservatives, who predictably vied with each other in denouncing Mary Wollstonecraft and her ilk as "the Amazonian band." It was also true of a radical like William Godwin, whose vindication of Mary Wollstonecraft—his erstwhile wife—sought to play down and explain away the "somewhat amazonian temper, which characterizes some parts of [her] book"—a temper that he too found to be distasteful—and to emphasize instead her "essential character," as "a woman, lovely in her person, and in the best and most engaging sense, feminine in her manners." Far from being an Amazon, an epithet that Godwin wished to renounce at all cost (Amazonian behavior was "absurd, indelicate, and unbecoming," he wrote a few years later), Wollstonecraft as he now reconstructed her turned out to have been a living reaffirmation—in a proper juxtaposition to her husband—of the basic gender distinctions between men and women.[18] Or take Godwin's friend, the painter James Barry: Barry too (writing the same year as Godwin) tried to defend Wollstonecraft's reputation, offering her together with her *Vindication of the Rights of Woman* as an example of "why the ancients . . . have chosen Minerva a female." But Barry proved unable to stick by this "feminist" stance for very long: on the next page we find his Minerva advocating "the superior

17. *Historical Magazine* 4 (1792): 40–42. Theophilus Swift, *The Temple of Folly, in Four Cantos* (London, 1787), 50, 69–72. John Bennett, *Letters to a Young Lady . . .* , vol. 1 (Warrington, 1789), 241. Ann Yearsley, *The Rural Lyre; A Volume of Poems* (London, 1796), frontispiece, 30–31, 113–14 (and see D. Landry, "Figures of the Feminine: An Amazonian Revolution in Feminist Literary History?" in *The Uses of Literary History*, ed. M. Brown [Durham, N.C., 1995], 107–28). *Poems, on Several Occasions, by Mary Collier, Author of the Washerwoman's Labour, with Some Remarks on Her Life* (Winchester, 1762), iv.

18. The phrase *the Amazonian band* was used by Richard Polwhele in his anonymous poem *The Unsex'd Females . . .* (London, 1798), 6n. William Godwin, *Memoirs of Mary Wollstonecraft*, ed. J. Middleton Murry (London, 1928), 55–56, 130–31. Godwin, *Fleetwood: Or, the New Man of Feeling* (1805), in *Collected Novels and Memoirs of William Godwin*, vol. 5, ed. P. Clemit (London, 1992), 55.

sentiment and graces of feminine softness . . . [which] as wives, mothers, daughters, sisters, citizens, and above all, as friends . . . could not fail of rendering [women] the graceful ornaments of all stations." Barry's turn-of-the-century Minerva, domesticated and properly feminine, was a far cry indeed from the Amazonian Minerva—with her "sternness that has much more of masculine than female in it"—that had been put forward by his eighteenth-century predecessors in art criticism, Shaftesbury and Spence.[19]

Similarly, the changing overtones of the Amazon can also be illustrated in a less freighted context through the successive editions of the *Encyclopaedia Britannica*. Whereas the discussions of Amazons in the first and second editions of the *Britannica* (1771 and 1778) had been neutral in tone, if not appreciative, by the third edition (begun in 1788) they were supplanted by a frankly critical essay, characterizing the Amazons as terrible, barbaric, and politically dangerous. Or take the correspondence of Horace Walpole (as good an indication as any of tremors in the tectonic plates of culture, given its extraordinary scale and continuity over so many years). In the years following the French Revolution, Walpole used the term *Amazonian* repeatedly to denounce those virago supporters of the Revolution, both in France and at home (and in fact this use can already be found in his letters of the mid-1780s). But twenty years earlier Walpole had actually written to a lady friend—a "heroine," in his words—in *appreciation* of her "real Amazonian principles." In the intervening years, as we have seen by now from a number of different angles, the meaning of *Amazon* shifted from an admiration for female heroism to a condemnation of female transgression; a sudden shift that did not go unnoticed by at least one (female) contemporary, who observed in 1793 that "Amazonian virtue" had recently gone out of fashion.[20]

Finally, to go back to queens, we can find a perhaps unexpected parallel to the transformation of the queen bee from Amazon to queen mother in yet another Amazonian monarch, one cast in this role—rather unflatteringly— by William Shakespeare in the third part of *Henry VI:* she was Margaret of Anjou, the "warlike Queen" of the feeble Henry, whose martial spirit and feisty exhortations egged the king on when he was ready to concede his son's right to the throne. In 1724, Theophilus Cibber—son of the better-known Colley Cibber—restaged Shakespeare's play in an "altered" form. Cibber's

19. James Barry, in his *Letter to the Dilettanti Society* (1798), as cited and discussed in J. Barrell, *The Birth of Pandora and the Division of Knowledge* (Basingstoke, 1992), 163–68. Spence, *Polymetis*, 59.

20. *Encyclopaedia Britannica*, 1st ed., vol. 1 (London, 1771), 131; 2nd ed., vol. 1 (Edinburgh, 1778), 279–80; and 3rd ed., vol. 1 (Edinburgh, 1797), 518–23 (but the first volume was actually completed in October 1788). For the detailed references in Walpole's correspondence, see Wahrman, "*Percy*'s Prologue." [Laetitia Matilda Hawkins], *Letters on the Female Mind, Its Powers and Pursuits . . .* (London, 1793), 117.

revised treatment of Queen Margaret's Amazonianism is suggestive: not only did he introduce Margaret's Amazonian behavior earlier and more prominently than Shakespeare's mise-en-scène, he also "cleansed" it of the negative connotations it had had in the original text—for instance, by replacing a hostile comment on Margaret as "an Amazonian trull" with an appreciative one (though uttered by Margaret's enemies) on "the bold Amazon Queen." Overall, Amazonian behavior is not condemned in Cibber's *Henry VI:* as the queen herself says—in another addition peculiar to this version of the play—such behavior on her part was not unnatural (this word she reserved for the king's willingness to disinherit his son), but rather merely a justifiable "disguise [of] fair nature" in order to attain a higher goal.[21]

But when Margaret came back on stage in another adaptation of Shakespeare's *Henry VI* in 1795, this one by Richard Valpy, the theatrically inclined head of Reading School, the effect was totally reversed. Gone was the feisty Amazonian behavior, gone (almost) was the intrepid female warrior charging to battle, gone was the woman who disguised nature in order to encourage the men to fight to the bitter end. In part Valpy achieved this simply by reducing considerably Margaret's active role in the play: she no longer spoke of going into battle, and the last remaining reference to "her more than manly spirit" was only hearsay. (Needless to say, the word *Amazon* itself was nowhere to be found.) Instead, on the couple of occasions that she did appear on stage to do what the story demands of her, namely encourage her weaker husband, she did so briefly and in a proper wifely fashion.[22] But this is not to say that once her Amazonian tendencies were muffled, Margaret in this version of 1795 remained with no heroic role to play. For in all the recountings of this story she also played the role of *mother*—first protective and then aching mother of the prince who is disinherited and

21. William Shakespeare, *Henry VI, Part III,* act 2, scene 1, line 123, and act 1, scene 4, line 114. Theophilus Cibber, *King Henry VI. A Tragedy . . . Altered from Shakespear, in the Year 1720,* 2nd ed. (London, 1724), 7, 16–17, 55, 57. This vindication of Margaret of Anjou was in fact common to other eighteenth-century representations: cf. her onstage characterization in 1723 as "In Feature Woman; but, in Heart, a Man:/Fair as the Queen of Beauty; Bold, as *Mars*" ([Ambrose] Philips, *Humphrey, Duke of Gloucester. A Tragedy . . .* [London, 1723], 5); or David Garrick's epilogue to [Thomas Francklin], *The Earl of Warwick. A Tragedy . . .* (London, 1766), which presented her as a courageous, defiant female warrior; or the rather curious production *The Goat's Beard. A Fable* (London, 1777), which listed Margaret among a series of valiant "Amazons" who had exhibited "the most heroic spirit" (pp. 17–18).

22. [Richard Valpy], *The Roses; Or King Henry the Sixth; An Historical Tragedy . . . Compiled Principally from Shakespeare* (Reading, [1795]), 4, 7. The point is not that these lines were necessarily new—they could be based on Shakespeare's own text (cf. *Henry VI, Part III,* act 2, scene 2, lines 56–57)—but that their selective use accentuated one meaning while obliterating the rest. Crucially, Valpy omitted a key moment in the earlier retellings of the story that proved Margaret's resolve: a dramatic moment in which she announces her intention to divorce King Henry for his weakness. In the 1795 script, by contrast, she stuck by her husband as a loyal, supportive wife.

ultimately killed. The climax of Margaret's maternal role, from Shakespeare onward, has been in her parting words over the body of her dead son. But whereas formerly this maternal pain had stood side by side with Margaret's no-less-powerful Amazonian actions, and without apparent contradiction, in Valpy's play Margaret's ultimate speech over her son's body completely eclipsed any other aspect of her performance. In sum, at least in this late-eighteenth-century production—a production that announced at the out-set its intent to tell the story in a way "neither offensive to delicacy, nor repugnant to the principles of modern taste"—we are back where we started: Margaret the Amazon queen, precisely like the queen bee, was also recast solely and unambiguously as a queen mother.[23]

The problem, however, was more intractable for those more closely accountable to the historical record, which might explain why an 1804 bio-graphical portrait of Margaret rather lost its bearings in trying to account for her mixture of Amazon and mother. With confusing inconsistency, this account characterized Margaret as a woman "tainted with ferocity," or as an unfortunate woman "unsexed" through situations beyond her control, but at the same time, miraculously, also as a woman exhibiting feminine devo-tion to "a husband and son she had so faithfully served." What a distance we have moved by now from the 1766 example of the same biographical genre, which could find no higher praise for Margaret than that "nature had en-dowed her with all the virtues of the men without their defects"—a mix that this mid-eighteenth-century portrait had seen as nature's generous gift, beneficial all around. Its 1804 counterpart, by contrast, made an effort to turn Margaret's Amazonian battles, in the final count, into little more than her own—albeit peculiar—way of fulfilling her proper duties in being what this text wanted her to be above all else: a good wife and mother.[24] And when a few years later a female author devoted almost five hundred pages of poetry to retelling the misfortunes of Margaret of Anjou, it was not as a warring saga (her Margaret heard the sounds of battle only from a dis-

23. [Valpy], *The Roses*, advertisement.

24. Matilda Betham, *A Biographical Dictionary of the Celebrated Women of Every Age and Country* (London, 1804), 546–47. *Biographium Fæmineum. The Female Worthies: Or, Memoirs of the Most Illustrious Ladies, of All Ages and Nations . . .* , 2 vols. (London, 1766), vol. 2, 89. The following page described how Margaret "commanded her army herself"; "rode thro' all the battalions"; "drew up her troops in order of battle, and encouraged them with a speech." In all these for-mulations there were unmistakable echoes of another queen in a widely acclaimed moment laden with Amazonian associations; that is, of course, Queen Elizabeth, in her famous horse-back speech to her troops at Tilbury, a speech that the *Biographium Fæmineum* itself reproduced in vol. 1, pp. 187–88. Although beyond the scope of this essay, it can be readily shown—as I hope to do elsewhere—that Elizabeth's reputation went through a transformation much like Margaret's: from considerable eighteenth-century appreciation for her Amazonianism (and by association for the manliness of her times, not least of the women), to turn-of-the-century rewritings of her history that tried to hide it as much as possible.

tance), but as a voyage of discovery of the "maternal softness" that suddenly "stole/With force resistless, o'er her soul," chasing away her more Amazonian tendencies:

> In Margaret's fierce and stormy breast
> A thousand warring passions strove,
> Yet now, unbid, a stranger-guest
> Dispers'd and silenc'd all the rest—
> Thy voice, Maternal Love!

Against the backdrop of this therapeutic apotheosis of maternal love we can return to the symbolic meaning of dedications. Whereas Joseph Warder had prefaced his early-eighteenth-century Amazons with a perhaps overdetermined dedication to his queen, one suspects even more of an overdetermined inevitability in the dedication of this early-nineteenth-century poet, who presented her anti-Amazonian *Margaret of Anjou*—how else—to "my dear Mother."[25]

The turn-of-the-century depictions of Queen Margaret, then, were torn between the seemingly incommensurable poles of Amazon and mother. It is worth reminding ourselves that there was nothing inevitable about this incommensurability: as the earlier portrayals of Margaret indicate, formerly Amazon and mother could have been imagined more easily to inhabit the same feminine body. As one more indication of this we can take the 1707 play *Thomyris, Queen of Scythia:* not only did this play center on a flattering image of an Amazon-cum-mother, its prologue—once again—made explicit the analogy between this double-sided heroine and Queen Anne, whose public image joined enthusiastic-but-unsuccessful motherhood with successful-though-unenthusiastic Amazonianism.[26]

Once Amazon and mother were cast as fundamentally incommensurate opposites, however, there was one particular image that embodied this supposedly natural truth more evocatively and literally than any other: their breasts, mutilated for the purpose of warfare by one, or cherished for the suckling of infants by the other. So when the novelist and educator Maria Edgeworth published in 1801 a highly didactic novel—she herself preferred to call it a "moral tale"—that set forth her moral vision and worldview for the coming century, she focused it precisely on this graphic antithesis. Looking more closely at this novel, *Belinda*, might therefore provide us with a good lead into the perceptions of maternity that form the other half of our bee-driven inquiry.

25. [Margaret] Holford, *Margaret of Anjou: A Poem. In Ten Cantos* (London, 1816), dedication, 58.
26. Peter Anthony Motteux, *Thomyris, Queen of Scythia. An Opera* (London, 1707).

Despite its title, *Belinda* was not so much a book about the eponymous heroine Belinda Portman—an unchanging (and really rather boring) paragon of virtue—as it was about her London patron, Lady Delacour. Following the loss of two children in infancy, Lady Delacour had renounced motherhood altogether and refused to nurse or to educate her surviving daughter, Helena. It was from this unnatural renunciation of her key feminine essence, that of a mother, that all her miseries ensued. The agent of Lady Delacour's corruption was the Amazonian "*man-woman*," a woman with "bold masculine arms" whose favorite pastimes included hunting, electioneering, sword-fighting, and above all, donning male clothes. Perhaps somewhat heavy-handedly, this newfound friend was named Mrs. Harriot Freke ("Who am I? only a Freke!" she cried on one occasion, when mistaken for "a smart-looking young man"). Cajoled by Freke, Delacour agreed to a crossdressed duel with a female enemy—a scheme that backfired, quite literally, inflicting on her what was to remain a "hideous" wound in one breast. The bad mother turned into a literal one-breasted Amazon: a point driven home by Lady Delacour's own words to Belinda, "there certainly were such people as Amazons—I hope you admire them." But of course "Amazon" in this novel was anything but admirable: quite the contrary, Lady Delacour's "Amazonian" wound proved her undoing, threatening to consume her body, her peace of mind, her independence, and ultimately her life.

In a particularly poignant scene, the relationship of the breast wound to that initial rejection of motherhood is underscored when Helena (brought home by Belinda) attempts to hug her mother. As "she pressed close to her mother's bosom," "Lady Delacour screamed, and pushed her daughter away"—thus linking most graphically her Amazonian body and her inability to mother.[27] The point to note about this exchange is its physicality: feminine maternal identity in *Belinda* is innate, physical, and impossible to shed at will. This is why Lady Delacour's rejection of her daughter must have resulted in a physical corollary on her very body—the mutilated breast; and this is why the resolution of the novel involves simultaneously the restoration of Lady Delacour to the role of mother *and* the almost-miraculous cure of her breast wound.[28] The antithesis drawn (or rather overdrawn) in

27. Maria Edgeworth, *Belinda*, 3 vols. (London, 1801), vol. 1, 60, 66–67, 87, 93–101, 113–22; vol. 2, 23, 76, 139. To leave little doubt as to the meaning of that last scene, it is soon followed by a freighted reference to "a comedy called 'The School for Mothers'" (p. 157). The Amazonian imagery in *Belinda* is discussed in much detail in Barker-Benfield, *Culture of Sensibility*, 386–92, though he may underestimate the extent to which the understandings of gender categories embodied in the novel were a new departure, distinct from previous notions of the eighteenth century. See also B. Kowaleski-Wallace, "Home Economics: Domestic Ideology in Maria Edgeworth's *Belinda*," *The Eighteenth Century* 29 (1988): 242–62.

28. Interestingly, in Edgeworth's first draft, Lady Delacour actually dies of breast cancer; in other words, her Amazonian state proves to be so innate as to be incurable. See M. Butler, *Maria Edgeworth: A Literary Biography* (Oxford, 1972), 282.

Belinda between idealized natural motherhood and unredeemable monstrous Amazonianism was hardly an unfamiliar one at this juncture: thus, Ann Yearsley resorted to precisely the same double-breasted imagery in conjunction with her aforementioned assertion that she was "no Amazon." On the one hand, Yearsley drew the blissful image of a baby at his mother's breast; on the other, the ominous image of a woman whose refusal to suckle her baby results in breast disease ("Too proud to nurse, maternal fevers came—/Her burthen'd bosom caught th'invited flame"). In fact, even a cursory search will readily establish the diseased breast as a recurrent trope in a variety of turn-of-the-century contexts, marking unfeminine—and unmaternal—behavior.[29]

More broadly, the closing years of the eighteenth century were strewn with ubiquitous assertions of the natural, biological-physical basis of maternity; assertions, for example, of women's natural "destiny of bearing and nursing children," which meant (in the words of this writer of 1787) that "the order of nature would be totally reversed" if a woman opted for "the cold, *forbidding* pride of a studious virginity." Another text of 1803, by the renowned Dr. William Buchan, not only insisted obsessively on the "naturalness" of motherhood, but went further to posit the maternal role as *the* key to feminine identity, determining the whole of women's physical and spiritual essence: "[no] virtue [can] take deep root in the breast of the female that is callous to the feelings of a mother"—a woman who thus renders herself an "unfeeling monster" by her "unnatural conduct." This, of course, was essentially the same perception of maternity qua femininity that Maria Edgeworth had put forward two years earlier in *Belinda*—all the way to the insistence on the physical injury to a woman's body that will necessarily ensue from her neglect of maternal breast-feeding.[30]

It is important to realize what I am *not* saying here. The emphasis on motherhood was of course not a novelty of the last two decades of the eighteenth century. Quite the contrary: the widely researched historical consensus, recently recapitulated by Felicity Nussbaum, is that "a distinctive and historically nuanced fascination with the maternal" had already characterized England by about the mid-century. The same was also the case for the increasing preoccupation with the maternal breast; most famously, perhaps, for Rousseau and Linnaeus, or for Dr. William Cadogan's influential

29. Yearsley, "To Mira, on the Care of Her Infant" (16 September 1795), in *The Rural Lyre*, 115–16. For examples of unfeminine women who contract breast disease, see, for instance, Robert Jephson, *Conspiracy, A Tragedy . . .* (Dublin, 1796), epilogue; G. H. Wilson, *The Eccentric Mirror: Reflecting a Faithful and Interesting Delineation of Male and Female Characters . . .* (London, 1806–7), vol. 2, no. 12, p. 21; vol. 3, no. 30, p. 30.

30. [John Bennett], *Strictures on Female Education . . .* (London, [1787]), 123–24. William Buchan, *Advice to Mothers, on the Subject of Their Own Health* (London, 1803), 99, 215–17 (quoted in part in Kowaleski-Wallace, "Home Economics," 253–56).

Essay upon Nursing and the Management of Children (1748).[31] But then the mother and the Amazon are not completely symmetrical: the mother, after all, was the normative figure, whereas the Amazon was always (even when tolerated or appreciated) the counternormative one. It is the *nonmother,* therefore, that is the more precise equivalent of the Amazon: and the question is, when did prevalent notions of maternity make the woman who chose *not* to mother a fundamentally unacceptable and disturbing figure? It is here, I want to suggest, that we can see again clear marks of the cultural shift of the late eighteenth century, which in this case produced the final and conclusive twist in the long-term advent of the new understandings of maternity that we may wish to call "modern." Dr. Buchan, for one, self-consciously recognized this change in his own writing: in the forty years that had passed between his earlier advice manual for mothers and that of 1803, he admitted, his shift of emphasis from the health of the child to the natural duties of the mother had led him to disallow any mother any deviation from the prescribed models he had set up formerly in general terms.[32]

The suggestion, then, is that the distinctive shift peculiar to the late eighteenth century was that from maternity as a general ideal, broadly prescriptive but allowing for individual divergences, to maternity as inextricably intertwined with the essence of femininity for each and every woman. In the latter understanding, what was ruled out was the possibility of *choice:* a woman choosing not to exercise these essential maternal instincts, rather than being forced into such a situation through circumstances beyond her control, was now most likely to be branded "unnatural." Earlier, however, one could readily find plenty of acknowledgments of women's ability—even right—to choose to remain single, and not to mother, without this choice necessarily reflecting damagingly on them. Thus, in contrast to the pre-

31. F. A. Nussbaum, *Torrid Zones: Maternity, Sexuality, and Empire in Eighteenth-Century English Narratives* (Baltimore, 1995), 24. Nussbaum, *The Autobiographical Subject: Gender and Ideology in Eighteenth-Century England* (Baltimore, 1989), 205–12. R. Perry, "Colonizing the Breast: Sexuality and Maternity in Eighteenth-Century England," *Journal of the History of Sexuality* 2 (1991): 204–34. L. Friedli, "'Passing Women'—A Study of Gender Boundaries in the Eighteenth Century," in *Sexual Underworlds of the Enlightenment*, ed. G. S. Rousseau and R. Porter (Manchester, 1987), 235–37. J. E. Sitter, "Mother, Memory, Muse, and Poetry after Pope," *ELH* 44 (1977): 312–36. On the eighteenth-century preoccupation with the breast and with breast-feeding, see also L. Schiebinger, "Why Mammals Are Called Mammals," in *Nature's Body: Gender in the Making of Modern Science* (Boston, 1993), 40–74. A. Hollander, *Seeing through Clothes* (Berkeley, 1993), 112–13. M. Yalom, *A History of the Breast* (New York, 1997), chap. 4. S. Wiseman, "From the Luxurious Breast to the Virtuous Breast: The Body Politic Transformed," *Textual Practice* 11 (1997): 477–92.

32. Buchan, *Advice to Mothers*, 1–3, and esp. 103. Compare his much less stringent (though no less committed) advocacy of breast-feeding in *Domestic Medicine*, 2nd ed. (London, 1772), 664–65. This shift is noted in L. Friedli, "Crossing Gender Boundaries in Eighteenth-Century England" (Ph.D. diss., University of Essex, 1987), 221.

scriptive texts of the turn of the century, which asserted in unison that motherhood and even marriage were "of natural instinct," mid-century contributions to the same conventional genre had been surprisingly undogmatic on this point. "She, who lives to be an old maid, against her will, is unfortunate," one popular conduct book told its readers in 1740; "but where this state results from a free choice . . . then it may properly be called a life of angels." No less. "I know nothing that renders a woman more despicable, than her thinking it essential to happiness to be married," echoed John Gregory in his even more popular conduct book of 1774; "besides the gross indelicacy of the sentiment, it is a false one, as thousands of women have experienced."[33]

In a different textual register, Sarah Scott's utopian novel *Millenium Hall* (1762) depicted a community of chaste, nonsexual women whose lives presented an alternative to marriage and biological motherhood; an alternative, crucially, that they followed by choice, not as a consequence of unfortunate circumstances. To be sure, the women of Millenium Hall "consider[ed] matrimony as absolutely necessary to the good of society"; but they saw it as "a general duty," of which individual women could "be excused by . . . substitut[ing] . . . others." The novel is consequently strewn with instances of motherhood (and occasionally fatherhood) being relegated, displaced, assumed, or renounced, with little consideration for the "natural" ties of biological parentage. Furthermore, tellingly, when Scott did introduce a mother characterized by unfeminine "boldness" combined with a lack of maternal feeling, she turned out to be not a prototype of Lady Delacour, who was deficient in her natural maternal instinct, but her precise opposite: in *Millenium Hall* the unnatural Amazonian mother was in fact a *stepmother*, and it was her unwillingness to *assume* the maternal role—to let her acquired duty overcome her lack of natural attachment—that had turned her into the narrative's villain.[34] It was perhaps a sign of things to come that by 1778 a critic of *Millenium Hall* not only dismissed its women as "neutral beings, with the outward parts of women cast in a masculine mould," but (somewhat inconsistently) also claimed that their unmarried situation was necessarily the result of unfortunate circumstances beyond

33. Wetenhall Wilkes, *A Letter of Genteel and Moral Advice to a Young Lady,* 8th ed. (1766; originally 1740), reproduced in *Women in the Eighteenth Century: Constructions of Femininity,* ed. V. Jones (London, 1990), 33–34. John Gregory, *A Father's Legacy to His Daughters,* 2nd ed. (London, 1774), 104–5. Cf. also [Dorothy Kilner], *Dialogues and Letters on Morality, Œconomy, and Politeness, for the Improvement and Entertainment of Young Female Minds* (London, [1780?]), 154, about a woman who might "happen to marry," and who might "chance to have children"—but then again, who might not.

34. Sarah Scott, *A Description of Millenium Hall,* ed. J. Spencer (New York, 1986), 37, 115. And note the contrast with Buchan's utter denial in 1803 of the possibility of transferring motherhood: *Advice to Mothers,* 362.

their control: even masculine women, for this critic, could not be imagined making a choice not to marry or to mother.[35]

We should not paint too rosy a picture: throughout the eighteenth century, to be sure, the lot of "old maids" was often a harsh and abusive one. But even vituperation has room for different configurations of possibility. Thus, *A Satyr upon Old Maids* (1713), one of the most vicious attacks of its kind in the eighteenth century, concluded with the surprising exculpation of those women "who continue *Maids* to *Old Age*, through Choice"; women who thus "deserve all the *Encomiums* [that] can be merited by the *Best* of their *Sex*." But when the poet William Hayley penned a well-wishing *defense* of single women in 1785, by contrast, his self-proclaimed posture as a "Friend to the Sisterhood" extended—as he hastened to explain—only to those women who remained unmarried "not as the effect of choice, arising from a cold and irrational aversion to the [married] state in general," but rather due to such unfortunate circumstances that can "lead even the worthiest of beings into situations very different from what they would otherwise have chosen." By choice, Hayley insisted, every acceptable woman would marry; and she who would not must be "utterly devoid of tenderness." So whereas the 1713 satirist had excluded from his blanket antipathy those women whom he respected for not fulfilling their roles as wife and mother through their own choice, the 1785 essayist excluded from his blanket empathy those very same women, who lost his respect by making precisely such a choice. Susan Lanser's recent investigation of attitudes toward single women in the eighteenth century has reached a similar conclusion: namely, that most of the century witnessed an unstable duality in the images of the single woman, hovering between the incompatible alternatives of appreciation and condemnation, only to be replaced in the 1780s by a unified negative (albeit humanely pitiful) synthesis that was to remain in place all the way to the twentieth century.[36]

Overall, then, we can see a recurrent shift in understandings of maternity

35. *Letters of Momus, from Margate* . . . (London, 1778), 28. It is also perhaps not a complete coincidence that after four successful editions between 1762 and 1778 the fortunes of *Millenium Hall* were reversed, and it went decisively out of print from the late eighteenth until the twentieth century.

36. *A Satyr upon Old Maids* (London, 1713), 12. [William Hayley], *A Philosophical, Historical, and Moral Essay on Old Maids. By a Friend to the Sisterhood*, 3 vols. (London, 1785), vol. 1, 12–14. S. S. Lanser, "Singular Politics: The Rise of the British Nation and the Production of the Old Maid," in *Singlewomen in the European Past, 1250–1800*, ed. J. M. Bennett and A. M. Froide (Philadelphia, 1999), 297–323. Although Lanser is more interested in the negative portrayal of single women, she readily admits the alternative for the period up to the 1780s. Other recent work on eighteenth-century maternity also seems in tune with the account suggested here. For some examples, note Susan Stare's account of the shift from mid-century controversy to turn-of-the-century consensus in the reception of the theme of maternal affection in John Home's 1756 tragedy *Douglas* ("Douglas's Mother," in *Brandeis Essays in Literature*, ed. J. Hazel Smith

mirroring the shift noticeable at the same time in the fortunes of the Amazons: in both cases, behavior or images that seemed to offer alternatives to dominant gender roles, or cracks allowing individuals to slip through gender boundaries, or perspectives that exposed how unreliable such boundaries really were, now lost their cultural ground. Before setting these observations within wider contexts that can endow them with broader meaning, however, I would like to flag one more late-eighteenth-century development that may well have partaken in the transformation suggested here, but in a rather different cultural domain: fashion. Metropolitan female fashions, to be precise.

Notoriously, the decades at the turn of the eighteenth century saw—often with a wincing eye—a conspicuous trend toward dresses that clung to the body, and toward fabrics that were more transparent than before; many contemporaries noted the resulting accentuation of the natural female body form. A key focus in these new fashions—including the radical discarding of the stays, and the suddenly increased use of false bosoms—was the maternal breast: a trend captured inimitably in James Gillray's print of 1796, *The Fashionable Mamma,—or—The Convenience of Modern Dress* (see the frontispiece to this volume). The print shows a fashionable lady in evening dress about to go out (a waiting carriage is visible through the window), fully equipped with feathered turban, gloves, and fan; and yet her "modern" dress is cut in such a way as to lend itself spontaneously to the suckling of an eager infant, presenting no obstacle to its demands, which she satisfies en route to the door. The dress of this "fashionable mamma" wore the precedence and the immediacy of the maternal role on its sleeve, as it were—a point that was further reinforced in a typically heavy-handed manner by a large picture of a breastfeeding woman hanging on the wall, titled *Maternal Love*.[37]

But nothing, perhaps, illustrates more graphically the new sartorial

---

[Waltham, Mass., 1983], 51–67); Ludmilla Jordanova's suggestion of a late-eighteenth-century shift in notions of reproduction to a "Xerox model of reproduction," resulting in an increasingly essentialized—even quasi-racial—conception of the role of the mother ("Interrogating the Concept of Reproduction in the Eighteenth Century," in *Conceiving the New World Order: The Global Politics of Reproduction*, ed. F. D. Ginsburg and R. Rapp [Berkeley, 1995], 369–86); and S. C. Greenfield and C. Barash, eds., *Inventing Maternity: Politics, Science, and Literature, 1650–1865* (Lexington, Ky., 1999), the chronology of which (although at times hazy) seems to confirm a late-eighteenth-century shift following a surge in interest throughout the century (see, e.g., the introduction, pp. 24–25).

37. The previous month, Gillray had made a similar point in another satire on women's fashion, titled *Ladies Dress, as It Soon Will Be*, which emphasized its exaggerated transparency, leaving the female body almost bare: see M. D. George, *Catalogue of Political and Personal Satires Preserved in the Department of Prints and Drawings in the British Museum*, vol. 7 (London, 1942), 303–4. For the fashion of false bosoms, see C. W. Cunnington and P. Cunnington, *The History of Underclothes* (London, 1951), 108–9; an example of contemporary humor at the expense of this trend is Mrs. [Anne] Thicknesse, *The School for Fashion*, 2 vols. (London, 1800), vol. 2, 119.

emphasis on femininity in its maternal form than a curious fashion that appeared in the streets of London in late 1792: a new contraption that women wore under their dresses, called "the pad," which gave them the distinct look of appearing to be many months pregnant. In spite of much ridicule from all sides (see the cover illustration to this volume), strong objections from the fashion-setting royal family, and even a play— The Pad— set in motion by mistaken assumptions about the pregnancy of various women, the pad became a fad, spreading to women of varied conditions, social and marital. "The fashion of dressing, at present," commented the Times in March 1793, "is to appear prominent . . . holding out a wish to be thought in a thriving way, even without the authority of the Arches Court of Canterbury." Or, as the Morning Chronicle put it, the pad "makes the barren Matron breed" while at the same time allowing maidens to be in love without "fear[ing] a swelling waist."[38] So what can we make of the fact that so many women, whether pregnant or not, were lining up to associate themselves with this visible sign of maternity? With due caution about the difficulties of the interpretation of fashion, it is at least suggestive to consider the pad as yet another indication of the extent to which maternity, albeit fabricated (or parodied—which amounts to the same thing), appears to have acquired an increased significance in defining womanhood at this juncture, an essential foundation of feminine identity, which is therefore shared by all women.

But fashions in the previous couple of generations had been distinctly different on all these scores. Broadly speaking, whereas the fashions of the closing decades of the century accentuated gender differences, with a distinct emphasis on ultra-femininity for women (as well as on masculinity for men), those of the earlier decades, for women as well as men, had been noticeably eroding or subverting clearly demarcated gender distinctions. In particular we can mention the popular female riding habits that had (to an eighteenth-century eye) distinctly masculine cuts. Before the abrupt disappearance of these riding habits in the 1780s, fashionable English women were increasingly donning them also as a walking costume, when traveling, or even when sitting for portraits.[39] Women in such habits were repeatedly

38. Times, 25 March 1793; quoted in John Ashton, Old Times: A Picture of Social Life at the End of the Eighteenth Century (London, 1885), 70. Morning Chronicle, 30 May 1793. Robert Woodbridge, The Pad, a Farce . . . (London, 1793). Compare also the ridicule heaped on the pad in the epilogue to Frederick Reynolds, How to Grow Rich: A Comedy . . . (London, 1793). On the pad, see L. Werkmeister, A Newspaper History of England 1792–1793 (Lincoln, Nebraska, 1967), 164–65, 328–30 (citing further contemporary reactions); Gelpi, Shelley's Goddess, 59–60; and Cunnington and Cunnington, History of Underclothes, 111, and p. 91 for a letter of Horace Walpole's that mentions female artificial protuberances worn in front "in imitation of the Duchess of Devonshire's pregnancy" as early as 1783.

39. This trend extended to greatcoat-dresses, which were likewise encoded as gender-transgressive—echoing masculine styles, for instance, in long tight sleeves, caped collars, and

described as "Hermaphroditical," "half-Men, half-Women," "most officer-like," and of course, "Amazonians." "On meeting a company on horseback now-a-days," one observer recycled an all-but-ubiquitous trope in 1760, "one shall hardly be able to distinguish, at first sight, whether it is composed of ladies or gentlemen. . . . They should be called Amazons."[40] Once again we encounter popular Amazonian resonances in the eighteenth century, resonances that were to be reversed (here, in the actual social practice of dress) in its closing decades.

And if the pad was the extreme form of those latter-day accentuations of the maternal female form, then the earlier pattern can be represented by the "lévite": a masculine-looking wrapping gown for women, common in the late 1770s, that partook of the sartorial subversion of gender differences at this point (Horace Walpole once described it sarcastically as "a man's night-gown bound round with a belt"). Most famously, the lévite was reputed to be effective in disguising pregnancies: that is, for *concealing* maternity—precisely the opposite effect of the pad that was soon to succeed it. Indeed, the subsequent shift to a completely different sartorial-cultural climate was too sharp to go unnoticed. As one provincial newspaper put it in 1794: "When our grandmothers were pregnant they wore jumps to conceal it. Our modern young ladies, who are not pregnant, wear pads to carry the semblance of it."[41] The only thing this newspaper got wrong was the time frame—the truth of the matter was that this reversal took place not over two generations, but over less than two decades; and the very fact that the former practices seemed now so very distant was in itself a telling sign of how effective this cultural transformation had been.

Let us now recall why we started on this whirlwind tour of some aspects of eighteenth-century culture in the first place. We were seeking a context

---

a double-breasted fastening or false-waistcoat front—all the more so when combined with new low-heeled shoes or with the increasingly fashionable boots. For discussion of these "masculine" female fashions, see A. Ribeiro, *Dress in Eighteenth-Century Europe, 1715–1789* (London, 1984), 155–57; Ribeiro, *Dress and Morality* (New York, 1986), 114; and Ribeiro, *The Art of Dress: Fashion in England and France, 1750 to 1820* (New Haven, Conn., 1995), 67–68. See also Cunnington and Cunnington, *History of Underclothes*, 83–85, and A. Buck, *Dress in Eighteenth-Century England* (London, 1979), 52–53.

40. [Charles Allen], *The Polite Lady: Or, a Course of Female Education . . .* (London, 1760), 103. For the characterizations of women in riding habits, see Wahrman, "*Percy's* Prologue," 120.

41. Walpole to Lady Ossory in 1779, cited in Ribeiro, *Dress in Eighteenth-Century Europe*, 155. *Chester Chronicle*, 1794, cited in Cunnington and Cunnington, *History of Underclothes*, 111. For another commentator noting—and celebrating—the happy demise of the former tendency of English women to hide pregnancies rather than display them with pride, see Buchan, *Advice to Mothers*, 78–79.

within which to understand the transformation in the descriptions of the beehive in the late eighteenth century; a transformation that led to a sudden unease about those aspects of bee society that did not conform to prevailing expectations about gender. For simplicity of analysis, we focused on the marked refashioning of the queen bee from Amazon queen—"the martial Dame" heading "the Female State," "Terrible to her Enemies," who wields absolute power and commands absolute loyalty from her subjects—to queen mother, "the only perfect female" who "boasts no military pride" and who "is to be considered in no other light than as a layer of eggs," the only way "by which she lays claim to royalty." We then located two parallel and complementary trends in late-eighteenth-century culture that seemed to intersect in this story. On the one hand we traced the reversal of fortunes in the reputations of the Amazons and in the connotations of things "Amazonian," which after decades of relative tolerance and often positive appreciation suddenly came to be seen as irredeemably negative, signifying a disturbing affront to nature. On the other hand we saw the simultaneous shift in the ramifications—and limits—of the eighteenth-century focus on maternity, a shift that essentialized maternity as an innate precondition of femininity, the renunciation of which became—again—an irredeemable affront to nature. Both shifts identified here, then, shared key characteristics in redefining prevailing gender norms as essential and natural, and in disallowing individuals to deviate from these norms. Together, they provide a wider pattern that explains (or at least situates) what was posited at the beginning of this essay as in need of explication.

But in what sense, or to what extent, can we take these parallel shifts further, as indicators of a "cultural revolution"? I would like to conclude this essay with some speculations on how far it may yet prove possible to push the story told in the above pages.

First, let us remind ourselves what cultural sites came within the scope of our itinerary. These included novels and poems, encyclopedias and biographical dictionaries, art criticism and mythographies, periodicals and didactic literature, plays (including the eighteenth-century engagement with Shakespeare) and fashion, and of course the language of natural history and the apiary manuals. If indeed the examples put forward here do represent wider trends in all these domains (and I believe they do), then we have one important precondition for a "cultural" revolution: namely, the broad range of cultural forms, sites, and genres in which this revolution was registered, reflecting not only the taut interconnectedness of eighteenth-century culture but also the far-reaching effects of the phenomenon that arguably transformed it.

A second, complementary precondition has to do with the meaning of "revolution": that is, the focus on a relatively short-term, sharp transformation. Again, if the evidence in this essay is anything to go by, these changes seem to have taken place within a matter of years, not generations, more like a seismic quake than like a glacial shift in the tectonic plates of culture.

But in the end the key to whether this was a cultural revolution is surely not a structural one—the extent or pace of change—but a substantive one: what was the proposed transformation *about,* and what difference did it make? I would like to suggest—albeit, given the space limitations of this essay, without the necessary evidence to really make the case—that in fact our cultural tour has taken us to the tip of an iceberg, the extensive contours of which are only beginning to become discernible.

To begin with, the transformations identified here were not isolated or random, but rather part of a much broader reconfiguration of understandings of gender in the late eighteenth century. As I have tried to show with more detail elsewhere, gender categories appear to have undergone a pervasive and radical transformation at this juncture. Throughout the first three quarters of the century, gender categories were characterized by a remarkable degree of looseness and playfulness. Although the expectations from "femininity" and "masculinity" were generally well defined, contemporaries did not perceive them as necessarily determining each and every individual, and could often be found to react to apparent subversions of these expectations with resignation, or tolerance, or—not infrequently— even appreciation. Occasionally, in other words, a person's gender was conceptually allowed to roam away from his or her sex. In the end, just as we have seen in the cases of both the manly Amazons and the women who chose not to mother—and as could have been similarly shown for, say, the female warrior, the female politician and orator, the lachrymose and tender man of feeling, and other common gender-transgressive figures— eighteenth-century Britons were on the whole not overly disturbed by the possibility that gender categories were limited, that gender boundaries could be proven porous and imperfect, and even that gender identities could occasionally become a matter of personal choice. And even when some contemporaries were anxious about such dissonances, their apprehension was joined with the admission, not denial, of the possibility of such gender play, which is precisely what made such behavior, in their critical eyes, so dangerous.[42]

But this relative playfulness of eighteenth-century categories of gender, allowing them to be imagined as unreliable, mutable, and even a matter of choice, disappeared with remarkable speed in the closing two decades of the century. In a sharp, uneasy reversal, one that I have called "gender

42. For more detailed evidence of these assertions, see Wahrman, "*Percy*'s Prologue," and "Gender in Translation: How the English Wrote Their Juvenal, 1644–1815," *Representations* 65 (winter 1999): 1–41.

panic," long-standing forms and practices that had capitalized on (and at times wallowed in) the former flexibility of gender boundaries now became culturally unintelligible and socially unacceptable. It was no longer seen as conceivable that a man would be able truly to inhabit femininity, or a woman masculinity. Cross-dressed heroes and heroines, for instance, formerly a stock trope in a variety of genres, now found themselves failing in their assumed roles, and frequently hastening to affirm their embarrassment at such "unnatural" masquerades, adopted for reasons beyond their control. Similarly, we have seen the various mental somersaults of the turn-of-the-century writers on bees as they tried to veil not only the Amazonian side of the queen, but also other gender-destabilizing aspects of the beehive: be it through the erasure of the femininity of the worker bees, or through the metamorphosis of the drones into self-sacrificing heroic males or caring fathers, or even through the invention of an imaginary king bee with whom the queen "cohabit[s] in a lawful and decorous manner."[43] It was crucial to the new understanding of gender categories that they were now seen as deterministic and immutable, and beyond one's free choice. Gender, the behavioral and cultural attributes of masculinity and femininity, collapsed into sex—that is, into the physicality inscribed on the body of every individual. There was thus no longer any individual escape through a play with gender from the dictates of the sexual body itself—or at least none without the most severe consequences; which, again, is precisely what we have seen for both Amazons and reluctant mothers as they came to be branded "unnatural."

So this putative late-eighteenth-century transformation in understandings of gender is one possible way to conceptualize the broader phenomenon touched upon in this essay. But is this broad enough? Is this story really, at bottom, about gender? Arguably not. The even bigger iceberg in these waters, perhaps, is not so much that of the transformation of *gender* as it is the underlying transformation involved in essentializing *identities*. This suggestion is one that I hope to substantiate in detail in the larger project of which this essay is part;[44] here I simply want briefly to flag the possibilities, in the spirit of preliminary speculation. En route I will also take a final, retrospective look at some common moves and hints made by several of the contributors to this volume, for possible affinities with the following speculations. (Needless to say, however, they may not necessarily agree with the thrust of what follows.)

Perhaps most obviously, consider the implications of David Bell's and Kathleen Wilson's essays regarding the conceptualizations of race at this period. Both essays gesture toward the beginnings, in the second half of the

43. This opinion of an apiarian from Essex is cited in Huish, *A Treatise*, 26.
44. D. Wahrman, *The Making of the Modern Self* (Yale University Press, forthcoming).

eighteenth century, of what Wilson describes as "the naturalization of certain kinds of identities whose traces refuse to disappear," that is to say, kinds of identities that were to become staples of European modernity. Both essays register signs of a gradual decline of former climatic and environmental notions of human diversity, malleable notions that ran against an increasing investment in demarcating "ineradicable otherness." These were the first steps, Bell proposes, toward "the essentializing of ethnic and racial differences."[45]

Now suppose that we can make a case for a structural homology between the transformation undergone by race in the late eighteenth century and that of gender. I say *homology* rather than *equivalence,* because race and gender have obviously evolved toward their modern understandings in different ways and different points in time. And yet, using cultural markers of change analogous to the bees and the queens, it is possible to show how both race and gender were jolted at this particular juncture in suggestively similar ways. Both, I want to suggest, were pushed along the axis from relatively porous and unstable categories (that were moreover recognized as such) to more rigid, essentialized ones with supposedly impermeable boundaries, while the opportunities for individuals to fall between the cracks were rapidly closing down. To give but one example illustrative of changing notions of race, consider the reports of the "greasing" practices of the relatively fair-skinned Khoikhoi—the "Hottentots"—of South Africa. Throughout the eighteenth century numerous observers attributed to greasing the deliberate function—in the words of the second edition of the *Encyclopaedia Britannica* (1778)—to "take care to make their children as black as possible . . . much blacker than they really are." But sometime toward the end of the century, reports of the Khoikhoi actively assuming blackness appear to have ceased, and greasing was now interpreted solely in functional terms (as enhancing skin protection, swift movement, etc). This fact was reflected (among many other examples) in the rewriting of the entry for "Hottentots" in the third edition of the *Britannica* in the 1790s, which turned the "obscur[ing]" of the Hottentot skin color through greasing into an unintended effect of their penchant for "filth and nastiness."[46]

45. See pp. 35, 66, and 90, above.

46. *Encyclopaedia Britannica,* 2nd ed., vol. 5, 3739; 3rd ed., vol. 8, 683–91. And see L. E. Merians, "What They Are, Who We Are: Representations of the 'Hottentot' in Eighteenth-Century Britain," *Eighteenth-Century Life* 17 (November 1993): 20–22. R. Elphick, *Khoikhoi and the Founding of White South Africa* (New Haven, Conn., 1975), 197. For recent work on race that appears in tune with these assertions, see, for instance, R. Wheeler, "The Complexion of Desire: Racial Ideology and Mid-Eighteenth-Century British Novels," *Eighteenth-Century Studies* 32, no. 3 (1999): 309–32; Wheeler, *The Complexion of Race: Categories of Difference in Eighteenth-Century British Culture* (Philadelphia, 2000); and S. C. Greenfield, " 'Abroad and at Home': Sexual Ambiguity, Miscegenation, and Colonial Boundaries in Edgeworth's *Belinda,*" *PMLA*

Could it be the case that in the interim between the publication of the second and third editions of the *Britannica*, the ability to conceptualize a deliberate manufacturing of blackness through choice was lost? What needs to be shown is how, in parallel to the developments in notions of gender, new understandings of race, buttressed as they might have been by the developing science of natural history and taxonomy, came to the fore in the late eighteenth century as the biological-physical substratum on which questions of human diversity were evaluated, gradually supplanting the role of cultural, mutable, and historical factors (such as "civilization").

Moreover, it seems that homologous shifts can be traced not only for race and gender, but for other categories and boundaries of identity at the same time. Thus, closely related to race was the boundary between human and animal. This boundary too was one that eighteenth-century people were occasionally willing to contemplate as porous and unstable. It allowed, for instance, for some groups of people to be represented as halfway between humans and apes (which may give us pause in reading Lesuire's 1760 characterization of the English as "mid-point between men and beasts," cited in this volume by Bell: was it necessarily, straightforwardly, simply metaphorical?); or for a woman who claimed to give birth to rabbits to go quite a long way, and carry conviction with quite a number of people, before her hoax was discovered; or for the ape exhibited in London in 1738–39 as "Madame Chimpanzee" to be the talk of the town (with the town's tongue only partly in cheek) as a well-dressed, well-behaved, perhaps human creature. But as Keith Thomas has already observed, this space for confusion along the human-animal divide closed down in the late eighteenth century (in a development linked to the rigidification of the categories of race); a fact reflected *inter alia* in the dismissive incomprehension with which the story of the rabbit-breeding woman was now universally laughed out of the room.[47]

More centrally, it can also be argued that *class* categories were transformed in or about the late eighteenth century from relatively flexible to

---

112, no. 2 (March 1997): 214–28 (which suggests that Maria Edgeworth's *Belinda* makes essentializing suggestions regarding racial boundaries and miscegenation that are closely analogous to those we have seen it make regarding gender boundaries). My discussion of race benefited greatly from personal communications with Linda Colley, Elizabeth Elbourne, Silvia Sebastiani, and Kathleen Wilson; I am grateful for their generous sharing of ongoing research.

47. On Mary Tofts the rabbit-breeder, her place within other eighteenth-century beliefs, and the inability of early-nineteenth-century people to comprehend how their forebears could have taken this story even semi-seriously, see L. Cody, "The Doctor's in Labour; or a New Whim Wham from Guildford," *Gender and History* 4, no. 2 (1992): 175–96. G. S. Rousseau, "Madame Chimpanzee," in *Enlightenment Crossings: Pre- and Post-Modern Discourses* (Manchester, 1991), 198–209. K. Thomas, *Man and the Natural World: Changing Attitudes in England, 1500–1800* (Harmondsworth, 1984), 135.

more holistic, essentialized (perhaps even "naturalized"), and totalizing ones, mirroring in some key respects the developments described here. (As one indication of this development, consider for instance those Scottish thinkers invoked by Carolyn Steedman in her essay, who linked people's social rank with their personal identity in civil society.) In my previous work I have charted the contingent introduction of the notion of "middle class" as a resonant key to the understanding of British society; a development driven by the exigencies of changing political configurations from the late eighteenth century to the 1830s, rather than by some inexorable pressures of transformations in social structure. But in fact it can be suggested further that while these political configurations can account for the particular appeal of the category of "middle class" at that specific juncture, this suddenly resonant appeal also relied on an anterior, more general shift in the meaning assigned to social categories. This was a shift, arguably, that led people to believe that social categories—not only "middle class," but also, say, "aristocracy" or "the poor"—could indeed have such essential, determinative significance (and, consequently, political power); and in this it was not far from those transformations in the meanings assigned to categories of gender or race.

The point, to repeat again, is not that these different categories of identity were somehow the same. Rather, it is to explore the possibility that they all went through the same late-eighteenth-century crucible, which exerted similar constraints on each one, even if its effects on—and meaning for—each category were different, depending on the internal history of each category's evolution up to this point. Thus, for gender this jolt appears to have been the final stage in a long process of transformation of understandings of sex and gender, and the relationship between them, from their premodern configuration in the seventeenth century (as described by Thomas Laqueur and Michael McKeon elsewhere) to a recognizably modern one.[48] For race, however, as well as for class, these decades seem to have heralded more the *beginnings* of such a process, dislodging premodern notions and launching a process of realignment that would end only decades later, in mid-nineteenth-century visions of modern class society or in the certitudes of scientific racism.

This, however, is not to say that *every* identity category went through the same transformation at this time. Others, such as nation or religion, did not undergo this development and thus arrived at the threshold of modernity in a different form. Once these divergent paths are laid out, they may help

---

48. T. Laqueur, *Making Sex: Body and Gender from the Greeks to Freud* (Cambridge, Mass., 1990). M. McKeon, "Historicizing Patriarchy: The Emergence of Gender Difference in England, 1660–1760," *Eighteenth-Century Studies* 28 (1995): 295–322. For a more detailed discussion, see Wahrman, "*Percy's* Prologue."

account for the different status of different identity categories as attributes of modern personal selfhood—how did racial identity come to be seen as more innate than national identity, for instance, or religious identity less of a burden of birth than that of class? This divergence may also help explain the perhaps overdetermined emphasis on the cluster of race, class, and gender—the often maligned "holy trinity" of recent scholarship—in the postmodern critique of this historically specific modern construction of selfhood.

In conclusion, then, what I would like to suggest is that a common thread runs from the shifts in representations of the beehive with which we started, through the broader simultaneous transformations in the specific categories used by contemporaries to map and define their social world, to a possible underlying transformation in the very understanding of "self" itself. For we should not assume an interior self to be a human given, a latent bud waiting patiently for the sun rays of modernity to wake it to life. Rather, we need to seek the historically specific context for how the modern notion of identity came to be synonymous with precisely such a self. I would like, therefore, to pursue the possibility that similarly to (but more fundamentally than) the categories of identity such as gender, race, and class, personal identity came to be seen in the late eighteenth century as an innate, fixed, determined core, indeed as tantamount to "self." In the process, collective categories—those that pinpoint a group ("women," "aristocracy," "Indians") rather than an individual—were transmuted into personal characteristics stamped on each and every individual. To early-nineteenth-century observers, indeed, these relatively playful, contingent, and unreliable aspects of the earlier, eighteenth-century notions of identity—what may be called identity's ancien régime—turned it into a distant, incomprehensible foreign country.

Indeed, one can catch further glimpses of the same common thread in observations made elsewhere in this volume. Thus, such a transformation may help account for the shift that Paul Friedland has identified in the understanding of theatrical representation: whereas actors in the early part of the eighteenth century were expected to go through a process of embodied metamorphosis that involved a suspension of their "self," during the latter part of the century the identity of the actor came to be seen as stable, an inner reality that remained unscathed beneath the assumed facades put on for the sake of acting. This bifurcation of inner core and outer facade of course brings to mind familiar images of Romanticism, possibly another late-eighteenth-century departure riding on the coattails of the same underlying transformation. Carla Hesse, for one, invokes this broader Romantic context when she too encounters the very same gap, "between inner feeling and its external representation," in her comments on women's responses to the essentializing discourses on gender during the closing years of the century; a gap "in which the self can be seen to exist independently from, and in a determining relation to, its external representations." How different is this picture, however, from that which surfaces in James Chandler's essay as characteristic of an earlier era: with the aid of Adam Smith, Chandler evokes eighteenth-century notions of personhood that involved "a certain division within—or redoubling of—the persons who compose it"—that is, not a bifurcation of essence and representation, but a fluid notion of personal identity that has no stable core.[49]

But if so (or even partly so), then we are indeed touching upon a "cultural revolution" in the fullest sense implied in this volume: a radical shift in the mental maps people employed to organize the most fundamental components of their worldview, of which none could have more import than their own sense of identity. And it is a "cultural revolution," moreover, that impinges directly on our understanding of "modernity." In the end, much of what we have been observing may well be but different facets of one phenomenon: the historical birth of that great ideological construct of modernity—the belief in the individual, centered subject with an essentialized, clearly demarcated, and always classifiable stable self.

49. See pp. 138 and 199, above. We can also speculate about whether the sudden urge precisely at this period to relocate urban cemeteries at a distance, an act that in Thomas Laqueur's view helped mask the ephemerality of the fundamental distinctions on which the late-eighteenth-century bourgeois worldview had been predicated, had something to do with the heightened investment at this particular juncture in the essential and absolute nature of these fundamental distinctions.

I have no space here to address the key question of national divergence—the extent to which the unfoldings of modern identity were shaped by specific, divergent national histories. I would argue that western European paths to modernity (and that in America) were broadly similar, but differed in their nationally specific triggers and precise chronology: for instance, there are some grounds—including observations made here by David Bell, Carla Hesse, and Sarah Maza—to hypothesize that some of the developments that took place in the English context around the 1780s were paralleled by French ones in the mid-1790s.

INDEX

Abelard, 31

absolutism: and devolution of power to individual, 178, 181–82, 188; and politics of marriage, 182–86; and the state, 178. *See also* Bodin, Jean; Locke, John

Addison, Joseph, 184, 185

Africans, 48, 49, 52, 59

Agnew, Jean-Christophe, 156, 158, 162

Alfred the Great, 91–92

Amazon: Margaret of Anjou as, 261–62; positive representations of, 256, 257–59, 273; queen bees as, 251–53, 255, 258–59; as unacceptable female identity, 256, 259–66, 273

America, Seven Years' War in, 33, 37

Anatomy Acts, 25

ancien régime, 4, 6, 35, 62; absolutism in, 238–40; *cahiers de doléance* in, 234, 246; emergence of modern nationalism in, 35–53, 59–61; emergence of modern political spectator in, 243–46; Estates-General as *corpus mysticum* in, 230–36, 246; female writers in, 190, 191; Malesherbes' remonstrances of the Cour des Aides, 241–44; *milice bourgeoises* in, 114–16; political culture of, 45, 52, 114–18, 218–36; print culture in, 45, 48; theories of political representation, 218–19, 229, 233–37, 240; and theories of theatrical representation, 218–29. *See also* absolutism; France

Anderson, Benedict, 119, 120n. *See also* community

Andress, David, 120, 121n

Anglophilia: French Anglomania, 45, 47, 52–54

Annales, 4, 14; *Annaliste*, 8; failure of, to engage with concept of discourse, 102–3; "first generation," 95; and history of *mentalités*, 8, 95–96; intellectual and institutional power of, 94; and *la longue durée*, 95–96; limitations of "convention" in historical explanation, 104; new category of "convention" and, 99–100, 102–5; new methodological individualism of, 97–98, 105; objectivist socioeconomic framework of, 96–97; reassessment within, 94; rejection of Foucault, 103; rejection of structuralism and modernization theory, 99, 100–101, 105; repudiation of unilinear narrative of modernity, 100; vision of history as indeterminate multiplicity, 99–100

Annual Register, 68

anthropology: anthropologists, 21, 79; foundations of modern, 58, 79, 80; "Geertzian," 7

apiary manuals, 252–56. *See also* beehives

Apotheosis of Captain Cook, 76

Ariès, Philippe, 17

Arnauld, Antoine: *Copy of the Anti-Spaniard*, 57

identity of, 78–93; scientific and historical representation of, 78–93; and theatrical representation of identity, 71–78. *See also* Pacific

Enlightenment, 9, 21, 23, 59, 64n; anthropology and, 58; and control of dead, 26, 27; empiricism and, 79, 81, 82; English imperialism as agent of, 76; French, 48, 49n, 58n, 64n; French, and non-European world, 48; and sciences of ethnic/racial difference, 60, 74–93; Scottish, 81, 83, 131, 278; and subjectivity, 132, 134, 178, 179, 193, 201, 280. *See also* civilization; modernity; primitivism

Eskimos, 85

essentialization, 16, 35, 59; gender and, 256, 266–73; and identities, 70, 275; and making of modern self, 279–80; maternity and, 262–68, 273. *See also* modernity

Estates-General, as *corpus mysticum* of France, 230–36, 246

Europe, 10; as cultural entity, 48, 49; English as "de-Europeanized," 50; Europeans, 51, 58; identity of, in relation to non-European peoples, 48, 64, 67, 80–82; as political unit, 47; Western, 15

Evans, John, M.D., 254

Evelyn, John, 23

Fairchilds, Cissie, 128

Falconer, William, 84, 89

Favart, Charles-Simon: *The Englishman in Bordeaux*, 54

Febvre, Lucien, 95. See also *Annales*

female writers: and assertion of fictive selves, 197–202; cultural contradictions of, 192; demand for intellectual and moral autonomy of, 195, 199, 201; in French Revolution, 190–92, 196–99; insistence on opacity of language of, 197–98, 201, 202; in Old Regime, 190, 191; and problems of publicity, 197, 200–202; Thermidorian reaction against, 193, 194, 199, 200, 202

feminism: and female poetics, 194, 201; and feminists, 10n, 205–6, 213–14; in French Revolution, 190; and historiography, 8–10, 14, 190; and Kantian subjectivity, 200–201; and misogyny, 203–6; politics of, 213–14; psychic history of, 14, 206; unconscious fantasies of, 204, 206, 214, 216, 217

Ferguson, Adam, 131. *See also* civilization

Fielding, Henry: *Joseph Andrews*, 154; *Tom Jones*, 154

Fitzgerald, Reverend Gerald: *The Injured Islanders*, 70

Fordyce, Dr. Alexander, 209

Forster, J. R., 80, 88; *Observations Made During a Voyage Round the World*, 82

Forster, Johann, 86

Fort Duquesne, 33

Fort Necessity, 33, 34, 42

Foucault, Michel: *Annalistes* rejection of, 103; historiographical influence of, 8, 12–13

Fox, George, 22

Fraisse, Genevieve, 192

France: army of, in America, 33, 34; as center of European civilization, 50–55; cultural influence of, 48; and "dual revolution," 3–7; in eighteenth-century historiography, 111; and French protestants, 38, 41; historiography of, 1–16, 94, 100; Louis XIV, king of, 44, 45; Louis XVI, king of, 121, 241; nationalism in, 35, 43–61, 120; as new Rome, 50; and perception of English, 36–58; Third Republic in, 101; wars of religion in, 37, 41, 57. See also *ancien régime*; *Annales*; French Revolution

Freemasons, and importance of oaths, 118. *See also* National Guard

French Revolution: as anti-aristocratic, 122; as bourgeois revolution, 2, 5, 107; citizenship and, 115–17; and Constituent Assembly, 55; and Convention, 56, 58; cultural institutions of, 190; as cultural revolution, 122–23; deregulation of print market during, 191–92, 201; and Directory, 193; discursive exclusion of women during, 192, 201; and "dual revolution," 1, 5, 9, 14, 15; female writers in, 190–202; feminism and, 190–202; Festival of the Federation, 120; martyrs of, 59; Marxist interpretation of, 107; and modern class system, 106; nationalism in, 35, 52, 55, 56; origins of racism in, 60–61; revolutionaries in, 11, 56; revolutionaries' self-perception in, 107–22; revolutionary assemblies, 112; and "Tennis Court Oath," 117; theatricality of politics in, 218, 246–50; and Thermidor, 192–94, 199, 200, 202; wars of,

private sphere *(continued)*
modernity, 188; as privation, 179; relation of, to Greek *oikos,* 179. *See also*
domestic sphere; public sphere
progress, 60, 65, 76, 78, 79; of human society, 81, 82; moral improvement and possibility of, 83, 85; rational capacity and
possibility of, 83, 85. *See also* civilization;
primitivism
psychoanalysis: Barbara Taylor and, 14,
214–15; Jacqueline Rose and, 214
public sphere: and analogy of spheres in
traditional political thought, 174; bourgeois, 5, 9n, 64n; and private sphere, 9,
14, 64n; and public sector, 179; relation
of, to Greek *polis,* 179; role of opinion in,
45. *See also* bourgeois; Habermas, Jürgen;
print culture
Pugin, A. W., 31
Purea, 72; as represented by character of
Oberea, 76

Quakers, 22, 28
Queen Anne: as Amazon, 251, 258, 259,
264; as mother, 264. *See also* gender
queen bees: representation of, as Amazons,
252–53, 256, 258; as mothers, 253–56

Rabaut Saint-Etienne, Jean-Paul, 109, 110
Rabelais, 95
race, 15, 16, 51, 59, 64; eighteenth-century
meanings of, 59; and English view of
themselves as "island race," 67; essentialization and, 60, 275–77; ethnicity and,
15, 35, 64, 65; French view of English as,
38, 39, 53, 55; and interracial sex, 51,
75; nationalism and, 35, 60; Pacific
Islanders as primitive, 82; racism, 35, 59,
60n; universal human, 61
Ramah Droog, 77
Ramazzini, Bernardino, 26
Raoul, Fanny: *Opinion d'une femme sur les
femmes,* 195
Reformation, 18, 59
Resolution, 72, 84
Revel, Jacques, 96
revisionism, 2, 5, 6, 7, 9, 11, 12n, 13
revolution: "Age of," 1–4, 106; bourgeois,
5; "dual," 1–3, 7–8; industrial, 1, 3, 6.
See also cultural revolution; French
Revolution
Reynolds, Joshua, 72

Riccoboni, Francois: *L'art du théâtre,* 221–22
Richards, George: *The Aboriginal Britons,* 89
Richardson, Samuel, 211; *Pamela* 171, 176,
177. *See also* domestic fiction
Riley, Denise, 10, 205
Rivarol, Antoine de: *L'université de la langue
francaise,* 50
Roach, Joseph, 71
Robespierre, Maximilien, 36, 55, 117
romanticism: and the self, 279–80; and sen-
timent, 139, 144
Rose, Jacqueline, 214. *See also* psychoanalysis
Rouget de Lisle, 56
Rousseau, Jean-Jacques, 11, 48, 118, 131n,
230n; *Considerations on the Government of
Poland,* 48; *Emile,* 210; and natural equal-
ity, 78; sexual attitudes of, 209; and
women as mothers, 211, 266
Royal Society, 68
Russia, 75

Saint-Just, 55
Sand, George, 201
savagery, 41, 51, 58, 60; of Africans, 48, 49;
of Americans, 49, 50, 61; of English, 52,
57; of Indians, 41, 48, 51; language of,
60; "noble savage," 72, 78n, 80; and
refinement, 67; South Sea islanders, 80
Schama, Simon, 11, 117n
Schiller, Friedrich: *Essay on Naive and Sentimental Poetry,* 139, 142, 145, 159
Schreiner, Olive, 205
Scots, as primitive peoples, 78, 88–90
Scott, Joan, 9n, 10, 12
Scott, Sarah: *Millenium Hall,* 268
Scott, Sir Walter: as admirer of Sterne, 152,
170; *Ivanhoe,* 153; and vehicular media,
153; Waverley novels of, 152
Selkirk, Alexander, 91
sentiment: and chance, 140, 168; comic
drama and, 137, 142, 155; commerce
and, 141, 144, 147, 156, 158, 163;
creation of modern, 137, 138, 139; face-
to-face encounters and, 155, 156, 158;
humanitarian, 155; hypallage as trope of,
146–47, 150, 165; and imaginative sympathy, 138–44, 159, 163; "mass culture"
and, 170; "movement" and, 143, 145–
51, 166, 168; national, 163–65, 170;
novel of, 141, 142, 153, 155, 156; print
culture and, 141, 142, 153–55, 158,
162, 163; Romanticism and, 139, 144;

Text:	10/12 Baskerville
Display:	Baskerville
Compositor:	BookMatters, Berkeley
Printer/Binder:	Maple-Vail Manufacturing Group